Media Ethics

Media Ethics

Issues and Cases

Tenth Edition

Lee Wilkins
University of Missouri

Chad Painter
University of Dayton

Philip Patterson
Oklahoma Christian University

ROWMAN & LITTLEFIELD
Lanham • Boulder • New York • London

Executive Editor: Natalie Mandziuk
Assistant Editor: Sylvia Landis
Sales and Marketing Inquiries: textbooks@rowman.com

Credits and acknowledgments for material borrowed from other sources, and reproduced with permission, appear on the appropriate page within the text.

Published by Rowman & Littlefield
An imprint of The Rowman & Littlefield Publishing Group, Inc.
4501 Forbes Boulevard, Suite 200, Lanham, Maryland 20706
www.rowman.com

86-90 Paul Street, London EC2A 4NE, United Kingdom

British Library Cataloguing in Publication Information Available

Library of Congress Cataloging-in-Publication Data Available

Names: Wilkins, Lee, author. | Painter, Chad, 1977– author. | Patterson, Philip, author.
Title: Media ethics : issues and cases / Lee Wilkins, University of Missouri, Chad
   Painter, University of Dayton, Philip Patterson, Oklahoma Christian University.
Description: Tenth edition. | Lanham, Maryland : Rowman & Littlefield, [2022] |
   Includes bibliographical references and index. | Summary: "The tenth edition of
   'Media Ethics: Issues and Cases' has been updated with the most pressing media
   issues of the past two years, including coverage of the 2020 pandemic and election.
   This authoritative case book gives students the tools to make ethical decisions in an
   increasingly complex environment"— Provided by publisher.
Identifiers: LCCN 2021006305 (print) | LCCN 2021006306 (ebook) |
   ISBN 9781538142370 (paperback) | ISBN 9781538142387 (epub)
Subjects: LCSH: Mass media—Moral and ethical aspects. | Communication—Moral and
   ethical aspects.
Classification: LCC P94 .M36 2022 (print) | LCC P94 (ebook) | DDC 175—dc23
LC record available at https://lccn.loc.gov/2021006305
LC ebook record available at https://lccn.loc.gov/2021006306

For Linda, David, and Laurel

Brief Contents

Contents

Foreword

Clifford G. Christians
Research Professor of Communication,
University of Illinois–Urbana

The playful wit and sharp mind of Socrates attracted disciples from all across ancient Greece. They came to learn and debate in what could be translated as "his thinkery." By shifting the disputes among Athenians over earth, air, fire, and water to human virtue, Socrates gave Western philosophy and ethics a new intellectual center (Cassier, 1944).

But sometimes his relentless arguments would go nowhere. On one occasion, he sparred with the philosopher Hippias about the difference between truth and falsehood. Hippias was worn into submission but retorted at the end, "I cannot agree with you, Socrates." And then the master concluded, "Nor I with myself, Hippias. . . . I go astray, up and down, and never hold the same opinion." Socrates admitted to being so clever that he had befuddled himself. No wonder he was a favorite target of the comic poets. I. F. Stone likens this wizardry to "whales of the intellect flailing about in deep seas" (Stone, 1988).

With his young friend Meno, Socrates argued whether virtue is teachable. Meno was eager to learn more after "holding forth often on the subject in front of large audiences." But he complained,

> You are exercising magic and witchcraft upon me and positively laying me under your spell until I am just a mass of helplessness. . . . You are exactly like the flat stingray that one meets in the sea. Whenever anyone comes into contact with it, it numbs him, and that is the sort of thing you seem to be doing to me now. My mind and my lips are literally numb.

Philosophy is not a semantic game, though sometimes its idiosyncrasies feed that response into the popular mind. *Media Ethics: Issues and Cases* does not debunk philosophy as the excess of sovereign reason. The authors

of this book will not encourage those who ridicule philosophy as cunning rhetoric. The issue at stake here is actually a somewhat different problem—the
Cartesian model of philosophizing.

The founder of modern philosophy, René Descartes, preferred to work
in solitude. Paris was whirling in the early 17th century, but for two years
even Descartes's friends could not find him as he squirreled himself away
studying mathematics. One can even guess the motto above his desk: "Happy
is he who lives in seclusion." Imagine the conditions under which he wrote
"Meditations II." The Thirty Years' War in Europe brought social chaos every-
where. The Spanish were ravaging the French provinces and even threatening
Paris, but Descartes was shut away in an apartment in Holland. Tranquility
for philosophical speculation mattered so much to him that, upon hearing
Galileo had been condemned by the church, he retracted parallel arguments of
his own on natural science. Pure philosophy as an abstract enterprise needed
a cool atmosphere isolated from everyday events.

Descartes's magnificent formulations have always had their detractors, of
course. David Hume did not think of philosophy in those terms, believing as
he did that sentiment is the foundation of morality. For Søren Kierkegaard,
an abstract system of ethics is only paper currency with nothing to back it up.
Karl Marx insisted that we change the world and not merely explain it. But
no one drew the modern philosophical map more decisively than Descartes,
and his mode of rigid inquiry has generally defined the field's parameters.

This book adopts the historical perspective suggested by Stephen Toulmin:

> The philosophy whose legitimacy the critics challenge is always the seventeenth
> century tradition founded primarily upon René Descartes. . . . [The] arguments
> are directed to one particular style of philosophizing—a theory-centered style
> which poses philosophical problems, and frames solutions to them, in timeless
> and universal terms. From 1650, this particular style was taken as defining the
> very agenda of philosophy. (1988, 338)

The 17th-century philosophers set aside the particular, the timely, the local,
and the oral. And that development left untouched nearly half of the philosophical agenda. Indeed, it is those neglected topics—what I here call "practical philosophy"—that are showing fresh signs of life today, at the very time
when the more familiar "theory-centered" half of the subject is languishing
(Toulmin, 1988, p. 338).

This book collaborates in demolishing the barrier of three centuries between
pure and applied philosophy; it joins in reentering practical concerns as the
legitimate domain of philosophy itself. For Toulmin, the primary focus of
ethics has moved from the study to the bedside to criminal courts, engineering
labs, the newsroom, factories, and ethnic street corners. Moral philosophers

are not being asked to hand over their duties to technical experts in today's institutions, but rather to fashion their agendas within the conditions of contemporary struggle.

All humans have a theoretical capacity. Critical thinking, the reflective dimension, is our common property. And this book nurtures that reflection in communication classrooms and by extension into centers of media practice. If the mind is like a muscle, this volume provides a regimen of exercises for strengthening its powers of systematic reflection and moral discernment. It does not permit those aimless arguments that result in quandary ethics. Instead, it operates in the finest traditions of practical philosophy, anchoring the debates in real-life conundrums but pushing the discussion toward substantive issues and integrating appropriate theory into the decision-making process. It seeks to empower students to do ethics themselves, under the old adage that teaching someone to fish lasts a lifetime, and providing fish only saves the day.

Media Ethics: Issues and Cases arrives on the scene at a strategic time in higher education. Since the late 19th century, ethical questions have been taken from the curriculum as a whole and from the philosophy department. Recovering practical philosophy has involved a revolution during the last decade in which courses in professional ethics have reappeared throughout the curriculum. This book advocates the pervasive method and carries the discussions even further, beyond freestanding courses into communication classrooms across the board.

In this sense, the book represents a constructive response to the current debates over the mission of higher education. Professional ethics has long been saddled with the dilemma that the university was given responsibility for professional training precisely at the point in its history that it turned away from values to scientific naturalism. Today one sees it as a vast horizontal plain given to technical excellence but barren in enabling students to articulate a philosophy of life. As the late James Carey concluded,

> [h]igher education has not been performing well of late and, like most American institutions, is suffering from a confusion of purpose, an excess of ambition that borders on hubris, and an appetite for money that is truly alarming. (1989, 48)

The broadside critiques leveled in Thorstein Veblen's *The Higher Learning in America* (1918) and Upton Sinclair's *The Goose Step* (1922) are now too blatantly obvious to ignore. But *Media Ethics: Issues and Cases* does not merely demand a better general education or a recommitment to values; it strengthens the communications curriculum by equipping thoughtful students with a more enlightened moral awareness. Since Confucius, we have understood that lighting a candle is better than cursing the darkness or, in Mother Teresa's version, we feed the world one mouth at a time.

Preface

In the past decade, media ethics has been asked to do increasingly heavy lifting. The realities of consolidating ownership, the relentless and shifting requirements of computer and platform adeptness, and the ongoing personal toll as our work meets with increased skepticism and borderline hostility are but three factors that demonstrate why sound ethical thinking is the core of excellence. We believe thinking ethically makes you a better person and a more valuable professional. It also helps you in other aspects of your life—being a parent, a community member, and a self-aware human being.

In its 10th edition, this book continues to begin and end with theory—moral philosophy and moral development, respectively. However, in response to our readers, we have subdivided the other chapters into two sections: foundations and applications. The foundation chapters focus on philosophy spanning all elements of the field. For example, strategic communication professionals lead the privacy discussion, and the role of documentary film is examined as part of truth telling. That philosophical foundation adds feminist ethics to classical theory and joins the concept of social justice with democratic functioning.

The application chapters examine some professional niches such as individual decisions in strategic communication or visual thinking, as well as institutional questions such as those raised by media economics or the pervasive role of art and entertainment.

In this edition, our bedrock assumption remains that the media and democracy need one another to survive. If there is a single animating idea in this book, it is this: No matter what your job, it is made easier in a functioning democracy. Whether your focus is news, entertainment, or strategic communication, or whether your role is a professional or a parent, democracy is both an enabler and a sustainer. And democracy functions best with a free and independent media ecosystem that spurs change, reifies culture, and provides opportunities to read, think, explore, and create. This book remains optimistic about the very tough times in which we find ourselves.

There also is content deliberately left out. First, you'll find no media bashing in this book. There's enough of that already, and, besides, it's too easy to do. This book is not designed to indict the media; it's designed to train its future practitioners. If we cite ethical lapses from the past, it is only to learn what we can from them to prevent similar occurrences in the future. Second, you'll find no conclusions in this book—neither at the end of the book nor after each case. No one has yet written the conclusive chapter to the ethical dilemmas of the media, and we don't presume to be the first.

The role of the cases is to propel your understanding of the issues. About half of them are new to this edition, and many are focused on local issues, as what happens nationally increasingly finds its way to local media markets propelled by social media. These cases begin with the actual details and then suggest "micro issues" (what would you do on this day with this set of facts?). The questions then broaden to larger issues and deeper questions, which we call "midrange issues." Finally, they conclude with some of the largest issues in society. We call these "macro issues." The questions are not answered in this textbook. It is left to the student and the professor to arrive at an answer—and there often is not one *right* or *correct* answer. The "right" answer is one that is justified by ethical underpinnings of the text.

This simple idea became popular, and each edition has added to the depth of the chapters and the recency of the cases. As the field changed and student majors within the field changed, so did this book. Some chapters came and went, including an "international" chapter and a "new media" chapter, with the material absorbed in other places in the book. "Public relations" became "strategic communication," with all the nuances that category entailed. Social media rocked our industry and changed our economic model. The book followed with the corresponding ethical issues and cases. At every stage, it remained a true media ethics textbook and not simply a journalism ethics book. It emphasizes connections and consistency across professional roles. Both the current chapters and the current cases bear that out.

This 10th edition brings with it some changes, the major ones being a new editor and a reordering of the coauthors. At least as important, the text was revised at a time of intellectual and professional ferment. A large portion of the text remains the same, as do several cases found in previous editions of this book. These decisions mirror the state of the field of media ethics: Some of the problems media professionals face today are new; others are as old as our professions.

Each of us bears a significant debt of gratitude to families, to teachers and mentors, to colleagues, to students, and to our delightful project editor and publisher. We acknowledge their contributions to our intellectual and moral development in making this book possible, and we accept the flaws of this book as our own.

1

An Introduction to Ethical Decision-Making

By the end of this chapter, you should be able to

- recognize the need for professional ethics in journalism and strategic communication;
- work through a model of ethical decision-making;
- identify and use philosophical principles applicable to professional practice.

MAKING ETHICAL DECISIONS

No matter your professional niche in mass communication, the past few years have been nothing short of an assault on the role you play in a democratic society, on the business model that supports your organization and pays your salary, or whether your job might be better done—and certainly more cheaply—by a robot or an algorithm.

Consider the following ethical decisions that made the news:

- "Don't make us write obituaries" read the headline in the Notre Dame student newspaper in early fall 2020, as the university administration wrestled with decisions about online versus in-person learning as part of its pandemic response. Dozens of college journalists helped news organizations, such as the *New York Times*, report on the impact of COVID-19 on campus. After months of a contentious relationship, the Foundation for Individual Rights in Education, the Native American Journalists Association, and the Student Press Law Center wrote to

1

Haskell Indian Nations University in October 2020 demanding that the federally operated university immediately and explicitly rescind its threats against its own award-winning student newspaper (Foundation for Individual Rights in Education, 2020). That letter noted that the university's leadership could be held personally and monetarily responsible for threatening freedom of speech and freedom of the press. Haskell president Ronald Graham capitulated on Nov. 20, though this was not announced until Jan. 13, 2021, due to an "administrative error," according to the Bureau of Indian Education.

- In October 2020, two student journalists—Satchel Walton and Cooper Walton—writing for their high school newspaper, the *Dupont Manual Redeye*, broke the story that the official Kentucky State Police training manual and slideshow used quotes from Adolf Hitler to support the warrior mindset it sought to inculcate in recruits. The manual included quotes promoting "ruthless" violence. The Kentucky State Police Commissioner resigned after the story broke; the state responded with an investigation of how state police and other police departments were trained. The training manual itself dated from 2013; the Hitler quotes were uncovered as the result of a Freedom of Information Act request. The context for the story included the shooting by Louisville police of Breonna Taylor, a Black medical worker, who became one of the foci of the Black Lives Matter movement.

- In September 2020, famed investigative reporter Bob Woodward released excerpts from his book *Fear*, in which he quoted President Donald J. Trump—with the support of audiotapes of the conversations—saying he was lying about the lethality of the coronavirus because "I don't want to create a panic." Woodward taped the president's comments in January and February of that year. Trump justified his actions as lies for the public good. Woodward said he was unable to place the statements in context until May and that his single biggest problem was determining whether President Trump was telling the truth about his repeated efforts to downplay the impact of the virus. Despite this rationale, many journalists, among them David Boardman, former editor at the *Seattle Times* and now dean at Temple University, said Woodward should have reported what he knew earlier because it could have saved lives.

- In June 2020, Quaker Oats announced that it would remove the controversial image of Aunt Jemima from its line of maple syrups, pancake mixes, and other foods starting at the end of 2020. "We recognize Aunt Jemima's origins are based on a racial stereotype," Kristin Kroepfl, vice president and chief marketing officer of Quaker Foods North America, said in a statement to NBC News. "While work has been done over the years to update the brand in a manner intended to be appropriate and respectful, we realize those changes are not enough."

Figure 1.1. Historical and contemporary images of Aunt Jemima branding.

- In September 2020, subscribers to *El Nuevo Herald*—sister publication to the *Miami Herald*—received an apology from both newspapers about the inclusion of an insert called "Libre." That insert included defamatory columns about Jews and the Black Lives Matter movement. Among the comments, a writer claimed American Jews support "thieves and arsonists" and equated Black Lives Matter protestors with Nazis.

     "What kind of people are these Jews? They're always talking about the Holocaust, but have they already forgotten Kristallnacht, when Nazi thugs rampaged through Jewish shops all over Germany? So do the BLM and Antifa, only the Nazis didn't steal; they only destroyed," author Roberto Luque Escalona wrote.

     When the issue came to light, *Herald* editors learned that the newspaper had been including the insert since January 2020.
- After months of rumors during 2019–2020, US tech firm Oracle apparently will be allowed to purchase Chinese-owned app TikTok, which is globally popular with younger social media users. Oracle's bid was supported by President Trump and several Republican senators. The president had initially labeled the social media app a national security

risk and had threatened to prohibit it from operating in the United States unless it were sold to a US buyer. Oracle's purchase announcement came just minutes after Microsoft, also making an offer, announced that TikTok's parent company had rejected its bid. As of this writing, the sale has yet to be completed.

- *Scientific American* endorsed Joe Biden in the 2020 presidential election, the magazine's first endorsement in its 175-year history. The first part of that editorial reviewed the missteps of the Trump administration and statements by President Trump himself on the lethality of COVID-19 and the potential impact of public-health measures on its spread. The magazine's editors concluded with this: "Joe Biden, in contrast, comes prepared with plans to control COVID-19, improve health care, reduce carbon emissions and restore the role of legitimate science in policy-making. He solicits expertise and has turned that knowledge into solid policy proposals."

- Despite the news media's insistence on truth telling, academic studies found that the profession was a major source of disinformation in the 2016 and 2020 elections. A Columbia University Tow Center for Digital Journalism study found that "news organizations play a major role in propagating hoaxes, false claims, questionable rumors, and dubious viral content" (Silverman, 2015). Why? Because journalists' routine methods of gathering and editing news mean that false claims are reported as news, particularly if they come from an authoritative source and are only subsequently fact-checked. A study by the nonprofit media watchdog Media Matters found two-thirds of the media's retweets of President Trump's false claims were passed along without noting that the claims were false.

- In December 2020, the *New York Times* retracted the core of the reporting for its hit podcast *Caliphate*, which reported on terrorism and how one person had been radicalized into terrorist activity. The podcast had won multiple awards, which the *Times* returned, and also had garnered new subscribers and listeners for the paper. The newspaper reassigned its star terrorism reporter, Rukmini Callimachi. "We fell in love with the fact that we had gotten a member of ISIS who would describe his life in the caliphate and would describe his crimes," *New York Times* executive editor Dean Baquet told National Public Radio (NPR). "I think we were so in love with it that when we saw evidence that maybe he was a fabulist, when we saw evidence that he was making some of it up, we didn't listen hard enough." However, the *Times*'s decision became controversial when, less than a week later, NPR also reported that the *Times*'s reporter writing the story about the podcast had asked well-known journalists not to call it a "retraction."

- Suicide, racism, bullying, mean girls, jock high school culture, and a host of other issues became the focus on the hit Netflix series *13 Reasons Why*, which was based on a 2007 novel. The popularity of the series (now in its fourth season) prompted junior high and high school administrations to buttress their counseling services; colleges were affected as well. The series also was widely criticized, particularly for the focus on teen suicide without accompanying information about how to detect it and what to do if a friend or loved one exhibits signs of potential suicide.

Each of these instances represents an ethical choice, decisions that most often begin with individuals but are then reinforced by the profit-making organizations for which they work or by the social organizations in which people willingly participate. Almost all of them include the element of melding roles—am I acting as a news reporter or as a consumer, as a private citizen or as a professional, as an audience member who understands that comedians can sometimes speak a certain sort of truth, or as an objective reporter for whom words that imply or state an opinion are forbidden? As young professionals, you are told to "promote your own brand" while simultaneously promoting your client, your news organization, or your profession. It's a staggering array of requirements and obligations, and it's made more difficult by the very public nature—and the potential public response—that your decisions inevitably will provoke.

The Dilemma of Dilemmas

The summaries above are dilemmas—they present an ethical problem with no single (or simple) "right" answer. Resolving dilemmas is the business of ethics. It's not an easy process, but ethical dilemmas can be anticipated and prepared for, and there is a wealth of ethical theory—some of it centuries old—to back up your final decision. In this chapter and throughout this book, you will be equipped with both the theories and the tools to help solve the dilemmas that arise in working for the mass media.

In the end, you will have tools, not answers. Answers must come from within you, but your answers should be informed by what others have written and experienced. Otherwise, you always will be forced to solve each ethical problem without the benefit of anyone else's insight. Acquiring these tools also will help prevent such dilemmas from spiraling into "quandary ethics"— the feeling that no best choice is available and that everyone's choice is equally valid. (For more, see Deni Elliott's essay following this chapter.)

Will codes of ethics help? Virtually all media associations have one, but they have limitations. For instance, the ethics code for the Society of

Professional Journalists could be read to allow for revealing or withholding information, two opposite actions. That doesn't make the code useless; it simply points out a shortfall in depending on codes.

While we don't dismiss codes, we believe you will find more universally applicable help in the writings of philosophers, ancient and modern, introduced in this chapter and throughout the text.

Some writers claim that ethics can't be taught. It's situational, some claim. Because every message is unique, there is no real way to learn ethics other than by daily life. Ethics, it is argued, is something you have, not something you do. But while it's true that reading about ethics is no guarantee you will perform your job ethically, thinking about ethics is a skill anyone can acquire.

While each area of mass communication has its unique ethical issues, thinking about ethics is the same whether you make your living writing advertising copy or obituaries. Thinking about ethics won't necessarily make tough choices easier, but your ethical decision-making can become more consistent with practice. A consistently ethical approach to your work as a reporter, designer, or multimedia story producer—regardless of your job title—can improve that work as well.

Ethics and Morals

Contemporary professional ethics revolves around these questions:

- What duties do I have, and to whom do I owe them?
- What values are reflected by the duties I've assumed?

Ethics takes us out of the world of "This is the way I do it" or "This is the way it's always been done" into the realm of "This is what I should do" or "This is the action that can be rationally justified." Ethics in this sense is "ought talk." The questions arising from duty and values can be answered a number of ways as long as they are consistent with each other. For example, a journalist and a public relations professional may see the truth of a story differently because they see their duties differently and because there are different values at work in their professions, but each can be acting ethically if they are operating under the imperatives of "oughtness" for their profession.

It is important here to distinguish between *ethics,* a rational process founded on certain agreed-on principles, and *morals,* which are in the realm of religion. The Ten Commandments constitute a moral system in the Judeo-Christian tradition, and Jewish scholars have expanded this study of the laws throughout the Bible's Old Testament into the Talmud, a thousand-page religious volume. The Buddhist Eightfold Path provides a similar moral framework.

However, moral systems are not synonymous with ethics. *Ethics begins when elements within a moral system conflict.* Ethics is less about the conflict between right and wrong than it is about the conflict between equally compelling (or equally unattractive) alternatives and the choices that must be made between them. Ethics is just as often about the choices between good and better or poor and worse as about right and wrong, which tends to be the domain of morals.

When elements within a moral system conflict, ethical principles can help you make tough choices. We'll review several ethical principles briefly after describing how one philosopher, Sissela Bok, says working professionals can learn to make good ethical decisions (see below).

BOK'S MODEL

Sissela Bok's ethical decision-making framework was introduced in her 1978 book *Lying: Moral Choice in Public and Private Life.* Bok's model is based on two premises: that we must have empathy for the people involved in ethical decisions, and that maintaining social trust is a fundamental goal. With this in mind, Bok says any ethical question should be analyzed in three steps.

First, consult your own conscience about the "rightness" of an action. *How do you feel about the action?*

A Word about Ethics

The concept of ethics comes from the Greeks, who divided the philosophical world into separate disciplines. For them, aesthetics was the study of the beautiful and how a person could analyze beauty without relying only on subjective evaluations. Epistemology was the study of knowing, debate about what constitutes learning and what is knowable. Ethics was the study of what is good, both for the individual and for society. Interestingly, the root of the word means "custom" or "habit," giving ethics an underlying root in behavior that is long established and beneficial to the advance of society. The Greeks were also concerned with the individual virtues of fortitude, justice, temperance, and wisdom, as well as with societal virtues such as freedom. Two millennia later, ethics has come to mean learning to make rational decisions among an array of choices, all of which may be morally justifiable, but some more so than others. *Rationality* is the key word here, for the Greeks believed, and modern philosophers affirm, that people should be able to explain their ethical decisions and that acting ethically could be shown to be a rational decision. That ability to explain ethical choices is an important one for media professionals whose choices are so public. When confronted with an angry public, "It seemed like the right thing to do at the time" is a personally embarrassing and ethically unsatisfactory explanation.

Second, seek expert advice for alternatives to the act creating the ethical problem. Experts, by the way, can be those either living or dead—a producer or editor you trust or a philosopher you admire. *Is there another professionally acceptable way to achieve the same goal that will not raise ethical issues?*

Third, if possible, conduct a public discussion with the parties involved in the dispute. These include those who are directly involved, such as a reporter or their source, and those indirectly involved, such as a reader or a media outlet owner. If they cannot be gathered—and that will most often be the case—you can conduct the conversation hypothetically in your head, playing out the roles. The goal of this conversation is to discover: *How will others respond to the proposed act?*

Let's see how Bok's model works in the following scenario. In the section after the case, follow the three steps Bok recommends and decide if you would run the story.

How Much News Is Fit to Print?

In your community, the major charity is the United Way. The annual fund-raising drive will begin in less than two weeks. However, at a late-night meeting of the board with no media present, the executive director resigns. Though the agency is not covered by the Open Meetings Act, you are able to learn most of what went on from a source on the board.

According to her, the executive director had taken pay from the agency by submitting a falsified time sheet while he was actually away at the funeral of a college roommate. The United Way board investigated the absence and asked for his resignation, citing lying about the absence as the reason, though most agreed that they would have given him paid leave had he asked.

The United Way wants to issue a short statement, praising the work of the executive director while regretfully accepting his resignation. The executive director also will issue a short statement citing other opportunities as his reason for leaving. You are assigned the story by an editor who does not know about the additional information you have obtained but wants you to "see if there's any more to it [the resignation] than they're telling."

You call your source on the board and she asks you, as a friend, to withhold the damaging information because it will hinder the United Way's annual fundraising effort and jeopardize services to needy people in the community because faith in the United Way will be destroyed. You confront the executive director. He says he already has a job interview with another nonprofit, and you will ruin his chances of a future career if you run the story.

What do you do?

The Analysis

Bok's first step requires you to *consult your conscience*. When you do so, you realize you have a problem. Your responsibility is to tell the truth, and that means providing readers with all the facts you discover. You also have a larger responsibility not to harm your community, and printing the complete story might well cause short-term harm. Clearly, your conscience causes you to be of two minds about the issue.

You move to the second step: *alternatives*. Do you simply run the resignation release, figuring the person can do no further harm and therefore should be left alone? Do you run the whole story but buttress it with board members' quotes that such an action couldn't happen again, figuring that you have restored public trust in the agency? Do you do nothing until after the fundraising drive and risk the loss of trust from readers if the story circulates around town as a rumor? Again, there are alternatives, but each has some cost.

In the third step of Bok's model, you will attempt to *hold a public ethical dialogue* with all of the parties involved. Most likely you won't get all the parties into the newsroom on deadline. Instead, you can conduct an imaginary discussion among the parties involved. Such a discussion might go like this:

EXECUTIVE DIRECTOR: "I think my resignation is sufficient penalty for any mistake I might have made, and your article will jeopardize my ability to find another job. It's really hurting my wife and kids, and they've done nothing wrong."

REPORTER: "But shouldn't you have thought about that *before* you decided to falsify the time sheet? This is a good story, and I think the public should know what the people who are handling their donations are like."

READER 1: "Wait a minute. I am the public, and I'm tired of all of this bad news your paper focuses on. This man has done nothing but good in the community, and I can't see where any money that belonged to the poor went into his pocket. Why can't we see some good news for a change?"

READER 2: "I disagree. I buy the paper precisely because it does this kind of reporting. Stories like this that keep the government, the charities, and everyone else on their toes."

PUBLISHER: "You mean like a watchdog function."

READER 2: "Exactly. And if it bothers you, don't read it."

PUBLISHER: "I don't really like to hurt people with the power we have, but if we don't print stories like this, and the community later finds out that we withheld news, our credibility is ruined, and we're out of business." [To source] "Did you request that the information be off the record?"

SOURCE: "No. But I never thought you'd use it in your story."

REPORTER: "I'm a reporter. I report what I hear for a living. What did you think I would do with it? Stories like these allow me to support my family."

EXECUTIVE DIRECTOR: "So it's your career or mine, is that what you're saying? Look, no charges have been filed here, but if your story runs, I look like a criminal. Is that fair?"

PUBLISHER: "And if it doesn't run, we don't keep our promise to the community. Is that fair?"

NEEDY MOTHER: "Fair? You want to talk fair? Do you suffer if the donations go down? No, I do. This is just another story to you. It's the difference in me and my family getting by."

The conversation could continue, and other points of view could be voiced. Your imaginary conversations could be more or less elaborate than the one above, but out of this discussion it should be possible to rationally support an ethical choice.

There are two cautions in using Bok's model for ethical decision-making. First, it is important to go through all three steps before making a final choice. Most of us make ethical choices prematurely, after we've consulted only our consciences, an error Bok says results in a lot of flabby moral thinking. Second, while you will not be endowed with any clairvoyant powers to anticipate your ethical problems, the ethical dialogue outlined in the third step is best when conducted in advance of the event, not in the heat of writing a story.

For instance, an advertising copywriter might conduct such a discussion about whether advertising copy can ethically withhold disclaimers about potential harm from a product. A reporter might conduct such a discussion well in advance of the time she is actually asked to withhold a name or an embarrassing fact from a story. Since it is likely that such dilemmas will arise in your chosen profession (the illustration above is based on what happened to one of the authors the first day on the job), your answer will be more readily available and more logical if you hold such discussions either with trusted colleagues in a casual atmosphere or by yourself well in advance of the problem. The cases in this book are selected partially for their ability to predict your on-the-job dilemmas and start the ethical discussion now.

GUIDELINES FOR MAKING ETHICAL DECISIONS

Since the days of ancient Greece, philosophers have tried to draft rules or guidelines governing how to make ethical choices. In ethical dilemmas such as the one above, you will need principles to help you determine what to do amid conflicting voices. While a number of principles work well, we will review six.

Aristotle's "Golden Mean"

Aristotle believed that happiness—which some scholars translate as "flourishing"—was the ultimate human good. By flourishing, Aristotle sought to elevate any activity through the setting of high standards, what he called exercising "practical reasoning."

Practical reasoning was exercised by individuals who understood what the Greeks called the "virtues" and demonstrated them in their lives and their callings. Such a person was the *phrenemos,* or person of practical wisdom, one who demonstrated ethical excellence in his or her daily activity. For Aristotle, the highest virtue was citizenship, and its highest practitioner the statesman, a politician who exercised so much practical wisdom in his daily activity that he elevated the craft of politics to an art. In contemporary terms, we might think of a *phrenemos* as a person who excels at any of a variety of activities—cellist Yo-Yo Ma, the late poet Maya Angelou, filmmakers Spike Lee and Steven Spielberg. They are people who flourish in their professional performance, extending our own vision of what is possible.

This notion of flourishing led Aristotle to assert that people acting virtuously are the moral basis of his ethical system, not those who simply follow rules. His ethical system is now called *virtue ethics*. Virtue ethics flows from both the nature of the act itself and the moral character of the person who acts. In the Aristotelian sense, in order to behave ethically, (1) you must know (through the exercise of practical reasoning) what you are doing; (2) you must select the act for its own sake, in order to flourish; and (3) the act itself must spring from a firm and unchanging character (see figure 1.2).

It is not stretching Aristotle's framework to assert that one way to learn ethics is to select heroes and try to model your individual acts and ultimately

Figure 1.2. Calvin and Hobbes © 1989 Watterson. Reprinted with permission of Andrews McMeel Syndication. All rights reserved.

Table 1.1. Aristotle's Golden Mean

Unacceptable Behaviors (Deficiency)	Acceptable Behaviors	Unacceptable Behaviors (Excess)
Cowardice	Courage	Foolhardiness
Shamelessness	Modesty	Bashfulness
Stinginess	Generosity	Wastefulness

your professional character on what you believe they would do. An Aristotelian might well consult this hero as an expert when making an ethical choice. Asking what your hero would do in a particular situation is a valid form of ethical analysis. The trick, however, is to select your heroes carefully and continue to think for yourself rather than merely copy behavior you have seen previously.

What then is a virtue? *Virtue lies at the mean between two extremes of excess and deficiency*, a reduction of Aristotle's philosophy and often called the "Golden Mean," as shown in table 1.1. Courage, for example, is a mean between foolhardiness, on one hand, and cowardice, on the other. But to determine that mean for yourself, you have to exercise practical wisdom, act according to high standards and in accordance with firm and continuing character traits.

In reality, therefore, the middle ground of a virtue is not a single point on a line that is the same for every individual. It is instead a range of behaviors—a range that varies individually while avoiding the undesirable extremes. Candor is a good example of a virtue that is most certainly contextual—what is too blunt in one instance is kind in another. Consider two witnesses to a potential drowning: One onlooker is a poor swimmer but a fast runner, the other is a good swimmer but a slow runner. What is cowardice for one is foolhardy for the other. Each can exhibit courage, but in different ways.

Seeking the Golden Mean implies that individual acts are not disconnected from one another, but collectively form a whole that a person of good character should aspire to. A virtue theory of ethics is not outcome-oriented. Instead, it is agent-oriented, and right actions in a virtue theory of ethics are a result of an agent seeking virtue and accomplishing it. As Aristotle wrote in *Nicomachean Ethics*,

> We learn an art or craft by doing the things that we shall have to do when we have learnt it: for instance, men become builders by building houses, harpers by playing on the harp. Similarly we become just by doing just acts, temperate by doing temperate acts, brave by doing brave acts.

Far from being old-fashioned, Aristotle's concept of virtue ethics has been rediscovered by a variety of professions. As Kenneth Woodward (1994) states in a *Newsweek* essay entitled "What Is Virtue?" a call for virtue is still relevant today:

> But before politicians embrace virtue as their latest election-year slogan, they would do well to tune into contemporary philosophy. Despite the call for virtue, we live in an age of moral relativism. According to the dominant school of moral philosophy, the skepticism engendered by the Enlightenment has reduced all ideas of right and wrong to matters of personal taste, emotional preference or cultural choice. . . . Against this moral relativism, advocates of the "ethics of virtue" argue that some personal choices are morally superior to others.

Confucius's Self-Cultivation

A similar, yet distinct, philosophy of ethical thought can be found through Confucius's teachings of self-cultivation.

Confucian philosophy is devoted to the cultivation of virtues. Specifically, self-cultivation is the key pathway to moral excellence, according to Confucius. While Confucian philosophy often is compared and contrasted with tenets of Western philosophy, especially Aristotle's concept of character building, the idea of self-cultivation as taught by Confucius was never a central theme in Western philosophy. Indeed, self-cultivation is fundamentally "different from the Western model where decision-making is the central concern" because the "approach places more emphasis on the project of understanding and cultivating the self" (Feng, 2020, p. 21).

The key difference is that self-cultivation is internal, not external. Self-cultivation is not practiced with a goal of acquiring psychological or material goods. This ultimate goal distinguishes Confucian teachings from Aristotle's virtue framework where individuals develop moral character by developing the ability to find pleasure in virtue and pain in vices.

For Confucius, self-cultivation is an expression of the self as a follower of the Way: *dao* (Feng, 2020).

> Several elements are key to the self-cultivation process: *zixing* (reflection/examination of the self), *li* (social rites), inspirational classics, music, family, and human relationships. Through self-cultivation, one is shaped and transformed by internalizing the social values through accumulative learning and repeated practices. (Feng, 2020, p. 13)

Kant's Categorical Imperative

Immanuel Kant is best known for his *categorical imperative*, which is most often stated in two ways. The first asserts that an individual should act as if the choices one makes for oneself could become universal law. The second states that one should act so that they treat each individual as an end and never merely as a means. Kant called these two rules "categorical" imperatives, meaning that their demands were universal and not subject to situational factors. Many readers will recognize the similarity between Kant's first manifestation of the categorical imperative and the Bible's Golden Rule: Do unto others as you would have others do unto you. The two are quite similar in their focus on duty.

Kant's ethical theory is based on the notion that it is in the act itself, rather than in the person who acts, where moral force resides. This theory of ethics is unlike Aristotle's in that it shifts the notion of what is ethical from the actor to the act itself. This does not mean that Kant did not believe in moral character, but rather that people could act morally from a sense of duty even if their character might incline them to act otherwise.

For Kant, an action was morally justified only if it was performed from duty—motive matters to Kant—and in Kant's moral universe there were two sorts of duties. The strict duties were generally negative: not to murder, not to break promises, not to lie. The meritorious duties were more positive: to aid others, to develop one's talents, to show gratitude. Kant spent very little time defining these notions, but philosophers have generally asserted that the strict duties are somewhat more morally mandatory than the meritorious duties.

Some have argued that consequences are not important in Kant's ethical reasoning. We prefer a somewhat less austere reading of Kant. While Kant's view is that the moral worth of an action does not depend on its consequences, those consequences are not irrelevant. For example, a surgeon may show moral virtue in attempting to save a patient through an experimental procedure, but the decision about whether to undertake that procedure requires taking into account the probability of a cure. This framing of Kantian principles allows us to learn from our mistakes.

The test of a moral act, according to Kant, is its universality—whether it can be applied to everyone. For instance, under Kant's categorical imperative, journalists can claim few special privileges, such as the right to lie or the right to invade privacy in order to get a story. Kant's view, if taken seriously, reminds you of what you give up—truth, privacy, and the like—when you make certain ethical decisions.

Utilitarianism

The original articulation of *utilitarianism* by Englishmen Jeremy Bentham and later John Stuart Mill in the 19th century introduced what was then a novel notion into ethics discussions: *The consequences of actions are important in deciding whether they are ethical.* In the utilitarian view, it may be considered ethical to harm one person for the benefit of the larger group. This approach, for example, is the ethical justification for investigative reporting, the results of which may harm individuals even though they are printed or broadcast in the hope of providing a greater societal good.

The appeal of utilitarianism is that it has proven to mesh well with Western thought, particularly on human rights. Harvard ethicist Arthur Dyck (1977, p. 55) writes of Mill:

> He took the view that the rightness or wrongness of any action is decided by its consequences. . . . His particular understanding of what is best on the whole was that which brings about the most happiness or the least suffering, i.e., the best balance of pleasure over pain for the greatest number.

The benefit of utilitarianism is that it provides a principle by which rightness and wrongness can be identified and judged, conflicts can be resolved, and exceptions can be decided. The utilitarian calculus also has made possible the "quantification of welfare," Dyck says, allowing governments to make decisions that create the most favorable balance of benefits over harms.

With its focus on the consequences of an action, utilitarianism completes a cycle begun with Aristotle (see table 1.2). Aristotle, in developing the Golden Mean, focused on the *actor*, as does Confucius. Kant, in his categorical imperative, focused on the *action*, while Mill, in his utilitarian philosophy, focused on the *outcome*.

Utilitarianism has been condensed to the ethical philosophy of the "greatest good for the greatest number." While this pithy phrase is a very rough-and-ready characterization of utilitarian theory, it also has led to an overly mechanistic application of the principle: Just tally up the amount of good and subtract the amount of harm. If the remaining number is positive, the act is ethical. However, when properly applied, utilitarianism is not mechanical.

Table 1.2.   The Shifting Focus of Ethics from Aristotle to Mill

Philosopher	Known For	Popularly Known As	Emphasized
Aristotle	Golden Mean	Virtue lies between extremes.	The actor
Kant	Categorical imperative	Act so your choices could be universal law; treat humanity as an end, never as a means only.	The action
Mill	Utility principle	An act's rightness is determined by its contribution to a desirable end.	The outcome

To do justice to utilitarian theory, it must be understood within a historical context. Mill wrote after the changes of the Enlightenment. The principle of democracy was fresh and untried, and the thought that the average person should be able to speak his mind to those in power was novel. Utilitarianism, as Mill conceived of it, was a profoundly social ethic; Mill was among the first to acknowledge that the good of an entire society had a place in ethical reasoning.

Mill was what philosophers call a *valuational hedonist*. He argued that pleasure—and the absence of pain—was the only intrinsic moral end. Mill further asserted that an act was right in proportion to how it contributed to the general happiness. Conversely, an act was wrong in proportion to how it contributed to the general unhappiness or pain. Utilitarianism can be subtle and complex in that the same act can make some happy but cause others pain. Mill insisted that both outcomes be valued simultaneously, a precarious activity but one that forces discussion of competing stakeholder claims.

In utilitarian theory, no one's happiness is any more valuable than anyone else's, and definitely not more valuable than everyone's—quantity and quality being equal. In democratic societies, this is a particularly important concept because it meshes well with certain social and political goals. In application, utilitarianism has a way of puncturing entrenched self-interest but, when badly applied, it can actually promote social selfishness.

Utilitarianism also suggests that moral questions are objective, empirical, and even in some sense scientific. Utilitarianism promotes a universal ethical standard that each rational person can determine. However, utilitarianism is among the most criticized of philosophical principles because it is so difficult to accurately anticipate all the consequences of a particular act. Philosophers have disputed how one calculates the good, rendering any utilitarian calculus fundamentally error prone.

While utilitarianism is a powerful theory, too many rely exclusively on it. Taken to extremes, the act of calculating the good can lead to ethical gridlock, with each group of stakeholders seemingly having equally strong claims with little way to choose among them. Carelessly done, utilitarianism may bias the user toward short-term benefit, which is often contrary to the nature of ethical decisions.

Pluralistic Theory of Value

Philosopher William David Ross (1930) based his ethical theory on the belief that there is often more than one ethical value simultaneously "competing" for preeminence in our ethical decision-making, a tension set up in the title of his book *The Right and the Good*. Commenting on this tension, ethicist Christopher Meyers (2003, p. 84) says,

> As the book title suggests, Ross distinguished between the *right* and the *good*. The latter term refers to an objective, if indefinable, quality present in all acts. It is something seen, not done. Right, on the other hand, refers to actions. A right action is something undertaken by persons motivated by correct reasons and on careful reflection. Not all right actions, however, will be productive of the good.

In acknowledging the competition between the good and the right, Ross differs from Kant and Mill, who both proposed only one ultimate value. To Ross, these competing ethical claims, which he calls duties, are equal, provided that the circumstances of the particular moral choice are equal. Further, these duties gain their moral weight, not from their consequences, but from the highly personal nature of duty.

Ross proposed these types of duties:

1. those duties of *fidelity*, based on my implicit or explicit promise;
2. those duties of *reparation*, arising from a previous wrongful act;
3. those duties of *gratitude* that rest on previous acts of others;
4. those duties of *justice* that arise from the necessity to ensure the equitable and meritorious distribution of pleasure or happiness;
5. those duties of *beneficence* that rest on the fact that there are others in the world whose lot we can better;
6. those duties of *self-improvement* that rest on the fact that we can improve our own condition; and
7. one negative duty: the duty of *not injuring others*.

We would recommend two additional duties that may be implied by Ross's list but are not specifically stated:

1. the duty to tell the truth, *veracity* (which may be implied by fidelity); and
2. the duty to *nurture,* to help others achieve some measure of self-worth and achievement.

Ross's typology of duties works well for professionals who often must balance competing roles. It also brings to ethical reasoning some affirmative notions of the primacy of community and relationships as a way to balance the largely rights-based traditions of much Western philosophical theory.

Like Kant, Ross divided his duties into two kinds. *Prima facie duties* are those duties that seem to be right because of the nature of the act itself. *Duty proper* (also called actual duties) are those duties that are paramount given specific circumstances. Arriving at your duty proper from among the prima facie duties requires that you consider what ethicists call the *morally relevant differences*. But Ross (1930, p. 24) warns that

> there is no reason to anticipate that every act that is our duty is so for one and the same reason. Why should two sets or circumstances, or one set of circumstances *not* possess different characteristics, any one of which makes a certain act our *prima facie* duty?

Let's take an example using one of Ross's prima facie duties: keeping promises. In your job as a reporter, you have made an appointment with the mayor to discuss a year-end feature on your community. On your way to the city hall, you drive by a serious auto accident and see a young child wandering, dazed, along the road. If you stop to help, you will certainly be late for your appointment and may have to cancel altogether. You have broken a promise.

But is that act ethical?

Ross would probably say yes because the specific aspects of the situation had a bearing on the fulfillment of a prima facie duty. You exercised discernment. You knew that your commitment to the mayor was a relatively minor sort of promise. Your news organization will not be hurt by postponing the interview, and your act allowed you to fulfill the prima facie duties of beneficence, avoiding harm, and nurturing. Had the interview been more important, or the wreck less severe, the morally relevant factors would have been different. Ross's pluralistic theory of values may be more difficult to apply than a system of absolute rules, but it reflects the way we make ethical choices.

Ross's concept of multiple duties "helps to explain why we feel uneasy about breaking a promise even when we are justified in doing so. Our uneasiness comes from the fact that we have broken a *prima facie* duty even as we fulfilled another" (Lebacqz, 1985, p. 27).

Feminist Theory

Feminist theory begins with a different set of assumptions about how human beings come to know what is ethical. Classical philosophy approaches ethical knowing—epistemology—as a thought experiment. Once the thinking is complete, and general principles understood, the resulting theory can be applied to "real life" situations. However, feminist epistemology—and hence feminist theory—begins with the lived experience. Only as real-life ethical choice is understood, and over many instances of choosing, does theory emerge. Because of this ground-up epistemic approach, feminist theory tends to embed contemporary problems in its theoretical work. It foregrounds women's interests and includes women's experiences as appropriate fodder for moral reflection.

Carol Gilligan's research was conducted in a Cambridge clinic with women who were deciding whether to abort. In this naturalistic setting, and faced with a consequential decision soon after abortion became legal in the United States, she interviewed 24 women about their choices—while they were making them. The resulting book, *In a Different Voice*, spanned fields. The different voice that Gilligan heard was women struggling to integrate into their moral calculus an emotional commitment to others—to care (Wilkins, 2009).

Gilligan asserted that moral development did not proceed in stages. Some people began their thinking at a relatively low level and remained there, others began in a morally sophisticated fashion, and some people began in one place and progressed to another.

In their initial thinking, many women began to decide whether to abort by engaging in what Gilligan called "moral nihilism"; they needed to protect themselves and find a way through the experience. They had no thought of "should." Instead, they focused entirely on a way to get what they wanted. This is care exclusively of and for self.

At the second strand of ethical thinking, Gilligan learned that women thought of goodness as self-sacrifice. The women thought the appropriate decision was to give others what they needed, often at the expense of self. Denise, 25, initially decided against abortion, but her married lover convinced her otherwise, arguing that a failure to abort would have disastrous consequences for himself and his wife. That argument made Denise begin to question her own moral worth, to feel manipulated, not just by her lover but also by the relationship itself. Goodness as self-sacrifice did not result in a sense of moral flourishing.

Finally, some of the women Gilligan interviewed moved to thinking that focused on "the responsibility of the consequences of choice." In the case of abortion, this meant acknowledging that any decision would result in great hurt on all sides of the question. It meant acknowledging that life's consequential ethical decisions are difficult and fraught and will remain so long after the decision itself is made. These choices have no comfortable answers.

> The criterion for judgment thus shifts from goodness to truth when the morality of action is assessed not on the basis of its appearance in the eyes of others, but in terms of the realities of its intention and consequence. (Gilligan, 1982, p. 150)

Unlike conventional goodness, the "truth" of this final understanding of care requires that people extend nonviolence to themselves and others. This universal and, in some senses, elemental understanding meant that women had learned to care for themselves and to include themselves among that group of people whom it is moral not to hurt.

The ethics of care has developed intellectually based on Gilligan's work. Nel Noddings, for example, has theorized that thinking about care most fundamentally reflects the mother–infant bond. Because Gilligan was writing about women, her subsequent work has emphasized that men, too, care. As Linda Steiner notes,

> Thus journalists are ethically obligated not only to be sensitive to the voice of care, but also to evaluate and help readers evaluate claims of care and suffering and to evaluate policies and proposals to ameliorate suffering.... This politicized version of care calls on media to privilege the problems, stories, and counter-stories of marginalized or subordinated peoples and others who deserve care and compassion. (2020, p. 445)

Caring is affirmative. Unlike some ethical theory that focuses on what not to do, the ethics of care foregrounds the need for action. In this, feminist theory asks ethical decision-makers to consider what might be possible.

THE "SCIENCE" OF ETHICS

Life in the 21st century has changed how most people think about issues, such as what constitutes a fact and what does or does not influence moral certainty. But ethical theory, with its apparent uncertainties and contradictions, appears to have taken a back seat to science. As people have become drawn to ethics, they seek "the answer" to an ethical dilemma in the same way they seek "the answer" in science. Consequently, the vagaries of ethical choice as contrasted with the seeming certainty of scientific knowledge cast an unfair light on ethics.

We'd like to offer you a different conceptualization of "the facts" of both science and ethics. Science, and the seeming certainty of scientific knowledge, has undergone vast changes in the past 100 years. Before Einstein, most educated people believed that Sir Francis Bacon had accurately and eternally described the basic actions and laws of the physical universe. Bacon, however, was wrong. Scientific inquiry in the 20th century explored a variety of physical phenomena, uncovered new relationships, new areas of knowledge, and new areas of ignorance. The "certainty" of scientific truth has changed fundamentally in those 100 years, and there is every reason to expect similar changes in the present century, especially in the areas of neuroscience, nanotechnology, and artificial intelligence. Science and certainty are not synonymous despite our tendency to blur the two.

Contrast these fundamental changes in the scientific worldview with the developments of moral theory. Aristotle's writing, more than 2,000 years old, still has much to recommend it to the modern era. The same can be said of utilitarianism and of the Kantian approach—both after 150 years of critical review. Certainly, new moral thinking has emerged, but such work tends to build on rather than radically alter the moral theory that has gone before. Ethical philosophers still have fundamental debates, but these debates have generally tended to deepen previous insights rather than to "prove" them incorrect. Further, thinking about global ethics uncovers some striking areas of agreement. We are aware of no ethical system, for example, that argues that murder is an ethical behavior, or that lying, cheating, and stealing are the sorts of activities that human beings ought to engage in on a regular basis.

From this viewpoint, there is more continuity in thinking about ethics than in scientific thought. When the average person contrasts ethics with science, it is ethics that tends to be viewed as changeable, unsystematic, and idiosyncratic. Science has rigor, proof, and some relationship to an external reality. We would like to suggest that such characterizations arise from a short-term view of the history of science and ethics. In our view, ethics as a field has at least as much continuity of thought as developments in science. And while it cannot often be quantified, it has the rigor, the systematic quality, and the relationship to reality that moderns too often characterize as the exclusive domain of scientific thinking.

SUGGESTED READINGS

Aristotle. *Nicomachean ethics*.

Bok, S. (1978). *Lying: Moral choice in public and private life*. New York: Random House.

Borden, S. L. (2009). *Journalism as practice*. Burlington, VT: Ashgate.

Gert, B. (1988). *Morality: A new justification of the moral rules.* New York: Oxford University Press.

Gilligan, C. (1982). *In a Different Voice*. Cambridge, MA: Harvard University Press.

Mill, J. S. *On liberty*.

Ross, W. D. (1930). *The right and the good*. Oxford: Clarendon Press.

ESSAY

CASES AND MORAL SYSTEMS

DENI ELLIOTT
University of South Florida St. Petersburg

Case studies are wonderful vehicles for ethics discussions with strengths that include helping discussants

1. appreciate the complexity of ethical decision-making;
2. understand the context within which difficult decisions are made;
3. track the consequences of choosing one action over another; and
4. learn both how and when to reconcile and to tolerate divergent points of view.

However, when case studies are misused, these strengths become weaknesses. Case studies are vehicles for an ethics discussion, not its ultimate destination. The purpose of an ethics discussion is to teach discussants how to "do ethics"—that is, to teach processes so that discussants can practice and improve their own critical decision-making abilities to reach a reasoned response to the issue at hand.

When the discussion stops short of this point, it is often because the destination has been fogged in by one or more myths of media case discussions:

Myth 1: Every opinion is equally valid.

Not true. The best opinion (conclusion) is the one that is best supported by judicious analysis of fact and theory and best addresses the morally relevant factors of the case (Gert, 1988). An action has morally relevant factors if it is likely to cause some individual to suffer an evil that any rational person would wish to avoid (such as death, disability, pain, or loss of freedom or pleasure), or if it is the kind of action that generally causes evil (such as deception, breaking promises, cheating, disobedience of law, or neglect of duty).

Myth 2: Since we can't agree on an answer, there is no right answer.

In an ethics case, it may be that there are a number of acceptable answers. But there also will be many wrong answers—many approaches that the group can agree would be unacceptable. When discussants begin to despair of ever reaching any agreement on a right answer or answers, it is time to reflect on all of the agreement that exists within the group concerning the actions that would be out of bounds.

Myth 3: It hardly matters if you come up with the "ethical thing to do" because people ultimately act out of their own self-interest anyway.

Any institution supported by society—manufacturing firms or media corporations, medical centers, and so on—provides some service that merits that support. No matter what the service, practitioners or companies acting only in the short-term interest (i.e., to make money) will not last long. Both free-market pragmatism and ethics dictate that it makes little sense to ignore the expectations of consumers and of the society at large.

The guidelines below can serve as a map for an ethics discussion. They are helpful to have when working through unfamiliar terrain toward individual end points. They also can help you avoid the myths above. While discussing the case, check to see if these questions are being addressed:

1. What are the morally relevant factors of the case?
    (a) Will the proposed action cause an evil—such as death, disability, pain, loss of freedom or opportunity, or loss of pleasure—that any rational person would wish to avoid?
    (b) Is the proposed action the sort of action—such as deception, breaking promises, cheating, disobedience of law, or disobedience of professional or role-defined duty—that generally causes evil?
2. If the proposed action is one described above, is a greater evil being prevented or punished by allowing it to go forward?
3. If so, is the actor in a unique position to prevent or punish such an evil, or is that a more appropriate role for some other person or profession?
4. If the actor followed through on the action, would he be allowing himself to be an exception to a rule that he thinks everyone else should follow? (If so, then the action is prudent, not moral.)
5. Finally, would a rational, uninvolved person appreciate the reason for causing harm? Are the journalists ready and able to state, explain, and defend the proposed action in a public forum, or would a more detached journalist be ready to write an exposé?

CASE

CASE 1-A

HOW TO READ A CASE STUDY

PHILIP PATTERSON
Oklahoma Christian University

When you look at the photo, it stirs your emotions. It's the last moment of one girl's life (the younger survived). It's a technically good photo—perhaps a once-in-a-lifetime shot. However, when you learn the backstory of this photo, a world of issues emerges and the real discussions begin. That's the beauty of cases as a way of learning media ethics.

For this case, here is what you need to know: One July afternoon, *Boston Herald* photographer Stanley Forman answered a call about a fire in one of the city's older sections. When he arrived, he followed a hunch and ran down the alley to the back of the row of houses. There he saw a 2-year-old girl and her 19-year-old godmother on the fifth-floor fire escape. A fire truck had raised its aerial ladder to help. Another firefighter was on the roof, tantalizingly close to pulling the girls to safety. Then came a loud noise; the fire escape gave way, and the girls tumbled to the ground. Forman saw it all through his 135 mm lens and took four photos as the two were falling (see figure 1.3).

The case study has several possible angles. You can discuss the gritty reality of the content. You can factor in that within 24 hours, the city of Boston acted to improve the inspection of all fire escapes in the city, and that groups across the nation used the photos to promote similar efforts. You can talk about the ingenuity and industry of Forman to go where the story was rather than remain in front where the rest of the media missed it. You can critique his refusal to photograph the girls after impact. You can debate why the Pulitzer Prize committee gave Forman its top prize for this photo and add in the fact that more than half of the various "Picture of the Year" awards over decades are of death or imminent death. You can discuss whether the *Boston Herald* profited off the death and injury of the girls and what Forman's role was once he witnessed the tragedy. And you can ponder what happens when this photo hits the internet, stripped of context.

You can talk about any or all of these issues or imagine others. That's the beauty of a case study—you can go where it takes you. From this one case, you can argue taste in content, media economics ("If it bleeds, it leads"), personal versus professional duty, and so forth.

Perhaps you will want to role-play. Perhaps you will ask yourself what Kant or Mill would do if he were the editor, or whether a communitarian would approve of the means (the photo) because of the end (better fire escape safety). Perhaps you want to talk about the "Post Toasties Test" for objectionable content in the morning paper, whether it passes the test, or whether the test ought to exist. Or what values led the paper to run the photo and the committee to give it an award.

During the semester, you can do more than just work through the cases in this book—you can find your own. All around you are cases of meritorious media behavior and cases of questionable media behavior. And, quite frankly, there are cases where good people will disagree over which category the behavior falls into. Good cases make for good discussion, not only now but also when you graduate into the marketplace.

So, dive in, discuss, and defend.

Figure 1.3.   Stanley J. Forman, Pulitzer Prize 1977. Used with permission.

PART I:
FOUNDATIONS

The first part of this book reflects the understanding that there are not different sets of ethical rules for different occupations. To provide just one example, public relations cannot achieve its goals without news, and without news stories that are truthful and are believed by readers and viewers. Thus, Part I begins with a discussion of truth, moves to the concept of privacy, and then to loyalty. All explore the professional reality that journalists and strategic communication professionals employ multiple ethical constructs in their daily work. That work takes place in a community—a democratic society—and hence has an impact beyond the individual. The goal of democracy is not merely to exist but rather, as the founding documents of the United States suggest, to promote a just self-government. Hence Part I of this book concludes with an examination of ethical issues centering on social justice. Students will find case studies representing every professional role in each of these chapters. The goal here is to understand and then be able to apply the same ethical theories to a range of specific ethical choices.

2

Information Ethics

A Profession Seeks the Truth

By the end of this chapter, you should be familiar with

- both the Enlightenment and pragmatic constructions of truth;
- the development and several criticisms of objective news reporting as a professional ideal;
- why truth in "getting" the news may be as important as truth in reporting it;
- how to develop a personal list of ethical news values.

Each traditional profession has laid claims to a central tenet of philosophy. Law is equated with justice, medicine with the duty to render aid. Journalism, too, has a lofty ideal: the communication of truth.

However, the ideal of truth is problematic. We often consider truth a stable commodity: It doesn't change much for us on a day-to-day basis, nor does it vary greatly among members of a community. However, the concept of truth has changed throughout history. At one level or another, human beings since ancient times have acknowledged that how truth is defined may vary. Since Plato's analogy of life as experienced by individual human beings as "truthful" in the same way that shadows on the wall of a cave resemble the physical objects that cast those shadows was first proposed more than 3,000 years ago, people have grappled with the amorphous nature of truth. Today, while we accept some cultural "lies"—the existence of Santa Claus—we condemn others, such as income tax evasion or fabricating an employment history. Most of the time, we know what the boundaries are, at least when we deal with one another face-to-face.

Compounding the modern problem of the shifting nature of truth is the changing media audience. When a profession accepts the responsibility of printing and broadcasting the truth, facts that are apparent in face-to-face interactions become subject to different interpretations among geographically and culturally diverse readers and viewers. Ideas once readily accepted are open to debate. Telling the truth becomes not merely a matter of possessing good moral character but something that requires learning how to recognize truth and conveying it in the least distorted manner possible.

A CHANGING VIEW OF TRUTH

One pre-Socratic Greek tradition viewed truth—*alethea*—as encompassing what humans remember, singled out through memory from everything that is destined for Lethe, the river of forgetfulness (Bok, 1978). Linking truth and remembrance is essential in an oral culture, one that requires that information be memorized and repeated so as not to be forgotten. Repeating the message, often in the form of songs or poetry, meant that ideas and knowledge were kept alive or true for subsequent generations. Homer's *Iliad* and *Odyssey* or much of the Bible's Old Testament served this function.

This oral concept of truth, as noted in table 2.1, was gradually discarded once words and ideas were written down. However, it has come to the fore with the advent of television and its computer cousins, such as YouTube, that allow viewers to hear the words of the president rather than wait for those words to be passed down to them. When we see something on television or our computer screen, we assume that it closely corresponds to reality. The maxim "seeing is believing" reminds us that truth has become entangled with pictures, an oral concept of truth that has been a dormant form of knowledge for hundreds of years until technology made "seeing" events live worldwide possible.

While the ancient Greeks tied truth to memory, Plato was the first to link truth to human rationality and intellect. In *Republic*, Plato equated truth with a world of pure form, a world to which human beings had only indirect access. In Plato's vision, there was an ideal notion of a chair—but that ideal chair did not exist in reality. What people thought of as a chair was as similar to the ideal chair as the shadows on the wall of the cave are to the objects illuminated by the fire. To Plato, truth was knowable only to the human intellect—it could not be touched or verified. We're living in the cave.

Plato's metaphor of the cave has had a profound influence on Western thought. Not only did Plato link truth to rationality, as opposed to human experience, but his work implies that truth is something that can be captured only through the intellect. Platonic truth is implicit within a thing itself; truth defined the "perfect form." Plato's concept of the truth separated the concept from the external world in which physical objects exist.

Subsequent centuries and thinkers adhered to Plato's view. Medieval theologians believed truth was revealed only by God or by the church. The intellectual legacy of the Reformation centered on whether it is possible for the average person to ascertain truth without benefit of a priest or a king. About 200 years later, Milton suggested that competing notions of the truth should be allowed to coexist, with the ultimate truth eventually emerging (see table 2.1).

Milton's assertions foreshadowed the philosophy of the Enlightenment, from which modern journalism borrows its notion of truth. The Enlightenment cast truth in secular terms, divorced from the church. and developed a "correspondence theory" of truth still held today. The correspondence theory asserts that truth should correspond to external facts or observations. The Enlightenment concept of truth was linked to what human beings could perceive with their senses harnessed through the intellect. Truth acquired substance. It was something that could be known and something that could be replicated.

This Enlightenment notion of truth is essential to the scientific method. Truth has become increasingly tied to what is written down, what can be empirically verified, what can be perceived by the human senses. Enlightenment truth does not vary among people or cultures. It is a truth uniquely suited to the written word, for it links what is written with what is factual, accurate, and important.

Truth and Objectivity

This Enlightenment view of truth is the basis for the journalistic ideal of objectivity. While objectivity has many definitions, minimally it is the requirement that journalists divorce fact from opinion. Objectivity is a way of knowing that connects human perception with facts and then knowledge. Objectivity is

Table 2.1. A Philosophy of Truth Emerges

Source	Truth Equals
Ancient Greeks	What is memorable and is handed down
Plato	What abides in the world of perfect forms
Medieval	What the king, church, or God says
Milton	What emerges from the "marketplace of ideas"
Enlightenment	What is verifiable, replicable, universal
Pragmatists	What is filtered through individual perception

also a process of information collection (Ward, 2004). Journalists view objectivity as refusing to allow individual bias to influence what they report or how they cover it. It is in journalism that all facts and people are regarded as equal and equally worthy of coverage "without fear or favor," as stated by the *New York Times*. Culture, an individual sense of mission, and individual and organizational feelings and views do not belong in objective news accounts. An Enlightenment view of truth allowed objectivity to be considered an attainable ideal, and objectivity was often linked to the end result of reporting and editing: the individual news story or media outlet.

However, philosophy was not the only reason that objectivity became a professional standard in the early 1900s. The early American press garnered much of its financial support from political advertising and most of its readers through avowedly partisan political reporting. America became more urban in the late 1800s, and publishers realized that they had to make certain their publications would be read in order to convince potential advertisers that their advertising would be seen by a large audience. Partisan publications could not ensure that, for strong views offended potential readers. What publishers at the turn of the 20th century needed was a product that built on an Enlightenment principle that guaranteed that facts would be facts, no matter who was doing the reading. Opinion would be relegated to specific pages, and both facts and opinion could be wrapped around advertising (Schudson, 1978). In this century, the niched political product has reemerged, first on cable television and then more robustly on the web. As advertising itself has become more targeted, financial support for political content that attracts some and repels others has not been a disadvantage.

The normative ideal of objectivity came along at an advantageous time for yet another reason. The mass press of the early 1900s was deeply and corruptly involved in "yellow journalism." Fabricated stories were common; newspaper wars were close to the real thing. Objectivity was a good way to clean up journalism's act with a set of standards where seemingly none had existed before. It fit the cultural expectations of the Enlightenment that truth was knowable and ascertainable. And it made sure that readers of news columns would remain unoffended long enough to glance at the ads.

The Enlightenment view of truth also was compatible with democracy and its emphasis on rational government. People who could reason together could arrive at some shared "truth" of how they could govern themselves. Information was essential to government, for it allowed citizens to scrutinize government. As long as truth was ascertainable, government could function. Citizens and government needed information in order to continue their rational function. Information, and the notion that it corresponded in some essential way with the truth, carried enormous promise.

The Enlightenment view of truth was challenged by the 20th-century pragmatists—most notably Americans John Dewey, George Herbert Mead, Charles Sanders Pierce, and William James. They held that the perception of truth depended on how it was investigated and on who was doing the investigating. Further, they rejected the notion that there was only one proper method of investigation—that is, the scientific method. Borrowing from Einstein, pragmatists argued that truth, like matter, was relative.

Specifically, the pragmatists proposed that knowledge and reality were not *fixed by* but instead were *the result of* an evolving stream of consciousness and learning. Reality itself varied based on the psychological, social, historical, or cultural context. Additionally, reality was defined as that which was probable, not as something intrinsic (the Platonic view) or something determined by only one method of observation (the Enlightenment view). Pragmatism found a comfortable home in the 20th-century United States. Under pragmatism, truth lost much of its universality, but it was in remarkable agreement with the American value of democratic individualism. Soon pragmatism filtered through literature, science, and some professions, such as law.

Pragmatism provided a challenge to objectivity. No sooner had the journalistic community embraced objectivity than the culture adopted more pragmatic notions of truth. That clash fueled criticism of objectivity. Pragmatism challenged the journalistic product: the individual news story and the media ecosystem in which it emerged. However, if objectivity is defined as a method of information collection—a systematic approach to gathering "facts" from many points of view—then this philosophical development provides support for defining objectivity as a process rather than as a result.

Postmodern philosophy has taken these questions to their logical extension, suggesting that the concept of truth is devoid of meaning. Postmodernism asserts that context is literally everything, and that meaning cannot exist apart from context, which is directly opposed to fact-based journalism.

The last decade of the 20th century and all the years of the 21st century have added yet another level of complexity to the problem: the information explosion. Facts and truth come to us quickly from all over the globe. While objective reporting is still *one* standard, it is not the *only* standard. With the advent of websites that include words and images aggregated from many sources, yet another notion of truth is resurfacing—what philosophers call the convergence or coherence theory of truth. Under this view, truth is discovered not through any single method of investigation but by determining which set of facts forms a coherent mental picture of events and ideas investigated through a variety of methods. Multimedia journalism, which uses sounds, images, and words to cover stories, is one professional response to the coherence theory of truth and the technological possibilities of the internet and the personal computer. Of course, multimedia journalism requires an active audience, and an active audience brings its preexisting beliefs, values, and context to every message. All too often, it is possible to be overwhelmed by the information available to us rather than to devote the time and effort required to make sense of it.

In short, objectivity has been deeply undermined by both a philosophical shift and technological innovation (Christians, Ferré, & Fackler, 1993). Telling your readers and viewers the truth has become a complicated business. As Sissela Bok points out:

> Telling the "truth" therefore is not solely a matter of moral character; it is also a matter of correct appreciation of real situations and of serious reflection upon them…. Telling the truth, therefore, is something which must be learnt. This will sound very shocking to anyone who thinks that it must all depend on moral character and that if this is blameless the rest is child's play. But the simple fact is that the ethics cannot be detached from reality, and consequently continual progress in learning to appreciate reality is a necessary ingredient in ethical action. (Bok, 1978, pp. 302–303)

WHO'S DOING THE TALKING ANYWAY?

The pragmatic's critique of objectivity has called attention to the question of who writes the news. Journalists—primarily male, Caucasian, well educated, and middle to upper class—are often asked to cover issues and questions that life experiences have not prepared them to cover. Stephen Hess (1981) noted that journalists (particularly the Eastern "elite" media), in terms of their socioeconomic status, look a great deal more like the famous or powerful people they cover than the people they are supposedly writing for. Research on the national press corps has shown similar results (Weaver, Beam, Brownlee, Voakes, & Wilhoit, 2007). Journalists generally are better paid and better educated than the audience for their product.

Almost every professional journalistic organization has developed programs specifically to attract and retain women and minorities, but with only incremental and sporadic success. For example, men receive 63 percent of byline credits in print, online, and wire news. Similarly, broadcast news is anchored by men 60 percent of the time (Women's Media Center, 2019). This lack of access to the engines of information has not been lost on a variety of groups—from religious fundamentalists, who have established their own media outlets, to racial minorities, who fail to find themselves as either owners or managers of media outlets, to political conservatives.

These groups argue that the result is news about middle-class Caucasians, for middle-class Caucasians, and liberal in political orientation. How individual journalists and the corporations they work for should remedy the situation is unclear. But as demographics change us from a culture that is predominantly Caucasian to one that is not, the mass media will play a decreasing role unless journalists find a way to report news that is of interest to the new majority. In this century, worldwide newspaper readership and broadcast viewership continue to decline in favor of the internet (including newspaper websites) and magazines that focus on celebrities rather than public affairs (Thorson, Duffy, & Schumann, 2007). Traditional journalists face an audience in open rebellion with no clear strategy to remain financially viable and provide the public with the information that civic engagement requires.

DEFINING AND CONSTRUCTING THE NEWS

More than 90 years ago, journalist Walter Lippmann (1922) said, "For the most part, we do not first see, and then define, we define first and then see." He added that we tend to pick out what our culture has already defined for us, and then perceive it in the form stereotyped for us by our culture.

In one classic study (Rainville & McCormick, 1977), a blind New York journalism professor claimed he could predict the race of football players being described in the play-by-play by what was said about them. Caucasian athletes were described as intellectually gifted while Black athletes were described as physically gifted. In a culture that values brains over brawn, Black football players were the subject of repeated stereotypical insults—all couched as praise. Even though the study is now more than 40 years old, the tendency to revert to these stereotypes continues on sports broadcasts today in which athletes across sports—basketball, baseball, football, soccer, golf, and various Olympic sports—are called "intelligent" and "leaders" while others are called "physically strong" and having "natural ability" (see Billings, 2003, 2004; Billings & Eastman, 2003; Denham, Billings, & Halone, 2002; Eastman & Billings, 2001; Halone & Billings, 2010; and Rada & Wulfemeyer, 2005). In the former, the quality was obtained by hard work; in the latter, it was a gift of genetics. Women, the elderly, and the LGBTQIA community have been the focus of studies with similar results. Their conclusion has been that while journalists maintain that they are objective, they (like their readers and viewers) bring something to the message that literally changes what they see and what they report (Lester, 1996). Further, researchers have found that audiences exposed to these racial stereotypes begin to internalize them (Ferrucci, Tandoc, Painter, & Leshner, 2013; Ferrucci, Tandoc, Painter, & Wolfgang, 2016).

How journalists do their work—what scholars call news routines—also has an impact on what readers and viewers "see." "Objectivity can trip us up on the way to truth," says Brent Cunningham (2003). "Objectivity excuses lazy reporting. If you're on deadline and all you have is 'both sides of the story,' then that's often good enough." Most recently, Wesley Lowery (2020) voiced the complaints and skepticism of many in the Black community "that most American media organizations do not reflect the diversity of the nation or the communities they cover" while confining coverage to the "crime of the day." Cunningham points to a study of 414 Iraq war stories broadcast on ABC, CBS, and NBC leading up to the 2003 conflict. All but 34 originated from the White House, the Pentagon, or the State Department. The result: The "official truth" becomes the received truth, and only the bravest journalists dare depart from it. Timothy Crouse, in his 1974 campaign memoir *The Boys on the Bus,* reported the same phenomenon. John Oliver's achingly funny take on reporting climate change repeats the criticism that objectivity misused can result in lies of staggering consequence (Nuccitelli, 2014).

Theodore L. Glasser (1992) argued that a strict adherence to objectivity could bias news coverage. First, "objective reporting is biased against what the press typically defines as its role in a democracy—that of a Fourth Estate, the watchdog role, an adversary press" (p. 176). Objectivity makes the press biased against its watchdog role because it forces reporters and editors to rely on official sources, and this reliance propagates the status quo by leading journalists to seek out established power holders as primary sources of news and comment. Second, "objective reporting is biased against independent thinking; it emasculates the intellect by treating it as a disinterested spectator" (Glasser, 1992, p. 176). In strict adherence to objectivity, journalists are forced to remain impartial and neutral, which means that they should just report the "facts" as they are told instead of interpreting events through a critical lens. Third, "objective reporting is biased against the very idea of responsibility; the day's news is viewed as something journalists are compelled to report, not something they are responsible for creating" (Glasser, 1992, p. 176). In this ideology, news exists as something for a journalist to gather "out there." A journalist has completed the job if he or she reports that a fact claim has been made; he or she can report such a claim "without moral impunity—even if he or she knows the content of the claim to be false" (Glasser, 1992, p. 176). Studies of how journalists have reported false statements in 2016 and 2020 noted in the opening anecdotes for this book confirm this 30-year-old insight.

News reflects certain cultural values and professional norms. In a classic study, sociologist Herbert Gans (1979) examined how stories became news at *Newsweek, Time,* NBC, and CBS and found that almost all news stories reflected six cultural values: (1) ethnocentrism, (2) altruistic democracy, (3) responsible capitalism, (4) individualism, (5) an emphasis on the need for and maintenance of social order, and (6) leadership. These dominant values helped to shape which stories were printed and what they said, what communication scholars call "framing."

Gans called these values the "para-ideology" of the media. He added that "the news is not so much conservative or liberal as it is reformist." Researcher James Carey (quoted in Cunningham, 2003) says that it is this para-ideology that results in charges of liberal bias against the media. "There is a bit of the reformer in anyone who enters journalism. And reformers are always going to make conservatives uncomfortable."

News stories about middle-class or upper-class people, those who tend to successfully adopt the culture's values, made the American news "budget," according to Gans. While Gans focused on journalism about the United States, other scholars have noted the same phenomenon, called *domesticating the foreign*, in international coverage (Gurevitch, Levy, & Roeh, 1991; Siegel, 2020). Journalists working for US media outlets tell stories about international events in cultural terms that Americans can readily understand but that also sacrifice accuracy. For example, routine coverage of elections in Britain or Israel is conveyed in horse-race metaphors even though both countries employ a parliamentary system where governing coalitions are common and who wins the horse race is not always so important.

Americans, and others globally, increasingly are entering into "news bubbles" or "echo chambers" where their preexisting beliefs are reinforced or amplified by voices that confirm those beliefs, ideas, and attitudes instead of being challenged by others who do not already hold their views. These bubbles reflect a coherence theory of truth while pinpointing the weakness inherent in the theory. Bill Kovach and Tom Rosenstiel (2010) dubbed the media echo chamber the "journalism of affirmation." Cable news pundits such as Sean Hannity or Anderson Cooper, for example, build loyalty by affirming the beliefs of their audiences, cherry-picking information that serves that purpose. Whether you call them news bubbles, echo chambers, or the journalism of affirmation, they distort discourse by limiting the scope of public discussion: News organizations no longer can identify a common set of issues. As former senator Daniel Patrick Moynihan said, "Everyone is entitled to his own opinion, but not his own facts."

E. J. Dionne (1996) claims that the press is in internal contradiction. It must be neutral yet investigative. It must be disengaged but have an impact. It must be fair minded but have an edge. The conflicts make objectivity virtually impossible to define and even harder to practice (see figure 2.1).

Figure 2.1. 1993, Washington Post Writers Group. Reprinted with permission.

PACKAGING THE STORY: NEWS AS MANUFACTURED PRODUCT

The goal of telling a "good story" also raises other ethical questions, specifically those that focus on packaging to highlight drama and human interest. These questions have intensified as all media channels—from newspapers to documentary film to entertainment programming—have focused on coherent storytelling and the need for a powerful story to capture audience interest. Current research suggests that narratives are memorable, but news narratives are not always neat, and the facts from which they emerge can be both chaotic and contradictory.

This drive to package has led to a profession that values finding an "event" to report and to be there first. Few consumers realize it, but news is "manufactured" daily. Journalists start the day with a blank computer screen and with deadlines looming. They produce a print story, a video package, a tweet, or a multimedia report—or often all four. Adding to the built-in tension of deadlines is the challenge to be fair, complete, accurate, and, above all, interesting. Whole industries—particularly public relations or strategic communication—have emerged to help journalists package their daily stories on deadline.

Finding an event to cover means that journalists have missed some important stories because they were not events but rather historic developments. Major social developments such as the civil rights and the anti-Vietnam War movements of the 20th century, and the Black Lives Matter and the Occupy Wall Street movements in the 21st century, were under-covered until their leaders created events for the media to report. Director Michael Moore said he began his career with the 1989 film *Roger and Me* about the devastation of General Motors layoffs in his hometown of Flint, Michigan, because he "didn't see on the silver screen or the television screen what happened to people like us" (Smith, 1992). The preoccupation with events also affects coverage of science, which is most frequently reported as a series of discoveries and "firsts" rather than as a process (Nelkin, 1987)—a decades-old criticism that has emerged with new force during the COVID-19 pandemic. Other stories are missed or misreported when they lack the easy "peg" editors look for. The *Washington Post*'s Pulitzer Prize-winning stories on conditions at Walter Reed army hospital emerged only after dismayed veterans and their families contacted the newspaper multiple times (Priest & Hall, 2007). When thousands of lives were lost in Bhopal, India, by a malfunctioning pesticides plant, coverage focused entirely on the picture-friendly event and not on the socioeconomic, scientific, and political causes that led to the disaster (Wilkins, 1987). A deeper look at news coverage of the 1986 Chernobyl nuclear disaster, something Charles Perrow calls a "normal accident" in his book of the same title, found that coverage echoed the stereotype of American superiority and Russian inferiority rather than an approach focusing on science and risk (Patterson, 1989). Phenomena not linked to specific events—such as climate change or the opioid crisis—went unreported for years waiting for an appropriate news peg. Truth is more than just a collection of facts. Facts have a relationship to one another and to other facts, forming a larger whole. However, analytic coverage of American institutions, of science and technology, of politics, and of social movements is rare.

What is more common—especially on cable news outlets—is to invite two or more parties with conflicting views, allot them too little time to discuss the issue at hand, and then sit back and let the resulting heated exchange take the place of reporting. Deborah Tannen (1999) dubbed this phenomenon argument culture, which she described as an adversarial frame that assumes blanket opposition is the best way to get anything done. Argument culture, at least in part, also allows bad actors into the marketplace of ideas, or at least allows outrageous conspiracies such as Pizzagate and QAnon to get a hearing in the marketplace.

Stephen Hess (1981) has argued that journalists need to engage in reporting that looks more like social science than storytelling. Gans (1979) argues for news that is labeled as originating from a particular point of view. Other scholars argue for news that is analytical rather than anecdotal, proactive rather than reactive, and contextual rather than detached. On a practical level, working reporters and editors insist that individual journalists need to do a better job of understanding their own biases and compensating for them.

The accumulated evidence, both anecdotal and scholarly, today strikes at the core of objectivity (Craft, 2017) and shows that, intellectually, we are living in a pragmatic era, but we seem to be unable professionally to develop a working alternative to the Enlightenment's view of truth. Because of this, mainstream media are increasingly seen as irrelevant, particularly to a younger audience for whom truth is more likely to be a segment on *The Daily Show* than a report on the networks' nightly newscasts.

ON THE ETHICS OF DECEPTION

Ethicist Sissela Bok (1978) notes that discerning the truth—and then telling it—is hard. Bok's book focuses intensely on human relationships. It would be fair to say that she did not anticipate algorithms, social media, and the like. In this decade, the confluence of a cultural shift about the nature of truth; the segmentation of an active audience, on the one hand, and the range of media outlets, on the other; the emergence of Facebook and Twitter as purveyors of news through sharing; and the increasingly sophisticated technology associated with computers and widely available software have led to the emergence of yet another challenge to journalism: what was once called "fake news" but now is more appropriately dubbed disinformation or misinformation.

So, let's begin with a definition. Bok defines lying in the following way: The lie must be stated, the liar must knowingly provide information that they are aware is incorrect or wrong, and the lie must be told in order to gain power over the person who is being lied to. For Bok and many other ethicists, lying as an act—like murder—starts out in the "moral deficit" column. The human default is "truth"; lying must be justified to be ethical, and satisfactory justification is rare.

We think the parallels between Bok's definition of lying and any definition of disinformation are strong. First, disinformation is "stated"—that is, publication on the internet, including the dark web, is the equivalent of saying something to a friend. Second, those who produce disinformation—or set its production in motion through the use of bots or other technological tools—are aware that it is wrong or inaccurate. This sets disinformation apart from a mistake (discussed later in this chapter), misleading or out-of-context information, clickbait, satire, propaganda, or conspiracy theories. Third, disinformation is developed and distributed to gain power—in this context, the economic power that comes from internet clicks linked to advertising content. The motive here is not better social relations or political activism; the goal is to gain power through wealth.

Disinformation also has become a lot more sophisticated since the 2016 US presidential election. For example, Russia's Internet Research Agency created a fake, left-wing news outlet with fictional editors. The innovation: They hired real, unwitting freelance journalists to report and write stories. Facebook eventually removed the stories. The social media site also deleted a doctored video featuring a supposedly drunk or drugged House Speaker Nancy Pelosi, but not before it was seen by more than 2 million people.

Journalists who unmask internet trolls—and thereby challenge their worldview—have themselves been threatened. Jared Yates Sexton, a *New York Times* contributor and assistant professor of creative writing at Georgia Southern University, shared with *HuffPost* several threatening messages directed at him since he unmasked an internet troll who created a video retweeted by President Donald J. Trump. In one, a Reddit user warns of a looming "journocaust"—presumably a holocaust for journalists. In another, a Twitter user says there's "a civil war coming" and that memes—specifically, the anti-Semitic one by the creator of the video that Trump shared—are "the least" of Sexton's problems. "There's a fever pitch to this dialogue that is dangerous to everybody," Sexton told *HuffPost*. "And it's the people who are mentally ill, who are unhinged, who are unwell—they pick up on this stuff. And they are really, really moved to act by it" (D'Angelo, 2017).

Bok's treatise on lying does not anticipate that those who tell the truth about lies will be physically threatened by those who lie. She assumes that, in civil society, the human need for truth in order to live an authentic life will triumph over the short-term need to ease difficult questions and difficult relationships by everything from fibbing to telling whoppers. However, as the above examples and many others suggest, getting "found out" about lying does not seem to deter the impulse, which can be fueled by a drive for wealth or notoriety or both.

As human beings, we are attracted to things that seem outlandish and strange. In a study that examined how tweets were shared, beginning in 2006 and continuing through 2013, social scientists found false tweets reached an audience of 1,500 or more six times faster than true tweets, a pattern that emerged as more than 126,000 individual news items were shared 4.5 million times among more than 3 million people. As one of the researchers noted, "The crazy stupid . . . is the one that goes massively viral" (Lazer et al., 2018). At least one site—Prank Me Not—even allows users to create fake tweets and Facebook posts. While the creators of the site explicitly state that it "may only be used for personal use," it's incredibly easy to create an extremely realistic fake tweet, take a screen capture, and then upload the image to Twitter with a message of "Can you believe what so and so said?" It's humorous, though potentially harmful, to create a fake tweet about your friend; it's potentially world changing, though, if it's "from" President Joe Biden.

Fake news is a new frontier for journalists. There are too many fake news stories to spend the time and resources to debunk every one. Debunking itself may put journalists and their news organizations in harm's way. Technological solutions (for example, the development of real-time algorithms that would spot the fake and label it as such) are in development but not yet in the world. We will discuss the impact of "fake news" on democratic decision-making in chapter 5, but for our purposes in this chapter, one principle stands out: It has never been more important for professional journalists to tell the truth in their reporting and to make every effort to continue to do so. Minimally, trust in the profession and belief in its credibility are at stake.

ON THE ETHICS OF DECEPTION: THE JOURNALIST'S PERSPECTIVE

In a profession that values truth, is it ever ethical to lie? To editors? To readers? To sources, who may be liars themselves? Are there levels of lying? Is flattering someone to get an interview as serious a transgression as doctoring a quote or photograph? Is withholding information the same thing as lying? If you can only get one side of the story, do you go with it? Does it matter today if opinion mingles with news?

Unearthing Fake News

One of the most basic tenets of journalism is "check it out." In previous eras, that has meant double-checking what human sources say with other human sources, seeing if documents support or contradict what human sources say, and, more recently, making sure that documents are both authentic and complete. But "fake news" calls for a different kind of checking, first by journalists and then by readers, viewers, and listeners. It calls for skepticism about every element of a news story—from the headlines to the visuals to the origin of the words themselves.

And, in what is sure to be an affirmative change in role, journalists need to educate their viewers, readers, and listeners on how to "check it out" for themselves. If veracity can be considered an ethical news value, something we suggest later in this chapter, then this sort of investigation of news stories themselves can become part of your journalistic routine.

Here is a checklist we think you should consider as you develop your own methods for verifying facts, sources, and images.

- Look up sources before posting or publishing.
- Check the URL. Can you tell where the story is from?
- Read the "About" page.
  Warning: If there is no "About" page or if it is not clear who is running the site, be skeptical and double-check everything.
  Warning: A URL pretending to be a news site—for example, ABCNews.com.co—is a tip-off for bogus content.
- Analyze the headline.
  Do the facts in the story match the headline?
  If there is a quote from a prominent/famous person, put the quote in a search engine and see what turns up.
  Are the quotes in the story in context?
  No quotes in the story—be very cautious. Journalists quote their sources.
- Does the story attack a general enemy (for example, "Washington," "the media," or "Trump supporters")?
- Check the author—stories with no author or written under a pseudonym deserve extra scrutiny.
- What's the support?
  Click the links on the story and see where they lead; links that don't exist or don't link to credible sources indicate a problem.

- Check the photos through a search engine such as Google images—who is really pictured?
- Check the date.
- Check your sense of humor—are you sure this isn't a joke?
- Check your biases.
  Is the story so outrageous you don't believe it?
  Is the story so good you must believe it?
  Stories that are too perfect, too good to be true, or that provoke an immediate and intense emotional reaction deserve a second and then a third look.
- Are other, reputable news sources reporting on the story?
  If you Google the URL and get a report back from Politifact or Snopes, the claim you searched is false.

  We also encourage you to beware of sudden popularity. Five years ago, going viral was a sort of gold standard for journalistic reports. But with bots, hackers, and troll farms at work, viral popularity is just as likely to be fool's gold.
  This checklist also can be made a prominent part of every news organization's website.

Crises of credibility have faced media outlets of all sizes, including spectacular instances at both *USA Today* and the *New York Times* that resulted in front-page editorial apologies and multipage retractions. In what is now a historic case for the *Times*, in 2002 a 27-year-old reporter, Jayson Blair, fabricated all or part of more than 40 stories. After his resignation from the paper, the *Times* ran four full pages of corrections documenting every error discovered in Blair's reporting. The *Times*'s correction made it clear that editors had failed to find and fix the problem in earlier stages despite many opportunities to do so. In a subsequent analysis of the case, many at the *Times* and other places suggested that one reason Blair's actions had been unchecked for so long was because of his race. Blair was Black, and he had been hired as part of the *Times*'s diversity program. His mentors at the paper, Executive Editor Howell Raines and Managing Editor Gerald Boyd, who also was Black, were among Blair's strongest supporters. Both eventually resigned in the fallout. While the *Times* denied that race was the reason that Blair had been promoted, Blair himself did not.

Errors in Journalism: Inevitability and Arrogance

Confounding truth and deception in journalism is the problem of errors. Inadvertent mistakes in stories are common. One freelance fact-checker (Hart, 2003) wrote in the *Columbia Journalism Review* (*CJR*), one of journalism's leading watchdog publications, that she had not experienced an error-free story in three years of fact-checking for *CJR*. Her calls to fellow fact-checkers at other publications led her to believe that articles with factual errors are the rule, not the exception.

However, mistakes are different from fabrication and do not indicate a lack of dedication to the truth. Some, if not most, mistakes are matters of interpretation, but others are outright errors of fact. In her article "Delusions of Accuracy," Ariel Hart says that hearing journalists proudly claim to have had no errors or fewer errors than the *Times* found in Blair's writing is "scary, not the least because it encourages delusions of accuracy."

One problem seems to be audience members being so disconnected from the media that they don't bother to correct journalists' mistakes or, worse, assume, as readers of the *Times* evidently did, that fabrication is de rigueur for journalists (see figure 2.2).

"Journalists surely make mistakes often, but I think we don't—or can't—admit it to ourselves because the idea of a mistake is so stigmatized. . . . So mistakes need to be destigmatized or restigmatized and dealt with accordingly. They should be treated like language errors," Hart argues.

However, Blair wasn't the only bad news for the *Times* during those weeks. Pulitzer Prize-winning reporter Rick Bragg also resigned from the paper after it became known that he, too, had published stories based largely on the reporting of stringers who did not receive a byline in the *Times*. Furthermore, some of his stories filed with non-New York datelines had been written on airplanes and in hotel rooms, where Bragg was functioning more as a rewrite editor rather than doing actual on-the-scene reporting. Bragg said his practices were known at the *Times* and common in the industry. That comment aligns

Figure 2.2. Pearls Before Swine © Stephan Pastis/Distributed by United Feature Syndicate, Inc.

with one heard frequently in the Blair incident that sources did not complain to the *Times* about incorrect stories since they felt that fictionalizing stories was just the way things were done. This cynical appraisal of journalism threatens our credibility, which is the chief currency of the profession.

So, how do journalists feel about deception? A survey of members of the nonprofit organization Investigative Reporters and Editors (IRE) provides some insight into the profession's thinking (Lee, 2005). Journalists think about deception on a continuum. At one end, there is almost universal rejection of lying to readers, viewers, and listeners. IRE members regard such lies as among the worst ethical professional breaches. At the other end, more than half of the IRE members surveyed said they approved of flattering a source to get an interview, even though that flattery could be considered deceptive and certainly was insincere.

In the same survey, lies of omission—such as withholding information from readers and viewers and also editors and bosses—were considered less of a problem than fabricating facts in a story or fabricating entire stories, which was almost universally condemned. IRE members were more willing to withhold information in instances when national security issues were involved. The journalists also said some lies were justified: They approved of lying if it would save a life or prevent injury to a source.

The journalists surveyed also noted that there were outside influences on these judgments. Broadcast journalists were more accepting of hidden cameras and altering video than were print journalists, although that difference might be changing as more print journalists get video experience via their newspaper's websites. Further, those who worked in competitive markets were more willing to accept deception than were those who saw themselves in less competitive environments. The more experienced a journalist was, the less likely he or she was to accept any form of deception. Finally, the survey revealed what journalists worry about is the impact such reporting methods have on the believability of news accounts and on journalists' ability to cover subsequent stories if caught in an ethical lapse.

Is it ethical to lie to liars? Is withholding information the same thing as lying? If not, under what circumstances might it be appropriate? If it is, are there ethically based justifications for such an act? Sissela Bok (1978) argues that such an act raises two questions. Will the lie serve a larger social good, and does the act of lying mean that we as professionals are willing to be lied to in return?

Bok suggests that most of the time, when we lie we want "free rider" status—gaining the benefits of lying without incurring the risks of being lied to. In other words, some journalists may believe it's acceptable to lie to a crook to get a story, but they professionally resent being lied to by any source, regardless of motive.

Lying is a way to get and maintain power. Those in positions of power often believe they have the right to lie because they have a greater than ordinary understanding of what is at stake. Lying in a crisis (to prevent panic) and lying to enemies (to protect national security) are two examples. In both circumstances, journalists can be—either actively or without their knowledge—involved in the deception. Do journalists have a right to counter this lying with lies of their own, told under the guise of the public's need to know? Does a journalist have the responsibility to print the truth when printing it will cause one of the evils—panic or a threat to national security—that the lie was concocted to prevent?

Then there is the "omission versus commission" issue. In the first, the lie is that some part of the truth was conveniently left out; in the latter, the lie is an untruth told purposefully. Bok asserts that a genuinely white lie may be excusable on some grounds, but that all forms of lying must stand up to questions of fairness and mutuality. According to Kant's categorical imperative, the teller of the white lie must also be willing to be lied to. Even lying to liars can have its downside as Bok points out:

> In the end, the participants in deception they take to be mutually understood may end up with coarsened judgment and diminished credibility. But if, finally, the liar to whom one wishes to lie is also in a position to do one harm, then the balance may shift; not because he is a liar, but because of the threat he poses. (1978, p. 140)

Reporting via the internet has given new urgency to the issue of lying by omission. In most instances, failing to identify yourself as a reporter when collecting information electronically from news groups, chat rooms, or other modes of public discussion is considered problematic. Journalists, when pressed, note that the US Supreme Court has ruled internet transmissions are public. The ethical issue emerges when most of those involved in the discussion are not aware of the legal standards and expect, instead, the more ethically based relations of face-to-face interactions. Ethical thought leaves journalists with difficult choices.

Reporting *on* the contents of the internet—and cable television—raises another series of challenges. How should journalists go about debunking internet rumors, which can sometimes be distinguished from disinformation? Conventional wisdom for legacy media holds that reprinting or rebroadcasting rumors only furthers them. News organizations in New Orleans covering Hurricane Katrina faced a series of difficult news decisions in the face of rumors sweeping the city. In some instances, they elected to print or broadcast rumors prevalent in the networked world that they could not substantiate. The same problems continue to plague journalists in stories as distinct as news of Kobe Bryant's death, terrorist attacks in Europe, or the latest "cure" for COVID-19.

Another equally serious challenge is how to treat information promulgated by well-known sources—information that is false. Calling someone a liar, at one level, seems the height of nonobjective journalism. However, when the facts suggest that a source is lying—even if that source is not held to the same standards of truth telling as journalists are—what becomes an acceptable professional mechanism to hold non-journalist sources to account? Fact-checking is one mechanism increasingly used by news organizations. PolitiFact, for example, rates statements by political and other figures on a six-point scale ranging from "True" to "Pants on Fire." The organization fact-checked more than 900 claims made by Donald Trump, finding that only 12 percent were "True" or "Mostly True" while 42 percent were "False" or "Pants on Fire." Barack Obama, by contrast, was fact-checked more than 600 times by PolitiFact, which found his statements "True" or "Mostly True" 47 percent of the time and "False" or "Pants on Fire" only 12 percent of the time.

ETHICAL NEWS VALUES

Most mass-media courses present a list of qualities that define news. Most such lists include proximity, timeliness, conflict, consequence, prominence, rarity, change, concreteness, action, and personality. Additional elements may include notions of mystery, drama, adventure, celebration, self-improvement, and even ethics. While these lists are helpful to beginning journalists, they probably will not help you decide how to report the news ethically.

We suggest you expand your journalistic definitions of news to include a list of ethical news values. These values are intended to reflect the philosophical tensions inherent in a profession with a commitment to truth. If news values were constructed from ethical reasoning, we believe the following elements would be emphasized by both journalists and the organizations for which they work.

- **Accuracy**—using the correct facts and the right words and putting things in context. Journalists need to be as independent as they can when framing stories. They need to be aware of their own biases—including those they "inherit" such as social class, gender, and ethnicity, as well as learned professional norms.
- **Confirmation**—writing articles that are able to withstand scrutiny inside and outside the newsroom. Media ethicist Sandy Borden (2009) refers to this as the "discipline of confirmation," a concept that reflects how

difficult it can be to capture even a portion of the truth in sometimes complex news situations.

Tenacity—knowing when a story is important enough to require additional effort, both personal and institutional. Tenacity drives journalists to provide all the depth they can regardless of the individual assignment. It has institutional implications, too, for the individual cannot function well in an environment where resources are too scarce or the corporate bottom line too dominant. In addition, news organizations need to trust journalists when they report independently rather than expect them to act as part of a pack.

Dignity—leaving the subject of a story as much self-respect as possible. Dignity values each person regardless of the particular story or the particular role the individual plays. Dignity allows the individual journalist to recognize that newsgathering is a cooperative enterprise where each plays a role, including editors, videographers, designers, and advertising sales staff.

Reciprocity—treating others as you wish to be treated. Too often, journalism is "writing for the lowest common denominator." Reciprocity demands respect for the reader. It also rejects the notion of journalism as benevolent paternalism—"We'll tell you what we think is good for you"—and recognizes that journalists and their viewers and readers are partners both in discovering what is important and in gleaning meaning from it.

Sufficiency—allocating adequate resources to important issues. On the individual level, sufficiency can mean thoroughness—for example, checking both people and documents for every scrap of fact before beginning to write. On an organizational level, it means allocating adequate resources to the newsgathering process. With virtually every media outlet suffering from declining readers or viewers, thanks mainly to the web, this is probably the central issue of the current media landscape.

Equity—seeking justice for all involved in controversial issues and treating all sources and subjects equally. Equity assumes a complicated world with a variety of points of view. Equity demands that all points of view be considered but does not demand that all sides be framed as equally compelling. Equity expands the journalistic norms of "telling both sides of the story" to "telling all sides of the story."

Community—valuing social cohesion. On the organizational level, a sense of community means that media outlets and the corporations that own them need to consider themselves as citizens rather than mere "profit centers." On the individual level, it means evaluating stories with an eye first to social good.

Diversity—covering all segments of the audience fairly and adequately. There appears to be almost overwhelming evidence that news organizations do not "look like" the society they cover. While management can remedy part of this problem by changing hiring patterns, individual journalists can learn to "think diversity" regardless of their individual heritages.

In 2013, the Corporation for Public Broadcasting decided to make an ethical news value—transparency—the cornerstone of its new standards and practices policy. However, no list of ethical news values should be considered conclusive. Collectively, they provide a framework within which informed ethical choices can be made.

SUGGESTED READINGS

Bok, S. (1978). *Lying: Moral choice in public and private life.* New York: Random House.

Gans, H. (1979). *Deciding what's news: A study of CBS Evening News, NBC Nightly News, Newsweek and Time.* New York: Vintage.

Jamieson, K. H. (1992). *Dirty politics.* New York: Oxford University Press.

Lippmann, W. (1922). *Public opinion.* New York: Free Press.

Plato. *Republic.*

Weaver, D. H., Beam, R. A., Brownlee, B. J., Voakes, P. S., & Wilhoit, G. C. (2007). *The American journalist in the 21st century: U.S. news people at the dawn of a new millennium (LEA's Communication Series).* Mahwah, NJ: Lawrence Erlbaum Associates.

CASES

CASE 2-A

RULES OF ENGAGEMENT: MARY LOUISE KELLY AND THE MIKE POMPEO INTERVIEW

LEE WILKINS
University of Missouri

Despite the apparent ease of asking questions via email, broadcast journalists still must get their sources on the record via sound and images. Most often this is done in person, although broadcasters make use of technologies such as Zoom, and radio journalists often use phone interviews. In many ways, these in-person requirements are dictated by the medium itself, although the history of print journalism includes extensive reliance on the in-person interview.

In January 2020, National Public Radio journalist Mary Louise Kelly interviewed Secretary of State Mike Pompeo about Iran. Kelly worked to make arrangements for the interview for more than a month, corresponding with Pompeo's staff via email to set up the interview. In those emails, which have become public, Kelly said she planned to devote most of what became a nine-minute interview to US policy toward Iran but that she would also ask about the Trump administration's relationship with Ukraine, which had become the focus of congressional impeachment hearings that were taking place at the same time as the interview. In none of the emails did she agree to make any part of the interview "off the record."

In the initial portion of the interview, Kelly pressed Pompeo for specifics on US foreign policy that would retard or prevent Iran from building nuclear weapons.

Kelly: How do you stop Iran from getting a nuclear weapon?
Pompeo: We'll stop them.
Kelly: How? Sanctions?
Pompeo: We'll stop them. The president made it very clear. The opening sentence in his remarks said that we will never permit Iran to have a nuclear weapon. The coalition that we've built out, the economic, military, and diplomatic deterrence that we have put in place will deliver that outcome. It's important [crosstalk] because this will protect the American people.
Kelly: Is there any new deal being developed? A new nuclear deal, something that would rein in Iran, something that they would agree to.

Pompeo: The Iranian leadership will have to make the decision about what its behavior is going to be.

At this point, Kelly turned the interview to Ukraine. Specifically, she asked Pompeo what he had done to defend former US ambassador Marie L. Yovanovitch from the campaign that ultimately led to President Donald J. Trump firing her.

"I've defended every single person on this team," Pompeo said. "I've done what's right for every single person on this team" (Breslow, 2020).

When Kelly asked if he could point to specific remarks in which he defended Yovanovitch, Pompeo said, "I've said all I'm going to say today. Thank you. Thanks for the repeated opportunity to do so. I appreciate that."

One of Pompeo's staff members then ended the interview. Kelly reported that the secretary of state glared at her as he left the room.

In a broadcast later on NPR, Kelly described what happened next.

She said the aide who had stopped the interview reappeared and asked her to come with her, with no recorder. Kelly said she was taken to Pompeo's private living room, where he was waiting, and "where he shouted at me for about the same amount of time as the interview itself had lasted."

"He was not happy to have been questioned about Ukraine," Kelly said. "Do you think Americans care about Ukraine? He used the f-word in that sentence, and many others."

Pompeo asked Kelly if she could find Ukraine on a map, and Kelly, whose reporting has taken her around the world, said, "Yes."

"He called out for his aides to bring him a map of the world with no writing, no countries marked," Kelly said. "I pointed to Ukraine. He put the map away. He said, 'People will hear about this.'"

Kelly reported the entire series of events, including her meeting with Pompeo in his private living room, on NPR the next day, including the fact that the US Department of State had been asked to comment but had not responded by airtime.

The next day, as reported by the *New York Times* and many other media outlets, Pompeo criticized the interaction as follows:

In a statement on Saturday, Mr. Pompeo responded to Kelly's account but did not deny that he used obscenities and shouted at her.

"NPR reporter Mary Louise Kelly lied to me, twice," Pompeo said. "First, last month, in setting up our interview and, then again yesterday, in agreeing to have our post-interview conversation off the record.

"It is shameful that this reporter chose to violate the basic rules of journalism and decency," Pompeo added. "This is another example of how unhinged the media has become in its quest to hurt President

Trump and this Administration. It is no wonder that the American people distrust many in the media when they so consistently demonstrate their agenda and their absence of integrity."

NPR stood by its reporting of the incident and supported Kelly in her journalistic conduct and decisions.

Micro Issues

1. Was it appropriate for Kelly to tell Pompeo the subject of her questions in the process of setting up the interview?
2. Do broadcast journalists face a different set of professional challenges in getting interviews than do journalists working in print or online? Should they? How do those challenges change the relationship between the interviewer and the interviewee?
3. Should Kelly have reported what happened after the formal interview concluded? Why or why not? Does Kelly's action constitute courage or foolhardiness, based on your understanding of Aristotle's virtue ethics?

Midrange Issues

1. Journalists must always balance getting a source to talk and so offending a source that an interview is concluded before the needed information is gathered. What guidelines have you received from your editors/news directors/professors on this issue? Do they make sense?
2. Should Kelly have taken her recording equipment with her into Pompeo's private living room after the on-air interview concluded? Why or why not?
3. Should journalists tell their readers/listeners/viewers about the specific conditions of interviews as part of the reporting on the interview itself? What ethical principle supports your response?

Macro Issues

1. When, if ever, is it appropriate for a journalist to report information gathered "off the record"?
2. What should journalists do when they are treated poorly by sources? Does the type of source—victim of a crime, elected public official, and so forth—make a difference?

3. Develop guidelines for you and others to go "off the record" with sources. Link those guidelines to the ethical philosophies of utilitarianism and the categorical imperative.
4. Was Kelly at a disadvantage because she was a woman? Some media outlets reported that Pompeo was a particularly confrontational interview subject with women journalists. Should NPR have asked a male journalist to do this interview instead?

CASE 2-B

DON'T TWEET ILL OF THE DEAD

CHAD PAINTER
University of Dayton

NBA legend Kobe Bryant and his 13-year-old daughter, Giana Maria-Onore Bryant, were among nine people killed in a Jan. 26, 2020, helicopter crash in Calabasas, California. Tributes and remembrances poured in from sports figures such as Bryant's ex-teammate Shaquille O'Neal, Michael Jordan, and LeBron James, as well as celebrities including Taylor Swift, Chrissy Teigen, and Jennifer Lopez.

One tweet, though, created a wave of backlash. Felicia Sonmez—a national political reporter for the *Washington Post* who covers breaking news from the White House, Congress, and political campaigns—tweeted a link to a 2016 *Daily Beast* article about Bryant's 2003 sexual assault case. In two follow-up tweets, Sonmez wrote:

> Well, THAT was eye-opening. To the 10,000 people (literally) who have commented and emailed me with abuse and death threats, please take a moment and read the story—which was written 3+ years ago, and not by me. Any public figure is worth remembering in their totality . . . even if that public figure is beloved and that totality unsettling. That folks are responding with rage & threats toward me (someone who didn't even write the piece but found it well-reported) speaks volumes about the pressure people come under to stay silent in these cases.

In July 2003, police in Eagle, Colorado, arrested Bryant after a 19-year-old hotel employee accused him of raping her at the Lodge and Spa at Cordillera in Edwards, Colorado. Bryant admitted having sex with the woman, but he claimed that it was consensual. Charges later were dropped after the woman refused to testify in the case. However, Bryant and the woman did settle a civil lawsuit out of court, and Bryant publicly apologized to her, his family, and the public while denying the allegations.

Sonmez is herself a survivor of sexual assault. In spring 2018, she detailed allegations against Jon Kaiman, the president of the Foreign Correspondents' Club of China. (At the time of the alleged 2017 assault, Sonmez was a foreign correspondent based in Beijing.) She wrote that Kaiman digitally penetrated her twice without her consent, attempted to take his pants off while she protested, and later had unprotected sex with her while she was too intoxicated to consent (Harris, 2019).

The *Post* responded to the backlash over Sonmez's tweets by suspending her. Managing Editor Tracy Grant said in a Jan. 26 statement,

> National political reporter Felicia Sonmez was placed on administrative leave while the *Post* reviews whether tweets about the death of Kobe Bryant violated the *Post* newsroom's social media policy. The tweets displayed poor judgment that undermined the work of her colleagues. (Stewart, 2020)

Sonmez said that Grant emailed her to say that the tweets didn't pertain to her area of coverage and were making it difficult for other *Post* reporters do their work (Stewart, 2020).

Post executive editor Marty Baron was even more blunt in an email he sent to Sonmez, which she shared with the *New York Times*. "A real lack of judgment to tweet this," Baron wrote. "Please stop. You're hurting this institution by doing this" (Abrams, 2020).

By Jan. 27, the *Washington Post* Guild, a union representing more than 1,000 employees, issued a statement supporting Sonmez and admonishing the *Post*. In the letter, the Guild called for the *Post* to "issue a statement condemning abuse of its reporters, allow Felicia to return to work, rescind whatever sanctions have been imposed and provide her with any resources she may request as she navigates this traumatic experience."

The *Post* reversed course and reinstated Sonmez on Jan. 28. In a statement, Managing Editor Grant wrote the following:

> After conducting an internal review, we have determined that, while we consider Felicia's tweets ill-timed, she was not in clear and direct violation of our social media policy. Reporters on social media represent *The Washington Post*, and our policy states "we must be ever mindful of preserving the reputation of *The Washington Post* for journalistic excellence, fairness and independence." We consistently urge restraint, which is particularly important when there are tragic deaths. We regret having spoken publicly about a personnel matter.

Micro Issues

1. Was the *Post* right in suspending Sonmez? In reinstating her?
2. Analyze Sonmez's tweets in relation to the *Washington Post*'s social media policy, which can be found online.
3. Sonmez was not the only person on Twitter and elsewhere who pointed toward Bryant's rape case. Why do you think her tweet received so much backlash?

Midrange Issues

1. Sonmez was suspended, in part, because of the online backlash to her and the *Post*. What impact, if any, should public comment and criticism play in a news organization's editorial decisions?
2. The *Post* extensively covered the Bryant rape case in 2003. How might *Post* editors have reacted if Sonmez posted the paper's reporting instead of a *Daily Beast* article?
3. The phrase "stick to sports" refers to the view that professional athletes should refrain from political or cultural commentary. Sonmez is a political reporter. So, should she "stick to politics"? Why or why not?

Macro Issues

1. Sonmez wrote "Any public figure is worth remembering in their totality . . . even if that public figure is beloved and that totality unsettling." What is the proper balance between truth telling and respect for the dead? Should there be a period of time before journalists begin reporting a person's past misdeeds?
2. When entering a newsroom, do journalists give up the privilege to express opinions online? Should they? How does your answer conform to or diverge from the concept of objectivity?
3. When former President Bill Clinton eulogized former President Richard Nixon, he failed to mention that Nixon had resigned the presidency in disgrace. Obituaries of Nixon noted this fact high in the story. Should the standards for political leaders apply to sports figures? Why or why not?

CASE 2-C

DR. DOOLITTLE NOT: DEBUNKING FAKE ANIMAL STORIES

LEE WILKINS
University of Missouri

The ratings demonstrate it: People like stories about animals. Such stories often close local—and sometimes national—television newscasts. News stories focusing on animals go viral with regularity. Animals are the long-term focus of advertising campaigns; even if you don't drink beer, you probably recognize the Budweiser Clydesdales.

And films as historic as *Old Yeller* or as contemporary as *The Secret Life of Pets* are popular, apparently for repeated viewings. Pandemic puppies are a real thing. According to the American Pet Products Association, Americans spent more than $72 billion on their animal companions in 2018.

But sometimes the stories aren't true.

Swans and dolphins have not returned to the polluted canals of Venice. Russian President Vladimir Putin did not let African lions loose in the streets of Moscow to enforce COVID-19 stay-at-home orders. A group of elephants did not stroll through a Chinese village, get drunk on corn wine, and pass out in the public square.

Debunking these online stories has more and more become a full-time job, especially for Natasha Daly, a reporter for *National Geographic*. Daly began reporting for the magazine five years ago because she believed that it was impossible for "animals to tell their own stories." She viewed her beat as one that focused on conservation, but she also covered the factual account of a Bronx Zoo tiger that tested positive for COVID-19.

Daly has online support. Paulo Ordoveza is a web developer and image-verification expert who runs the Twitter account @picpedant. Ordoveza says the "greed for virality" has driven the widespread sharing of such misinformation. The high that comes from thousands of likes and retweets is just too much for some to resist.

Kaveri Ganapathy Ahuja's retweet about the swans returning to Venice got more than a million likes, a personal social media record Ahuja says she would not like to delete. The New Delhi resident said she composed the tweets combining photos she saw on social media, unaware that the swans already lived in Italy before the coronavirus hit that country. "The tweet was just something that brought me joy in gloomy times," she told *National Geographic*.

For others, it was a need to return to order in 2020—a year that felt like chaos on wheels. The theme of nature returning to normal, which underlies many of the fake animal stories, gives people some sense that nature has the power to rise above the pandemic.

Daly says she believes that it's her responsibility as a journalist to tell her readers the truth, even when they push back about her debunking efforts. False stories can have a deleterious impact on conservation efforts, Daly notes. When humans change ecosystems to the point where they cannot recover with human intervention, false stories give the impression that such efforts aren't needed because life will eventually find a way to survive.

However, Daly also takes pride in telling "the real" animal stories. "I always want to empower readers to come away from it feeling like there's actually something they can do in their own lives to protect animals."

Micro Issues

1. In 2020, a year of COVID-19 and a contentious US election, what is the ethical rationale for ending newscasts on a "happy" note?
2. Should social media websites mark untrue animal story posts as misinformation?
3. Social psychologist Erin Vogel said that feel-good fake stories can make people even more distrustful of news when they learn that they are not true. Evaluate this statement in light of the theories of truth outlined earlier in this chapter.

Midrange Issues

1. Is debunking fake animal stories an appropriate use of journalistic resources?
2. Are such fake animal stories a triumph of emotion over reason? How would strategic communication professionals respond to such a question? Those who are focused on news?
3. Evaluate Ahuja's rationale for declining to retract her tweet. How should Twitter respond to users who think this way?
4. How does a willingness to believe such animal stories make you think about your readers/viewers/listeners as ethical decision-makers?

Macro Issues

1. What is the role of the news media in verifying internet rumors?
2. Are such animal stories too trivial to consider in light of the significant and serious news events in contemporary political culture?
3. Do narrative films such as *The Jungle Book* and *Lion King* trivialize the real issues of conservation and global climate change by anthropomorphizing animal welfare?
4. Use TinEye or Google's reverse image search to fact-check an animal-based story carried on a local news outlet. After your fact-check, evaluate the truthfulness of the images. Do fabricated images harm readers and viewers?

CASE 2-D

ANONYMOUS OR CONFIDENTIAL: UNNAMED NEWS SOURCES IN THE NEWS

LEE WILKINS
University of Missouri

They are characterized in many different ways. Frequently, there are no names, just blurred references to job duties.

From the *New York Times* on Dec. 9, 2017, as it reported on President Donald J. Trump's daily routine:

> One adviser said that aides to the president needed to stay positive and look for silver linings wherever they could find them, and that the West Wing team at times resolved not to let the tweets dominate their day.

Other times, they are slightly more anonymous. From the *New Yorker's* reporting by journalist Ronan Farrow about the Harvey Weinstein sexual abuse/harassment scandal:

> Two sources close to the police investigation said that they had no reason to doubt Gutierrez's account of the incident. One of them, a police source, said that the department had collected more than enough evidence to prosecute Weinstein. But the other source said that Gutierrez's statements about her past complicated the case for the office of the Manhattan District Attorney, Cyrus Vance Jr. After two weeks of investigation, the district attorney's office decided not to file charges.

There are those who have made journalistic history, such as Watergate's anonymous source, who was known for decades only as "Deep Throat." Journalists Bob Woodward and Carl Bernstein kept Deep Throat's identity a secret for more than 30 years until FBI agent W. Mark Felt, shortly before his death, announced that he had played this pivotal "follow the money" role in the investigation.

And sometimes they even make it to the US Supreme Court, as in *Cohen v. Cowles Media Co.*, 501 US 663 (1991), when the court ruled that journalists could not allow sources to remain confidential if such promises would violate normally applicable laws. *Cohen v. Cowles* changed the way newsrooms operated.

Anonymous sources may even change the course of history. Judith Miller, a former *New York Times* reporter who protected her anonymous sources in her reporting on the alleged existence of weapons of mass destruction in Iraq in 2002 and 2003, was lionized by her profession until being ultimately vilified when it was revealed that those sources were, in fact, former president George W. Bush administration officials who had demanded anonymity in return for access. The weapons of mass destruction, of course, did not exist, and both Miller and the *Times* had to face the historic impact of erroneous reporting that supported the US decision to invade Iraq.

Anonymous sources are also used as political bludgeons. If a story is sourced anonymously, it's tantamount to "fake news." A reader voiced what many other were thinking in a February 2017 *New York Times* piece that reflected on its own sourcing practices, something that the newspaper has been criticized for since at least the early 1990s. The *Times*'s article included the following:

> Gene Gambale of Indio, Calif., is among the readers who wrote to complain in recent weeks. "I have noticed a continuous and disturbing trend of relying upon unnamed sources," Gambale said. "I believe that is poor journalism and deprives the reader of any way to evaluate, on their own, the credibility of those sources or the accuracy of the statements they make."

Anonymous sources have become so much a part of what the public believes it knows about how journalists operate that every beginning reporter has faced this question, whether it comes from average citizens, or local elected, appointed, or nongovernmental officials: "I'd like to tell you this, but I don't want you to use my name."

How to handle such requests, and under what circumstances, has been a continual professional debate that dates back to the founding of the US republic when Benjamin Franklin used multiple "noms de plume" such as Silence Dogood and Richard Saunders, who published respectively in the *New England Courant* and as the author of the *Poor Richard's Almanac*. Ethical decision-making asks journalists to balance potential harm to sources—for example, ratting out a drug cartel in a news story is a life-threatening decision—with the need for the public to know consequential information and to evaluate it. These decisions involve truth telling, transparency, and the ability for news organizations to defend their decisions in court—something that multiple news organizations have had to do since the Cohen decision, and which is often threatened by the subjects of unflattering and often investigative pieces.

Micro Issues

1. How would you respond to a city councilperson who requests anonymity before speaking with you about an important local issue? Why?
2. Many journalists believe that the Cohen ruling is an example of "bad law" overriding important ethical principles. Evaluate this claim. What is the role of trust between a journalist and her supervising editors in such decisions? Between a journalist and the news organization's corporate owners?

Midrange Issues

1. How would you respond to the reader who wrote to the *New York Times* to question that paper's use of anonymous sources?
2. Is there a distinction between sources who are unknown to the general public but well known to the major players in specific stories and sources such as Deep Throat who are known only to journalists? Why?
3. The names of rape and sexual harassment victims are often allowed to remain anonymous. Evaluate this professional norm.

Macro Issues

1. Investigative journalist and *Washington Post* editor Bob Woodward has said that some institutions, such as the military and the courts, could not be covered were it not for anonymous sources. Assuming that Woodward is correct, what should journalists agree to in order to cover these important beats?

2. Judith Miller spent three months in jail rather than reveal the sources of her stories on weapons of mass destruction. Would you be willing to take such a stand? Do you think news organizations should support journalists who do make such decisions?

CASE 2-E

DEATH AS CONTENT: SOCIAL RESPONSIBILITY AND THE DOCUMENTARY FILMMAKER

TANNER HAWKINS
Oklahoma Christian University

Eric Steele's documentary *The Bridge* tells the story of the Golden Gate Bridge—the leading location for suicide in the world—and the people who travel from around the nation to end their lives there. The documentary also features interviews with the families of the deceased and a lone jumper who survived.

Steele's crew spent 365 days recording the bridge and documented 23 of the 24 suicides that occurred in 2004. According to Steele, he and his crew were often the first callers to the bridge patrol office to report jumpers, but they never stopped recording during incidents with potential jumpers and those that followed through. To accurately portray the number of suicides that take place annually at the bridge, Steele and his crew did not personally interfere with any of the jumpers.

In the United States, approximately 30,000 people kill themselves each year. The average age for a person who commits suicide by jumping from the Golden Gate Bridge is in the 20s. Eleven men died building the structure. In an interview, Steele said he had once considered suicide. "It's that Humpty Dumpty moment when it's all going to fall apart," he said. "For me and many others, it didn't come. For the people in this film, it did" (Glionna, 2006).

Soon after Steele's crew wrapped up filming, the *San Francisco Chronicle* reported that multiple government officials claimed that Steele lied about the intentions of his documentary. When applying for a permit to film in the Golden Gate National Recreation Area, Steele said he planned to film the "powerful and spectacular interaction between the monument and nature." He later emailed bridge officials to confess the true intentions of his documentary, knowing there was little they could do.

Many critics lambasted the documentary, claiming that featuring the bridge as a prominent suicide destination in such a somber manner would only increase the number of suicides. It was called "voyeuristic," "ghastly," and "immoral" in various reviews and the equivalent of a "snuff film" by one San Francisco supervisor.

"This is like a newspaper carrying a front-page photo of someone blowing his head off; it's irresponsible, exploitive," said Mark Chaffee, president of Suicide Prevention Advocacy Network California.

Other detractors rebuked the film for failing to include interviews with any mental illness experts or psychologists. The review on the BBC website noted that "despite the shocking, up-close look, we're no closer to a real understanding of the terrible urge to end it all" (Mattin, 2007).

The *New York Times* took a middle road, observing that *The Bridge* raises inevitable questions about the filmmaker's motives and methods and whether he could have tried harder to save lives (Holden, 2006). It "raises age-old moral and aesthetic questions about the detachment from one's surroundings that gazing through the camera's lens tends to produce." The author went on to say that such discussion was beyond the scope of a movie review.

However, just as many supporters came to the defense of the documentary, arguing that the film brought awareness to an important topic that is not discussed openly enough in society. Reviewer Jim Emerson (2006) wrote about the film for Roger Ebert's website:

> *The Bridge* is neither a well-intentioned humanitarian project, nor a voyeuristic snuff film. It succeeds because it is honest about exhibiting undeniable elements of both. It's a profoundly affecting work of art that peers into an abyss that most of us are terrified to face.

Following the release of the film, the city of San Francisco voted to spend $2 million on a study to examine building a pedestrian suicide barrier, a move it had resisted in the past (Glionna, 2006).

Micro Issues

1. Should the makers of the documentary have tried to intervene in any of the 20-plus suicides they witnessed? Why or why not? Justify your answer.
2. If a news crew had been on the bridge at the time of a jumper, would their obligations be any different from a documentarian?
3. Because suicide is a crime, did the filmmakers have a duty to report the jumpers as they climbed to the top of the bridge?

Midrange Issues

1. Does the recording of the last moments of nearly two dozen lives violate the privacy of individuals suffering from severe mental illness? The privacy of their families? If so, is this violation justified?
2. Does Steele's dishonesty in obtaining a permit to film the bridge and the jumpers negate the integrity of his documentary? Discuss your answer in light of utilitarian theory.
3. Is there any merit to complaints that the documentary might encourage "copycats" among those struggling with suicidal thoughts? Justify your answer.
4. Do you agree with the comments by Chaffee that the film is equivalent to a newspaper printing a photo of someone blowing his head off? In what way is the comparison right or wrong in your opinion?

Macro Issues

1. Is there a difference between how a utilitarian such as John Stuart Mill would view the decisions made by the documentarians and how they would be viewed by a deontologist such as Immanuel Kant? If so, discuss how they would differ.
2. Other documentarians have had to make decisions that allowed harm to come to their subjects or decisions to not render aid to their subjects in pursuit of a truthful outcome on film. What is the "greater good" in situations such as this? Is there a universal principle for all documentaries, or should it be decided on a case-by-case basis?
3. Many believe that the decision by the city to finance a study to examine ways to prevent future suicides was motivated by the film. Does this change your opinion of the film in any way? If so, how?

CASE 2-F

WHEN IS OBJECTIVE REPORTING IRRESPONSIBLE REPORTING?

THEODORE L. GLASSER
Stanford University

Amanda Laurens, a reporter for a local daily newspaper, covers the city mayor's office, where she attended a 4 p.m. press conference. The mayor, Ben Adams, read a statement accusing Evan Michaels, a city council member, of being a "paid liar" for the pesticide industry.

"Councilman Michaels," the mayor said at the press conference, "has intentionally distorted the facts about the effects of certain pesticides on birds indigenous to the local area."

"Mr. Michaels," the mayor continued, "is on the payroll of a local pesticide manufacturer," and his views on the effects of pesticides on bird life "are necessarily tainted."

The press conference ended at about 5:15 p.m., less than an hour before her 6 p.m. deadline. Laurens quickly contacted Councilman Michaels for a quote in response to the mayor's statement. Michaels, however, refused to comment, except to say that Mayor Adams's accusations were "utter nonsense" and "politically motivated." Laurens filed her story, which included both the mayor's accusation and the councilman's denial. Laurens's editor thought the story was fair and balanced and ran it the following morning on the front page.

The mayor was pleased with the coverage he received. He thought Laurens had acted professionally and responsibly by reporting his accusation along with Michaels's denial. Anything else, the mayor thought, would have violated the principles of objective journalism. The mayor had always believed that one of the most important responsibilities of the press was to provide an impartial forum for public controversies, and the exchange between him and the councilman was certainly a bona fide public controversy. Deciding who's right and who's wrong is not the responsibility of journalists, the mayor believed, but a responsibility best left to readers.

Councilman Michaels, by contrast, was outraged. He wrote a scathing letter to the editor, chiding the newspaper for mindless, irresponsible journalism. "The story may have been fair, balanced, and accurate," he wrote, "but it was not truthful." He had never lied about the effects of pesticides on bird life, and he had "never been on the payroll of any pesticide manufacturer," he wrote. "A responsible reporter would do more than report the facts truthfully; she would also report the truth about the facts." In this case, Michaels said, the reporter should have held off on the story until she had time to independently investigate the mayor's accusation, and if the accusation had proved to be of no merit, as Michaels insisted, then there shouldn't have been a story. Or if there had to be a story, Michaels added, "it should be a story about the *mayor lying*."

By way of background: The effects of pesticides on bird life has been a local issue for nearly a year. Part of the community backs Mayor Adams's position on the harmful effects of certain pesticides and supports local legislation that would limit or ban their use. Others in the community support Councilman Michaels's position that the evidence on the effects of pesticides on bird life is at best ambiguous and that more scientific study is needed before anyone proposes legislation. They argue that pesticides are useful, particularly to local farmers who need to protect crops, and because the available evidence about their deleterious effects is inconclusive, they believe that the city council should not seek to further restrict or prohibit their use. The exchange between Mayor Adams and Councilman Michaels is the latest in a series of verbal bouts on the subject of pesticides and the city's role in their regulation.

Micro Issues

1. Did Laurens do the right thing by submitting her story without the benefit of an independent investigation into the mayor's accusations about Councilman Michaels?
2. Is the mayor correct in arguing that Laurens acted responsibly by providing fair and balanced coverage of both sides of a public controversy without trying to judge whose side is right and whose side is wrong?
3. Is the councilman correct in arguing that Laurens acted irresponsibly by concerning herself only with reporting the facts truthfully and ignoring the "truth about the facts"?

Midrange Issues

1. Is it sufficient when covering public controversies to simply report the facts accurately and fairly? Does it matter that fair and accurate reporting of facts might not do justice to the truth about the facts?
2. Does the practice of objective reporting distance reporters from the substance of their stories in ways contrary to the ideals of responsible journalism?
3. If reporters serve as the eyes and ears of their readers, how can they be expected to report more than what they've heard or seen?

Macro Issues

1. What distinguishes fact from truth? For which should journalists accept responsibility?
2. If journalists know that a fact is not true, do they have an obligation to share that knowledge with their readers? And if they do share that knowledge, how can they claim to be objective in their reporting?
3. Justify or reject the role of objectivity in an era where more media outlets are available than ever before.

3

Privacy

Looking for Solitude in the Global Village

By the end of this chapter, you should

- appreciate how the logic of contemporary technology is changing how we think about privacy, particularly in strategic communication;
- understand the concepts of discretion, right to know, need to know, want to know, and circles of intimacy;
- understand potential justifications for privacy invasion;
- understand and apply Rawls's veil of ignorance as a tool for justice-based ethical decision-making

WHY PRIVACY IN THE NEW MILLENNIUM?

Advertising historically has been thought of as more art than science. Popular culture affirms this view. Don Draper in *Mad Men* invents slogans and visual images for iconic products. Mel Gibson in *What Women Want* employs personal experience to understand his target audience. In *Ford vs. Ferrari*, Matt Damon and Christian Bale spend millions to promote Ford as fast and cool, an image campaign designed to sell Mustangs. You probably enrolled in a strategic communication course believing that creativity would be among the tools that cut through the clutter of our mediated lives. If you are like a lot of strategic communication majors, courses in marketing, statistics, and data analysis—now often required for graduation—are most often classes to be endured rather than understood as the bedrock of a profession.

However, on the other side of campus in colleges of engineering and departments of computer science, advertising itself has changed beyond anything Don Draper would have recognized. We experience that change on laptops and mobile phones while only vaguely connecting it to strategic communication or to how journalistic organizations make money. Thanks to computers, data analytics, and a cultural shift to a modernity that emphasizes the individual, we have entered the world of surveillance capitalism (Zuboff, 2019), where products and services are not the objects of value exchange. Instead, consumers are being bought and sold, most often to advertisers but sometimes to political movements and individual political candidates. Further, what is being sold is a prediction of our *future behaviors* based on information that has been stored and scraped from everything from specific information searches and posts on social networking sites to online purchases.

Surveillance capitalism employs technology, but it cannot be reduced to technology. Rather, it is the logic of the technology that defines the concept, a field that is characterized by asymmetries in knowledge and the power to retain that knowledge and repurpose it to make a profit.

> In the march of institutional interests . . . the very first citadel to fall is the most ancient: The principle of sanctuary[,] . . . The crucial developmental challenges of the self-other balance cannot be negotiated adequately without disconnected time and space for the ripening of inward awareness . . . reflection on and by oneself. *The real psychological truth is this: If you've got nothing to hide, you are nothing.* (Zuboff, 2019, pp. 478–479, italics in the original)

Sanctuary is the physical place where individual privacy can be sustained. For the first time in the intellectual history of mass communication, how we think about privacy now is the purview of strategic communication more than news.

PRIVACY AS AN ETHICAL CONSTRUCT

The ethical basis for privacy historically has been linked to natural rights, rights that we possess by being human. Philosophically, privacy has two components: control over information about the self and control over the context in which that information is understood. In much Western philosophy, privacy is linked to protecting the individual from larger, more powerful persons or institutions. Search engines aided by algorithms, what Zuboff and others call machine learning, is one such powerful tool employed by corporations as large as Facebook or as consequential as Cambridge Analytica. However, it is impossible to think about privacy outside of community.

Communitarians see the myth of the self-contained "man" in a state of nature as politically misleading and dangerous. Persons are embedded in language, history, and culture, which are social creations; there can be no such thing as a person without society. (Radin, 1982)

Responsibility for keeping things private is shared: Individuals have to learn when to share or withhold information, while the community has to learn when to avert its eyes. "A credible ethics of privacy needs to be rooted in the common good rather than individual rights" (Christians, 2010). The role of the community in avoiding "the unwanted gaze" can be understood through Talmudic law, according to legal scholar Jeffrey Rosen:

> Jewish law, for example, has developed a remarkable body of doctrine around the concept of *hezzek re'iyyah*, which means "the injury caused by seeing" or "the injury caused by being seen." This doctrine expands the right of privacy to protect individuals not only from physical intrusions into the home but also from surveillance by a neighbor who is outside the home, peering through a window in a common courtyard. Jewish law protects neighbors not only from unwanted observation, but also from the possibility of being observed. . . . From its earliest days, Jewish law has recognized that it is the uncertainty about whether or not we are being observed that forces us to lead more constricted lives and inhibits us from speaking and acting freely in public. (Rosen, 2000, pp. 18–19)

The last sentence is important: Fear of being observed causes us to partially shut down our lives where we are celebrating, mourning, or just going about our daily pattern. The injury caused by seeing is not fleeting. In 2019, students at Harvard University supported a lawsuit by the descendant of two slaves who had been photographed in the 1860s to support supposed academic work proving that Blacks were biologically inferior. These may be the oldest existing images of slaves. The suit alleged that Harvard had made money from the images and that the descendant of the two slaves was injured by the selling of the photographs and the publishing of them in various books (Su, 2020). In 2020, retired British royals Harry Windsor and Meghan Markle won a privacy suit against one of the largest paparazzi agencies in California for drone photography it had taken and sold of their 14-month-old son, Archie Harrison Mountbatten-Windsor. As part of the settlement, the X17 agency agreed to destroy all photographs and not to take any more "in any private residence or the surrounding private grounds" (Barnes, 2020). Regardless of historic era, Talmudic law is detailed and strict. If your window looks into your neighbor's private courtyard, you are morally obligated to avert your gaze.

PHILOSOPHICAL TOOLS TO DISTINGUISH
BETWEEN SECRECY AND PRIVACY

While Rosen's work begins in community, most of Western philosophy has focused on the individual. The injury caused by seeing foregrounds two separable and individually oriented concepts: privacy and secrecy. Secrecy can be defined as blocking information intentionally to prevent others from learning, possessing, using, or revealing it (Bok, 1983). Secrecy ensures that information is kept from *any* public view. Privacy, however, is concerned with determining who will obtain access to the information. Privacy does not require that information never reach public view, but rather who has control over the information that becomes public. Secrecy often carries a negative connotation, particularly for journalists. However, secrecy is neither morally good nor bad. Privacy and secrecy can overlap but are not identical. "Privacy need not hide; and secrecy hides far more than what is private. A private garden need not be a secret garden, a private life is rarely a secret life" (Bok, 1983, p. 11). Many people think of their information searches as both private and ephemeral. The opposite is true: Machine learning demands data on everything from your location to your search habits. Corporations such as Google admit to retaining that information "for a very long time."

CIRCLES OF INTIMACY

Legal rulings have provided some tools to understand the philosophical basis of privacy, again focusing first on the individual. In *Dietemann v. Time* (1971), jurist Alan F. Westin viewed privacy as the ability to control one's own "circles of intimacy." If you conceive of privacy as a series of concentric circles, as figure 3.1 illustrates, in the innermost circle you are alone with your secrets, fantasies, hopes, reconstructed memories, and the rest of the unique psychological "furniture" we bring to our lives.

The second circle you probably occupy with one other person, perhaps a sibling, a spouse, a parent, a roommate, or a loved one. You might hold several "you plus one" circles simultaneously in life and the number and identity of these "you plus one circles" might change at various times in your development. In that circle, you share your private information, and for that relationship to work well, it needs to be reciprocal—based on trust.

The third circle contains others to whom you are very close—probably family or friends, perhaps a lawyer or clergy member. Here, the basis of relationships is still one of trust, but control over the information gets trickier. As the ripples in the pond of intimacy continue to spread, what you reveal

PUBLIC   PUBLIC

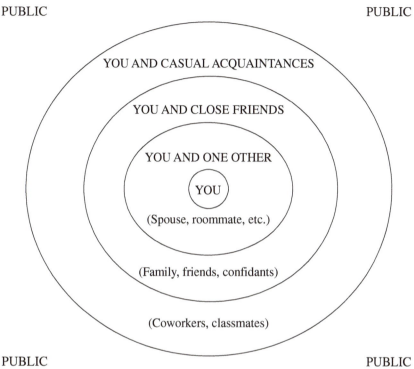

PUBLIC   PUBLIC

Figure 3.1. The Concept of Circles of Intimacy

about yourself becomes progressively more public and less intimate, and you lose progressively more control over information about you.

Using this model, privacy can be considered control over who has access to your various circles of intimacy. Invasion of privacy occurs when your control over your own circles of intimacy is wrestled from you by people or institutions. Facebook has a history of providing much information to online "friends" without first asking the permission of those who generated the information. In almost all instances, Facebook has had to walk back those decisions after substantial user blowback. Doxxing is a contemporary example of privacy invasion—intensified because of the nature of social media. The original doxxing provides one sort of injury, but as the information spreads and is used in a variety of ways, the original injury is repeated and sometimes intensified.

Journalists sometimes invade circles of intimacy either accidentally or purposefully. Awareness of the concept will allow you to consider the rights and needs of others as well as the demands of society, particularly when the issue is newsworthy. Under at least some circumstances, invasion can be justified. Part of ethical growth is to know when the rule applies and when the exceptions should occur.

DISCRETION: WHETHER TO REVEAL PRIVATE INFORMATION

With the distinction between privacy and secrecy in mind, the next problem confronting the ethical journalist is "discretion"—a word not usually associated with journalism. Bok (1983) defines discretion as "the intuitive ability to discern what is and is not intrusive and injurious" (p. 41).

We all decide at times to reveal private information, and doing so wisely is a mark of moral growth discussed in the final chapter of this book. Discretion demands moral reasoning. Once a source decides to reveal private information, a reporter's discretion remains the sole gatekeeper between that information and a public that might need the information or might merely want the information. Take, for instance, the journalist covering the California wildfires who gets answers to questions about resettlement and potential restitution while the interviewees are clearly in shock and in no condition to be making complex decisions like the cost and benefits of granting an interview. Journalists routinely interact with people following traumatic events such as the death of a loved one or the loss of a home to fire. Reporters, then, must take those factors into account as they ask questions and turn those answers into a story. Reporters also must be cognizant of the distinction—both journalistically and ethically—between interviewing politicians, celebrities, and other public figures who routinely interact with the press and know the process and "normal" people for whom a journalistic interview is a novel and sometimes nerve-wracking experience. Kantian theory would suggest that the journalist treat even the indiscreet source as the journalist herself would wish to be treated, making publication of the indiscretion less likely. Yet many journalists claim that, in practice, everything is "on-the-record" unless otherwise specified. This is the approach that is reflected in "machine learning": Everything done on the web is "on the record" in the sense that the data it generates can be used for other purposes, most often to produce targeted ads.

In the culture of surveillance capitalism, people don't own their own data, the corporation that collected it does. Both strategic communication and news can summon a series of duties: How should vulnerable audiences be treated? What would best inform readers/viewers/listeners? What might an employee owe the corporation paying them? Ross's list of prima facie duties could be helpful. However, machine learning has yet to be able to calculate discretion; human thinking and feeling appear to be required.

WHEN THE RIGHT TO KNOW IS NOT ENOUGH

Just as the distinction between secrecy and privacy is easily confused, there is also a misunderstanding among professionals and the public about the concepts of "right to know," "need to know," and "want to know." These three concepts are distinct and not interchangeable.

Right to know is a legal term often associated with open-meeting and open-record statutes. These laws are a legal, not ethical, construct. Journalists have a legal right to the same information that other members of the public may obtain—for example, the transportation of hazardous materials through their communities.

Ethical problems can emerge from right-to-know information. Is it ethical to print everything a journalist has a legal right to know? For instance, police reports routinely carry the names of suspects, victims, and witnesses to a variety of crimes. If a reporter has information that might harm, on the local level, the right to a fair trial or, on the federal level, national security, should it be withheld?

Need to know originates in the realm of philosophy. One function of mass media is to provide information that will allow citizens to go about their daily lives in society, regardless of political outlook.

Too often, when journalists assert the public has a "right to know," what they mean is that citizens "need" the information to get along in their daily lives. For example, the average citizen cannot examine bank records—those records are specifically excluded from the Freedom of Information Act. But what happens when government fails? Consider the 2007–2009 turmoil in the financial sector. Investors lost billions in a New York-based Ponzi scheme. Major banks wrote off billions of losses. Investment banks faltered. Enron became a synonym for bad corporate management. Because of the "carnage" left behind when these events happen, journalists could reasonably argue that at least some information about the health of financial institutions and the character of those who run them is needed by the public to make informed economic decisions. Need to know requires a tenacious journalist and an acknowledgment that some laws need to be changed in order for the public to get needed information.

Grcic (1986) asserts that privacy can be negated by more compelling rights. In simpler times, the right to invade privacy belonged almost exclusively to the government. For the survival of the entire political community, the government demands that its citizens provide it with certain information that is otherwise private. Specific rules govern such disclosure. The government cannot legally give your tax return information—which under penalty of law must include much private financial information—to other interested

parties. Such a check on government power theoretically allows the maintenance of some level of individual privacy. There also is an important conceptual distinction between traditional privacy—typically defined as the right
to keep certain personal facts from public view—and contemporary privacy,
which the courts carved out starting in the late 1960s. Contemporary privacy recognizes a person's right to engage in personal activities—including
marriage, procreation, contraception, and abortion—without governmental
interference (Sandel, 1996).

However, the government is not the only institution today that can demand
and receive private information. Banks, credit companies, doctors, and attorneys all request (and usually receive) private information, the bulk of it willingly disclosed. And, of course, there are Facebook and other social media
sites. Inevitably, such disclosure is one-directional. When you buy a house or
apply for a job, the information industry disgorges huge amounts of legal and
financial information about you with about a 40 percent chance of some error,
according to some industry figures. And even when consumers are given a
free chance to look at and correct their credit information, only a small percentage do. While you are expected to provide your physician with your medical history to ensure proper treatment, your physician might be surprised if
you inquired about her success rate with a particular surgical procedure, and
she certainly is not required to give it to you. Doctors in states where laws
requiring such information be made available to patients have been debated
usually go on record as being against disclosure, saying that the information
devoid of context can be deceptive or outright wrong.

Need to know is the most ethically compelling argument. Need to know
demands that an ethical case be constructed for making known information
that others wish to keep private. Need to know also means that a case be
made that the journalist is not engaging in mere voyeurism. When an argument is framed in terms of right to know, it reduces the journalist to an ethical legalism: I will do precisely what the law allows. When an argument is
framed in terms of need to know, however, it means that counterbalancing
forces have been weighed and that bringing the information to light is still
the most ethical act.

Finally, there is the issue of *want to know*, which speaks to the curiosity
in all of us. Want to know is the least ethically compelling rationale for
acquiring and disseminating information. We all want to know a lot of things:
what our neighbors do in the evening hours; how much money other people
earn; what products might be available and of interest. The books a person
ordered on wedding planning and dog sports might be personal, but they are
not private to Amazon, which will recommend additional volumes on these
same subjects within days of the initial browsing or purchase. While we may

want that information, we don't really need it thrust on us in the midst of other activities, and we most certainly have no right to it.

Journalists—especially bloggers—have become sources for much "want to know" information. Nearly a century ago, *Police Gazette* titillated its readers with information they wanted to know that no other media outlet provided. Today that function is filled by slick websites and syndicated television shows such as TMZ. Surveillance capitalism provides a similar sort of information—with the significant addition that such information may never have been requested by the end user in the first place. Instead, the end user (as understood through big data) is the real endpoint in the economic transaction.

As the foregoing paragraphs suggest, the concept of privacy in the United States has intersected with and emerged from law, particularly constitutional law. Employing legal concepts to elucidate an element of philosophy dominated much 20th-century thinking about privacy. Professionals needed to know in general terms when privacy claims are justified. "Since a right to privacy imposes obligations and restrictions on others, it is important that the right be circumscribed in a non-arbitrary manner" (Nissenbaum, 2010, p. 72). These law-based constraints focused on the individual harm—intrusion on a person's solitude, the public disclosure of embarrassing facts, or the misappropriation of a person's name or likeness for personal advantage.

However, thinking of privacy through a legal lens was problematic for two reasons. First, in the United States, state and federal courts have made divergent rulings about the concept. Journalists are caught between what the law allows and what their consciences will permit. This confusion has led to ethical bungling on a scale that undermines the profession's credibility by feeding the stereotypical notion that journalists will do anything to get a story and that audiences will willingly consume anything the journalist—or a social media website—delivers. Second, the law is always post hoc: Legal remedies occur only after harm has been inflicted. In almost every instance, ethical thinking prior to broadcast or publication is preferable to a court battle and a potential monetary award.

INFORMATION PRIVACY: SHIFTING THE FOCUS OF THE ACT

The law assumes that a specific and concrete individual is harmed in privacy issues. However, the notion of surveillance capitalism shifts the concept of harm away from an act that is based exclusively in individuals and instead can focus on groups of individuals—voters, those who consume specific products, social media acquaintances and friends. Corporations are included among these "groups." Helen Nissenbaum, one of the foremost scholars on the subject, argues that social media and many other forms of technology have erased the public/private dichotomy. Nissenbaum's sophisticated thesis is that privacy is neither a right to secrecy nor a right to control information, but rather a right that individuals have to "control . . . the appropriate flow of personal information" in a variety of contexts (Nissenbaum, 2010, p. 127).

The individual history and professional roles of the parties potentially affected by any decision to release information illustrate what scholars call "context-relative informational norms." The norms for a corporation such as Facebook or Google, both of which are profit-making entities, might be different from those of the local police department or your campus student services office as it tracks COVID-19 cases. Because these contexts are so different, any analysis of privacy questions will seldom result in a rule that fits all cases and all eventualities. This shift in focus on the nature of the act of invading privacy, occurring as it does in our data-soaked information age, has led to the following philosophically based categorization of 21st-century harms of privacy invasion:

- informational harm such as identity theft;
- informational inequality, such as governments and corporations amassing large amounts of data about individuals without their knowledge or consent;
- informational injustice—for example, transferring data from your financial records to the local newspaper without appropriate contextual information; and
- encroachment on moral autonomy, "the capacity to shape our own moral biographies, to reflect on our moral careers, to evaluate and identify with our own moral choices, without the critical gaze and interference of others" (Van den Hoven, 2008, p. 49). In this new type of information age, Pederson (1999) has defined privacy as a boundary control process, including both seeking and restricting interaction. His studies suggest that privacy is essential for psychological health, a kind of health that allows individuals to flourish and contribute to families, communities, and society at large.

The central role of technology also influences contemporary theory. Scholars note that individual control over the bits and bytes of private information is much more difficult to accomplish (some assert impossible) for the average individual, particularly if that person is coerced by economic or political necessity (Marx, 1999). European scholars have linked privacy with a capitalist market economy, on the one hand, and the interventions of the welfare state, on the other. "What does privacy mean to the homeless and the unemployed? Is there a point to privacy if people do not have the means and the power to enjoy freedom?" (Gutwirth, 2002, p. 52).

Thinking about privacy as embedded in community summons different philosophical understandings than individual harms. Information inequality and injustice require thinking about privacy questions through the lens of justice in addition to the more traditional approach of individual rights.

The Need for Privacy

The so-called right to privacy has been widely debated and written about, but the arguments are made more problematic by the fact that the term never appears in the US Constitution. Relatively little has been written about the "need for privacy." Philosopher Louis W. Hodges writes on the need for privacy, saying that "without some degree of privacy, civilized life would be impossible" (Hodges, 1983).

Both a personal and a societal need for privacy exists, Hodges claims. First, we need privacy to develop a sense of self. Constance T. Fischer (1980) states that people need privacy to "try out" new poses, future selves, and so on, without fear of ridicule by outsiders. If we are to become the person we wish to be, we need a certain degree of privacy to develop that person apart from observation. Religious cults that seek cognitive control over their members do so in part by depriving the members of any real degree of privacy, restricting both growth and reflection.

Second, society needs privacy as a shield against the power of the state. As the state gains more information about its citizens, it is increasingly easy to influence, manipulate, or control each one. Precisely because the state is feared, limitations on the power of the state, such as the Bill of Rights, were established to protect private life (Neville, 1980). Throughout history, totalitarian regimes have used extensive government surveillance—the near absence of privacy—as a major component of any attempt to create a uniformly subservient citizenry, a subject that dominates Orwell's *1984*. Third, society needs privacy as a shield against internet sites such as Facebook and others that demand large sums of data about you to enter into their site.

Therefore, while much of the debate focuses on the right to privacy, an equally compelling argument must be made for the need for privacy. Privacy is not a luxury or even a gift of a benevolent government. It is a necessary component of a democracy.

MELDING FIELDS: COMBINING LAW, PHILOSOPHY, AND ECONOMICS

The concept of privacy thus is not what philosophers term an "a priori right." An individual right to privacy—or, as philosophers would say, a need for privacy—can be overridden by other, consequential claims. In the 21st century, the result is a tension between thinking about privacy as an economic good or as something that money can only incompletely capture or explain. Deciding among the competing demands is difficult. Legal scholar Margaret Radin (1982, 1993, 1996) provides a way to resolve the competing claims by using the theory of contested commodities. Her explanation begins with theory of the self—articulated by philosophers David Hume, Thomas Hobbes, Immanuel Kant, John Stuart Mill, and feminist philosophy—and then engages with contemporary market economics where the concept of personhood and private property that can be bought and sold are inextricably joined.

When the self is understood expansively so as to include not merely undifferentiated Kantian moral agency but also the person's particular endowments and attributes, and not merely those particular endowments and attributes, either, but also the specific things needed for the contextual aspect of personhood, then this understanding is a thick theory of the self (Radin, 1996). In the crudest of senses, what algorithms attempt to do is create an artificial "self" indirectly by examining purchasing and searching decisions. Radin embodies the community in the self but also situates the self within community, noting that a thick theory of the self and the traditional concepts of market-driven economics do coexist within contemporary culture, but that there is a group of "goods"—contested commodities—for which market economics does not provide complete explanatory power. Private information that emerges from human beings acting within a cultural context constitutes a contested commodity, one that market forces may intrude upon but that are incompletely accounted for by examining only market transactions.

Privacy as a contested commodity fits well with 21st-century lived experience at the individual level—that privacy is a right that individuals can chose to trade away, or to retain, based on individual needs and desires. The concept of contested commodity also notes that the "contest" takes place not just within an isolated individual but within an individual who also is embedded in a cultural and economic system. Finally, that "contest" is in the service of human capabilities that can be actualized in a community and within certain sorts of markets but also are separable from them in individual circumstances. Radin's thinking would mean that corporate demands would be every bit as subject to restriction as government regulations and for the same reason—the health of the community that, in turn, supports the flourishing of individuals. Radin's thinking also suggests that philosophy needs to consider an institution-based theory of privacy (Wilkins & Patterson, 2020). Currently, the European Union has enacted multiple laws that restrict what corporations may do with information about individuals; philosophy has no theory that articulates how institutions can or should be held accountable to individuals and to communities over their control of individual private information. Christians (2010) considers control over commercial data banks, along with government surveillance and invasive news coverage of victims of tragedy, as the most important privacy questions emerging in the 21st century. Scholars note that privacy is related to human experience but the concept itself is not relative. "Privacy's moral weight, its importance as a value, does not shrink or swell in direct proportion to the numbers of people who want or like it or how much they want or like it" (Nissenbaum, 2010, p. 66). Perhaps the best example of this fundamental philosophical importance is Article 12 of the Universal Declaration of Human Rights: "No one shall be subjected to arbitrary interference with his privacy, family, home or correspondence, nor to attacks upon his honour and reputation. Everyone has the **right** to the protection of the law against such interference or attacks."

Privacy's moral weight also is not proportional to the number of people who are aware of the initial invasion. That is one of the points of the 2019 documentary *The Great Hack*, which chronicles how the UK-based political consulting firm Cambridge Analytica employed "political voter surveillance" through the collection of data points about individuals to influence elections in more than 20 countries. The firm's first US effort was in support of the 2016 failed presidential campaign of Texas Republican Sen. Ted Cruz. Cambridge Analytica acquired its data through Facebook; the corporation denied that it had been aware of the uses to which the firm put the information it obtained. The film documents how investigative reporters, "average" people portrayed by a college professor who simply "wants his data back," and ultimately the British government all must cooperate to understand how the firm worked and what the potential outcome of those efforts might have been. In addition to "micro-targeting" specific groups of voters and attempting to influence their intention to vote and to vote for specific candidates, Cambridge Analytica interfered with multiple elections, among them the UK vote to leave the European Union (Brexit), and influenced the outcome in another election by convincing voters *not* to vote as part of a supposedly authentic, anti-government social movement. Unfortunately, all of this information emerged only after the various elections on which the firm "consulted" were held. Ultimately, Cambridge Analytica went bankrupt, but the use of these techniques and others continues on various social media platforms, including Facebook.

JOHN RAWLS AND THE VEIL OF IGNORANCE

Preserving human dignity in times of crisis is a difficult task. Political philosopher John Rawls, an articulate proponent of the social contract theory of government, has provided a helpful exercise to make decisions about particularly thorny privacy issues (Rawls, 1971).

Rawls's theory of "distributive justice" takes the best from utilitarian theory while avoiding some of its problems. It begins with the premise that justice should be equated with fairness. In order to achieve fairness, Rawls suggests an exercise he calls the "veil of ignorance." In the exercise, before a community can make an ethical decision affecting its members, the community must consider the options behind a veil of ignorance. Behind the veil, everyone starts out in an "original position" as equals. According to Rawls (1971), "no one knows his place in society, his class position or social status; nor does he know his fortune in the distribution of natural assets and abilities, his intelligence and strength, and the like."

Rawls suggests that, behind the veil, rational people would be willing to make and to follow decisions when individual distinctions such as gender or socioeconomic status are laid aside. For example, if the issue is whether to photograph or interview survivors at the scene of an airline crash, you could gather many people with diverse views behind the veil. Among them could be a reporter, a photographer, a survivor, a victim's family, an average reader or viewer, the management or owner of the media outlet, the owner of the airline, paramedics at the scene, the flying public, and others. Behind the veil, in the original position, none of the participants would know what their status would be when they emerged. *Their arguments would then be free of bias that comes from points of view.* The participants would argue the pros and cons of the public's need to know and the victim's right to privacy without knowing whether they would emerge as a reporter, a reader, or a victim.

When people begin their deliberations behind such a veil, Rawls suggests that two values emerge. We will first act so that *individual liberty is maximized*; however, we will also act so that *weaker parties will be protected*. We will look at each concept separately.

First, Rawls suggests the liberty of all will be valued equally. Behind the veil, freedom of the press (a liberty journalists cherish) becomes equal to freedom from intrusion into private life (a liberty readers cherish). How you retain both becomes a debate to be argued from all points of view, free of bias.

Second, behind the veil, the weaker party is usually protected. Few participants would make an ethical decision that might not be in the interest of the weaker party unless the evidence was overwhelming that it would better the lot of the entire group. Behind the veil, participants would be forced to weigh the actual and potential harm that journalists, as a powerful group representing powerful institutions, could inflict on people who are less powerful.

It is important to note that behind-the-veil consensus is not required, and maybe even not expected. The veil of ignorance is designed to facilitate ethical discussions, not stymie them by lack of unanimity. Using the veil of ignorance, the ethical decision-maker arrives at what Rawls calls "reflective equilibrium," where some inequalities are allowed. However, they will be the inequalities that contribute in some significant way to the betterment of most individuals in the social situation. For instance, the consensus of the group behind the veil might be to run a photo of a victim of tragedy if it might prevent a similar tragedy from occurring.

Reflective equilibrium summons what Rawls calls our "considered moral judgment." Balancing the liberties of various stakeholders while protecting the weaker party allows for an exploration of all of the issues involved, which utilitarianism sometimes fails to address.

Using the concepts of contested commodities embedded in a culture of surveillance capitalism and understanding the distinctions among right to know, need to know, discretion, and circles of intimacy may give you the tools to begin to articulate how informational justice might be distributed behind the veil of ignorance. These tools will enable you to better justify your choices, to make decisions systematically, and to understand what went wrong when mistakes occur.

SUGGESTED READINGS

Bok, S. (1983). *Secrets: On the ethics of concealment and revelation.* New York: Vintage.

Grcic, J. M. (1986). The right to privacy: Behavior as property. *Journal of Values Inquiry, 20*, 137–144.

Nissenbaum, H. (2010). *Privacy in context: Technology, policy and the integrity of social life.* Stanford: Stanford Law Books.

Orwell, G. (1949). *1984.* San Diego: Harcourt, Brace, Jovanovich.

Rawls, J. (1971). *A theory of justice.* Cambridge, MA: Harvard University Press.

Rosen, J. (2000). *The unwanted gaze: The destruction of privacy in America.* New York: Random House.

Schoeman, F. D. (ed.). (1984). *Philosophical dimensions of privacy: An anthology.* New York: Cambridge University Press.

Zuboff, S. (2019). *The age of surveillance capitalism: The fight for a human future at the new frontier of power*. New York: Public Affairs, Hachette Book Group.

CASES

CASE 3-A

HARRY AND MEGHAN: CONTEXT AND CONTROL

LEE WILKINS
University of Missouri

In the pre-mediated olden days, royalty was also celebrity. In the English-speaking world, this was particularly true for British kings and queens whose lives, loves, and origin stories became the stuff of national myth reverberating into the 21st century.

The British royal family, among the richest of the world's monarchies and supported by British taxpayers, has served as both cultural glue and national fault line. No one more personified Britain's uneasy relationship with its contemporary monarchy than Diana, Princess of Wales, who married the heir to the throne in 1981 in what was described as a storybook wedding. Princess Diana came under increasingly intense media focus during the next decade, in which her marriage collapsed, she gave birth to the "heir and a spare" to the British throne, and she was informally crowned the people's princess.

Diana died in an early-morning car crash on Aug. 31, 1997, when she and her current boyfriend were traveling at a high speed through a tunnel in Paris while being pursued by dozens of paparazzi. At the time, many asserted that this particular wing of photojournalists had been the proximate cause of her death. One of the most recognizable images of the 1990s was the photograph of her two sons walking behind her casket.

"My mother had just died, and I had to walk a long way behind her coffin, surrounded by thousands of people watching me while millions more did on television," Harry said during an interview with *Newsweek* (Levin, 2017). "I don't think any child should be asked to do that, under any circumstances. I don't think it would happen today."

It came as no surprise when, almost 20 years later, Prince Harry's romance and marriage to American Meghan Markle came under equivalent and intense media scrutiny, particularly from the British tabloid press. Those stories—and there were thousands of them—focused on Markle's mixed-race heritage, on her relationship with her estranged father, and on how well Markle would or would not meld with the existing royal family. Many of the stories included malicious gossip, focused on Markle's racial heritage in the most insulting terms, and generally blamed her for the problems that had plagued the royal family since long before Diana's death. The relationship with the four dominant British tabloids—the *Sun*, the *Daily Mirror*, the *Daily Mail*, and the *Daily Express*—was accurately described as poisonous.

What was surprising was that Prince Harry decided to fight. He sued the *Sun* and the *Daily Mirror*, alleging that they hacked his cell phones as far back as the early 2000s. After Harry and Meghan, known in the United Kingdom as the Duke and Duchess of Sussex, announced that they were stepping back from their royal obligations and relocating, ultimately to the Los Angeles area, they took more aggressive steps. The couple announced they would boycott the Royal Rota, the press pool that covers the royal family. In April 2020, they wrote a letter to the editors of the four tabloids stating that they would no longer deal with them. The letter summarized Harry and Meghan's view of the tabloid coverage as "distorted, false, or invasive beyond reason." Meghan also filed suit against the *Daily Mail* for its publication of a letter to her father prior to her 2018 wedding. The couple also hired a Hollywood public relations firm to handle their image. All of this occurred while Britain was dealing with the first, vicious surge of COVID-19, and the duke and duchess were publicly criticized for royal self-absorption at a time of national crisis.

In November 2020, the world learned that Markle had suffered a miscarriage. The story was not broken by a tabloid, but by Markle herself in a Nov. 25 op-ed column in the *New York Times*. It recounted her July miscarriage, her grief and pain in a year in which "loss and pain have plagued every one of us in 2020, in moments both fraught and debilitating."

Markle said she was moved to reveal these obviously private facts in hope of promoting healing for herself and others. She said she was inspired by a question from a journalist: "Are you okay?"

Micro Issues

1. Based on Markle's actions, how do you think she defines privacy?
2. Should the *New York Times* have run the op-ed at a time when deaths from COVID-19 were rapidly escalating in the United States?
3. How do Markle's actions and news coverage of them reflect the distinction between privacy and secrecy? Respond to the same questions that arise as a result of their 2021 interview with Oprah Winfrey.
4. If you were in charge of Meghan and Harry's public relations account, what advice would you provide? What ethical concepts inform your strategy?

Midrange Issues

1. What sort of stories should the tabloids publish about the royal family?
2. Are Meghan and Harry a means for the *New York Times* to boost readership and circulation? How would you respond to this question if a British paper were involved?
3. Access coverage of Princess Diana's death and Harry and Meghan's courtship and wedding. Evaluate it, using the concepts of right to know, need to know, and want to know.

Macro Issues

1. Research libel law in the United Kingdom. How is it distinct from US law? Why do Harry and Meghan stand a better chance in the UK courts?
2. Miscarriages are something that happens to many women and their partners. What sort of coverage does this issue merit? If you think the issue is newsworthy, how would you report and produce such a story?
3. What do you know about the British monarchy? Where did you pick up the knowledge? If you listed entertainment programming such as the film *The Queen* or the television series *The Crown*, do you believe that what you learned in those programs is true?

CASE 3-B

GUILTY BY GOOGLE: UNPUBLISHING AND CRIME REPORTING IN THE DIGITAL AGE

DEBORAH L. DWYER
University of North Carolina at Chapel Hill

The documentary *Out of Omaha* chronicles the struggles of identical twins Darcell and Darrell Trotter, two Black men fighting to escape a life of systemic inequality, poverty, and hopelessness in a downtrodden area of North Omaha, Nebraska. Darcell hoped moving to another part of the state would help him put his teenage years—spent affiliated with a gang, selling drugs, and multiple arrests—behind him.

However, a series of events would threaten to thwart the twins' plans for a better life, and the internet would not let them forget it.

In 2012, Darcell and Darrell were arrested and charged with first-degree sexual assault, a second-degree felony. Several news outlets, including the local ABC affiliate KHGI Nebraska TV and the *Lincoln Journal Star*, covered the story, using the brothers' names and mugshots.

Soon after, the alleged victim recanted her statement, saying that the twins did not assault her. She was charged with filing a false police report, and all charges against the Trotters were dropped.

The articles about Darcell and Darrell's arrests, however, were still available online. "They never retracted that . . . they just left it up there," Darcell said. "My whole purpose of moving out here was to do something different."

Five years later, Darcell contacted one of the news organizations to ask that the story be removed. The editor asked, "Did we run a story when the charges were dropped too?" Darcell said no. He told the editor he felt like his being Black was a factor.

"We should have had a follow-up story if the charges were dropped," the editor said. "Give me some time to look into it."

In 2019, a *Columbia Journalism Review* article noted that the *Lincoln Journal Star* article was still available online. A year later, the link returned a 403 error, and the page was not available through the Internet Archive's Wayback Machine.

Darcell and Darrell's story is not unique. Every day, newsrooms across the country report on people who are arrested for crimes large and small, creating a "digital scarlet letter" for those named in the news. Journalism ethics call for balancing the public's right to know with minimizing harm to those involved, but finding that balance in the age of the internet has become more difficult.

People increasingly are contacting newsrooms to ask that stories about them be "unpublished," or deleted from the news website and ultimately from search engines such as Google. Sometimes the person claims the information is inaccurate, the reporting is unfair, the publicity violates their privacy, or that the article simply does not represent who they are today.

Adding to the problem is the simple fact that criminal charges often change. They may be dropped, as in the Trotters' case, or the severity of the initial charges could be reduced. Even if the charges stand, the accused might be found not guilty after a trial. Further, a person found guilty of a crime might successfully petition a court to expunge it later. Regardless, the initial news report that remains online can haunt the person in their present-day life, making finding a job or even a romantic partner difficult. What is the point of being declared innocent in court if Google still says you are guilty?

Newsrooms have not found an agreed-upon practice when it comes to unpublishing requests. Some news organizations refuse to consider them, while others are more sympathetic to those asking for help. Journalists typically determine how to handle such requests on a case-by-case basis. Although most newsrooms are reluctant to unpublish except in extreme circumstances, many do—but they do not necessarily disclose that to the public. Some editors will agree to update a report if the person can prove the information has changed, but journalism's norms of accuracy and the profession's identity as custodians of the public record make altering "the first draft of history" difficult to swallow.

Micro Issues

1. Darcell Trotter previously was affiliated with a gang, sold drugs, and had been arrested multiple times. What role, if any, should such information play in a decision to unpublish?
2. Is it fair for journalists to address requests only of those people who contact them? Is it equitable? What about those who don't know they can even ask? Or don't know how to ask?
3. If a news organization chooses to unpublish a story, should it disclose that information to readers/viewers/listeners? Why or why not?

Midrange Issues

1. Journalism ethics call for balancing the public's right to know with minimizing harm to those involved. How should a news organization balance those obligations when deciding whether to unpublish a news story?
2. Develop a set of newsroom practices regarding crime coverage. Should nonviolent crimes such as a misdemeanor drug possession or DUI be excluded from regular crime reports? Is it appropriate to report on criminal cases if your newsroom does not intend to follow the court hearing/verdict? Should daily crime reports be removed from public view online after a certain period of time?
3. How should newsrooms handle differences between public and private figures when it comes to unpublishing? How should a newsroom consider unpublishing requests if a private person could at any time become public (e.g., could run for office)?

Macro Issues

1. How might an editor's decision to unpublish be influenced by the requester's race, gender, or socioeconomic status? How might

unpublishing exacerbate problems such as systemic racism in matters of criminal justice?

2. The European Union and countries such as Argentina have established a legal right to be forgotten, which allows individuals to request information about themselves be omitted from search-engine results. Should such a law exist in the United States? Why or why not?

CASE 3-C

DRONES AND THE NEWS

KATHLEEN BARTZEN CULVER
University of Wisconsin

News outlets, along with a number of other kinds of businesses and organizations, are increasingly using unmanned aerial vehicles (UAVs) as part of their professional activities. Commonly known as "drones," UAVs are tightly regulated by the Federal Aviation Administration (FAA), especially for commercial uses, which the agency defines as including journalism. News organizations primarily use drones to capture video and still images but also can mount them with sensors to collect data, such as air pollution or water quality.

In 2016, the FAA issued the Small Unmanned Aircraft Rule—known as Part 107—and established an operator's certificate for commercial users. The certificate requires users to pass a test covering basics of airspace and aeronautics. According to the Center for Journalism Ethics at the University of Wisconsin–Madison, Part 107 also established specific restrictions, barring

- commercial use of UAVs weighing more than 55 pounds;
- UAV flights above 400 feet in most cases;
- night flights;
- flights over people not involved in the operation of the UAV;
- reckless or careless operation;
- flights in restricted airspace without permission (airspace restrictions vary based on size and location of an airport); and
- flight beyond the operator's visual line of sight (Culver & Duncan, 2017).

As more newsrooms were exploring deployment of drones in compliance with FAA rules in 2017, Kentucky Gov. Matt Bevin used social media to challenge the ethics of such uses by Louisville news outlets. Bevin was under fire based on his purchase of a house and surrounding property that had been owned by a prominent campaign donor who also owned a company that did business with the state. Bevin bought the estate from Neil Ramsey in March 2017 for $1.6 million. A county property evaluation estimated the property's worth far higher, at $2.97 million, when including nine adjacent acres Bevin did not buy. The transaction prompted two ethics complaints, but a later ruling by an assessment appeals body cleared the governor.

In the midst of the controversy, the Board of Assessment Appeals inspected Bevin's home as part of the appeal he filed but denied access to reporters seeking to attend the inspection and report on it. The *Louisville Courier-Journal* later filed a complaint alleging the action violated the Kentucky Open Meetings Act (Loftus, 2017a).

The day of the inspection, Bevin used Twitter to lash out at Louisville news media (see figures 3.2 and 3.3). He tweeted that two organizations— the *Courier-Journal* newspaper and the Wave3News television station— used a UAV to fly over the mansion and capture video of his children. "Drones again flying directly over and around my home filming my children . . . @wave3news @courierjournal #PeepingTom Loftus," Bevin wrote, referring to political reporter Tom Loftus as "Peeping Tom."

Staff from both named news outlets immediately responded that they did not, in fact, use a drone in reporting on the mansion assessment controversy, with the *Courier-Journal* editor tweeting that the paper neither owns nor operates drones in its reporting and Wave3News stating that it had not flown at the governor's property.

Just after these replies, the governor identified WDRB News as the responsible outlet.

News Director Barry Fullmer tweeted that his station had operated the drone in accordance with FAA requirements and did not capture video footage of the governor's children. The posted video bears this out, with lofty images of the home (see figure 3.4), outbuildings, and lush green landscape (Andrews, 2017).

The WDRB story quotes Bevin saying he bought the massive home so his nine children would have room and privacy. It's the latter consideration that appears to have prompted the governor to call out news media outlets for their use of drones. In a recorded press conference, he repeatedly critiqued outlets for "breathlessly" reporting on the controversy and using drones and helicopters over his property (Loftus, 2017b).

Even though the news station appears not to have captured footage of Bevin's children and certainly did not publish any, drones do have vast capabilities to venture where reporters on foot cannot and to

Figure 3.2.

Figure 3.3.

Figure 3.4.

record high-definition video that makes individuals easily identifiable. Organizations such as the Center for Journalism Ethics, the Poynter Institute, the Drone Journalism Lab at the University of Nebraska, and the National Press Photographers Association encourage news outlets to consider privacy when developing ethics standards to guide their drone use. They highlight the Society of Professional Journalists' ethics code in noting, "Balance the public's need for information against potential harm or discomfort. Pursuit of the news is not a license for arrogance or undue intrusiveness."

Bevin said he sought out his home in part for the privacy it afforded his children and accused news media of intruding upon that privacy by using a new technology. News media instead argued they were covering an issue of public importance involving one of the state's most powerful political figures. In the balance between the public's need for information and the potential harm from privacy invasions, clearly the two sides came out seeing the weight on different ends of the scale.

Micro Issues

1. Is an assessment controversy involving a public official a valid public controversy requiring robust news media coverage?
2. Is it fair to fly a drone over private property to capture images of a home and surrounding grounds at any time? Does it matter that the property is owned by a public official or the subject of an assessment dispute?

Midrange Issues

1. Should privacy considerations differ when children are involved?
2. Use this case to contrast the concepts of right to know, need to know, and want to know.
3. Does the governor have a responsibility to the truth when using Twitter? If not, why not? If so, how does that apply to this case?

Macro Issues

1. Rawls considers justice as fairness. Was WDRB fair to the governor in this case? What other stakeholders should be considered in this case? Was the news outlet fair to them? Were the governor's actions fair?

2. Apply the veil of ignorance to this case. How would you articulate the positions of the journalists, governor, and public if you did not know in which condition you would end up?
3. What other ethical considerations beyond privacy are important in drone journalism?

CASE 3-D

DOXXER, DOXXER, GIVE ME THE NEWS?

MARK ANTHONY POEPSEL
Southern Illinois University Edwardsville

Tiki torches blazed in the night on Aug. 11, 2017, in Charlottesville, Virginia, and images of screaming white supremacists burned paths through our social media consciousness. Cable and online news outlets covered the story as evidence of the rising threat of white nationalism in the context of a broader protest to maintain Confederate monuments in Charlottesville and elsewhere.

Monuments to the Confederacy and to white supremacy were being removed or relocated across the country as various groups, in particular those representing people of color, objected to their prominent display. Opponents also argued that the monuments maintain a narrative of white supremacy that was particularly threatening as the speeches and tweets of Donald Trump seemed to support white supremacist ideas and nationalist rhetoric that threaten safety and security.

The tiki-torch protest, startling enough for many Americans, grew into an even bigger story on Aug. 12. On that day, James Alex Fields drove his car into a group of counter-protestors in Charlottesville, killing Heather Heyer, 32, of Charlottesville (Caron, 2017).

President Trump sent signals of tacit support to white supremacists after Heyer was killed. He stated that blame rested "on both sides" of the Charlottesville protest—a claim he maintained a month later (Landler, 2017). To many, the president's comments were reinforcement of a narrative that white nationalists, also known as neo-Nazis, are only as threatening as those who oppose them. While there had been acts of violence on the part of anti-fascist protestors, in their defense they note that they must prepare for violence because white supremacists would attack even peaceful protestors (Shihipar, 2017).

Heather Heyer was one such peaceful protestor standing up in her home city against those who wield torches and shout hateful speech.

Her killing added urgency to efforts to "dox" the white supremacists who had made Charlottesville a battleground.

Ethicist David M. Douglas (2016) defines doxxing as "the intentional public release onto the Internet of personal information about an individual by a third party, often with the intent to humiliate, threaten, intimidate, or punish the identified individual." The practice is used by, and against, members of extremist groups to exact a form of vigilante justice. Not all doxxers are extremists, but they are generally interested in punishing those they feel are not being punished or are not being caught fast enough by existing institutional law enforcement agencies.

The Twitter account @YesYoureRacist, run by Logan Smith of Raleigh, North Carolina, published photos highlighting the faces of white supremacist demonstrators in Charlottesville (Cain, 2017). According to *Wired*, he gained more than 300,000 followers in a single weekend. By implication, it invited doxxing of those depicted. Smith argued it was necessary to expose participants in the white supremacist rally.

According to the *Raleigh News & Observer*, Smith said,

> And these people aren't afraid anymore. They're not hiding behind their hoods like they did before the civil rights era. They are out and proud. I think if they are so proud of their beliefs and proud to stand shoulder-to-shoulder with neo-Nazis and KKK members and white supremacists of all stripes, then I think their communities need to know who they are. They're not random faces in the crowd, they're your neighbors, they're your coworker, they're the people you pass in the grocery store. (Cain, 2017)

The problem, of course, is that Smith and those who use the photos he publishes can and do make mistakes. *Wired* reported:

> Kyle Quinn was more than 1,000 miles away from Charlottesville at the time of the protest—a case of mistaken identity that brought a wave of threats and accusations of racism so large that Quinn felt unsafe in his home. (Ellis, 2017)

Again from *Wired*:

> [A]s doxing continues to evolve as the preferred tactic of both far right and left wing internet factions, it's important to take a hard look at what each side is trying to accomplish. While the two sides use different logic to justify their actions, the true result is the same and even cumulative— leading to an arms race of financially incentivized, shame-slinging vigilantes. (Ellis, 2017)

Using crowdfunding tools, doxxers, and those who organize them, often seek financial assistance from the public. This opens the opportunity for a digital war on identity that journalists must be aware of when reporting on doxxers and information they develop and disseminate.

Micro Issues

1. Is doxxing, as it was used in this case, ethical? Justify your answer.
2. Is your answer based on whether you feel that the ones doing the doxxing are on *your* preferred side of the issue? If, as *Wired* points out, doxxing becomes the preferred tactic for both sides of an issue, does your opinion change on the ethics of doxxing?
3. Critique this statement by Smith: "I think their communities need to know who they are."

Midrange Issues

1. Many communities have seen tabloids crop up where people who are arrested on violations such as drug possession or DWI have their mugshot put into that tabloid for sale near the cash register of a convenience store even before the individuals are formally charged with a crime. In what way, if any, does doxxing differ from this practice?
2. What could be the "greater good," if any, that would justify doxxing in a case such as this?
3. Logan Smith is a private individual who runs a Twitter site. Should the Raleigh newspaper have given his decision to publish photos of bystanders in the Charlottesville crowd a larger audience through an article in their pages? Does their article imply endorsement of what he did?

Macro Issues

1. The Charlottesville protest was one of the biggest news stories of 2017. After you look up this incident online, critique the "blame on both sides" statement by Donald Trump.
2. The author of the *Wired* quote says that the two sides of the racial divide apply "different logic" to justify their use of the tactic. What, exactly, are the two sides, and what would be the logic that each would use in reaching a decision to use doxxing as a tactic?

CASE 3-E

LOOKING FOR RICHARD SIMMONS

LEE WILKINS
University of Missouri

Beginning in 2016, one of the trendiest "new media" was actually a reboot of some of the most popular programming long before television was invented.

This was the radio serial, weekly adventures of everyone from the Lone Ranger to the Shadow, which attracted huge audiences during the 1920s and 1930s. President Franklin D. Roosevelt reassured a nation on the brink of war with his "fireside chats," broadcast on the radio. Edward R. Murrow began his career as a radio reporter covering World War II before he became one of the early giants of the new medium of television. And Orson Welles's radio program *The War of the Worlds* gave rise to the first empirical research on media effects and is still broadcast today as part of annual Halloween celebrations.

Podcasts were the next-generation radio serial. They combined the intimacy of radio with the on-demand qualities of computers and smartphones. Even the best podcasts were relatively inexpensive to produce. Podcasts provided a way for media organizations, including news organizations such as National Public Radio, to repurpose content, and they were becoming increasingly popular. Downloaded from places such as iTunes, the most popular podcasts of 2017—for example, *This American Life*—could net more than $50,000 per episode.

Fitness guru Richard Simmons, who led exercise classes that were televised in the 1970s and 1980s, was an early crusader for weight loss at a time when Americans were beginning to expand to unhealthy proportions. With an on-air personality that combined some natural shyness with ebullience, Simmons had been a celebrity for more than three decades.

And then he decided he wanted a quieter life. A life out of the public spotlight. Simmons no longer wanted to be a celebrity.

Enter former *Daily Show* producer Dan Taberski, who said he was an acquaintance of Simmons and a regular at Simmons's Beverly Hills workout studio. Taberski said he was concerned enough about Simmons's three-year absence from mediated life that he wanted to find out what had caused him to withdraw to the backstage.

In February 2017, Taberski's podcast *Missing Richard Simmons* had its debut. The six episodes were framed as a mystery. Simmons refused to be interviewed for the podcast, but Taberski interviewed—or tried to interview—friends and relatives. After the podcast began, and because some of the content focused on Simmons's physical and mental health, the Los Angeles Police Department, based in large part on the speculations about Simmons's condition included in the podcast, made a wellness check at Simmons's home. He was fine.

In the second episode of the podcast, Taberski urged listeners to drive to Simmons's home for a "stakeout." The *New York Times* reported that Taberski justified the tactic this way: "I don't want him to feel like I'm invading his privacy. On the other hand, I'm Richard's friend."

During the time the podcast was being produced and aired, Simmons called NBC's *Today Show*, saying that he was fine. On his Facebook page, he also disparaged the podcast's claims.

However, Taberski encouraged podcast listeners to call in with "any theory you think we missed." Those tips included assertions that Simmons was bereaved from the loss of his pets or that he was depressed. (Simmons had acknowledged previously that he had suffered from depression.) At one point, Taberski intimated that Simmons was transitioning to a woman, only to discard the idea in the next episode.

The podcast topped the iTunes charts for four straight weeks.

Ultimately, if there was a mystery surrounding Simmons, Taberski didn't solve it. As of this writing, Simmons remains alive and living a more private life.

Micro Issues

1. Using the concepts of privacy, secrecy, right to know, need to know, and want to know, analyze whether the podcast invaded Simmons's privacy.
2. Would your answer be different if the wellness check by the Los Angeles police had found Simmons in some sort of physical danger or suffering from a physical illness?
3. Should Taberski have spiked the project when Simmons refused to speak with him?

Midrange Issues

1. Taberski's podcast told a narrative of a "missing person." Evaluate this narrative for truthfulness. Are there times when "telling a story" is not the most accurate way to provide readers and viewers with information about events and people?

2. How would you categorize podcasts such as *This American Life*? Are they journalism, entertainment, some new genre?
3. How do you think Taberski's background on Comedy Central influenced the narrative choices he made?

Macro Issues

1. The *New York Times* called the show the "morally suspect podcast." How do you evaluate the critic's characterization?
2. Can celebrities such as Simmons have privacy? Can public figures such as Supreme Court Chief Justice John Roberts have privacy? If your answers are different for different categories of people, explain.
3. Should iTunes or programs such as TMZ be responsible ethically for content such as that provided in the *Missing Richard Simmons* podcast? How should that responsibility be exercised?

CASE 3-F

CHILDREN AND FRAMING: THE USE OF CHILDREN'S IMAGES IN AN ANTI-SAME-SEX MARRIAGE AD

YANG LIU
University of Wisconsin

The brief ballot measure read, "Only marriage between a man and a woman is valid or recognizable in California" (voterguide.sos.ca.gov, 2008), but it was packed with potential for conflict. So when the parents of some San Francisco first graders recognized their sons' and daughters' faces in an advertisement promoting California's controversial 2008 Proposition 8, which successfully sought to outlaw marriage for same-sex couples in the state (protectmarriage.com, 2008), they were shocked.

The ad picked up two scenes from a website news video clip originally produced by the San Francisco *Chronicle* for a news story that described 18 students attending their lesbian teacher Erin Carder's wedding (sfgate.com, 2008). The newspaper story was a feature piece that took no position on Proposition 8. The story included an account of the wedding, which was held on Oct. 10, 2008. In the newspaper piece, and on the 80-second accompanying video, the children's participation was described as "tossed rose petals and blow bubbles . . . giggling and squealing as they mobbed their teacher with hugs" (sfgate.com, 2008). The story noted that it was a parent who suggested the trip, and because every student needed parental permission to attend, two students did not accompany their classmates to the wedding.

However, the central message of the advertisement was "children will be taught gay marriage unless we vote Yes on Proposition 8," using two scenes with the children's images. The first showed the children in a group, and their faces are somewhat difficult to distinguish. The second showed a single child looking into the camera. The ad did not include the scenes of the children hugging their teacher that were part of the original news story. In addition, the creators of the ad altered the color tones in the scenes with children to be somewhat darker than the original news story as posted on the *Chronicle* website. The ad featuring the video clip of the wedding was one of several similar ads run in support of Proposition 8.

After viewing the ad, four of the parents of the children involved wrote a letter to the Yes-on-Proposition-8 campaign, demanding that the campaign stop running the ad. Their request was denied. The *Chronicle* did not question the use of the copyrighted material in the ad, nor did it make a request that the ad be discontinued.

Micro Issues

1. How would you evaluate the truthfulness and accuracy of the video accompanying the political advertisement?
2. Three days after the ad began airing, law professor Lawrence Lessig said in an NPR interview that the law "should not stop the ability of people to use material that has been publicly distributed." Evaluate this statement using ethical theory.
3. Do children constitute a vulnerable audience when it comes to privacy?

Midrange Issues

1. All advertisements, by virtue of their brevity, engage in selective use of facts. Evaluate whether this ad is within that professional mainstream in an ethical sense.
2. What should the *Chronicle* do about the use of news material for the purpose of political persuasion, regardless of the specific issue?

Macro Issues

1. How would you evaluate the statement that this ad constitutes protected political speech?
2. It has been argued that the children do not have the ability to reason about the politics of same-sex marriage in this wedding, so they were not expressing consent to the same-sex marriage but only expressing affection for their teacher. Is their participation in the wedding a private matter without political meaning or not? Justify your answer.

4

Loyalty
Choosing between Competing Allegiances

By the end of this chapter, you should

- understand why the articulation of loyalties is important in professional ethics;
- know Royce's definition of loyalty, the major problems with that conceptualization, and why loyalty also can be considered a virtue;
- understand how journalists' role in society provides them with an additional set of loyalties to consider;
- be familiar with and able to use the Potter Box as a justification model for ethical decision-making.

LOYALTY AS BOTH VIRTUE AND THEORY

Decisions involving loyalty occur routinely for media professionals. When social media executives decide to block, label, or promote certain kinds of content, they have chosen a loyalty. The same is true for those who develop and then broadcast social-media content, whether they are called bloggers, journalists, or friends.

Loyalty also occupies an intriguing place in philosophy. Some argue loyalty is a virtue of individual character, simultaneously capable of nobility and ignominy within the same sets of facts.

Our loyalties are important signs of the kind of persons we have chosen to become. They mark a kind of constancy and steadfastness in our attachments. . . .

Real loyalty endures inconvenience, withstands temptation, and does not cringe under assault. (Bennett, 1993, p. 665)

When loyalty is lodged in individual character, it should be transparent, meaning visible to others. Individual loyalties can be discarded as well as affirmed. It is possible for people to sustain—and to jeopardize—multiple loyalties with a single act or related set of actions.

The original discussion of loyalty in Western culture was written by Plato in *The Trial and Death of Socrates* (see Russell, 1967). In Plato's *Phaedo*, Socrates bases his defense against the charges and his determination to continue teaching philosophy on his loyalty to divinely inspired truth, a loyalty that coincided with his loyalty to the city state of Athens. Plato quotes Socrates's explanation as follows:

> Men of Athens, I honor and love you: but I shall obey God rather than you, and while I have life and strength I shall never cease from the practice and teaching of philosophy, exhorting any one whom I meet[,] . . . and I believe that no greater good has ever happened in the State than my service to God.

Loyalty allows people to express what philosophers call epistemic partiality. A loyal person can be, and most often is, loyal to one group or one idea at the expense of others. If loyalty is a virtue, as philosophers beginning with Aristotle and continuing through Alastair McIntyre and Phillipa Foot have argued, then it is the virtuous individual who can be expected to understand loyalty and hence act in an ethical way.

The exclusive focus on the individual reveals one of the problems in defining loyalty as a virtue: While the virtue itself may be laudatory, how it is expressed cannot be universalized or generalized within an individual life or a particular society. After all, Socrates drank hemlock because his fellow citizens viewed his teaching as seditious. If loyalty is a philosophical principle, then even an unvirtuous person could reason her way into loyal—and hence ethical—choices. By elevating loyalty to principle, a broader set of potential choices and influences emerges. In principle, even a person of strong ethical character could make mistakes by failing to think through issues of loyalty. This definitional tension within the concept—virtue or principle—is one of the stumbling blocks that has kept loyalty from playing a major theoretical role in philosophy for many, but not all, philosophers.

A second problem with defining loyalty exclusively as a virtue is that the multiple loyalties that professionals must maintain produce an inevitable clash. These clashes are most often summarized as conflicts of interest. Conflicts of interest are exceptional: They are the only area in philosophy where the appearance of a problem can be every bit as troubling as the actual existence of the problem. If your listeners *believe* you have a conflict of interest, the actual facts of the case may not matter in their evaluation of your work. Further, the remedies for conflict-of-interest problems are, at best, partial. Philosophers recommend two alternatives: withdrawing from the activity creating the conflict or appearance of conflict, or publicizing the elements of the conflict, thus allowing others to determine whether professional conduct has been undermined. As the chapter case studies suggest, these alternatives can create as many problems as the original conflict—sometimes in the same layer or loyalties, and sometimes in different ones. Some professions (for example, law) have an extensive discussion of how law firms may avoid conflict of interest outlined in codes of ethics. Journalism and strategic communication as professions have no such strictures; however, some news organizations and strategic communication firms do include guidance as part of their codes of ethics.

THE CONTRIBUTIONS OF JOSIAH ROYCE

American theologian Josiah Royce, who taught at Harvard in the early 1900s, believed that loyalty could become the single guiding ethical principle. In *The Philosophy of Loyalty* (1908), Royce wrote, "My theory is that the whole moral law is implicitly bound up in one precept: 'Be loyal.'" Royce defined loyalty as a social act: "The willing and practical and thoroughgoing devotion of a person to a cause." Royce would be critical, therefore, of the journalist who gets a story at all costs and whose only loyalty is to himself, or the public relations professional who lets loyalty to an employer cause her to bend the truth in tweets, posts, press releases, or annual reports. To Royce, loyalty is an act of choice. A loyal person, Royce asserted, does not have the leisure not to decide, for in the act of not deciding, that person has cast his loyalty.

Loyalty also promotes self-realization. As a contemporary of Sigmund Freud, Royce spent much of his academic career fascinated with the new findings in psychology. He viewed loyalty in the light of psychology. As a person continued to exercise loyalty, Royce believed, he or she would develop habits of character that would result in systematic ethical action. Like other aspects of moral development (see the last chapter of this book), loyalty can be learned and honed, Royce theorized.

Loyalty as a single ethical guide has problems. *First*, loyalty, incompletely conceived, can be bias or prejudice thinly cloaked. *Second*, few people maintain merely a single loyalty, and, if loyalty is to become a guiding ethical principle, we need to develop a way to help distinguish among competing loyalties. *Third*, in a mass society, the concept of face-to-face loyalty has lost much of its power. *Finally*, the most troubling question: whether it is ethical to be loyal to an unethical cause—for example, racism or gender discrimination.

However, Royce suggested a way to determine whether a specific cause was worthy of loyalty. A worthy cause should harmonize with the loyalties of others within the community. For Royce, community was all-important to his philosophy and inextricable from it. He wrote that "individuals without community are without substance, while communities without individuals are blind" (Royce, 1908). Royce's thought here echoes political philosophy. Social contract theorist and monarchist Thomas Hobbes theorized loyalty to the crown was the solution to the natural selfishness of humans. In *The Leviathan*, Hobbes (1651/1985) embedded the necessity for a social contract in human nature rather than arrangements that are divinely inspired and enforced. Loyalty to the crown gave rise to the "social contract," a thought experiment whereby people would agree to be ruled in order to avoid a life that is "solitary, poor, nasty, brutish, and short." Hobbes acknowledged that people could have more than one loyalty at a time and might be forced to choose among them. He became the first political philosopher to assert that loyalty has limits. Loyalty to the ruler stops when continued loyalty would result in a subject's death—the loyalty to self-preservation being higher than loyalty to the ruler.

In the 21st century, journalism is essential to political community, and it is logical that both Royce and Hobbes would connect journalistic loyalties to readers as opposed to elites. Similarly, loyalty to the advertising agency should not conflict with the loyalty of either its client or the consumer. However, it's possible that journalistic loyalties might come into conflict with those of strategic communication professionals in certain areas—for example, political campaigns. How might loyalty to democracy be best expressed over issues such as campaign finance regulation that significantly impact not just political advertising but also news coverage of those ads, the candidates who benefit from them, and the financial health of the media outlets that carry them?

Royce provided an answer. The true problem of loyalty as an ethical principle was not the poor choice of loyalties but failure to adhere to proper loyalties: "The ills of mankind are largely the consequence of disloyalty rather than wrong-headed loyalty" (Royce, 1908). Causes capable of sustaining loyalty, Royce noted, have a "super-individual" quality, apparent when people become part of a community. A spirit of democratic cooperation is needed for Royce's view of loyalty to result in ethical action.

Royce's thought has been criticized on a number of grounds. First, some philosophers assert that Royce's concept of loyalty is simplistic and that the adoption of loyalty as a moral principle may lead to allegiance to troubling causes. For instance, the advertising copywriter who scripts distorted television spots about a political opponent in the belief that she must get her candidate elected is demonstrating a troubling allegiance to a politician over the democratic process. Similarly, a reporter who must get the story first, regardless of its completeness or accuracy, would be demonstrating a misplaced loyalty to beating the competition.

Second, others have noted that Royce provides no way to balance among conflicting loyalties. Media professionals are faced daily with a barrage of potential loyalties—the truth, the audience, the sources, the bottom line, the profession—and choosing among them is among the most basic of ethical decisions. Other professions have similar dilemmas, such as the documentarian who must be loyal to the truth in her art while at the same time being loyal to the producers who want large numbers of the ticket-buying public to see the final product.

Third, it is unclear how Royce's ethical thinking would balance majority notions against minority views. Strictly interpreted, Royce's notion of loyalty could inspire adherence to the status quo or strict majority rule. For instance, advertisements that stereotype groups of people despite evidence to the contrary help perpetuate incorrect images. The ads work because they appeal to the majority, but by stereotyping, they have crowded out more accurate impressions.

Yet, despite these criticisms, Royce's thought has much to recommend it. First, Royce speaks to the development of ethical habits. Second, he reminds us that the basis of loyalty is social and that loyalty requires we put others on an equal footing with ourselves. Most important is the overriding message of Royce's work: *When making ethical choices, it is important to consider what your loyalties are and how you arrived at those loyalties.*

LOYALTY AND PROFESSIONAL ROLE

Since Royce wrote more than 100 years ago—years of war, revolution, the emergence of civil rights, human rights, and populism as global social movements—two distinct approaches to loyalty have emerged (Fletcher, 1993):

- Do not betray me.
- Be one with me.

It's worth unpacking some distinctions. Philosophers assert that people must have the ability to make autonomous choices in order to be considered ethical. Societies protect groups of people (for example, children) who are assumed by qualities of role, age, or station in life to have less autonomy. Cultures, the legal system, and role also can circumscribe choice. "I was just following custom . . . or orders . . . or the ways of my ancestors" are reasons based in loyalty wherein autonomy appears to be circumscribed by external influences. Although both internal and external pressures regarding ethical choice are acknowledged to exist, autonomy allows for independent action.

"Do not betray me" foregrounds the costs of abandoning one set of loyalties to adopt another. Social groups become primary in our thinking. It is only within that community that we are willing to exercise the virtue of an impartial loyalty.

> Our wide and narrow loyalties define moral communities or domains within which we are willing to universalize moral judgments, treat equals equally, protect the common good, and in other ways adopt the familiar machinery of impersonal morality. (Oldenquist, 2002, p. 178)

The in-group, out-group dynamic is essential to understanding how we act out loyalty. Leaving an in-group, the core of the act of whistleblowing, exacts a psychological price (Keller, 2007). The complicated ethical relationship between journalists and whistleblowers is outlined by Stephenson Waters (2020) with the acknowledgment that "Journalists are well aware that whistleblowing is dangerous" (p. 233). In this relationship, it is assumed that both the journalist and the whistleblower have significant levels of autonomy that often are negotiated as part of the reporting process. Working a source as part of an investigative effort, as described in the Jodi Kantor and Megan Twohey book *She Said*, provides multiple examples of how journalists worked with sources and asked sources to work with them in order to complete the investigation of Harvey Weinstein's long history of sexual harassment as a means of power and control in the film industry. Autonomy was foundational in this decision-making.

However, the second definition of loyalty—*be one with me*—undermines autonomy. "Be one with me" helps human beings create an identity. Once that identity is in place, loyalty can make us willing not only to do harm but also to *be* harmed by engaging in unethical acts without autonomous reflection and thus suffering the emotional and psychological consequences of such choices. In the 21st century, we sometimes summarize this definition as "blind" loyalty or "unthinking" loyalty. Perhaps the best documented instances of this "dark side" of loyalty are the genocides of the 20th century. Genocide not only harms specific groups but also dehumanizes those who perpetrate the slaughter.

Between these two poles is a range of possibilities for allegiance and for corresponding media behavior. One of the problems modern news media face is that a large percentage of the US public subscribes to the notion that if the media are not maximally loyal—that is, one with government, with a particular political candidate, or with the military and so forth—then they are traitorous. The media have been called disloyal by politicians, often for no greater sin than fulfilling the watchdog role. In *Unbelievable: My Front Row Seat to the Craziest Campaign in American History*, MSNBC journalist and now anchor Katy Tur (2017) recalls the days she spent on the 2016 campaign trail covering candidate Donald Trump. His rally speeches included wild swings between criticizing her reporting and lavishing praise, and at one point a kiss, depending on whether he was pleased with her recent reporting. As it has been used in 2020, "fake news" is now shorthand for routine and investigative reporting that questions politicians and their statements and choices. If you are not "one with me," then you are fake, a denial of both professionalism and humanity that establishes an in-group/out-group dynamic that characterizes and sustains identity formation.

This in-group/out-group dynamic can reinforce loyalty to *my* tribe. Loyalty, psychological affiliation with a group, helps shape responses to ethical transgressions. Consumer research suggests that consumers may be motivated to give more leniency to an in-group transgressor because the "bad actor" is more "like me" and hence less psychologically distant. Harsher punishments were reserved for those who were perceived to be "outside" the group (Liberman, Trope, & Stephan, 2007). This sort of thinking may help explain everything from the persistence of brand loyalty to the positive impact of admitting wrongdoing and asking for forgiveness in instances such as product recall.

Loyalty can be linked to role. A role is a capacity in which we act toward others. It provides others with information about how we will act in a structured situation. Some roles are occupationally defined: account executive, screenwriter, editor. Others are not: mother, spouse, daughter. We all play multiple roles, and they help us to define ourselves and to know what is expected of us and others.

When the role you assume is a professional one, you add the ethical responsibilities of that role. Philosophers claim that "to belong to a profession is traditionally to be held to certain standards of conduct that go beyond the norm for others" (Lebacqz, 1985, p. 32), and journalism qualifies as one of those professions with a higher expected norm of conduct.

Journalists and their employers have debated whether journalism should be considered a profession (Craft, 2017). Advocates of professionalism assert that professionalism among journalists will provide them with greater autonomy, prestige, and financial rewards. Critics see the process of professionalization as one that distances readers and viewers from the institutions that journalists often represent. The internet—blogs, street tapes, memes—has blurred what was perhaps a too fine distinction to begin with.

Despite these debates, we sense that journalists have two central responsibilities that are distinct in modern society. First, they have a greater responsibility to tell the truth than members of most professions. Second, journalists also seem to carry a greater obligation to foster political involvement than the average person.

Philosophers note that while ethical dilemmas are transitory, roles endure. Roles require individual virtue in exercising them and principled understandings of the institutions in which roles are defined and survive. Role expectations carry over from one situation to another. Loyalty to the profession means loyalty to the *ideals* of the profession, to being the best television producer or multimedia reporter you can be.

LAYERED LOYALTIES

As you can see, we are no longer talking about merely a single loyalty. We live in an age of layers of loyalties, creating added problems and complications.

Sorting through competing loyalties can be difficult, particularly when loyalties in one role appear to conflict with the loyalties of another. Much has been written about this issue, and we have adapted one such framework from William F. May (2001). He offers four types of loyalty.

1. Loyalties arising from shared humanity:
   - Demonstrate respect for each person as an individual.
   - Communicate honestly and truthfully with all persons.
   - Build a fair and compassionate environment that promotes the common good.
2. Loyalties arising from professional practice:
   - Fulfill the informational and entertainment mission of the media.
   - Understand your audience's needs.
   - Strive to enhance professional development of self and others.
   - Avoid the abuse of power and position.
   - Conduct professional activities in ways that uphold or surpass the ideals of virtue and competence.
3. Loyalties arising from employment:
   - Keep agreements and promises, operate within the framework of the law, and extend due process to all persons.
   - Do not squander your organization's resources or your public trust.
   - Promote compassionate and humane professional relationships.

- Foster policies that build a community of ethnic, gender, and socio-economic diversity.
- Promote the right of all to be heard.
4. Loyalties arising from the media's role in public life:
    - Serve as examples of open institutions where truth is required.
    - Foster open discussion and debate.
    - Interpret your professional actions to readers, viewers, customers, and consumers.
    - Serve as a voice for the voiceless.
    - Serve as a mirror of society.

The problem of conflicting loyalties is evident in the reality that most media professionals work for a corporation. They owe at least some loyalty to their corporate employers. However, such loyalty seldom involves a face-to-face relationship. Corporations demand employee loyalty but are much less willing to be loyal in return. The fear is that one's allegiance to the organization will advance the interest of the organization without any reciprocal loyalty to the employee. This is emphatically true now when many news organizations, particularly newspapers and magazines, have gone out of business or suffered severe economic cutbacks.

Most ethical decisions, however, are not about loyalties to corporations or loyalty to an abstract concept such as freedom of the press or the public's right to know. Most everyday loyalty decisions are about how you treat the subject of your interview or how you consider the consumer of your advertising. Such ethical decisions bring to the forefront the notion of *reciprocity*. Simply articulated, reciprocity requires that loyalty should not work against the interest of either party.

Even in a time of shifting loyalties, there are some loyalties that should only be reluctantly abandoned such as loyalty to humanity and loyalty to truth. *Virtually no situation in media ethics calls for inhumane treatment or withholding the truth.* You can probably articulate other loyalties you would rarely, if ever, abandon. Even if you can't foresee every possible conflict of loyalty, knowing where your ultimate loyalties lie is a good start to thinking through inevitable conflicts.

THE POTTER BOX

Ethical decision-making models, such as the one in chapter 1 by Sissela Bok, help you make an ethical choice. In this chapter, you will learn a second decision-making model, one that incorporates loyalties into the reasoning process. The model was developed by Harvard theologian Ralph Potter and is called the Potter Box. Its initial use requires that you go through four steps to arrive at an ethical judgment. The case below will be used to help familiarize you with the model.

> You are the editor of a newspaper of about 30,000 circulation in a Western city of about 80,000. Your police reporter regularly reports on sexual assaults in the community.
>
> While the newspaper has a policy of not revealing the names of rape victims, it routinely reports where assaults occur, the circumstances, and a description of the assailant, if available.
>
> Tonight, the police reporter is preparing to write a story about a rape that occurred in the early-morning hours yesterday on the roof of the downtown bus station. Police report that the young woman who was raped went willingly to the roof of the bus station with her attacker. Although she is 25, she lives in a group home for people with educable intellectual disabilities in the city, one of seven women living there.
>
> She could not describe her assailant, and police have no suspects.
>
> Your reporter asks you for advice about how much detail, and what detail, he should include in the story.

The Potter Box has four steps that should be taken in order (see figure 4.1). They are (1) understanding the facts, (2) outlining the values inherent in the decision, (3) applying relevant philosophical principles, and (4) articulating loyalties. You proceed through the four steps in a counterclockwise fashion, beginning with the factual situation and ending at loyalties. We will examine each step individually.

Step One: Understanding the facts of the case. In the scenario, the facts are straightforward. You have the information; your ethical choice rests with how much of it you are going to print.

Step Two: Outlining values. Values is a much-abused word in modern English. People can value everything from their loved ones to making fashion statements. In ethics, however, values take on a more precise meaning. When you value something—an idea or a principle—it means you are willing to give up other things for it. If, as a journalist, you value truth above all things,

Figure 4.1.   The Potter Box

then you must sometimes be willing to give up privacy in favor of it. In the case above, such a value system would mean that you would print every detail because you value truth, and you would risk invading the privacy of a person who is in some important ways unable to defend herself. If, as a journalist, you value both truth and privacy, then you may be willing to give up some truth, the printing of every detail, to attempt to preserve the victim's privacy.

Values often compete. An important element of using the Potter Box is to be honest about what you really do value. Both truth and privacy are lofty ideals. A less lofty ideal that most of us value is keeping our jobs. Journalists often value getting the story first or exclusively. A forthright articulation of all the values (and there will be more than one) in any particular ethical situation will help you see more clearly the choices that you face and the potential compromises you may have to make.

Step Three: Applying philosophical principles. Once you have decided what you value, you need to apply the philosophical principles outlined in the first chapter. For example, in the previous scenario, a utilitarian might argue that the greatest good is served by printing a story that alerts the community to the fact that some creep who rapes women who cannot defend themselves is still out there. Ross would argue that a journalist has duties both to the readers and to the victim, and they must be weighed before making a decision.

Aristotle's Golden Mean might counsel a middle ground that balances printing every detail against printing no story at all. Kant would suggest that the maxim of protecting someone who cannot protect herself is a maxim that could be universalized, making a decision to omit some information justifiable. Feminist ethics would suggest much the same approach with the additional emphasis that a rape is newsworthy. Both Kant and multiple feminist scholars also would argue not to use the woman as a means to your end—an exclusive story, in this instance.

In this case, application of several ethical principles leads to the general conclusion that the newspaper should print some story, but not one that inadvertently reveals the victim's identity or that makes her out to be hopelessly naive in her trust of strangers.

However, you should be alert that while different ethical principles in this scenario lead to the same conclusion, many, if not most, ethical dilemmas may not produce such a happy result. The principles point to different and even mutually exclusive actions on your part, leaving you to decide your ultimate loyalty. But this is why the Potter Box demands that you apply more than one ethical principle, so that if (or when) they vary, you are able to explain why.

Step Four: Articulating loyalties. The ultimate destination of the Potter Box is to arrive at a loyalty. Potter viewed loyalty as a social commitment, and the results of using the Potter Box reflect that ethic. In the fourth step, you articulate your possible loyalties and decide whether they are in conflict. In the case above, you have a loyalty to the truth, to the community, to the victim, and to your job—just for starters.

However, your loyalties are not in severe conflict with one another unless you adopt an absolutist view of the truth or privacy. It is possible to counsel your reporter to write a story that tells the truth but omits some facts (for example, the woman's residence in a group home and her intellectual disability), alerts the community to a danger (there's a creep out there who police haven't caught), protects the victim's privacy (you won't print her name or where she lives), and allows you to take pride in the job you've done (you've told the truth and not harmed anyone).

Using the Potter Box, though, often highlights a conflict between loyalties. In these instances, we refer you to Royce's concept: What you choose to be loyal to should be capable of inspiring a similar loyalty in others who are both like and unlike you. Journalists often are accused of being "out of touch" with their viewers or readers, a fact for which we are highly criticized, and proper attention to loyalties can help to bridge this gap wherever it exists.

Our experience with the Potter Box has been that the vast majority of ethical decisions will allow you to sustain a variety of loyalties—they are sometimes not mutually exclusive as we saw above. However, those decisions that are most troubling are ones where a loyalty becomes so dominant that you are forced to abandon other loyalties that once seemed quite essential.

While you may initially find the stepwise process of the Potter Box somewhat cumbersome, as you learn to use it, you will become fluent in it. The following case study—"The Pimp, the Prostitute, and the Preacher"— illustrates how you might use the Potter Box when making an ethical decision.

The Pimp, the Prostitute, and the Preacher

You are the court reporter for a daily newspaper in a city of about 150,000 in the Pacific Northwest. About a year ago, the local police force began to crack down on prostitutes working the downtown mall. However, the department sought to limit prostitution by arresting pimps rather than by arresting either the prostitutes or their customers. The first of those arrests has now come to trial, and your paper has assigned you to cover it.

In his opening statement, the local assistant district attorney tells the jury that in order to convict a person of pimping under state law, the state must prove first that money was exchanged for sexual favors, and second that the money was then given to a third party, the pimp, in return for protection, continued work, etc. During the first two days of the trial, he calls as witnesses four young women, ages 14 to 16, who admit they have worked as prostitutes in the city but are a great deal less clear on the disposal of their earnings. Your story after the first day of the trial summarizes the details without disclosing their names.

Near the end of the second day, the prosecutor calls as witnesses men caught paying one or more of the women to have sex with them. Among those who testify is a middle-aged man who in an almost inaudible response to a question lists his occupation as a minister at one of the more conservative Protestant churches in the city. He admits to having paid one of the young women for sex, and that day's portion of the trial ends soon after his testimony is complete.

About 45 minutes later, you are back in the office to write the story when the newsroom secretary asks you if you have a few minutes to speak with "Reverend Jones." You look up and realize you are facing the minister who testified earlier. In the open newsroom, he begs you, in tears and on his knees, not to print his name. He even holds out a copy of the story you wrote on page 1 of this morning's paper outlining why the names of the prostitutes had not been used. He asserts that, should a story with his name appear, his marriage will crumble, his children will no longer respect him, and he will lose his job.

After a few minutes, the paper's managing editor realizes what is happening and calls you, the minister, and the news editor into his office for a conference.

Using the Potter Box, determine how you would report this story. Your decision will reflect a set of loyalties as well as the values and principles you have chosen. Others may choose differently. A justification model such as Potter's or Bok's does not eliminate differences. What it will do, ideally, is ensure that your choices are grounded in sound ethical reasoning and will be justifiable on demand.

When you are finished, the final casting of loyalties will inevitably create another fact for the first quadrant of the box. For instance, in this case, if the decision is to run the name, anything that might subsequently happen to the minister as a result—firing, divorce, even possible suicide—is now a hypothetical "fact" for the first quadrant of the Potter Box, and you go through it again. If you decide not to run the minister's name and his parishioners discover his actions, the newspaper loses credibility. This is also a "fact" to be entered into the first quadrant of the Potter Box. Considering these additional although hypothetical "facts," you may want to go through the process again to see if your decision will remain the same. Regardless of your initial decision about the story, would the possibility of that subsequent "fact," obviously not known to the journalist at the time, make a difference in a later use of the Potter Box?

Now that you've made a decision about revealing the name of the minister based on the facts, we'd like to introduce additional facts. Read them and go through the Potter Box again, focusing less on the minister and more on larger issues that affect how the story is written and how it is run in the newspaper. This time, think about the notions of stereotyping, how minorities are portrayed in news reports, and what exactly we mean by "objectivity" and "truth."

As the trial continues, it becomes clear that there are other factors at work. In your largely Caucasian community, the only people arrested for pimping have been Black. All the young women who work as prostitutes are Caucasian, as are the customers who testify. As far as prostitution goes, your Pacific Northwest version is relatively mild. There are no reports of drug use among the prostitutes and their customers, and none of the prostitutes has complained of physical violence. Further, the prosecuting attorney cannot make any of the young women admit under oath that they ever gave the pimps any money. The jury verdict in this case is not guilty.

Do the new facts change your loyalties? Do they change the way you look at the trial? If so, in what way?

We recommend that you try using both the Bok and the Potter justification models at various times in your ethical decision-making. Becoming a competent practitioner of both methods will provide you with greater flexibility and explanatory power. We also recommend, regardless of the approach you use, that an unvarnished and critical discussion of loyalty become part of your ethical dialogue. We believe it will enable you to anticipate situations as well as react to them.

SUGGESTED READINGS

Fletcher, G. P. (1993). *Loyalty: An essay on the morality of relationships.* New York: Oxford University Press.

Fuss, P. (1965). *The moral philosophy of Josiah Royce.* Cambridge, MA: Harvard University Press.

Hanson, K. (1986). The demands of loyalty. *Idealistic Studies, 16,* 195–204.

Hobbes, T. (1651/1958). *Leviathan.* New York: Bobbs-Merrill.

Oldenquist, A. (1982). Loyalties. *Journal of Philosophy, 79,* 73–93.

Powell, T. F. (1967). *Josiah Royce.* New York: Washington Square Press.

CASES

CASE 4-A

CUOMO INTERVIEWS CUOMO

CHAD PAINTER
University of Dayton

Andrew Cuomo became a media star in 2020. The third-term New York governor became one of the most prominent, visible, and popular faces of the COVID-19 pandemic with more than 100 daily press briefings that were aired nationally. The spring 2020 briefings provided viewers with split-screen experiences as Gov. Cuomo provided a distinct and often contradictory portrait of the nation's health during the pandemic's first wave. Cuomo's briefings were a contrast to those of the daily Coronavirus Task Force briefings frequently led by former President Donald J. Trump.

Gov. Cuomo's briefings spawned social media parody and "Cuomo bingo." He also was interviewed on *Good Morning America*, *CBS Sunday Morning*, *Ellen*, *The Howard Stern Show*, *The Daily Show*, *The Late Show with Stephen Colbert*, *The Tonight Show Starring Jimmy Fallon*, and *Late Night with Seth Meyers*. It was during one of these briefings that Gov. Cuomo announced that his younger brother Chris had tested positive for the virus and would ride it out in his basement while continuing to anchor his CNN news show, a decision Gov. Cuomo called courageous. Multiple interviews resulted. Chris Cuomo's ratings doubled.

CNN had barred Chris from interviewing Andrew from 2013 to 2020 (though he had interviewed him prior to 2013). However, that restriction was lifted in March 2020 when the COVID-19 pandemic first hit New York.

The Cuomo brothers are the sons of former New York Gov. Mario Cuomo. Andrew was sworn in as governor in January 2011. He previously served as New York Attorney General from 2007 to 2010 and as the US Secretary of Housing and Urban Development from 1997 to 2001. Chris has been an anchor and commentator for CNN since February 2013. He previously worked at ABC (including stints on *Good Morning America* and *20/20*), CNBC, MSNBC, and Fox News. Both were educated as attorneys, but one of the things viewers learned during the spring was that Chris had made an active decision to pursue journalism instead of law, a choice his older brother said he supported.

The major question surrounding such interviews, of course, is whether a younger brother could ever conduct an evenhanded interview with his older sibling—whether the issue is excessive toughness or going too easy on his brother (Graham, 2020). The brothers jokingly discussed old arguments—who is their mother's favorite child, who works harder, who's better at basketball, whose clothes fit better (Graham, 2020). The Cuomo brother interviews were funny but became serious when Chris tested positive for COVID-19; his older brother was obviously moved and simultaneously worried. It all made for great television.

There were major advantages to the interviews. The ratings for *Cuomo Prime Time* doubled from the year before (Graham, 2020). Andrew Cuomo, a respected but not beloved governor, became more humanized, in part because of how he conducted his daily briefings. His approval ratings increased 32 points during the pandemic, according to FiveThirtyEight, though some of that can be attributed to a "rally around the flag" effect that leads to increased support for leaders during times of crisis.

Media critics also generally were okay with the interviews. *The Washington Post*'s Margaret Sullivan wrote, "To a nation inured to nepotism by the likes of First Son-in-Law Jared Kushner spouting ill-informed policy views from a White House podium, this is pretty harmless stuff." Ben Smith, writing for *The New York Times*, not only didn't see an issue but also thought that this type of programming could be the future of news:

> They are, in their way, answering the endlessly debated question of how to restore trust in media. Do you strive to project an impossible ideal of total objectivity? Or do you reveal more of yourself, on Twitter or Instagram and in your home?

However, there also were major disadvantages, especially regarding accountability in terms of New York's response to the pandemic. Gov. Cuomo, at least initially, received relatively little criticism regarding the timing of the initial lockdown in New York, and the number of deaths among those in nursing homes and the general public. As of Jan. 15, 2021, there had been 1.19 million COVID-19 cases and 39,997 deaths in New York State.

Micro Issues

1. How would you prioritize Chris Cuomo's loyalties? Would your priorities change if Andrew Cuomo had been the one diagnosed with the virus?

2. Ratings for *Cuomo Prime Time* doubled in part due to the interview segments with Andrew Cuomo. What role, if any, should an increase in ratings play in decisions to allow Chris to interview his brother?
3. What role, if any, should Chris Cuomo play in holding Andrew Cuomo accountable to the public? Should he have aggressively questioned him about his decisions related to the COVID-19 pandemic in New York? How would you respond to this question if it were directed at journalists working for the *New York Times*?

Midrange Issues

1. Should CNN have lifted the ban of Chris Cuomo interviewing his brother Andrew? Use your answer to inform how local media outlets should decide whether to interview friends or family members of journalists working in those communities?
2. *New York Times* media columnist Ben Smith wrote, "Do you strive to project an impossible ideal of total objectivity? Or do you reveal more of yourself, on Twitter or Instagram and in your home?" Answer these questions in terms of loyalty.
3. To viewers, the conflict of interest with one brother (a journalist) interviewing another (a prominent politician) is obvious. Does the obviousness of the conflict mitigate the problem? Do you think revealing conflicts of interest at the local level would have the same impact?

Macro Issues

1. The vast majority of Andrew Cuomo's interviews were conducted by entertainers. Chris Cuomo, however, is a news anchor. How is his role similar to and different from late-night hosts such as Stephen Colbert and Jimmy Fallon?
2. Analyze Chris Cuomo, Andrew Cuomo, and CNN's decisions in terms of Josiah Royce's definition of loyalty.
3. Repeat this analysis when the subject changes to whether Andrew Cuomo has committed multiple acts of sexual harassment during his terms as governor. How does this new set of facts change—or fail to change—your analysis of the micro and midrange issues in this case?
4. Loyalty to a profession means loyalty to the *ideals* of the profession. What are the ideals of journalism? Did Chris Cuomo uphold those ideals while interviewing Andrew Cuomo?

CASE 4-B

TO WATCH OR TO REPORT: WHAT JOURNALISTS WERE THINKING IN THE MIDST OF DISASTER

LEE WILKINS
University of Missouri

Millions saw it live. A CNN crew including Ed Lavandera, producer Jason Morris, and cameraman Joel De La Rosa filmed and then helped volunteer first responder Austin Seth as he pulled 86-year-old Elmore Jones, his 83-year-old wife, JoAnne, and his daughter, Pam, from their Houston home in the aftermath of Hurricane Harvey.

Lavandera wasn't the only journalist to make this choice. "I'm a journalist, but I'm also a human being," said David Begnaud, who helped Houston residents out of a flooded house and into a rescue boat where he had been riding. The whole event was streamed live on CBSN digital.

The Weather Channel's Jim Cantore made the same decision. While on the air, he interviewed a man who was waiting for his daughter's family to be evacuated. Later, some residents who decided to leave the area told Cantore they had done so because of what he had said on television. His Weather Channel colleague was broadcast holding a crying baby, the youngest member of the family to be evacuated.

"I learned this 12 years ago to the date with Katrina's landfall," Cantore said in a *Washington Post* story. "When people are in trouble, you just do what you can to help. I could give a crap about TV at that point."

A woman struggling with a television set interrupted a live shot with Matt Finn, a Fox News reporter who was covering the hurricane from Port Arthur, Texas. Finn motioned the camera away from the woman and helped her when the shot ended. Finn also provided exhausted firefighters with transportation—a detail that did not make it into his news coverage.

"I'm not making myself the story, and I'm not a hero," he said. "The people I'm looking at right now—the police officers and the firefighters—are the heroes."

Micro Issues

1. Kelly McBride, vice president of the Poynter Institute, said that a reporter's job is to inform. "Any time you spend your energy on helping someone, that is energy and resources not spent on telling

the story to the audience." Evaluate this statement in light of the journalists' actions and rationale outlined above.
2. How does your evaluation differ from the "shoot now, edit later" decision that sometimes explains how still photographers decide which images to capture?

Midrange Issues

1. Less than two weeks later, Hurricane Irma pounded the state of Florida. Coverage included multiple journalists broadcasting live in the teeth of the storm while simultaneously airing government instructions to evacuate. Evaluate these actions in light of the cases outlined above. What philosophical theory supports your decision?
2. Should journalists broadcast (e.g., on personal Twitter feeds) photos or videos shot by citizens at the scene of a hurricane or other disaster despite the fact that those citizens have been encouraged to evacuate or take other measures to remain safe?

Macro Issues

1. How are the actions described above distinct from stating a personal opinion in a news story?
2. These decisions by news reporters occurred during a time when the media were being called the "enemy of the people" by President Donald J. Trump. Should footage of these actions be used to promote the profession as part of a public relations campaign?

CASE 4-C

PUBLIC/ON-AIR JOURNALIST VERSUS PRIVATE/ONLINE LIFE: CAN IT WORK?

MADISON HAGOOD
Oklahoma Christian University

On Oct. 9, 2017, viewers tuned in to ESPN's 6 p.m. *SportsCenter* only to find that one of the hosts, Jemele Hill, had been suspended from the ESPN airwaves for two weeks for running afoul of the network's social media policy. Almost immediately, the question of whether public figures should be able to express their private political opinions on social media came under scrutiny in ESPN's handling of *SportsCenter* co-host Hill's series of tweets from her personal Twitter account.

Hill, who first got a chance to co-host ESPN's flagship program in February 2017, came under fire that September when she called President Trump a "white supremacist who has surrounded himself with other white supremacists" in a tweet that has since been deleted. Hill also claimed Trump was the "most ignorant, offensive president of [her] lifetime," a "bigot," and "unqualified and unfit to be president."

Despite issuing an apology for her tweets, which "painted ESPN in an unfair light," Hill found herself serving a two-week suspension after a second breach of ESPN social media conduct, when she encouraged "paying customers" to "boycott" Dallas Cowboys owner Jerry Jones's advertisers in light of the ongoing 2017 NFL controversy concerning player conduct during the national anthem.

Following the lead of ex-San Francisco 49ers quarterback Colin Kaepernick from the 2016 season, many NFL players had chosen to sit, kneel, or stay in the locker room during the playing of the anthem in the fall of 2017. Jones, however, had orchestrated his team's protest carefully—a well-televised knee before the anthem and respect during it. He had even participated in the pseudo-event himself. Later, Jones had been quoted as saying that any Cowboy who did not stand for the anthem would be benched. At that point, Hill took to social media.

"If they don't kneel, some will see them as sellouts," Hill said in a series of tweets on her personal account on Oct. 8, 2017.

> By drawing a line in the sand, Jerry put his players under more scrutiny and threw them under the bus. . . . If the rationale behind JJ's stance is keeping the fan base happy, make him see that he underestimated how all of his fan base feels.

ESPN, which has a partnership with the NFL through 2021, told ThinkProgress that the key factor in Hill's suspension was the reference to a boycott of Cowboys' sponsors, many of which also sponsor the network (Legum, 2017). In a statement, an ESPN spokesperson said that in the aftermath of Hill's suspension, "all employees were reminded of how individual tweets may reflect negatively on ESPN and that such actions would have consequences."

ESPN and other networks have encouraged their commentators and personalities such as Hill to "build their personal 'brand' through commentary." However, ESPN public editor Jim Brady told the *Washington Post* that "media companies are simultaneously asking many of their personalities to be active and engaging on social media but not partisan or opinionated. It's a line that is, at best, blurry and, at worst, nonexistent" (Farhi, 2017).

Through two sets of guidelines for its employees, "Social Networking" and "Political and Social Issues," ESPN (2017) encourages its employees to

avoid personal attacks and inflammatory rhetoric. . . . Think before you tweet. Understand that at all times you are representing ESPN, and Twitter (as with other social sites) offers the equivalent of a live microphone. Simple rule: If you wouldn't say it on the air or write it in a column, don't post it on any social network.

Employees of companies such as ESPN are held responsible, not only for the content they post on their personal accounts but also for the audience their posts reach and the potential effects of an improper post. ESPN's *Outside the Lines* anchor Bob Ley told *Sports Illustrated* following Hill's first breach in social media policy:

The usual standard of saying only what you would with a microphone in your hand apparently no longer applies. These are emotional, political times. There are important responsibilities that come with the many perks, and chief among those these days is realizing your words carry the weight of your platform. You speak for more than yourself. (Deitsch, 2017)

Hill left *SportsCenter* in January 2018. She now writes for *The Atlantic*.

Micro Issues

1. Was it right for Hill to be suspended by ESPN for tweets published on her personal account? Justify your answer.
2. As an employee, do you believe you represent your employers, even when you are "off the clock"?
3. Should one be forced to sign a social media policy to gain employment?

Midrange Issues

1. If Hill had not been previously warned about social media after her tweets about President Trump, do you believe her calling for a boycott of Jerry Jones would have been enough by itself for a suspension by the network? Justify your answer.
2. Hill is a Black woman. Do you see any hints of either sexism or racism in this case, and, if so, where? Would a popular male anchor have been treated differently?

3. If Hill had a lesser role within ESPN, do you think her punishment would have been as severe?

Macro Issues

1. Is a sport event's integrity lost if there is no playing of the national anthem beforehand?
2. In the context of the Black Lives Matter movement and the protests in Charlottesville in 2017, do you believe minority television personalities' comments and views are met with more scrutiny than those of Caucasian commentators?

CASE 4-D

WHEN YOU ARE THE STORY: SEXUAL HARASSMENT IN THE NEWSROOM

LEE WILKINS
University of Missouri

By the time you read this case study, this list will be longer:

Roger Ailes, Fox News
Matt Lauer, NBC's *Today Show*
Mike Oreskes, NPR
Charlie Rose, CBS
David Sweeney, NPR
John Hockenberry, WNYC
Leonard Lopate and Jonathan Schwartz, WNYC
Harvey Weinstein, The Weinstein Company
John Lasseter, Disney/Pixar
Glen Thrush, *New York Times*
Bill O'Reilly, Fox News
Garrison Keeler, *The Prairie Home Companion*

The names on *this* list epitomize a series of important questions. The first: How to report a story when your own organization, and specifically your own newsroom, is involved?

NBC chose to announce Matt Lauer's firing on the *Today Show* less than 12 hours after the initial complaint surfaced. *Today Show* host Savannah Guthrie fought back tears as she read the announcement, noting, "This is a sad morning at NBC News." The show's ratings jumped after the announcement. Lauer waited a little more than two days to respond and then released a statement that read,

> There are no words to express my sorrow and regret for the pain I have caused others by words and actions. To the people I have hurt, I am truly sorry. As I am writing this I realize the depth of the damage and disappointment I have left behind at home and at NBC.

Fox played it differently. Charges against Bill O'Reilly dated back to 2002, and his contract was continually renewed, while some of the women involved received financial settlements totaling about $13 million. It was only after those settlements were reported in the *New York Times* that O'Reilly was fired. Months later, the *Times* reported that O'Reilly had settled yet another claim for $32 million right before he signed another contract renewal with the network. O'Reilly characterized his firing as a "political and financial hit job." He added, "There were a lot of other business things at play at that time, still today, that 21st Century [Fox] was involved with" (Media Matters Staff, 2017).

NPR played it yet a third way. On Nov. 19, 2017, it aired an hour-long special, reported by women at NPR, in which the network's response to sexual harassment claims was part of the focus of the in-depth coverage. That coverage explored why sexual harassment had become a flash point at this time in history, explored how men felt about the issue, and defined sexual harassment in the workplace. NPR's reporting about the issue, even when it involved other news organizations, always included a mention that NPR itself is involved in the harassment scandal.

In December 2017, the #MeToo movement was named a person of the year by *Time* magazine.

Micro Issues

1. Is sexual harassment a legitimate news story?
2. Evaluate the distinct approaches of the news organizations outlined above, as well as others that you may be familiar with, in terms of transparency and privacy (discussed in chapters 2 and 3, respectively).
3. If you were to write a "best practices" guide to how news organizations should report on sexual harassment within the organization, what would you suggest? Why?
4. Compare the reporting about sexual harassment by the news organizations outlined above with that conducted by the *Boston Globe* and described in the "Spotlight" case in chapter 6.

5. How does the fact that other news organizations are reporting on sexual harassment charges in news organizations that compete with them influence your response?

Midrange Issues

1. In most jurisdictions, certain kinds of sexual harassment are also criminal conduct. In the United States and in criminal cases, people are considered innocent until proven guilty. Do charges of sexual harassment carry a different standard of proof and evidence? Why or why not?
2. Sexual harassment is the most obvious and vicious form of misogyny in contemporary culture. How are changes in tolerance of acts of sexual harassment likely or unlikely to change underlying patterns of discrimination and marginalization of women, either in the workplace or as the focus of news and entertainment programming?

The second set of questions these responses to sexual harassment raise is more philosophical in nature. In general, they center on the role and effectiveness of punishment in human relationships, from the political to the personal. Most people consider being fired over charges of sexual harassment a form of punishment. In the current climate, Emily Lindin, a columnist at *Teen Vogue*, summed up one view concisely on Twitter: "I'm actually not at all concerned about innocent men losing their jobs over false sexual assault/harassment allegations," she wrote. "If some innocent men's reputations have to take a hit in the process of undoing the patriarchy, that is a price I am absolutely willing to pay." Lindin, who was criticized for this comment, noted that women had been afraid for decades and disbelieved and discounted when they attempted to report the issue. Lindin voiced the anger many women felt and continue to feel about the issue.

Feminist philosopher Martha Nussbaum notes that in any society, in situations of profound oppression and systematic injustice, trust is nonexistent. "It is very easy for the oppressed to believe that trust is impossible and that they can win their struggle only by dominating in their turn." In her 2016 book *Anger and Forgiveness: Resentment, Generosity, Justice*, Nussbaum examines the lives and work of Gandhi, Martin Luther King, and Nelson Mandela as examples of revolutionary justice. Nussbaum sees more potential in Mandela's approach, noting, "A nation torn by horrible acts may find itself unable to move forward. Angry feelings may have such a deep grip on people's minds that they cannot be changed to forward-looking projects and feelings" (Nussbaum,

2016, p. 244). With Mandela, Nussbaum suggests that anger itself, while understandable, is a philosophical error, one that replicates the dominant/dominated relationship that produced it in the first place. Instead, she recommends generosity and reciprocity. Nussbaum notes, "If this book achieves anything, I hope it achieves that sort of square-one reorientation, getting its readers to see clearly the irrationality and stupidity of anger" (Nussbaum, 2016, p. 249).

> Our institutions should model our best selves, not our worst. . . . Furthermore, when there is great injustice, we should not use that fact as an excuse for childish and undisciplined behavior. Injustice should be greeted with protest and careful, courageous strategic action. But the end goal must remain always in view: As King said so simply, "A world where men and women can live together." (Nussbaum, 2016, p. 249)

Macro Issues

1. Evaluate this statement: Sexual harassment is an expression of power that has been confounded with sex.
2. How might news organizations that have been plagued by sexual harassment and other forms of misogyny develop the "forward-looking projects and feelings" of which Nussbaum speaks?
3. Is Nussbaum's approach too idealistic for the current cultural climate? If your answer is yes, what alternative do you believe might be effective?

CASE 4-E

WHERE EVERYBODY KNOWS YOUR NAME: REPORTING AND RELATIONSHIPS IN A SMALL MARKET

GINNY WHITEHOUSE
Eastern Kentucky University

Everybody is a source when you're covering an agricultural town with a population under 12,000.

However, Sunnyside Police Sergeant Phil Schenck had not been a source for Jessica Luce when he asked her out on a date during a Halloween party in 1999. Luce had worked as a general assignment reporter at the *Yakima Herald-Republic* for almost a year. Sunnyside, Washington, was one of four communities she covered in this first job out of college. The two spent time together infrequently over the next two months.

"I was interested in him, we had fun, but if I had been asked what was going on, I would have said we were friends," Luce said.

Nonetheless, a coworker was incredulous.

"You can't go out on a date with a source," Luce remembers him saying. "It's one of the biggest taboos in journalism!"

The *Herald-Republic*'s four-page code of ethics advises staff to avoid conflicts of interest but offers no specifics on personal relationships that might cause conflicts of interest.

Luce decided to keep her relationship with Schenck quiet. She had never needed Schenck as a source and never thought the occasion would arise.

Schenck's boss, however, was another matter. Sunnyside Police Chief Wallace Anderson had been accused of shooting a great blue heron outside the police station, storing explosives at the station house, and of having a threatening temper. Following a lengthy and expensive investigation, Anderson resigned in November.

By New Year's Day, Luce and Schenck decided they were definitely dating.

"I kept my relationship under wraps save for a few confidants at work," Luce said. "I felt the relationship would be perceived as something wrong, but I didn't see it interfering with my job.

"Phil and I didn't talk about work as much as normal couples might. We knew it wasn't fair to either one of us."

In mid-February, Schenck was named acting captain, the No. 2 position in the Sunnyside Police Department, and the official media spokesman. Luce realized she needed to be pulled off the Sunnyside police beat immediately. Her editors agreed.

"It was hard to talk with them about my private relationship," Luce said, "and I was forced to define things about the relationship that I hadn't even done for myself."

Craig Troianello, her city editor, sat her down for a long conversation.

"Jessica made it easy because she was straightforward," Troianello said. "We didn't ask intimate questions—that's irrelevant in this case, [and] by taking the proactive ethical stand that she did, it was easy for us to deal with this."

Luce said Troianello emphasized that he was not questioning her integrity. However, he had to make sure he hadn't overlooked something that could be perceived as a conflict by readers.

"This was a lesson on perception versus reality," Luce said.

Luce's reporting did not affect Schenck's promotion, nor had Schenck ever implied that a story should or should not have been covered. Nonetheless, Schenck benefited from the chief's departure.

Troianello said he was never worried that Luce's reporting was compromised, but he wanted to make sure the newspaper was above suspicion.

"Issues involving the police department were in the forefront of the news," Troianello said. "People could read anything into it—that she was protecting the chief, that she was trying to bring the chief down. Those kinds of spins drove my concern."

However, Schenck questions whether a strict conflict-of-interest standard is realistic in a small town.

"Everybody is a potential source—even the clerk at the grocery store," Schenck said. "We eat food. If her husband or boyfriend is a farmer, you could say she is promoting eating. This is an ideal that might be somewhat impractical.

"If you can't be a real person, how can you report on real people?"

Luce says, if she had to do it all over again, she would not have kept the relationship a secret as long as she did. Nonetheless, it would still be hard to talk to a supervisor about dating. Troianello said he understands the complexities of a journalist's personal life but would rather Luce had brought the relationship to the newspaper's attention by New Year's Day, when the two began dating.

However, he understands the dynamic of the situation.

"She's in a small town where the number of people with four-year degrees and professionals is small," Troianello said. "It seems like there will be some mixing at some point. Relationships could occur as naturally as it does in the newsroom. I married a copy editor."

Once their relationship went public (they were later engaged), Luce was surprised at how supportive the community and city officials were, including the new police chief (someone other than Schenck).

"What we as journalists see as an ethical problem and conflict of interest isn't necessarily going to be seen as an ethical problem by the public."

However, Luce never heard comments one way or another from the former chief or his supporters. On several occasions, city officials have questioned whether Schenck leaked information to Luce or *Herald-Republic* reporters. Schenck simply explained that he had not.

"I deal with stuff every day that Jessica would love to get her hands on," Schenck said. "But we just don't talk about it."

Luce now covers education in the city of Yakima.

Micro Issues

1. Did Luce have a responsibility to tell her editors about her relationship with Schenck? If so, when should Luce have informed them?
2. What responsibility did the *Yakima Herald-Republic* editors have to explain expectations on conflicts of interest? Is spelling out those expectations necessary or appropriate in a code of ethics?
3. How would the ethical questions have changed if Schenck worked in another capacity for the city, such as being a teacher?
4. How would the ethical questions have changed if Luce and Schenck had remained only friends?

Midrange Issues

1. What aspects of their lives should journalists be able to keep private?
2. Is public perception of an ethical problem truly relevant?
3. Journalists spend most of their time with two groups: their sources and their coworkers. Considering those limitations, is dating possible or advisable?
4. NBC *Dateline* correspondent Maria Shriver took a leave of absence as her husband, Arnold Schwarzenegger, ran a successful race for governor of California. As she returned to her duties, what limitations, if any, should have been imposed on her reporting? Justify your decision.

Macro Issues

1. Can journalists cover communities effectively if they are expected to remain remote and removed?
2. How specific should codes of ethics be on conflicts of interest?

CASE 4-F

QUIT, BLOW THE WHISTLE, OR GO WITH THE FLOW?

ROBERT D. WAKEFIELD
Brigham Young University

Anyone who spends sufficient years in public relations will face a crisis of conscience. Practitioners are trained for the tenuous task of balancing institutional advocacy with the "public interest" (Newsom, Turk, &

Kruckeberg, 1996). Yet this role can lead to personal conflict, as it did in my case.

The setting was an urban school district with about 40 schools and more than 35,000 students. Its superintendent had a national reputation for innovative community outreach, and he was a media favorite. I worked with him for five years before he accepted a statewide position. His replacement was a quiet man with conservative views who, along with the administrative team he brought with him, believed that educators were trained to run the schools and could do so best with minimal interference.

Like most inner-city school districts, the system was losing students as people moved to the suburbs. In the previous decade, a student population that once filled four high schools could now fill only three.

The seven-member school board had approached—and then abandoned—the question of closing one of the schools because the proposal aroused such strong feelings among students, faculty, and parents. However, the new administration, trying to balance those responses against the financial drain of supporting an additional high school on taxpayer dollars, decided to broach the question again.

Promised a tumultuous situation, the new administrators aggravated the problem by how they handled it. Rather than sharing the issue with the community or with school faculties to seek a mutually agreeable solution, they tried to resolve the entire problem behind closed doors.

I first learned about the closed-door approach at a "study meeting" with the school board. The new superintendent held these informal meetings during his earliest days in the district; they tended to be so boring and ambiguous that journalists seldom attended.

Before the meeting in question, the superintendent asked me whether any media would be present. I told him one reporter might come late. As the meeting began, I was surprised to hear him tell the board and the few staff members, "If any reporter shows up, I will change the subject—but today we're going to talk about closing a high school." He then outlined the results of meetings he had already held on the issue, discussed a proposal from a local community college to buy the building so it would not be abandoned, and sought the support of the four high school principals.

Thus began my ethical conundrum. I agreed that the enrollment problem was serious and that closing a school was probably the best alternative, but I opposed the administration's method of resolving the issue. As public relations officer, I believed that public institutions must be open and that involving those affected by the closure in the actual decision-making process would eventually generate long-term support for whatever decision was made. I was appalled at the attempts to exclude the public, but I said nothing.

Closed doors can quickly swing ajar, and it took less than one day for news of the decision to leak. The school targeted for closure was one of the oldest in the state. It had recently received a US Department of Education award as an exemplary inner-city school, but its community was the least affluent and arguably the least politically powerful.

The day after the "study session," and with a regular board meeting scheduled for the same evening, reporters called to verify what they were hearing.

Chief executives often forget that supervisors of individual units within the system have their own allegiances. In this case, one of the high school principals left the "study meeting" and informed his teaching staff that they would be receiving transfer students "from that inner-city school." The rumors began.

After the phone calls, I asked the superintendent what he planned to say at the board meeting and was told, "We will discuss space utilization needs." I told him about the calls and that our jobs would be threatened if we were not truthful with the community. To his credit, he responded quickly and openly. The evening meeting unfolded as expected. The room was jammed with district patrons and with the media. The expected lines were drawn. Underlying the fervor was a common theme: Closing a traditional high school was awful enough, but the secretive way in which the administration had reached its conclusions was unforgivable.

The next several weeks were an intense period of work for a young public relations officer. I did media interviews, talk shows, and forums to explain the situation. I also met with dozens of teachers, parents, and citizens, both to hear their comments and to take their suggestions. I had to be careful that my words represented the district instead of myself. I had worked with some local reporters for several years and felt comfortable giving them background so they could seek additional materials without revealing me as the original source. It was a personal risk, but the reporters never betrayed my trust.

Two additional incidents epitomized my ethical struggles. The first occurred after the initial board meeting, when a top administrator said the community misunderstood why decisions were made behind closed doors. I lobbied for openness. The administrator admonished me to remember who paid my salary, a rebuke that confirmed the new administration did not share my own values.

The second incident occurred when I was asked to meet with a man who had been chosen to speak on behalf of the community. I had taken only a few steps into his office when he said to me, "You don't agree with your administration, do you?" My response was silence while he explained his position.

For some reason, it was this encounter that forced my crisis of conscience: Do I quit, blow the whistle, or keep quiet? I had a wife and child to support; the employment picture at the time was not robust. Right or wrong, I surmised that the various relationships I had developed could appease many angry feelings. I also believed in the importance of education. So, I decided to stay through the crisis, and then seek new employment.

About one month into the crisis, the board retained a consultant who, like me, believed in open communication. Two weeks later, four board members came to my office and requested a meeting. Because this constituted a majority of the board, such an assembly violated the law requiring the meeting be made public. I violated the law and invited them to stay. They said they were worn down by the constant tension and asked what I, as a public relations practitioner, thought they should do.

To me, the answer was straightforward. Relying on basic public relations formulas and common sense, I suggested that they could diffuse the tension by reverting to what should have been done in the first place: announce that selected representatives from throughout the city would form a committee to help review the situation and come to a decision that would then be discussed by the board.

To my surprise, the board members took this advice to the administration, and much of what I recommended was done. A few months later, the school was closed in a tearful farewell. And, five weeks after the school closed, I accepted a job with a local public relations firm.

Micro Issues

1. What sort of press releases or other talking points should Wakefield have prepared once the rumors began?
2. Should Wakefield have gone off the record with reporters he trusted?
3. Are there some sorts of decisions governmental bodies make that really should be kept from the media and hence the public? Is this one of them?
4. How should Wakefield have responded to the racial subtext of some of the protests about the closing of the school?

Midrange Issues

1. Should Wakefield have "blown the whistle" on the board members who requested an illegal meeting?
2. Was it appropriate for Wakefield to advise the board to take an approach different from that suggested by the superintendent?
3. How much does Wakefield's previous experience with a different superintendent influence his understanding of how the district works? How did this "workplace" socialization influence his ethical thinking?

Macro Issues

1. To whom should Wakefield be loyal?
2. Should he ever have told members of the community of his own personal views?
3. How does Wakefield's job compare with that of a press secretary for a political figure?
4. Is it ever appropriate to keep journalists in the dark about how political decisions are made?

5

Mass Media in a Democratic Society

Keeping a Promise

By the end of this chapter, you should

- reflect on and justify what you believe is the philosophical goal of journalism and strategic communication in a modern democracy;
- know how "fake news" can influence politics and a checklist for spotting it;
- understand the various institutional roles the media play in governing;
- be able to evaluate all forms of political communication through a single, ethically based framework.

THE WITHERING FOURTH ESTATE

Media organizations are expected to act as watchdogs on government. Edmund Burke, in a speech in Britain's House of Commons during the late 1700s, first called the media the "fourth estate" (Ward, 2004) because it performed this role. The founders protected the press in the Bill of Rights as the guardian of the public's interest despite the bitter, partisan nature of broadsheets in 1789. What goes unstated is that, for the fourth estate to be effective, the other three estates—legislative, executive, and judicial—need to work. Further, the human beings who animate those institutions need an overarching loyalty to democracy itself rather than a particular policy view or form of political leadership. For democracy to survive and thrive—Athenian democracy lasted less than 100 years—which the founders of the US constitutional government hoped for, the institutions involved and the people who inhabit them need to be willing to act within established patterns, some dictated by law and others by cultural norms. The Bill of Rights supported a clearly articulated—and experimental—political system. Journalists could not go it alone. In their analysis of *Why Democracies Die*, political scientists Steven Levitsky and Deniel Ziblatt theorize based on historical evidence from multiple nations that democracies die imperceptibly at the ballot box, beginning with political leaders who fail to prevent demagogues from gaining elected power. They note that elected autocrats intentionally subvert multiple democratic institutions, and the news media is included. In a 2018 editorial, scholars noted that in these instances,

> Newspapers still publish but are bought off or bullied into self-censorship. Citizens continue to criticize the government but often find themselves facing tax or other legal troubles. This sows public confusion. People do not immediately realize what is happening. (Levitsky & Ziblatt, 2018)

With this in mind—that journalism functions as part of a political system that relies on other systemic actors in order to achieve its goal of contributing to self-government—consider the following report from NPR media correspondent David Folkenflik:

> Newsrooms have been buzzing about the scenario for weeks: How would they handle covering a president in real time who makes false claims about his own reelection? The answer proved to be fact-checking, in some cases during his remarks from the White House, and tough criticism after he finished.
> A bit before 2:30 a.m. ET Wednesday morning, that scenario became reality. President Trump baselessly alleged Democrats were committing fraud. Trump also claimed he "did win the election," even though some pivotal swing states have not yet been projected for him by the AP or any of the major television networks.
> NBC and MSNBC broke into his remarks, as did NPR, to correct the record. "There have been several statements that are just not true," NBC's Savannah Guthrie said, noting his false claims of taking Georgia, Pennsylvania and Michigan.
> MSNBC's Brian Williams said, "Our presidents don't select our victors. . . . We always allow a lot on election night, hyperbole. But when it veers into falsehood—we have not called the states he claimed for victories."
> MSNBC did not return to Trump's remarks live.
> CBS and ABC returned to their studios once Vice President Pence stepped forward. "The president of the United States [is] castrating the facts of the election results that have been reported tonight," said Norah O'Donnell of CBS.
> "We've never had a situation like this in the country," said John Dickerson of CBS. "The president is a steward of the American electoral system. . . . And he is trying to undermine it while the count is still going on."

"If we were watching this in another country, we would be shocked," said CNN's Abby Phillip. "It's a sign our democracy is in peril."

Fox News anchor Bret Baier told viewers most of the president's claims were accurate. Then Fox's Chris Wallace weighed in: "This is an extremely flammable situation; the president just threw a match into it. He hasn't won the states [he claimed]. Nobody is saying he won the states. The states haven't said that he's won." (Folkenflik, 2020c)

Obviously, the networks as well as individual journalists were making multiple ethical decisions. The fact that these decisions were similar suggests that the fourth estate as an institution was trying to hold other institutions in the same political system to account. Furthermore, journalists knew that many in their audiences would be unlikely to believe them and to ascribe the worst of motives to the choices. In October 2017, one national poll found that 46 percent of registered voters believe that the news media fabricate stories about President Donald J. Trump. Only 37 percent believe the news media do not make up stories. The Politico Morning Consult poll of almost 2,000 Americans also found that a mere 51 percent of voters believe that the federal government should not be able to revoke the broadcast licenses of those news organizations who promulgate fabricated news (Shepard, 2017).

These sorts of polling results come as part of a decades-long decline in trust in government and other institutions by US citizens. That trend is global. Also in 2017—and for the first time in 17 years—a survey that spanned thousands of people and dozens of countries found that a majority of citizens said they did not trust government, the media, nongovernmental organizations, and business "to do what is right."

For one institution to check the power of another, belief in the institution itself and what it represents is essential. Yet journalists today are working in an environment where the general public is skeptical to the point of cynicism, not only about whether the news media can get stories "right" but also regarding whether individual journalists and the news organizations for which they work are motivated by professional norms. If the other institutions are in the process of ignoring existing norms or developing new ones, what motivates professionals becomes even more central.

There are, of course, multiple reasons for this situation, but in keeping with the focus of this book, we would like to suggest three philosophically based roots of the problem.

First, an Enlightenment vision of truth, reviewed in chapter 2, has not found a ready replacement in the 21st century. Humanity finds itself in the middle of an epistemological shift. While we know that truth is complex, we do not have a grasp on how to summarize that complexity in a way that spans points of view, methods of inquiry, or the causes that such complexity must serve.

Second, and unique to American culture, is the First Amendment itself and the normative role of the media as an institution. What is often left unsaid is that the Bill of Rights (and its First Amendment) was approved as a mechanism to further the larger goals of governing—that the First Amendment and all the others constitute a means to an end. That end, as outlined first in the Declaration of Independence and then in the Preamble to the Constitution, is "We the People of the United States, in Order to form a more perfect Union, establish Justice, ensure domestic Tranquility, provide for the common defence, promote the general Welfare, and secure the Blessings of Liberty to ourselves and our Posterity, do ordain and establish this Constitution for the United States." Thus, in both a political and an ethical sense, the goal of free speech in the American context is the promotion of justice within political community.

While other nations have turned to the government as a way of checking the power of the news media, Americans considered free speech so powerful that they outlawed such a partnership at the beginning of the republic. In fact, efforts to protect free speech have added an almost Wild West quality to what is said on the internet while erecting profound economic disincentives to actually control some of what is produced and said there. Furthermore, the US Supreme Court—in its 2010 *Citizens United* decision—equated money with speech. In a country that constitutionally cannot regulate speech by governmental means, economic means become not just the driver but also the decider of who speaks and how big a microphone that person wields. The autonomy from government that the founders sought to protect is now threatened by powerful economic interests, some of which own media organizations that could be expected to counterbalance government power—the historic role of the fourth estate.

Third, and most deeply philosophical, is a vision of the purpose of political power. Philosophers such as Plato, and millennia later St. Thomas Aquinas, wrote that the purpose of government was to provide security to the populace so that it would act in such a way as to conform to a higher authority. For Plato, this authority was the philosopher king. For Aquinas, it was the Judeo-Christian God. Both were considered wise and infallible. Political philosophers, beginning in 1600, lodged political authority more and more in those who were ruled rather than their rulers. This is true even for Marx. And all assumed that the form of political power they articulated would promote happiness in the larger populace. Only Plato, in his discussion in *The Republic* of "the declination of the state," and Marx, who postulated a societal disintegration with the workers at war with the owners of capital, considered what would happen if the current system failed. For Plato, that failure led to anarchy. For Marx, the failure was a necessary step to the creation of a communist utopia (see figure 5.1).

Figure 5.1. "Facebook News Feed" cartoon originally published Nov. 12, 2017 © Adam Zyglis.

Most philosophers, however, assumed their systems would "work." However, as the above NPR report describes, there are no clear guidelines for the news media when one element in a powerful system ignores political norms in such a way as challenges fundamental concepts of truth or seeks to overbalance a constitutional system that relies on balance among competing forces. The goal of that system is not merely to exist, but rather to make human flourishing within a just human community a potentially achievable goal.

DISINFORMATION: THE TRANSFORMATION TO JUNK NEWS

In chapter 2, we defined fake news and disinformation and linked it to philosophical definitions of lying. We also connected disinformation to a drive for profit. Sissela Bok (1978), in her definition of lying, notes that the reason people lie is to gain power; lies allow liars to define situations in ways that give them an advantage. In 2020, the lies became a particular kind of political framing: a meta-conspiracy theory called QAnon, which postulated a global,

Satan-worshipping, child-molesting Democratic Party cabal ensconced in political power that only then-President Donald J. Trump could thwart. In the QAnon universe, with its internet roots, fake news became news that you didn't like, news that arose from outside your "bubble," and news that may have questioned your very identity.

It's only a small step from whole-cloth fabrication to the concept of junk news—news that isn't exactly a total fabrication but that can be a sensationalizing of some facts, the substitution of trivial content for more important and consequential information, or an attempt to provide opinion without weighing *all* of the evidence. Junk news consists of alternate facts, stories that ignore evidence, often for political gain, or content that functions as clickbait rather than providing a genuine attempt to inform.

Lies that demonize and degrade for political ends are pernicious for citizens as individuals and for the political community as a whole. This is true whether the focus of the comment is immigrants or members of a profession such as journalists. Junk news is the "bad" content that takes up so much bandwidth on the internet and so much journalistic effort to debunk that it closes the professional "window" on the production of quality, evidence-based content.

On Oct. 30, 2017, Facebook executives told Congress that they believed as many as 126 million Americans had received fake news stories initiated by Russia as part of their Facebook newsfeeds (Fiegerman & Byers, 2017). A study conducted by the Oxford University Computational Propaganda Project found that in 11 of 16 swing states—including Wisconsin, Michigan, and Pennsylvania—that provided President Trump with his 2016 Electoral College victory margin, Twitter users received more fake and junk news than authentic political coverage in the two weeks before the November election (Wooley & Howard, 2017).

The congressional testimony marked both a watershed and an about-face for the builders and owners of social-media platforms and the corporations that have emerged from them. In the weeks before the 2016 election, the then president Barack Obama warned Facebook CEO Mark Zuckerberg about the potential impact of political disinformation, only to be countered by Zuckerberg's insistence that the problem was not widespread. Facebook executives continued to downplay the problem until their congressional testimony more than a year after the Obama–Zuckerberg conversation. When Zuckerberg testified before Congress, he admitted to "mistakes" but sidestepped the pointed questions about how the platform was going to counteract them. More than a year later, and after a torrent of criticism that included calls to regulate and break up the publishing platform, Zuckerberg announced that Facebook would block some websites (including those that pronounced that the Holocaust never happened), would discontinue "new" political advertising in the week before the 2020 presidential election, and was in favor of "some" form of regulation.

Scholars who have begun to study the effect of widespread junk news have concluded that junk news did make—and will continue to make—a difference in how Americans frame politics and hence think about political problems. "Adding fake news producers to a market has several potential social costs," say economists Hunt Allcott and Matthew Gentzhow (2017). They argue that leaders who mistake a junk-news outlet

> for a legitimate one have less accurate beliefs and are worse off for that reason. Second, these less accurate beliefs may . . . undermine the ability of the democratic process to select high-quality candidates. Third, consumers may also become more skeptical of legitimate news producers. . . . Fourth, a reduced demand for high-precision, low-bias reporting will reduce the incentives to invest in accurate reporting and truthfully report signals.

Although the history is recent, Facebook's architecture allows users to divide themselves into "friends" and "not friends." In almost any other setting—and certainly in one focused on ethics—this structure of "in group" versus "out group" would be considered problematic. It would raise questions about how "friends" can form a political community with those who are "not friends." For the Greeks, the answer was political debate, and for much of the history of British and US democracy, it has been a republican government serving an increasingly better-informed and more active electorate. The media had an institutional role in governing. However, Zuckerberg, in particular, has resisted having Facebook labeled a media company despite the findings in multiple studies that more and more Americans were getting their news from Facebook. The platform's institutional role had become that of a media company; it facilitates discussion about government, and it collaborates with those in power and those who seek power. Facebook takes advantage of protections afforded only to individuals and media organizations in the United States, specifically, the First Amendment. However, by maintaining that Facebook is not a media organization, the corporation is able to dodge the ethical obligations and legal strictures incumbent on journalists and news organizations.

This complicated and entwined analysis indicates that scholars need to develop some new ways of thinking. That thinking needs to place ethics at its core, not merely in describing what roles are but in imagining what they should be if democratic functioning is to be maintained. Individual journalists will need to exhibit courage as they do their daily work. What role a courageous institution should perform in a 21st-century democracy has yet to be determined. However, we suggest that an ethically based approach is one that balances freedom with justice and that helps citizens to understand both the history and the possibilities of such standards.

THE MEDIA'S POLITICAL ROLE

In a less complicated time, Americans viewed the written word as essential to political society. Writing in the *Federalist Papers*, Madison, Hamilton, and Jay expected citizens to be informed and to participate in politics. They knew that political debate, including what was printed in the press, would be partisan and biased rather than objective, but they also believed that from this "noisy" information the rational being would find the truth. Unfettered communication was essential to building a new nation. Citizens had an obligation to read such information; the press had an obligation to provide it.

The founders were thinking about the press of the day as an important institution in the emerging democracy. At this level, it is not the individual story or single ad but the aggregation of all of them that matters, and it received specific protection as the first bulwark against political authority outlined in the Bill of Rights.

Scholars such as John C. Merrill (1974) assert that the First Amendment should be interpreted purely as a restriction on government, emphasizing freedom of expression and downplaying any notion of reciprocal journalistic responsibility. In other words, freedom of speech is not extended to only speech written or uttered by "mainstream" media. Free speech also extends to minority voices, even those that are decidedly unpopular (see figure 5.2).

Others, including Alexis de Tocqueville (1985), who studied our democracy in the mid-19th century, viewed the press of the day as an essential antidote to a culture that valued liberty over community. The press, de Tocqueville said, was an incubator of civilization, an idea that political philosopher John Dewey would further for the mass media of his day a century later.

Figure 5.2. Mother Goose & Grimm (New) © 1999 Grimmy, Inc. King Features Syndicate.

Recent scholarship outlines four normative roles for the media in democratic political systems (Christians, Glasser, McQuail, Nordenstreng, & White, 2009). *Normative* used in this way means a description of how the media ought to behave. In real life, and in real theory, individual organizations can fulfill multiple roles simultaneously. These roles are as follows:

- The *radical role* operates when the media provide an alternate vision to the current political and social situation in a country.
- The *monitorial role* is what citizens most often think of when they speak of the watchdog function of the news media.
- The *facilitative role* is perhaps best captured by news coverage of elections and political advertising about candidates and public issues. Both news and ads can facilitate governing, although how well that role is accomplished is the source of much analysis and debate.
- The *collaborative role* is when the media promote the views of the state. Broadcasting weather forecasts can serve this role as can much less benign forms of collaboration.

These various roles have been the focus of scholarship for more than 75 years. However, emerging as they do from the academy, they are slow to reflect contemporary political reality. Beginning in 2019, then-President Donald J. Trump described another role for the media: "the enemy of the people." On April 5, 2019, Trump tweeted:

The press is doing everything within their power to fight the magnificence of the phrase, MAKE AMERICA GREAT AGAIN! They can't stand the fact that this Administration has done more than virtually any other Administration in its first 2yrs. They are truly the ENEMY OF THE PEOPLE! (capitalization in the original)

In the ensuing months, journalists were attacked, sometimes arrested, at one point hit with a rubber bullet, and jeered at by crowds attending Trump rallies and other protests. Trump rescinded individual reporters' credentials; he mocked others, particularly women broadcast journalists. In September 2020, Trump again emphasized that he believed journalists deserved to be attacked. Trump's treatment of the news media percolated through the political system. State and local officials sometimes took their cues from the president, often by failing to respond to media requests for information, locking out reporters from certain meetings, and sometimes publicly browbeating individual journalists for their coverage in various public forums. This new normative role might be best characterized as *political witness* from the democratic citizenry's point of view.

While Trump's vociferous criticism of the media, linking it to a conspiracy-fueled "deep state," is not how journalists like to think of themselves, history suggests that in the past century, the national press corps has been a player in the policy process by reporting "leaks" and granting "off-the-record" interviews (Linsky, 1986). Certainly, the owners of media companies are considered members of the power elite. Government officials, both elected and appointed, use journalists to leak a story to find out how others will react to it. Sometimes leaks take the form of whistleblowing when a government employee believes the public good is not being served by the system. Watergate's famed (and now named) source, "Deep Throat" (W. Mark Felt), apparently was so motivated when he leaked key parts of the government investigation into the Watergate break-in to *Washington Post* reporters Bob Woodward and Carl Bernstein, who wrote a series of articles that helped bring about the resignation of President Richard Nixon. More recently, the initial information about the 2003 Abu Ghraib prison abuse scandal in Iraq came to journalists in emails from servicemen and women who were alarmed at the treatment of Iraqis held at the prison and at the military command's unwillingness or inability to change the system. Edward Snowden's 2013 leaks revealed secret policy decisions by the US National Security Agency that were designed to forestall additional terrorist attacks by making everyday communication the subject of government surveillance. Scholar Elizabeth Stoycheff's work has documented that the act of surveillance is more detrimental to free speech than government censorship (Stoycheff, 2016). And, in 2017, the release of the "Paradise Papers," reported by a consortium of more than 150 news organizations worldwide, revealed the breadth and depth of individual, corporate, and institutional efforts to stash money in offshore accounts, thereby dodging tax laws and inflating earnings in everything from retirement accounts to university endowments. Based on the history of the past decade, it is difficult to assert that the journalists who undertake to report such leaks do so unaware of the potential those leaks have to change everything from individual lives to political and economic policy at the national and international levels.

The administration of former President Donald J. Trump leaked with great regularity, including stories from multiple whistleblowers or disgruntled cabinet officials, often after they had resigned. The best known was the anonymous author of a *New York Times* op-ed piece published in 2018 that characterized Trump as erratic and dangerous and claimed there was a resistance inside the White House to curb his actions. More than a year later, Miles Taylor, who had served in the Department of Homeland Security under the Bush and Obama administrations, revealed that he authored the piece.

As originally conceived, journalism was a public service. Yet, as academic studies have shown, and the former president's rhetoric emphasizes, the belief that journalists operate in the public interest is not universally accepted. Critical reporting—which can include a refusal to collaborate in spreading lies by powerful figures as emphasized by the NPR report—is sometimes viewed as a fundamental disloyalty to the system, one worthy of being dismissed from it.

Political reporter E. J. Dionne, in *Why Americans Hate Politics* (1991), argues that defining news as conflict (as virtually every journalism text does) inevitably reduces political debate to a shouting match. In the world of "fake news" and "alternative facts," there is always the chance that critical coverage of government will be labeled "unpatriotic," particularly by those in power. This is not a problem exclusively confined to the US system as documentaries such as *Control Room* (2004)—an in-depth look at the al-Jazeera newsgathering operation—make clear.

Dionne agrees with Plato, who said that democratic politics, while a "degenerative" form of government, was probably the best available system considering that human beings were its primary components. The same can be said of the humans who cover the governing process. Media critic James Fallows (1996) goes one step further. He holds journalism directly responsible for voter apathy, congressional gridlock, and government via opinion polls rather than via political leadership. In a quote that rings just as true today as it did when he made it before the turn of the century, Fallows claims:

> The harm actually goes much further than that, to threaten the long-term health of our political system. Step by step, mainstream journalism has fallen into the habit of portraying public life in America as a race to the bottom, in which one group of conniving, insincere politicians ceaselessly try to outmaneuver another. The great problem for American democracy . . . is that people barely trust elected leaders or the entire legislative system to accomplish anything of value. . . . Deep forces in America's political, social and economic structures account for most of the frustration of today's politics, but the media's attitudes have played a surprisingly important and destructive role. (p. 7)

Media critic Kathleen Hall Jamieson (1992) suggested that, when it comes to politics, journalists should get themselves a new definition of news. Instead of emphasizing events and conflict, Jamieson believes, news stories could equally revolve around issues and multiple policy perspectives. Fallows and others insist that implicit in the right to report on politics is that successful governing is an outcome for which the media are partially responsible. The cynical assumptions that government can never act for the public good, and that journalists and the media are somehow outside and perhaps even above the political system, are almost nihilistic. Further, we would like to add that an emerging responsibility is continuing in-depth reporting on people "who are not your Facebook friends." Whether this means people who are unlike you—in class, race, gender, or a multiplicity of such orientations—only by discovering their lives is it possible for our circle of friends to widen. If freedom and justice are the goals of democracy, then such ethically informed practice would allow journalists and their media consumers to become more conscientiously involved in the evolution of the American democratic political system.

GETTING ELECTED

For any politician to enact change, he or she must first be elected and, in our mass society, that means turning to the mass media to reach the electorate. In one classic study, voters admitted learning more about candidates' stands on issues from advertising than they did from news (Patterson, 1980). Considering that modern presidential campaigns place ads only in contested states, many voters get little exposure to even the limited and one-sided information coming from ads unless they access them online.

In the past few presidential campaigns, websites have become increasingly important. In 2020, it was possible to enter "Trump world" exclusively online, a phenomenon that was not limited to the presidential race. These websites were never intended to "make it" to the mainstream media but rather to "fire up the base." Similar websites, designed to look as if they represented citizen activism but were really the creation of powerful corporations that made their profits from fossil fuels, also were prominent in the 2020 race. Because such websites are under the control of the candidate or interest group and not bound by any constraints of objectivity or completeness, they too qualify as advertising. So today, more than 30 years after the first studies indicated it to be true, advertising is still the leading source of information for most people in most campaigns—not just about candidates but about policy issues as well.

Because ads are a leading source of campaign information, factual accuracy must be the starting point for ethical political advertising. As philosopher Hannah Arendt has noted, "Freedom of information is a farce unless factual information is guaranteed and the facts themselves are not in dispute" (Arendt, 1970).

News stories about elections emphasize strategy and tactics rather than stands on issues, forcing voters who want to become informed about the candidate's policy choices to get their information from ads, often "negative" or "attack" ads framed by the other side. Policy analysis, when it is present at all, is more frequently found on candidate websites, where spin and incomplete data are the foundation for content.

Contemporary voters can discern the various types of political ads, according to election studies. Comparative ads, ones that contrast candidate positions on specific issues, were viewed as information-rich, and voters view them as an appropriate part of political discourse. Attack ads, ones that are personal and negative, that contain no "positive" or "issue-oriented" information, were disliked and distrusted in the studies. A few years ago, a majority of political ads were either positive or contrasted stances of the candidates (Benoit, 1999). Another study from the same time showed that voters were able to distinguish among negative, comparative, and positive or biographical ads (Jamieson, 2000).

Today, "ad watches" put the claims in political ads to the tests of truthfulness and of context. Anecdotal evidence suggests that aggressive journalism reporting on attack ads and negative campaigning can have an impact on the voters' knowledge of particular candidates. Ideally, political advertising would be factual and rational. The use of emotional arguments designed to stir listeners or viewers "to set aside reason" is a "violation of democratic ethics" (Haiman, 1958, p. 388). However, there may be times when valid issues have strong emotional content, such as the ongoing debate over immigration, gun control, and the need for government to insure health care for all. The melding of emotion and issue in such cases is not unethical, but totalitarian regimes have historically used emotional rather than rational appeals to either gain or retain power (see figure 5.3).

Seeking the evidence behind political assertions has historically been the role of the news media. When this sort of journalism is lacking, it begins a cycle that was foreseen by Walter Lippmann:

Figure 5.3.   Ed Stein © The Rocky Mountain News. Reprinted by permission of Andrews McMeel Syndication for UFS. All rights reserved.

In the absence of debate, restricted utterance leads to the degradation of opinion[;] . . . the more rational is overcome by the less rational, and the opinions that will prevail will be those which are held most ardently by those with the most passionate will. (Lippmann, 1982, p. 196)

If political advertising is indeed a "special case" (Kaid, 1992), then journalists and their audiences should demand higher standards, more regulation, or both. While some of the solutions do run afoul of current legal standards such as the *Citizens United* decision, they are worthy of discussion. They include the following:

- Allot limited amounts of free time to qualified candidates for major office to level the playing field for candidates.
- Strengthen state regulations against corrupt campaign practices and find ways to enforce those regulations.
- Encourage journalists to stop covering the "horse race" aspect of campaigns and focus on problems and solutions. This is particularly essential since polling—designed to designate a front-runner among other things—appeared fatally flawed in both 2016 and 2020 at the national and state levels.
- Hold candidates accountable for their ads and for the ads of political action committees or other groups such as moveon.org.
- Teach journalists to read and report on the visual imagery of a campaign, and to ask candidates questions about it.
- Allow attack ads only if they include the image of the candidate directing the attack.
- Reject unfair or inaccurate ads created by political action committees.
- Conduct ad watches as part of media coverage of a campaign, analyzing the ads for omissions, inconsistencies, and inaccuracies.

It takes money to buy ads, and in contemporary democratic societies that means the candidate with the most money often has the loudest voice. Many argue the influence of money in the political system is pervasive and corrosive. In the 2012 election cycle, following the *Citizens United* decision, the Supreme Court essentially allowed supporters of candidates—including corporations and unions—to collect and spend unlimited amounts of campaign funds. While the impact was most noticeable at the presidential level, Senate and House races and even state legislative races also were influenced by an influx of campaign cash, much of it from supporters outside the geographic boundaries of specific legislative districts. It can be argued that money buys elections, especially in the light of evidence that the most heavily funded campaign wins more often than not. However, it also can be argued that monetary gifts are merely precursors to votes, and the most popular candidate in gifts is often the most popular in votes as well. Whether the money brings the votes or popularity brings the money, the lower the level of the race (state legislators, judges, etc.), the more impactful these outside gifts can be.

How to deal with the influence of money in elections is an important policy question, but there seem to be few answers. Politicians are too tied to the existing system to seek change, and the media that could presumably investigate political money and its negative influence are compromised by the act of receiving so much of the cash in the form of ad buys. The problem cannot be "solved" in this brief chapter, but it is worth considering whether a media system in a democracy might not be able to be a part of the solution rather than a part of the problem.

LEARNING ABOUT LEADERS AND THEIR CHARACTER

Too Much and Never Enough: How My Family Created the World's Most Dangerous Man was the title of Mary Trump's 2020 book. A psychologist by training and professional practice, Mary Trump provided her readers with a psychological portrait of her uncle, Donald J. Trump. Mary Trump understood that a representative democracy rests on the Greek concept of *aidos*, a concern for the good opinion of others. In addition to providing voters with facts, something that is generally assumed to be the role of news, the media provide citizens with a framework to understand those facts. Mary Trump's book received more "free media"—and hence public discussion—because its controversial assertion made news.

Cultivating that good opinion is the focus of not just election-season politics but governing as well, and the entertainment media exerts considerable influence on the public's opinion. For example, former California governor Arnold Schwarzenegger announced his candidacy on the *Tonight Show*. Former President Barack Obama appeared multiple times on *The Daily Show*, and news coverage of some of his interactions with White House correspondents revealed his comedic timing as well as his ability to sing on key. The good opinion of the public is cultivated in more traditional, and more predictable, ways. The person who covers the winning candidate for a network will almost assuredly become the White House correspondent for the next four years. Journalists covering a national election have almost as much at stake as the candidates they cover. Journalists treat front-runner differently than they do the remainder of the candidate pack (Robinson & Sheehan, 1984). Front-runners are the subject of closer scrutiny, but those examinations are seldom about issues. Candidates and their paid consultants have developed strategies that will allow them either to capitalize on front-runner status and image or to compensate for a lack of it. In the 2011 movie *The Adjustment Bureau*, Matt Damon portrays a young and good-looking candidate who uses his concession speech early in the film to poke fun at the absurd amounts his staff paid to test his shoes, his ties, and so forth. The movie makes a good point: Television-friendly candidates are more likely to receive free media—the Sunday morning programs, the nightly news, the higher-rated cable news shows, and so forth. Candidates have mastered the "photo opportunity" and, for incumbents, the "Rose Garden strategy" designed to thwart anything but the most carefully scripted candidate contact with the voting public.

At the same time as candidates try to script their every move, the media have the right, and the responsibility to get "behind the curtain" (Molotch & Lester, 1974) to the real candidate. What happens after the curtain is down often makes news in ways the candidates could not have foreseen, as Mary Trump's book did. It all goes back to the Greek notion of *aidos*. However, just because the information is available and even accurate does not automatically mean that it is relevant and ethical to broadcast or print it.

Conceptualizations of character have changed significantly since the founding of the republic, when character was defined in Aristotelian terms—an observable collection of habits, virtues, and vices. Freudian psychology has altered that definition to include motivation, the subconscious, and relationships that help to form all of us as people. What journalists cover is "political character," the intersection of personality and public performance within the cultural and historical contexts. Character is dynamic—the synergy of a person within an environment (Davies, 1963). Journalists who explore character often do so for an ethical reason despite apparent invasions of privacy.

Political figures are powerful people. Ethicist Sissela Bok (1978) has noted that when an unequal power relationship is involved, it is possible to justify what would otherwise be considered an unethical act. To paraphrase Bok, investigation of the private character of public people is validated if the person investigated is also in a position to do harm. In those cases, invading privacy in an attempt to counter that threat is justified. However, that invasion also needs to meet some tests (Schoeman, 1984):

- The invasion must be placed in a larger context of facts and history and must include context to provide meaning.
- The revelation of private facts about political figures should meet the traditional tests of journalism and needs to be linked to public, political behaviors before publication or broadcast becomes ethically justifiable.
- The invasion of privacy must further the larger political discourse and must meet the most demanding ethical test: the "need to know."

Even reporting that passes the three tests above must be filtered through discretion. Reporters covering political character should be aware that there are several building blocks of character, including the

- politician's development of a sense of trust;
- politician's own sense of self-worth and self-esteem;
- development of a politician's relationship to power and authority;
- early influences on adult policy outlook;
- way a politician establishes contact with people;
- flexibility, adaptability, and purposefulness of mature adulthood; and
- historical moment.

The media's current emphasis on covering political character provides the best illustration of the need to balance the demands of governing with privacy. No culture has ever expected its leaders to be saints; in fact, some cultures have prized leadership that is decidedly unsaintly. In American culture, the concept of public servant—which is the work of politics—has been replaced by the epithet "politician"—synonymous with "crook," or "liar," a caricature reinforced in popular culture by iconic films such as *Mr. Smith Goes to Washington* or *All the King's Men* or more recently *Games of Thrones* and *House of Cards*. However, Americans were reminded that public service can be a high calling, as shown by the first responders to the 9/11 tragedy or the thousands of healthcare workers who have staffed nursing homes and hospitals during the COVID-19 pandemic, many of whom lost their lives. The late Senator Edward Kennedy described his job as public service. Such service, dating as far back as Athens, was considered the mark of a life well lived.

EVALUATING POLITICAL COMMUNICATION

For the Greeks, who gave birth to democracy, the art of politics was considered a gift from the gods, who provided men with *aidos*, a sense of concern for the good opinion of others, and *dike*, a sense of justice that makes civic peace possible. In the ancient myth, these gifts were bestowed on all citizens, not just some elite. All free men were able to exercise the art of politics through rhetoric and argument in the assembly, a form of direct democracy that survived for only a few years in Athens. The Greeks called it *polity*, which translates as community.

Evaluating all this political information—news, advertising, and entertainment—is a problem for both media consumers and journalists. Furthermore, as news blends into entertainment and persuasion leaches into both genres, providing a consistent way of examining every political message becomes essential in ethical analysis. Political scientist Bruce A. Williams (2009) has begun this process with a four-part test he believes will help you determine when information has political relevance:

- First, is the information **useful**—does it provide citizens with the kind of information that helps individual and collective decision-making?
- Second, is the information **sufficient**—is there enough of it and at enough depth to allow people to make informed choices?
- Third, is the information **trustworthy**?
- Fourth, who is the **"audience"**—the political "we" on which the ancient Greeks placed so much emphasis?

Information that meets these criteria should be considered politically relevant, mediated information regardless of genre or source, Williams says. Under this test, a John Oliver newscast or a Stephen Colbert monologue could be considered politically relevant communication every bit as much as a campaign ad or an investigative piece. Under this sort of analysis, cable news programming, which often features dueling opinions by talking heads speaking over each other (often unsubstantiated by evidence), *would actually fare less well* than the comedy monologue.

In a famous dust up with cable news personality Tucker Carlson, Comedy Central comedian Jon Stewart took on the entire genre of punditry. Stewart suggested that his show was more truthful and politically relevant. Interestingly, Stewart has made that claim in other arenas—that Comedy Central actually has political clout—and adds that it personally frightens him, which gets a good laugh but makes a poignant point.

Putting all political communication into the same arena also has another virtue: Every message can be evaluated along the same standard. Here, again, Williams (2009) suggests four criteria.

- **Transparency**—Does the audience know who is speaking? This has become a major problem in recent elections with the rise of PACs and groups not bound by campaign finance rules and rarely bothered with the total accuracy of their claims.
- **Pluralism**—Does the media environment provide an opportunity for diverse points of view, either in different messages that are equally accessible or within a single message? Does every side have access to the engines of information that are now the modern equivalent of the face-to-face rhetoric of ancient Greece?

- **Verisimilitude**—Do the sources of the messages take responsibility for the truth claims they explicitly and implicitly make, even if these claims are not strictly verifiable in any formal sense?
- **Practice**—Does the message encourage modeling, rehearsing, preparing, and learning for civic engagement? Does it encourage activities such as voting or less direct forms of political activity such as thinking about issues, looking at websites, blogging, or talking to neighbors face-to-face? Is the ad or article empowering, or does it contribute to the cacophony that has dominated recent political campaigns?

We acknowledge that this framework places a premium on rationality and fact. However, it also acknowledges context and point of view. In addition, it assumes autonomy—not just in the voting booth but in choosing what to access through various web portals—while requiring community. This framework's foundation is an ethical one, and, like the Greeks, it asserts that politics is essential to human flourishing.

SUGGESTED READINGS

Christians, C. G., Glasser, T. L., McQuail, D., Nordenstreng, K., & White, R. A. (2009). *Normative theories of the media: Journalism in democratic societies.* Champaign: University of Illinois Press.

Dionne, E. J. (1991). *Why Americans hate politics.* New York: Simon & Schuster.

Fallows, J. (1996). *Breaking the news: How the media undermine American democracy.* New York: Pantheon.

Fry, D. (1983). *The adversary press.* St. Petersburg, FL: Modern Media Institute.

Jamieson, K. H. (2000). *Everything you think you know about politics . . . and why you're wrong.* New York: Basic Books.

Linsky, M. (1986). *Impact: How the press affects federal policymaking.* New York: W. W. Norton.

Madison, J. S., Hamilton, A., and Jay, J. *The Federalist papers.*

Ward, S. (2004). *The invention of journalism ethics.* Montreal: McGill–Queen's University Press.

CASES

CASE 5-A

MURDER THE MEDIA: ETHICS ON JANUARY 6, 2021

LEE WILKINS
University of Missouri

PART 1

There were warning signs. Reporters whose beat was the internet, the dark web, or national security were aware of online chatter about coming to Washington, D.C., on Jan. 6, 2021, to protest Congress's count of the Electoral College votes, which declared Joseph R. Biden the winner of the 2020 presidential election. Some reporters informed their editors. At least one suggested alerting the FBI (see figure 5.4).

Figure 5.4.   AP Photo/Jose Luis Magana.

Micro Issues

1. Journalists are not normally considered an information source for law enforcement. Was it appropriate for journalists to alert law enforcement agencies of the results of their reporting? What ethical theory supports your response?

2. Would a similar response be appropriate in your state capital? In these instances, would you be willing to turn over notes or source names to law enforcement?

PART 2

In the days and weeks after the Nov. 3, 2020, election, then-President Donald Trump and many supporters asserted that the presidential election had been rigged. The first "Stop the Steal" Facebook group was formed on Nov. 4, 2020. These assertions continued despite recounts in multiple states and court decisions that found the statements had no basis in fact. Beginning in mid-December, Trump encouraged his supporters to show up for a "big rally" in Washington, D.C., in early January. The Monday before the rally, he urged his supporters in Georgia to come to Washington to take back "what was taken from us."

Micro Issues

1. Should these claims have been reported? Whom would you consider an appropriate source? How should the lack of evidence in support of the election fraud claims have been treated? Would it be appropriate to call Trump and those who supported him "liars"?
2. How should submitted "street video" showing angry voters confronting public officials have been reported? How would you authenticate such video?
3. Some broadcast outlets—for example, national Fox News and local stations owned by the Sinclair Broadcast Group—aired opinion pieces and other programming that supported the allegations of election fraud. Should those news and opinion stories have been reported by other media outlets? Is there an ethical distinction between local and national news organizations in your answer? How would you respond to viewers/readers who believed this news coverage?
4. How much effort should local journalists have made to get their elected representatives on the record about these erroneous assertions? How should those news stories have been framed? How should local journalists have handled a refusal to comment about the issue by local officials?

Midrange Issue

1. For how long and in what form should these stories be cached on news organizations' websites?

PART 3

On the morning of Jan. 6, 2021, President Trump opened an hour-long speech to a crowd of supporters on the National Mall with the following:

> Media will not show the magnitude of this crowd. . . . But you don't see hundreds of thousands of people behind you because they don't want to show that. . . . We have hundreds of thousands of people here, and I just want them to be recognized by the fake news media. Turn your cameras please and show what's really happening out here because these people are not going to take it any longer. They're not going to take it any longer. . . . I just want to see how they covered. I've never seen anything like it. But it would be really great if we could be covered fairly by the media. The media is the biggest problem we have as far as I'm concerned, single biggest problem. The fake news and the big tech.

Trump went on to tell those gathered:

> All of us here today do not want to see our election victory stolen by emboldened radical-left Democrats, which is what they're doing. And stolen by the fake news media. That's what they've done and what they're doing. We will never give up, we will never concede. . . . You don't concede when there's theft involved.

A few minutes later, Trump added:

> Republicans are constantly fighting like a boxer with his hands tied behind his back. . . . And we're going to have to fight much harder. . . . And after this, we're going to walk down, and I'll be there with you, we're going to walk down, we're going to walk down. . . .
>
> Because you'll never take back our country with weakness. You have to show strength and you have to be strong. We have come to demand that Congress do the right thing and only count the electors who have been lawfully slated, lawfully slated. . . . I know that everyone here will soon be marching over to the Capitol building to peacefully and patriotically make your voices heard.

After speaking for more than an hour, Trump left the podium and returned to the White House, where he remained for the rest of the day. The crowd marched down the National Mall to the US Capitol. Once there, some stormed the building, breaking down doors and windows to get in, destroying property, ransacking offices, and sacking the building. Many were heavily armed. Some chanted "Hang Mike Pence." Others attempted to find Speaker of the House Nancy Pelosi. When that was impossible, they ransacked her office. Secret Service agents took Pence to a safe location less than a minute before part of the crowd reached the door to the Senate floor. After about five hours of confusion, threats, and numerous injuries, Washington Mayor Muriel Bowser established a 6 p.m. curfew, and the building ultimately was cleared. Congress went back into session at 4 a.m. the next morning and counted the Electoral College votes, officially making Joe Biden president. In that session, 147 Republican representatives and 8 Republican senators objected to the count in certain states.

Micro Issues

1. How should the crowd that stormed the US Capitol be characterized? A mob? Insurgents? Protestors? Insurrectionists? Domestic terrorists? Use ethical theory to support your word choice.
2. Should Trump's speech have been broadcast live? Excerpted? What are the harms and loyalties that inform your answer?
3. How much should journalists attempt to appear objective, considering the opening of Trump's speech?
4. Is appearing objective a truthful recounting of the day's events?

Midrange Issues

1. The phrase "murder the media" was scratched on a wooden door at the entrance to the Capitol. What are the ethical arguments for using that image with this case study compared to the image printed with it?
2. How long should television news continue to rebroadcast the Jan. 6 events? What ethical theory justifies your choice?
3. Many journalists covering the event said they were frightened; some of them were attacked verbally and physically. What is an ethical response for the individual journalist in this situation? What should their news organizations have done?
4. Many of the images shot by journalists covering the event included images of racist and anti-Semitic slogans and images. How should that footage have been edited in the first hour after the event? Twelve hours after the event? In the week after the event?

Macro Issues

1. Pundits on outlets such as CNN and MSNBC were among the first to note that the response of law enforcement to the Capitol insurrection was distinct from the response of law enforcement to Black Lives Matter protests. Is this an important element of the story? Is it opinion? Is it news? Support your answer using ethical reasoning.
2. Should journalists have waited for President-elect Biden to make the same comparison of law enforcement's response before reporting it?

PART 4

In the week after these events—in which five people died and dozens were injured—President Trump was de-platformed, first by Twitter and then by YouTube, Facebook, and other social media sites. Facebook also deleted tens of thousands of accounts associated with QAnon. Twitter deleted tweets and sometimes the accounts associated with them if they contained language that prompted violence.

Micro Issues

1. Is de-platforming a form of censorship? Is it appropriate in this case? How do you justify your answer using ethical theory?
2. Should journalists continue to use Twitter and Facebook as reporting tools? To promote their own stories?

Midrange Issues

1. How much coverage should journalists and news organizations be giving to continuing threats of violence?
2. How should journalists report on members of white supremacist organizations? Outline potential stories, interview questions, and visual images, and provide an ethical justification for them.

Macro Issues

1. During the week of these events, more than 20,000 Americans died from COVID-19. Which is the more significant news story? How would you stack a newscast or design a front page considering the entire news agenda for the week?

2. The journalists covering these events in Washington, D.C., were experienced local journalists responding to the same crises that occurred in the earliest years of their careers. What did the experienced reporters do that beginners can adopt in local media markets? What mistakes did they make that younger journalists can avoid?
3. Should the concept of free speech apply not just to government but also to privately owned social media companies?

CASE 5-B

A SECOND DRAFT OF HISTORY: THE *NEW YORK TIMES*'S 1619 PROJECT

LEE WILKINS
University of Missouri

Journalism has been described as the first, rough draft of history. In August 2019, the *New York Times* and reporter Nikole Hannah-Jones took a swing at a second draft, a social history of the United States that revolves around how slavery has shaped American political, social, and economic institutions. You may have read some or all of the project as part of the high school curriculum it spawned. The journalistic "nut graph" for the project is as follows: How would history look, and how would it be written, if 1619, the year enslaved Africans were first brought to the British colonies, was considered the year of the nation's birth?

However, chances are the 1619 Project looks little like the history you learned in high school and may be learning in college. For many decades, US history has been taught through the eyes of great men. Women and people of color are absent, and the events that shaped their lives omitted or downsized. In 2018, the Southern Poverty Law Center found that few American high school students know that slavery was the cause of the Civil War, that through the three-fifths clause the US Constitution protected slavery without mentioning it, or that ending slavery required a constitutional amendment.

While many elements of the 1619 Project were criticized, among the most controversial were Hannah-Jones's statements in the opening essay: "one of the primary reasons the colonists decided to declare their independence from Britain was because they wanted to protect the institution of slavery" as opposition to that practice began to take hold in Britain. Other flash points included sociologists Matthew Desmond's essay likening the crueler practices of American capitalism to similar practices under slavery.

Soon after the *Times* published the 1619 Project, Princeton historian Sean Wilentz began circulating a letter objecting to it. Wilentz's letter eventually was signed by James McPherson, Gordon Wood, Victoria Bynum, and James Oakes, all leading academics. They sent the letter to three of the *Times*'s top editors. A version of the letter was published in the *Times* on Dec. 4, 2019, along with a rebuttal from Jake Silverstein, editor of the *New York Times Magazine*, in which the 1619 Project had originally been published.

The academics' letter questioned some of the statements and noted that the 1619 Project reflected "a displacement of historical understanding by ideology." The letter did not criticize the *Times*'s attempt to cast accepted historical facts in a different light, nor did it assert that the re-envisioning of American history was somehow inappropriate or should not be attempted by journalists as opposed to academic historians. In fact, the letter said that all the signatories "think the idea of the 1619 Project is fantastic."

However, the deepest issue that was central to the disagreement was what Dr. Martin Luther King called the "arc of history." US history, as it is traditionally taught, frames the American experiment as a long, halting, and imperfect progression to a more perfect union that does not yet exist. Academic historians note that some of the interpretations made in the project—for example, that protecting slavery was one of the primary reasons for the colonists to break away from the British—do not deeply reflect the newness of antislavery ideology in the 18th century. In general, the academic authors of the letter accepted the progressive and optimistic view. So did Dr. King, who said on multiple occasions that the arc of history bends toward justice. Mohandas Gandhi also espoused this view.

On the other side of this debate, the authors of the 1619 Project are pessimistic that a majority of white people will abandon racism and work toward a more egalitarian political, social, and economic system. They wrote that slavery places such a heavy and enduring hand on American culture that the creation of a "different" society may ultimately be impossible.

Micro Issues

1. Journalists are not historians. Was it appropriate for the *New York Times* and its reporters and editors to undertake such a project?
2. Look at your local news media. Can you find stories that focus on the history of specific events—for example, significant floods or other

natural disasters? How do these stories employ history to inform their coverage? Should journalists produce more such coverage?
3. Nell Irvin Painter, a professor emeritus of history at Princeton, decided not to sign on to the letter because, she said, "I felt that if I signed on to that, I would be signing on to the white guy's attack of something that has given a lot of Black journalists and writers a chance to speak up in a really big way." Evaluate this statement.

Midrange Issues

1. Former Speaker of the House Newt Gingrich called the 1619 Project "a lie." Gingrich, who holds a doctorate in history, argued that several hundred thousand white Americans died during the Civil War to free the slaves. Evaluate this statement. Does such criticism belong in the project itself?
2. James Oakes, one of those who signed the letter, said in an interview on the World Socialist website, "The function of those tropes is to deny change over time. . . . The worst thing about it is that it leads to political paralysis." Evaluate this statement in a contemporary context. How do you believe it might inform coverage of the Black Lives Matter movement? Of criticisms of that movement?
3. How does the statement "a displacement of historical understanding by ideology" reflect the Enlightenment and pragmatic theories of truth?

Macro Issues

1. Journalism asks reporters and editors to become "expert" in complex questions. What are some of the tools journalists can ethically employ to report on such complexity?
2. Develop a 1619 Project-like series for your home community. What arguments would you use to promote the project with an editor or news director?
3. Evaluate books such as Shane Bauer's *American Prison: A Reporter's Undercover Journey in the Business of Punishment*, which relies on history as well as contemporary accounts. Is this journalism? Is it history? What normative theories of the press do you think are exemplified by this effort? Apply the same criteria to Isabel Wilkerson's book *Caste: The Origins of Our Discontents* and Fawn Brodie's *Jefferson: An Intimate History.*

CASE 5-C

WHEN JOURNALISTS QUESTION ALGORITHMS AND AUTOMATED SYSTEMS

XERXES MINOCHER AND KATHLEEN BARTZEN CULVER
University of Wisconsin–Madison

Algorithms are becoming more prevalent as a way of doing work in a variety of professions and disciplines. Often associated with technologies called "artificial intelligence," algorithms are best understood as mathematical models that follow a set of rules to solve or perform a task. What might take a human days or even weeks to do, algorithms combined with computers and large datasets can do in seconds.

The US criminal justice system is one place where algorithms and automated problem-solving are being deployed. For example, algorithms are used in courtrooms to assign scores to defendants in an attempt to determine how likely they are to commit a crime again. Based on information collected by the court, the algorithm produces what is known as a "recidivism" or "risk-assessment" score. These scores are then used to help determine bond amounts or even the lengths of criminal sentences.

In 2016, a journalistic team at ProPublica released the results of their investigation into the use of one risk-assessment algorithm in Broward County, Florida. The journalists investigated more than 7,000 individual cases, finding that "The formula [algorithm] was particularly likely to falsely flag Black defendants as future criminals, wrongly labeling them this way at almost twice the rate as white defendants. . . . White defendants were mislabeled as low risk more often than Black defendants" (Angwin, Larson, Mattu, & Kirchner, 2016).

BIAS IN ALGORITHMS

The findings by the ProPublica team were among the first to document a larger trend: the possibility of racial biases being embedded into artificial intelligence technologies. As Julia Angwin and her journalistic team describe it:

> Northpointe's core product is a set of scores derived from 137 questions that are either answered by defendants or pulled from criminal records. Race is not one of the questions. The survey asks defendants such things as: "Was one of your parents ever sent to jail or prison?" "How many of

your friends/acquaintances are taking drugs illegally?" and "How often did you get in fights while at school?" The questionnaire also asks people to agree or disagree with statements such as "A hungry person has a right to steal" and "If people make me angry or lose my temper, I can be dangerous."

Even though the questions used in the risk-assessment algorithm do not ask about race, in 21st-century America, responses that increase a defendant's "risk score" are inherently tied to social and class position. Given the history of systemic racism within and throughout the United States, these questions are highly racialized, even as they avoid explicitly asking the race of a defendant. Indeed, as the ProPublica team found, Black defendants consistently scored higher—or more at risk of flight or repeat offenses—than white defendants.

As Napa County Superior Court Judge Mark Boessenecker remarked, "A guy who has molested a small child every day for a year could still come out as a low risk because he probably has a job. . . . Meanwhile, a drunk guy will look high risk because he's homeless" (Angwin et al., 2016). A reliance on these algorithmic risk scores without attention to other factors in an individual's life seems more likely to affect those experiencing poverty or homelessness instead of those with a high likelihood to commit another crime or offense.

In response to ProPublica's story, Northpointe—the company that produced the algorithmic scoring system—challenged the journalists' statistical analysis. ProPublica responded and even academic researchers and some other news outlets joined the debate.

The key issue was summarized in October 2016 by an analysis in the *Washington Post*'s "Monkey Cage" section, which provides space for social scientists to weigh in on public issues. Writing about the debate, Sam Corbett-Davies and his team of academic researchers said, "It's easy to get lost in the often-technical back and forth between ProPublica and Northpointe, but at the heart of their disagreement is a subtle ethical question: What does it mean for an algorithm to be fair?" The details of both the system and ProPublica's analysis reveal two different definitions of fairness:

> Northpointe contends they are indeed fair because scores mean essentially the same thing regardless of the defendant's race. For example, among defendants who scored a seven on the COMPAS scale, 60 percent of white defendants reoffended, which is nearly identical to the 61 percent of black defendants who reoffended. . . .
>
> But ProPublica points out that among defendants who ultimately did not reoffend, blacks were more than twice as likely as whites to

be classified as medium or high risk (42 percent vs. 22 percent). Even though these defendants did not go on to commit a crime, they are nonetheless subjected to harsher treatment by the courts. ProPublica argues that a fair algorithm cannot make these serious errors more frequently for one race group than for another. (Corbett-Davies, Pierson, Feller, & Goel, 2016)

Ultimately, the challenge becomes the impossibility of satisfying both definitions of fairness simultaneously. If the algorithm achieves fairness by Northpointe's standard, it is unfair as identified by ProPublica. If it achieves fairness by ProPublica's standard, it fails Northpointe's definition. In the end, it is up to courts and judges to decide whether to use the system.

Micro Issues

1. Is the fairness of algorithms news? If your answer is yes, in what context? If your answer is no, why not?
2. Are there other areas of human behavior—for example, making a medical diagnosis or paying bills on time—where an algorithm might be helpful? Is this use of artificial intelligence news?
3. Does the collection of data used with algorithms invade privacy? Do algorithms used to predict behavior pose other privacy concerns?

Midrange Issues

1. The ProPublica story required extensive time and journalistic resources. Could a smaller journalistic organization—say, your local television station or newspaper—be expected to investigate this use of artificial intelligence? What values are reflected by a decision to undertake such enterprise reporting?
2. Is one definition of fairness more equitable than the other?
3. Some have argued that university-based journalism programs should join with local news organizations to conduct analyses such as this. Do you think your program would be able to contribute to such an effort? Why or why not?
4. Algorithms are often used in sales—for example, Amazon or Netflix recommendations. Is such a use of algorithms ethically distinct from the use investigated by ProPublica? What ethical theory supports your answer?

Macro Issues

1. Ethicists maintain that "fairness" is a dangerous concept. Contrast your understanding of fairness with your understanding of justice as outlined by John Rawls or Amartya Sen in chapter 6. Which concept—fairness or justice—do you think is a better explanation for ProPublica's story? The criticisms of it?
2. What is the social responsibility of corporations, including journalistic ones, that develop and use artificial intelligence in their work?
3. In the courtroom, algorithms are used to streamline an adversarial process that historically has involved exclusively human judgment. When is data an appropriate substitute for human-based reflection? Ground your answer in the ethical concept of flourishing and in ethical theory.

CASE 5-D

WATCHDOG OR HORNDOG: *DAILY MAIL*, REVENGE PORN, AND KATIE HILL

CHAD PAINTER
University of Dayton

The Katie Hill scandal began on Oct. 18, 2019, when the conservative political blog *RedState* reported that Hill was having an "inappropriate" relationship with Morgan Desjardins, a 24-year-old who worked for Hill's congressional campaign. *RedState* included two photos—including one of Hill and Desjardins kissing—as well as several text exchanges between Hill, Desjardins, and Hill's husband, Kenny Heslep. Hill and Heslep married in 2010; they divorced in 2019. The blog stated that Hill, Heslep, and Desjardins were having a three-way relationship.

Hill was a first-term congresswoman representing California's 25th Congressional District, which includes northern Los Angeles County and southern Ventura County. She defeated incumbent Republican Steve Knight in the November 2018 midterm elections.

The scandal escalated on Oct. 24 when the British tabloid the *Daily Mail* published a series of photos—including three depicting a naked Hill, one of which shows her brushing Desjardins's hair and another showing her smoking a bong. The *Daily Mail* story also states that Heslep posted Hill's photos to wife-sharing websites in 2016.

Heslep released the photos while he and Hill were in divorce proceedings. Hill, California's first openly bisexual US representative, broke off her relationships with both Heslep and Desjardins in May 2019, saying that she wanted to focus on her congressional work. Heslep also accused Hill of having an affair with her legislative director, Graham Kelly, which would have been a congressional ethics violation. That allegation, however, was false.

Hill called the photos an invasion of privacy and said that her estranged and abusive husband was trying to humiliate her. She also said that her political opponents were exploiting a personal matter for political gain.

On Nov. 3, 2019, Hill announced that she would resign from Congress, writing on Twitter, "This is the hardest thing I have ever had to do, but I believe it is the best thing for my constituents and our country" (Bowen, 2019).

"I'm leaving because of a misogynistic culture that gleefully consumed my naked pictures, capitalized on my sexuality and enabled my abusive ex to continue that abuse, this time with the entire country watching," Hill said. "I'm leaving, but we have men who have been credibly accused of intentional acts of sexual violence and remain in boardrooms, on the Supreme Court, in this very body and, worst of all, in the Oval Office" (Haddad, 2019).

Hill's last act before resigning was to vote in favor of formally launching impeachment proceedings against then-President Donald Trump.

Hill vowed to advocate for victims of revenge porn, or the sharing of explicit or sexual images or videos without the consent of the person in the image.

The *Daily Mail*'s decision to publish the sexually explicit photos stands in sharp contrast to decisions made by news organizations during the Anthony Weiner scandal. Weiner, then a New York congressman, admitted to sexting several women through his Twitter account. He resigned from Congress in June 2011 but continued to sext women until 2017, when he was convicted of sending nude photos to a 15-year-old girl. Several publications ran photos of Weiner. Some photos showed him wearing jockey shorts, but none showed his unclothed genitalia.

Micro Issues

1. Is it ever appropriate for a news organization to publish sexually explicit photos?

2. Photos do depict Hill abusing a power imbalance with a staffer, and they do show her smoking marijuana (at the time a crime in California). Does that make the photos newsworthy? Why or why not?
3. At the time of this writing, 38 states and Washington, D.C., have laws addressing nonconsensual pornography. Analyze the law in your state or an adjacent state.

Midrange Issues

1. Compare and contrast the decisions to publish photos in the Anthony Weiner and Katie Hill scandals.
2. Hill is openly bisexual. What impact, if any, do you think that had on *RedState* and the *Daily Mail*'s decisions to publish the photographs of her and Desjardins?
3. Hill is a Democrat. What role, if any, do you think her political affiliation played in the conservative blog *RedState*'s decision to publish photos and text exchanges?

Macro Issues

1. Hill stated that she was resigning "because of a misogynistic culture that gleefully consumed my naked pictures, capitalized on my sexuality and enabled my abusive ex to continue that abuse, this time with the entire country watching." What is the role of the public to look away and not consume these images?
2. How should journalists balance the needs for truth and privacy? Does the watchdog role of the press extend to a public official's private life? Under what circumstances would reporting on a public official's private life be acceptable and unacceptable?
3. Contrast the decision you made in response to the "Harry and Meghan" case (in chapter 3) with the decisions you have made in this case. Support your choices with philosophical theory.

CASE 5-E

MAYOR JIM WEST'S COMPUTER

GINNY WHITEHOUSE
Eastern Kentucky University

The quiet, conservative city of Spokane, Washington, woke up to a surprise on Thursday, May 5, 2005, as residents opened their newspapers. They discovered that Mayor Jim West had used his city computer to solicit young men in gay chat rooms and that two men claimed West had sexually molested them as children.

In the months prior, West had been e-chatting on Gay.com with someone he believed to be an 18-year-old recent high school graduate. West offered him a city hall internship, sports memorabilia, help getting into college, and excursions around the country. In reality, he had been corresponding with a forensic computer expert hired by the *Spokesman-Review*.

Reporter Bill Morlin had spent two years along with reporter Karen Dorn Steele tracking down allegations from the 1970s that West had sexually molested boys while he was a county sheriff's deputy and a Boy Scout leader. West had been close friends with fellow deputy David Hahn and fellow Scout leader George Robey, who both committed suicide after sexual abuse allegations were brought against them in the early 1980s.

In 2002, the reporters discovered links to West while investigating abuse by local Catholic priests. West was at that time Republican majority leader in the Washington State Senate and was considering running for what he called his "dream job"—being mayor of his hometown, Spokane. During the campaign, the reporters did not believe they had enough information to confirm any allegations. Eventually, they received tips from both anonymous sources and sources who would later go on the record and swear in depositions that West had abused them. One man, Robert Galliher, said West molested him at least four times as a child, and he was assaulted repeatedly by Hahn. Galliher, who says he has struggled with drug addiction as a result of the molestations, said he was in prison in 2003 when West visited him and sent him a message to keep his mouth shut. In addition, other young men reported that they had sex with West after meeting him on gay chat lines and had been offered favors and rewards.

Spokesman-Review editor Steven Smith and his staff spent days agonizing over creating a fictional character to go online at Gay.com and consulted with ethics experts at the Poynter Institute and elsewhere as they considered options. Smith told Spokane readers that the newspaper would not ordinarily go to such lengths or use deception, "But the seriousness of the allegations and the need for specific computer forensic skills overrode our general reluctance." Most important, Smith said the *Spokesman-Review*'s decisions were based on concerns about abuse of power and pedophilia, and not whether the mayor was homosexual.

The forensic expert, who previously worked for the US Customs Office, followed strict guidelines. The expert posed online as a 17-year-old Spokane high school student and waited for West to approach him. The expert did not initiate conversation about sex, sexuality, or the mayor's office. In the months that followed, the high school student supposedly had an 18th birthday. West then requested meetings with the fictional young man and arrived in a new Lexus at an agreed-upon spot—a golf course. His picture was taken secretly and the forensic expert broke off contact.

West was told about the forensic investigator in an interview with *Spokesman-Review* staff the day before the story broke. He admitted to the offers made within the chat room but denied abusing or having sex with anyone under age 18. When asked about the abuse allegations from the two men, West told the *Spokesman-Review* editors and reporters, "I didn't abuse them. I don't know these people. I didn't abuse anybody, and I didn't have sex with anybody under 18—ever—woman or man."

West insisted that he had not abused his office and that he was not gay. After the story broke, local gay rights advocate Ryan Oelrich, a former member of the city's Human Rights Commission, told the newspaper that he had resigned after coming to the conclusion West appointed him in an effort to pursue a sexual relationship. Oelrich said West offered him $300 at one point to swim naked with him in his swimming pool. Oelrich declined.

A conservative Republican, West blocked antidiscrimination provisions in housing for homosexuals and voted against health benefits for gay couples while he served in the Washington state legislature and as mayor. He supported legislation barring homosexuals from working in schools or day care centers and called for bans on gay marriage. He told the *Today Show* that he was merely representing his constituents' views.

West asserted a message that he would repeat eventually on CNN, MSNBC, and in a host of other national broadcasts: "There is a strong wall between my public and my private life."

Many political scientists disagreed with West's interpretation. Washington State University political science professor Lance LeLoup said using an elected position for personal benefit is both unethical and "a misuse of power." Gonzaga University political science professor Blaine Garvin told the *Spokesman-Review,* "I think it's a pretty bright line that you don't use your command over public resources to earn personal favors. That's not what those resources are for."

At the same time, some media critics criticized the newspaper's choice to use deception. The public cannot be expected to believe journalists and the veracity of their stories if lies are told to get at information, said Jane Kirtley, director of the Silha Center for Media Ethics and Law at the University of Minnesota. Speaking at a Washington News Council Forum on the *Spokesman-Review*'s coverage, Kirtley asserted that police officers can practice deception as part of their jobs but journalists should not.

"It's one thing for the police or the FBI to pose as a 17-year-old boy," William Babcock, journalism department chair at California State University-Long Beach, told the *Seattle Post-Intelligencer.* "It's another for a journalist to take on the role of junior G-man and do something that essentially is considered police work." Babcock insists that the *Spokesman-Review* should have gotten the information through traditional reporting methods, but he agreed that no one, particularly a city mayor, should expect privacy in an online chat room.

Poynter ethicist Kelly McBride, who previously was a reporter at the *Spokesman-Review,* said deception should not be normal practice but that the newspaper considered key ethical obligations: that the issue is grave and in the public interest; alternatives are explored; the decision and practice are openly shared with readers; and the mayor is given the opportunity to share his story.

Jeffrey Weiss, a religion reporter for the *Dallas Morning News,* said he rarely believes that the end justifies the means, "but some do."

The FBI investigated West on federal corruption charges but did not find his actions warranted prosecution. Special Counsel Mark Barlett said in a media conference, "Our investigation did not address whether Jim West's activities were ethical, moral, or appropriate. . . . We did not attempt to determine whether Jim West should be the mayor of Spokane."

In December 2005, Spokane voters ousted the mayor in a special recall election. West later said the newspaper had created a "mob mentality" and that considering the accusations, even he would have voted against himself. On July 22, 2006, West died following surgery for colon cancer, a disease he had been fighting for three years. He was 55.

Micro Issues

1. Do you agree that police officers are ethically permitted to use deception, but journalists are not?
2. Was the *Spokesman-Review* justified in using deception? Under what other extreme circumstances do you believe deception might be justified?

Midrange Issues

1. Some critics claimed that West's story only would come out in a provincial, conservative community and that his story would not have been news had he been the mayor of Chicago or Miami. Do you agree?
2. Sissela Bok says deception might be permitted if the act passes the test of publicity. Does the *Spokesman-Review* meet that standard?
3. Should the use of a forensic computer expert in this case be characterized as the ends justifying the means? Why or why not?

Macro Issues

1. Should there be a wall between the public and private lives of public officials? At what point do public officials' private lives become public concern? Is public officials' sexuality always part of their private lives?
2. The *Spokesman-Review* is locally owned by the Cowles Publishing Company. The family business includes a downtown mall with a parking garage, which was developed in financial partnership with the city of Spokane. The garage has been subject to repeated lawsuits and controversy. Some critics believed that the *Spokesman-Review*'s delay in reporting about the mayor was due to a conflict of interest. Editor Steve Smith insists that the story was reported as the facts became evident. How do locally owned media companies manage covering their own communities without incurring conflicts of interest?

CASE 5-F

FOR GOD AND COUNTRY: THE MEDIA AND NATIONAL SECURITY

JEREMY LITTAU
Lehigh University
MARK SLAGLE
University of North Carolina at Chapel Hill

The ethical issues involving the intersection of the media and national security typically revolve around the question of duties and loyalties. Those questions, as the following three-part case demonstrates, are long-standing. They also allow journalists to evaluate the consistency of their reasoning over time—something that good ethical thinking is supposed to promote. How journalists respond to these cases also may depend on the differing philosophies individual journalists and their news organizations adhere to.

With this introduction, decide each of the following three cases, all of which have an important role in the history of journalism ethics. As you resolve the various issues in each case, ask yourself whether you have been consistent in your decision-making and what philosophical approach or approaches best support your thinking.

CASE STUDY 1: THE BAY OF PIGS

In 1961, an anti-communist paramilitary force trained and supplied by the CIA was preparing to invade Cuba and topple Fidel Castro. Although the desire of the American government to overthrow Castro was no secret, the specifics of the invasion plan were not known to the public. On April 6, a *New York Times* reporter filed a story with his editors that declared the invasion was "imminent." The paper prepared to run the story with a page-one, four-column slot using the word "imminent" in the text and the headline.

After much discussion, *Times* managing editor Turner Catledge and publisher Orvil Dryfoos decided to remove the word "imminent" from the story and shrink the headline to a single column. These changes were made, in part, in response to a phone call from President John F. Kennedy, asking the paper to kill the story. On April 17, the anti-Castro forces landed at Cuba's Bay of Pigs, where all group members were either taken prisoner or killed. The botched invasion was a major embarrassment for Kennedy, who later told Catledge that if the *Times* had run the story as planned, it might have prevented the disastrous invasion (Hickey, 2001).

Micro Issue

1. Did the *Times* act ethically in downsizing and downplaying the story?

Midrange Issue

1. Are there certain categories of information (for example, troop movements or the development of new weapons) that journalists, as a matter of policy, should either downplay or not publish at all?

Macro Issue

1. How should journalists respond if government officials request that specific "facts" (which are not true) be printed as part of a disinformation campaign to confuse our enemies?

CASE STUDY 2: OSAMA BIN LADEN

Since the 9/11 attacks until his death at the hands of the US military in 2012, Osama bin Laden and his deputies released a series of video and audio tapes containing speeches about their ongoing operations. Many of them first aired on Al Jazeera, the Arabic-language news channel that broadcasts in the Middle East but also can be received in many American and European markets. The US government, specifically President George W. Bush, urged the US media not to rebroadcast these tapes, arguing that they might contain coded messages to al-Qaeda "sleeper cells" and could result in more attacks. Most broadcast networks acquiesced to the request, although it was never made clear whether any of the tapes did, in fact, contain such messages (Spencer, 2001).

Micro Issue

1. How is this request like and unlike President Kennedy's request to the *New York Times*?

Midrange Issues

1. Does the fact that other news agencies in other countries broadcast the tapes have any bearing on what US broadcasters should do?
2. Should US broadcasters have agreed to this request in October 2001? Should they agree to the request today? Why or why not?

Macro Issue

1. How would you respond to a viewer who says that broadcasting the tapes is unpatriotic and puts American lives at risk?

CASE STUDY 3: MAKE NEWS, NOT WAR?

In 1991, CNN correspondent Christiane Amanpour arrived in the Balkans to cover the breakaway of Slovenia and Croatia from Yugoslavia. After witnessing several brutal battles, including the siege of Dubrovnik, she moved on to Bosnia to cover the hostilities there for almost two years. Troubled by the lack of coverage the war was receiving, Amanpour encouraged her editors to devote more time to the issue. In 1994, Amanpour appeared via satellite on a live television broadcast with President Bill Clinton. She asked the president if "the constant flip-flops of your administration on the issue of Bosnia set a very dangerous precedent." Amanpour's pointed questions embarrassed the administration and generated more coverage of the war and of American foreign policy. Amanpour later admitted she wanted to draw more attention to the plight of the Bosnian Muslims (Halberstam, 2001).

Micro Issues

1. Should Amanpour consciously have tried to influence US foreign policy in this way?
2. If she had not tried to influence US policy, would she have been complicit in the genocide that followed?

Midrange Issues

1. Are some issues, such as genocide, so ethically reprehensible that journalists should speak out as citizens in addition to fulfilling their professional responsibilities?
2. Is it appropriate for journalists to testify at war crimes trials when they have witnessed and reported on atrocities?

Macro Issues

1. Is it naive for journalists to continue to say that "we just let readers make up their minds" on these issues? If you answer yes, what does that say about the ethical dilemmas that come with the power we have as journalists?

2. More than a half century ago, media theorist Marshall McLuhan predicted that wars of the future would be fought with images rather than bullets. How true has that prediction become in the ongoing war on terror?

6

Informing a Just Society

By the end of the chapter, students should

- be able to explain why social justice can be understood by examining institutions as well as individuals;
- be able to outline four ways of thinking about social justice;
- understand how diversity can influence coverage of issues such as crime and the reporting process;
- understand the concept of fault lines and how they can aid in evaluating professional performance.

ATHLETES AND ACTIVISM

The wildcat strike began Aug. 26, 2020, when the National Basketball Association's (NBA's) Milwaukee Bucks refused to take the court for a playoff game against the Orlando Magic.

The Bucks' decision led to the cancellation of all NBA and Women's National Basketball Association (WNBA) basketball games, as well as games across Major League Baseball and Major League Soccer. Tennis star Naomi Osaka did not play in the Western & Southern Open.

The strike was triggered by a police officer shooting Jacob Blake in the back seven times in Kenosha, Wisconsin.

"We are calling for justice for Jacob Blake and demanding the officers be held accountable," said Bucks guard George Hill, who read from a prepared statement on behalf of his teammates. "For this to occur, it is imperative for the Wisconsin state Legislature to reconvene after months of inaction, and take up meaningful measures to address police accountability, brutality, and criminal justice reform" (Mahoney, 2020).

On Jan. 5, 2021, the Kenosha, Wisconsin, district attorney declined to file charges against officer Rusten Sheskey.

Hill's teammate, Sterling Brown, who stood beside him during the announcement, had firsthand knowledge of police brutality. In 2018, Milwaukee police officers assaulted and tased Brown—including one officer putting his knee on Brown's neck—because he double-parked his car in a Walgreens parking lot. The city attorney offered Brown, who is the son of an Illinois police officer, a $400,000 settlement, which he refused.

Athletes from Muhammad Ali to Jim Brown to Tommie Smith and John Carlos (and many, many more) have used their public platforms to address societal issues. Starting in the 2016 season, San Francisco 49ers quarterback Colin Kaepernick and other NFL players began kneeling during the national anthem in an effort to draw attention to police brutality and racial injustice.

These protests and the resulting responses have been highly mediated, unlike the brutality and injustice—including lynchings in the 19th and 20th centuries—that often were not considered news. The murder of Emmett Till by white supremacists in 1955 was not fully explored until 50 years later. The police beating of Rodney King in 1991 is among the first uses of street tapes, explored in chapter 8. Seventeen-year-old Trayvon Martin was shot and killed by a self-proclaimed neighborhood watch volunteer in 2012. When George Zimmerman later was acquitted for that shooting, Alicia Garza went on Facebook and wrote a post that ended, "black lives matter." A movement was born. The *Washington Post* began an interactive database of people shot and killed by police in 2015; in 2019, the number of fatalities reached 999.

Social movements don't happen without debate, including labeling decisions such as the NBA's part of the "cancel culture." Like many slogans, "cancel culture" is so vague that it invites people to interpret it in ways most familiar to them. While our interpretation may not be the intent of those who originated and used such phrases, we suggest that these phrases ask important questions about justice, among them how might it be defined, and if injustice is historic, how might it be restored? These issues are the focus of news, strategic communication, and entertainment programming. The very first photo in this book, Stanley Foreman's prize-winning image of a child and her 19-year-old godmother falling to their deaths, tells a story rooted in history and justice: Would this have happened to a Caucasian child, and what is our collective responsibility to make certain such a calamity is less likely to happen to anyone today?

COVERING CRIME: MORE THAN A MATTER OF BLACK AND WHITE

Crime is one of the most prevalent issues in the news, and the media's constant reporting of crime cultivates widespread fear and concern (Gross & Aday, 2003; Iyengar, 1991). Crime reporting, however, also perpetuates racial stereotypes and biases because Blacks most frequently are depicted as criminals, victims, or dependents on society (Leshner, 2006). In contrast, most news stories and entertainment programming feature Caucasians, so audiences tend to associate Caucasians with a variety of topics, including business, technology, and science (Dixon & Linz, 2000). Local news also often over-represents Black criminals while under-representing Caucasian and Latino criminals as well as Black victims (Dixon & Linz, 2000). Further, Blacks are more often shown in handcuffs, and Black mugshots, often without names included, were shown four times more than Caucasian mugshots (Entman & Rojecki, 2000; Leshner, 2006). Gannett, the United States's largest newspaper chain, removed mugshot galleries from its websites in 2018 and continued that policy when it merged with Gatehouse Media in 2020. A company press release reads:

> We have made an editorial decision to discontinue the publication of mugshot galleries, or mugshot photos that are not associated with a story or other editorial content, effective immediately. Mugshot galleries presented without context may feed into negative stereotypes and, in our editorial judgment, are of limited news value. (Hare, 2020)

This emphasis on Blacks as criminals, especially men, has real-world consequences. Go back 50 years, and Detroit erupted in five days of unrest in which 43 people died and hundreds were arrested. The Detroit "riot" or "rebellion" (the proper terminology is still being debated) was the subject of the 2017 documentary *12th and Clairmount* and of the fictional film *Detroit*.

Brian Kaufman, a reporter for the *Detroit Free Press* and the co-editor of *12th and Clairmount*, said, "What we tried to do was get to the heart of why this happened, and it happened for several reasons, police brutality being one of them, housing segregation being another, and lack of jobs being the third." Through crowdsourcing, including notes from reporters working in the city at the time, archival news footage, and home movies that were first culled and then digitized to be edited into the film, viewers learned about the actions of a cadre of four Detroit police officers, known locally as the Big Four, who beat, intimidated, arrested on false pretenses, and terrorized Black Detroiters for years before the riots broke out. Most of this was little known and underreported in 1967.

Among the things you probably think you do know about Detroit is that it is a city with a high poverty rate and that it is predominantly Black. You would be right—about Detroit (where the population is about 79 percent Black) but not about the rest of Michigan or the rest of the United States. And that is the root of the problem. Covering poverty in Detroit represents a singularly difficult problem for journalists: how to cover poverty without racializing it. In other words, how can contemporary news stories break the unfounded connection between race and poverty that has characterized news coverage for the past 50 years?

Indeed, in total numbers, there are more Caucasians in poverty than any other racial group. The overall poverty rate—calculated as those earning less than $24,600 for a family of four—was 10.5 percent, or 35 million people in 2019 (US Census Bureau, 2020). That number is expected to rise following the economic collapse due to the COVID-19 pandemic.

One popular misconception is that poverty is a mainly urban problem. However, 48 of the 50 US counties with the highest child poverty rates are in rural America, according to the Annie E. Casey Foundation. Further, almost one in five rural kids is poor, and rates of rural child poverty are higher than urban child poverty for all kids and every minority group.

Many low-income families, especially those in high-poverty communities, pay too much for life's necessities, a phenomenon the Annie E. Casey Foundation dubs "the high cost of being poor." For example, families in low-income rural communities often pay nearly 20 percent more than the USDA-recommended budget for basic food items. The same upcharge is true for clothing, furniture, and appliances. This surplus charge occurs because small-scale local businesses operate outside of the economies of scale that allow larger businesses such as Walmart or Target to offer more options and charge less for products.

In 1999, Martin Gilens wrote that

> from 1964 to 1965, the percentage of African-Americans who appeared in news pictures of the poor jumped from 27 to 49 percent, at a time when the actual percentage of African-Americans among those whose income placed them among the poor was about 30 percent.

Gilens argued that "distorted coverage found in newsmagazines reflects a broader set of dynamics that also shapes images of the poor in the more important medium of television news."

Gilens's study also found that the tone of that coverage changed beginning in the mid-1960s. In his study, stories about mismanaged welfare programs included more visual images of Blacks as sometimes corrupt and often lazy and undeserving, a concrete symbol of the "Welfare Mess." However, stories that focused on the economic downturns of those decades, which also threw middle-class workers into poverty, were more sympathetic in tone and featured visual images of Caucasians.

The trends that Gilens and other scholars have been documenting for more than four decades still accurately describe many news stories. Gilens wrote,

> Most journalists consciously reject the stereotype of African-Americans as lazy. But in the everyday practice of their craft . . . these same journalists portray poor blacks as more blameworthy than poor whites. (cited in Green, 1999)

Some scholars directly connect public attitudes about the poor and changes in public policy about poverty to media coverage and images of the poor (Rose & Baumgartner, 2013).

That's the whole point of Black Lives Matter and the "cancel culture" rejoinder. We are no longer concerned with the actions of an individual journalist or public relations practitioner, but rather how those actions contribute to the ideals and assumptions of society at large.

PHILOSOPHICAL APPROACHES TO SOCIAL JUSTICE

These questions all center philosophically in the broad area of social justice, that branch of philosophy and political philosophy that connects individual acts to their societal consequences and the societal understanding to a range of possible individual actions. It's a philosophical feedback loop that places community on an equal footing with the individual. Thinking about social justice, unlike issues of truth telling or privacy, requires understanding the following foundational assumptions.

Social justice is comparative. It asks not just about the individual but about all the others as well. If Blacks are portrayed inaccurately as poor and lazy in a preponderance of news reports about poverty, how does that portrait influence all individuals in a community and their access to the "goods" that living in that community may provide?

Social justice is relational. While it can speak to individual decisions, it also can speak equally well to policies that cover a number of decisions. Take, for example, the Associated Press's decision about how the words "terrorist," "Islamist," and "migrant" are to be appropriately used in news stories. Contrary to what some critics have alleged, the Associated Press made these style decisions in an attempt to equalize and destigmatize certain groups of people. The folks at the Associated Press had read and understood the research about stereotyping, stigma, and the racialization of poverty that has emerged in the past 20 years. They have decided to provide an alternative view—one based on a concept of social justice—literally one word at a time.

"Justice is the first virtue of social institutions, just as truth is of systems of thought," writes philosopher John Rawls.

> A theory however elegant and economical must be rejected or revised if it is untrue; likewise laws and institutions no matter how efficient and well-arranged must be reformed or abolished if they are unjust. . . . An injustice is tolerable only when it is necessary to avoid a greater injustice. Being first virtues of human activities, truth and justice are uncompromising. (Rawls, 1971, pp. 3–4)

Thinking about social justice explores—and attempts to connect—distinctive ethical questions to one another. The three Enlightenment-based approaches to justice, philosopher Michael Sandel notes, begin in different places.

One branch of theory examines the maximization of welfare—something you were introduced to in chapter 2. Utilitarianism is deeply connected to this approach—doing the greatest good for a community of your fellows does maximize the welfare of all. In 2017, the US government, after decades of litigation, required US tobacco companies to develop and then pay for the broadcasting and printing of advertisements that informed consumers of the negative health effects of cigarettes and other tobacco products, as well as admit that those same firms used just enough nicotine in cigarettes to make them addictive. This act maximizes public health and welfare through the use of media messages. Even though the tobacco companies might be financially hurt by this advertising campaign, the larger good of the community was promoted: fewer deaths through tobacco-related illness. As contentious as the decision is, it is fundamentally grounded in a sense of social justice that speaks equally to both the community and the individuals within it.

A second branch of social justice theory focuses on freedom and individual rights, and Americans particularly are familiar with the broad range of the individual rights debate. On the one hand, some who examine social justice through the individual rights lens assume a type of laissez-faire position that justice consists of respecting and upholding the voluntary choices made by consenting adults. This argument is often, but not exclusively, framed in economic terms, and most Americans would connect this way of approaching social justice with the contemporary Libertarian political movement. However, freedom and individual rights also may be thought of as the need for there to be some rules so that all individuals would have access to the "goods"—material and otherwise—available to those living in the community. For those who subscribe to this approach to social justice, markets are not always the best regulators of individual welfare and may apportion the "goods" of society in a decidedly unfair way. I may be "free" to drive down

the left-hand side of the road, but that choice could have disastrous consequences for myself and others depending on whether I am driving in London
or New York. Some rules are needed to govern my access to and use of the
highway system—again, so that all may have access and that the "good life"
will be more widely available to all.

Finally, a third way of thinking about social justice is to connect it to
virtues. A just society affirms certain virtues, whether they are arrived at
through contemplation or religious instruction. However, it is not difficult
to imagine that certain sorts of societies might make upholding the virtues
easier—or more difficult—than other societies.

Rawls's concept of justice as fairness is among those concepts most widely
applied to issues of social justice. His approach, because it combines utilitarian thinking with the concept of freedom of access for societal "goods,"
provides a way of considering social justice that melds both utilitarianism and
freedom and, through the veil of ignorance, devises a way of coming up with
some institutional policies that might speak to social justice issues before
specific questions occur.

More recently, Indian philosopher Amartya Sen has provided a distinctive
insight into theorizing about social justice. Sen argues that much of Western
philosophy has been preoccupied with questions of what is the *most* just society.

"If a theory of justice is to guide reasoned choice of policies, strategies or
institutions, then the identification of fully just social arrangements is neither
necessary nor sufficient" (Sen, 2009, p. 15).

Sen bases much of his thinking in social-choice theory, a political theory that
focuses on a rational and often mathematical comparison among alternatives.
Sen's approach employs practical reason as the tool for comparison and
requires that reasoning be "public." His theory stipulates that thinking about
social justice requires accepting the "inescapable plurality of competing
principles," encourages re-examination of existing arrangements, allows
for partial solutions, and accepts a diversity of interpretation. By diversity
of interpretation, Sen acknowledges that different principles and individual
preferences may yield different specific results, but that all such results should
withstand clear and precise logical inquiry (Sen, 2009, p. 106–111). For Sen,
behavior—not some theoretical ideal—is the goal of justice.

Thinking about social justice using this approach would allow for multiple
solutions to questions of justice, solutions that, for example, could take both
culture and history into consideration without allowing them to determine any
specific outcome. Under this reasoning, the very different professional norms
and laws that govern how crime and the courts are covered in the United
States and Great Britain, both developed democracies, could be equally just
without descending into relativism. One approach is not better than the other,

and both can be re-examined in the light of new information, policies, laws, and regulations.

These four approaches to justice speak deeply to moving a society from a less-just to a more-just set of institutions, including government and the media. Feminist philosopher Martha Nussbaum provides an affirmative vision of what such a society might look like in her books *Creating Capabilities: The Human Development Approach* (2013), *Political Emotions: Why Love Matters for Justice* (2015), and *Upheavals of Thought: The Intelligence of Emotions* (2001).

> Thus the capabilities approach feels free to use an account of cooperation that treats justice and inclusiveness as ends of intrinsic value from the beginning, and that views human beings as held together by many altruistic ties as well as by ties of mutual advantage. (Nussbaum, 2006, p. 158)

Many of Nussbaum's 10 capabilities focus on the communication that must occur to allow groups and individuals to develop and flourish. This most certainly would include news, persuasive messages, and the communication inherent in art and entertainment. These capabilities include the development of emotions that allow people to attach to others outside themselves: affiliation—being able to live in a group and show concern for others; play and creation; and control over one's environment, particularly political control, including the right to political participation, free speech, and association. Nussbaum argues that careful attention to "language and imagery" (Nussbaum, 2006, p. 413) allows individuals to reconceptualize their relationship—both actual and metaphoric—to others. She acknowledges that her capabilities approach includes the affirmative—things that people should do, ways that people might be encouraged to imagine and act—which contrasts markedly with other articulations of justice that focus more on prohibitions and restrictions.

Nussbaum's affirmative vision of justice would support in-depth reporting of issues such as poverty and race, two contemporary problems she has written about extensively. Her capabilities approach also would encourage journalists to experiment with coverage, a recommendation that would apply equally to documentary filmmakers and strategic communication professionals. The creativity inherent in journalism and strategic communication finds a home in the capabilities approach, providing it is used in the service of the moral imagination.

SOCIAL JUSTICE IN A DEMOCRATIC SOCIETY

Just as there are members of a power elite, there also are those who feel excluded from political society. One popular interpretation of US history has been to track the gradual extension of power to ever more diverse publics. But the process has been uneven and contentious. All minority groups seek access to the political process and, because mass media have become major players in that process, they seek access to media as well.

Journalists say diversity matters. The marketplace of ideas—conceptualized by John Milton, John Locke, and John Stuart Mill, and Americanized by Thomas Jefferson and Oliver Wendell Holmes—is incomplete and inadequate when and if voices are left out of the discussion. One component of seeking and reporting truth, according to the Society of Professional Journalists code of ethics, is to tell "the stories of diversity and magnitude of the human experience. Seek sources whose voices we seldom hear." That statement echoes a similar one made by the Hutchins Commission in its report *A Free and Responsible Press*, which included the charge to project a "representative picture of the constituent groups in society." More contemporary thought, from the facilitative role in which media seek to promote dialogue among constituent groups (Christians, Glasser, McQuail, Nordenstreng, & White, 2009) to the mobilizer role where media incorporate citizens into the news process (Weaver & Wilhoit, 1996), also incorporates ideas of diverse voices.

Further, journalists should care because diverse voices help both the byline and the bottom line. Journalists need to appeal to a wide variety of audiences, and this is true whether you write for newspapers, magazines, or online; broadcast on radio or television; or work in advertising, marketing, or public relations. Economically, journalists cannot eliminate segments of the audience by appealing to one gender, race, class, or age group. For example, while Caucasians are still the majority population in the United States (with 63.7 percent of the population, according to the 2010 Census), they represent the only major racial or ethnic group with a declining population (down from 75.1 percent in the 2000 Census). Similarly, while advertisers typically target the 18–44-year-old demographic, 63.5 percent of the US population is either younger or older than that age group. Still, there are major issues, both in terms of newsroom employment and in the use of sources. For example, Wisconsin Public Radio reported that almost 90 percent of the 3,700 sources its reporters used between August 2019 and August 2020 were white, though the gender split was much more representative (Haynes & Dargan, 2020).

Byline diversity also could aid in improving coverage. However, women accounted for only 40 percent of print and online news bylines, and only 30 percent of newswire (e.g., Associated Press and Reuters) bylines in 2019. Similarly, only 37 percent of prime-time newscasts featured female anchors or correspondents in 2019 (Women's Media Center, 2019). The thoughts, feelings, and experiences of women are not monolithic, so greater numbers of women in the newsroom, for example, might ensure greater diversity by allowing various women's perspectives to be represented while also better reflecting culturally diverse communities (Harp, Bachmann, & Loke, 2014; Len-Ríos, Hinnant, & Jeong, 2012). A more robust representation also could influence editorial content, framing, sources, format, tone, and newsroom culture. Similarly, greater racial and ethnic diversity could influence a wide range of topics, from immigration to gun violence. For example, scholars found that media focused on the 2007 Virginia Tech shooter's Korean ethnicity and immigration status. Asian American journalists were among the first to alert the public and the journalism community of potentially excessive racialization of the shooting. With more common representations of Asian Americans, they argued, the shooter's race might have escaped the reporters' attention (Park, Holoday, & Zhang, 2012). The races of the 1999 Columbine High School shooters, by contrast, were virtually absent from media coverage (Zillman, 1999). The internet also enhances the number of differing opinions available in the marketplace of ideas. For a legacy news organization, then, it's better to have those voices represented in your news coverage than to be competing against them.

Media ethicists suggest these political and social out-groups provide mass media with a further set of responsibilities. They assert that mass media, and individual journalists, need to become advocates for the politically homeless. Media ethicist Clifford Christians suggests that

> justice for the powerless stands at the centerpiece of a socially responsible press. Or, in other terms, the litmus test of whether or not the news profession fulfills its mission over the long term is its advocacy for those outside the socioeconomic establishment. (Christians, 1986, p. 110)

COMMUNITARIANISM AND SOCIAL JUSTICE

Communitarian thinking urges that justice is the ethical linchpin of journalistic decision-making. If justice becomes the fundamental value of American journalism, then the media have the goal of transforming society, of empowering individual citizens to act in ways that promote political discussion, debate, and change (Christians, Ferré, & Fackler, 1993).

Communitarianism, which has its roots in political theory, seeks to provide ethical guidance when confronting the sort of society-wide issues that mark current political and business activity. Consider the environment. On many environmental questions, it is possible for people to make appropriate individual decisions—today I drive my car—that taken together promote environmental degradation. Communitarianism returns to Aristotle's concept of the "polis"—or community—and invests it with moral weight. People begin their lives, at least in a biological sense, as members of a two-person community. Communitarian philosophy extends this biological beginning to a philosophical worldview. "In communitarianism, persons have certain inescapable claims on one another that cannot be renounced except at the cost of their humanity" (Christians et al., 1993, p. 14).

Communitarianism focuses on the outcome of individual ethical decisions analyzed in light of their potential to impact society. When applied to journalism, you have a product

> committed to justice, covenant and empowerment. Authentic communities are marked by justice; in strong democracies, courageous talk is mobilized into action. . . . In normative communities, citizens are empowered for social transformation, not merely freed from external constraints. (Christians et al., 1993, p. 14)

While scholars have focused on news, it is possible to see how such thinking could be applied to strategic communication, particularly the work of public information officers.

Communitarianism asserts that social justice is the predominant moral value and elevates values such as altruism and benevolence. Communitarians recognize the value of process but are just as concerned with outcomes. Under communitarianism, the ability of individual acts to create a more just society is an appropriate measure of their rightness, and outcomes are part of the calculus. Indeed, Nobel Prize-winning work in game theory has empirically demonstrated that cooperation, one of the foundation stones of community, provides desirable results once thought to be possible only through competition (Axelrod, 1984). Cooperation is particularly powerful when the "shadow of the future," an understanding that we will encounter the outcome of our decisions and their impact on others in readily foreseeable time, is taken into account.

Any notion of a communitarian community begins with the framework of individual membership in the community.

> For them, community describes not just what they have as fellow citizens but also what they are, not as a relationship they choose (as in a voluntary association) but an attachment they discover, not merely an attribute but as a constituent of their identity. (Sandel, 1982, p. 150)

A communitarian community resembles family more than it resembles town.

Under communitarianism, journalism cannot separate itself from the political and economic system of which it is a part. Communitarian thinking makes it possible to ask whether current practice (for example, a traditional definition of news) provides a good mechanism for a community to discover itself, learn about itself, and ultimately transform itself. These are questions that necessarily implicate social justice, whether it is a set of "ideal" arrangements or a discussion among multiple alternatives, none of which is perfectly just but all of which may promote incremental steps in favor of just relations. Communitarianism would not ban the coverage of crime but would demand context that would help viewers or readers decide if they need to take action. Political stories would focus on issues, not the horse race.

What makes journalists uneasy is that this role shift smacks of a kind of benevolent paternalism. If individual human beings carry moral stature, then assigning one institution—in this case, the mass media—the role of social and political arbiter diminishes the moral worth of the individual citizen. Mass media become a kind parent and the citizen a sort of wayward child in need of guidance. However, linking justice and truth as the two irreducible ethical values, as Rawls does, provides a kind of philosophical alignment that may help journalism as a profession develop a rationale beyond objectivity that would justify its central, and protected, place in American democracy.

INTERNET INFLUENCE ON SOCIAL JUSTICE

The original journalists in America were citizens who stepped into the role of pamphleteers or publishers based on a desire to shape an emerging nation. Most of them, such as Benjamin Franklin or Thomas Paine, had sources of income outside of their role as citizen journalists. During the next 100 years, the role of professional journalist emerged in the new democracy and, for the next century, the delivery of information was primarily considered the role of the full-time professional.

However, no formal education or license is required to be a journalist in the United States. Toward the end of the 20th century—propelled by the internet—it became evident that the role of "journalist" no longer belonged exclusively to the trained writer working at a recognizable institutional media outlet. Professional strategic communicators were replaced by "influencers." Both functions had moved to social media.

The web is great for getting people together in a common cause, whether it's mobilizing to vote or tracking down a stolen bicycle by asking "friends" to keep an eye out for it. Social media is particularly adept—it appears—in separating people into groups, a superficially benign process when it's tracking down a lost pet in your neighborhood but a much more malevolent one when used to plan a violent insurrection at the US Capitol.

Social media, however, does not appear to be an effective organizing tool in the sort of activities, such as forming a government after a revolution, that require face-to-face interaction over a long period of time with people who are like and unlike "you" in significant ways. The sustained commitment to building a "new" social and political structure of almost any sort demands time and face-to-face interaction. While social media can promote some of that effort, the technology itself appears to make some sorts of human activity no more possible than it was in other eras.

In the early 21st century, social media seems to be separating two roles that about 400 years of media history had previously blended. The role of information provider and collector—what some scholars and professionals now refer to as the "first informer" role—can be done by citizens as well as journalists. But citizen journalism lacks one important component that traditional media had: information verification. It is this second role—verifying information and placing it in a social, political, and cultural context—that is becoming more and more the work of journalism.

The "first informer" role values speed. The information verification role is what makes the initial fact into something reliable and accessible to all. The information verification role values truth, context, and equality. It can and does employ social media as a corrective—and sometimes an essential one. However, it is the ethical values of truth and inclusive access that will continue to fund professional performance in this internet age. Indeed, if professionals lose their adherence to these values, there will be little to separate them from "first informers" and less to separate the institution of the mass media from its role as check and balance on the other powerful actors such as the modern nation-state and the multinational market.

EXCELLENT JOURNALISM AND FAULT LINES

Once journalists understand why social justice and diversity are important in their work, they next turn to how to incorporate the concepts into their stories, packages, and campaigns. Two useful tools are excellent journalism, developed by Keith Woods at the Poynter Institute, and Robert C. Maynard's fault lines. Woods argues that journalists need to ask four questions when writing stories:

First, does it provide context? The story needs to provide enough historical context—time, place, environment, social and cultural background, political history, legal history, and economic implications—for the audience to be able to make sense of what is happening.

Second, does it embrace complexity? Woods argues that stories need to rise above one-dimensional explanations and polarized framing to reveal gray truths. By moving past simplistic frames, journalists uncover multiple layers to people and their actions, develop fuller opinions, and expose a fuller picture of a story. As Westover notes,

Social media has flooded our consciousness with caricatures of each other. Human beings are reduced to data, and data nearly always underrepresent reality. The result is this great flattening of human life and human complexity. We think that because we know someone is pro-choice or pro-life, or that they drive a truck or a Prius, we know everything we need to know about them. Human detail gets lost in the algorithm. Thus humanity gives way to ideology. (cited in Goldberg, 2019)

Third, do we hear the voices of the people? Stories should bring the voice of people to the listener, reader, or viewer; quotes and sound bites should be purposeful and clear and should advance the story by conveying character and personality or revealing new truths.

Finally, does it have the ring of authenticity? The reporting needs to be broad and deep enough, the details fine enough, and the opinions open enough to provide insight.

One tool to develop authentic stories is through the use of fault lines. Maynard originally conceived of five fault lines: race and ethnicity, class, gender and sexual orientation, geography, and generation. Subsequent scholars have expanded the list to include religion, disability, and political affiliation as potential fault lines. Maynard argued that we, both as journalists and as members of society, cannot and should not pretend that differences do not exist. The key, then, is providing context and history. That context and history occur through understanding and utilizing fault lines. For journalists, fault lines can better help them reflect the interests, decisions, and actions of sources in a different social group. Fault lines also can provide a way to identify missing cultural voices, as well as story angles and perspectives that could offer a way to reframe a story or add complexity. The questions to ask: What fault lines are reflected in my sources, and how do those fault lines affect their comments, interests, decisions, or actions? Arguably more important, what fault lines are missing, and are they needed to help readers better understand the relevance of the information?

SUGGESTED READINGS

Jewkes, Y. (2011). *Media & crime: Key approaches to criminology.* Thousand Oaks, CA: Sage.

Len-Ríos, M., & Perry, E. L. (eds.). (2019). *Cross-cultural journalism: Communicating strategically about diversity* (2nd ed.). New York: Routledge.

Morgan, A. L., Woods, K., & Pifer, A. E. (2006). *The authentic voice: The best reporting on race and ethnicity.* New York: Columbia University Press.

Nussbaum, M. (2015). *Political emotions: Why love matters for justice.* Cambridge, MA: Belknap Press.

Shirky, C. (2009). *Here comes everybody: The power of organizing without organizations.* New York: Penguin Group.

CASES

CASE 6-A

THE *KANSAS CITY STAR* IN BLACK AND WHITE: A NEWSPAPER APOLOGIZES FOR 140 YEARS OF COVERAGE

LEE WILKINS
University of Missouri

Kansas City is the birthplace of jazz legends. Its barbeque is unsurpassed. President Harry Truman's home and presidential library are housed in the suburb of Independence, and visitors are encouraged to discover the Negro Leagues Baseball Museum downtown. Hallmark is headquartered in Kansas City, and by the time you read this case study, Kansas City Chiefs quarterback Patrick Mahomes has played in multiple Super Bowls.

Unlike many cities its size, Kansas City (which includes Kansas City, Kansas, as well as Kansas City, Missouri) retains a robust media ecosystem, including a local newspaper, the *Kansas City Star*. The *Star* has won multiple Pulitzer Prizes; its investigative unit is one of the finest in the United States. As of this writing, it has not suffered the economic devastation that has characterized newspaper ownership, particularly beginning in 2010.

So, it was surprising to many in the news business that on Dec. 20, 2020, the *Star* and its staff apologized to contemporary readers for its own work, which it characterized as "a powerful local business that has done wrong."

That conclusion was the culmination of an idea from reporter Mara Rose Williams, who suggested that the *Star* and its staff analyze its coverage of Kansas City's Black community and place that coverage in context. To do so, the staff examined not just what the newspaper itself had reported and published but also court records, congressional testimony, digital databases, and coverage of simultaneous events reported in the Black press of the era.

The result of the *Star*'s analysis—what students might know as a case study based in a textual analysis—disturbed and sickened the *Star*'s current staff.

> In the pages of *The Star*, when Black people were written about, they were cast primarily as the perpetrators or victims of crime, advancing a toxic narrative. Other violence, meantime, was tuned out. *The Star* and

The Times wrote about military action in Europe but not about Black families whose homes were being bombed just down the street.

To provide just two examples, jazz legend Charlie "Bird" Parker was not mentioned in the pages of the *Star* until his death in a story in which his name was misspelled and his birthdate incorrect. Baseball legend Jackie Robinson's move to the majors, the all-white National League, could be found in the *Star* on page 18. In times of disaster, including a historic 1977 flood, the *Star's* coverage focused on the white-owned Plaza and the segregated suburbs. The experience of Kansas City's Black families, who were far more economically and physically devastated by the event, could not be found.

Through what the staff photographed and wrote about—and what it did not—"it disenfranchised, ignored and scorned generations of Black Kansas Citians. It reinforced Jim Crow laws and redlining. Decade after early decade, it robbed an entire community of opportunity, dignity, justice and recognition." Perhaps most egregiously, it deprived white Kansas Citians a chance to know their neighbors as equal human beings and to make decisions about the political and social community of Kansas City based on that knowledge.

"We are sorry," the opening piece in the series noted.

That piece also noted that the *Star* had been an all-white and all-male newsroom for decades. When given the opportunity to cover the civil rights movement of the 1950s, the newspaper's desegregation coverage was "appalling and biased," according to interviews with current community members and staff. The *Star* began to change in the 1960s, but there were still major mistakes, all of which ignored the experience of Black Kansas Citians, misrepresented it, or downplayed it. Instead, white business owners and community leaders continued to get a "lot of ink."

Having documented its historic shortcomings, the *Star* staff also vowed to take steps to do better. Among these steps are increasing attention to staff diversity, exploring uncovered or under-covered stories (such as continuing racist language in housing covenants in the city), and a November 2020 three-part series exploring racism in the Kansas City, Missouri, Fire Department. The *Star* partnered with the city's public library to introduce its work to the public, to seek additional community comment, and to take advice on what the next steps should be. The paper also announced the formation of the *Kansas City Star* Advisory Board, which would meet monthly with newsroom leaders to provide advice and insight on the "issues of the day."

Kansas City, Missouri, Mayor Quinton Lucas acknowledged the *Star* for the "positive step" forward. However, Lucas, who is Black, said more was needed by other local media to address the city's past detachment from how Black stories were told.

"Now I hope my friends in the local TV business do the same," he tweeted.

Micro Issues

1. Journalists are taught that they are not the story. Is the *Star*'s effort an appropriate exception to that rule?
2. Are there "minority" communities in your hometown that you think may have been subject to the sort of coverage the *Star* described? How about in the town/city where your university is located?
3. Does the ethnicity of the reporter who suggested the series or the editors who supervised it matter? Should it?

Midrange Issues

1. The *Star*'s efforts were widely covered as news. Was this appropriate?
2. Evaluate Mayor Lucas's statement. What ethical principles are implied?
3. Examine coverage of Vice President Kamala Harris in your local media. How does this coverage reflect or fail to reflect the patterns in the *Kansas City Star*?

Macro Issues

1. President Harry Truman desegregated the US armed forces in 1948. How do you think the *Star* covered that policy decision? Other newspapers?
2. Evaluate whether you believe the advisory board established by the *Star* will have a negative impact on the paper's independence.
3. How would you design a similar evaluation of news coverage in a major media outlet in your community?
4. Does the penetration of social media into news coverage make the sort of community-wide evaluation of the impact of news coverage on the development of a community impossible? More likely?

CASE 6-B

JOURNALISM AND ACTIVISM? WHEN IDENTITY
BECOMES POLITICAL

REBECCA SMITH, HEALTH AND WELLNESS REPORTER
KBIA

Every semester, I begin my ethics lesson with my freshman college students by asking them: Should a journalist vote? Declare a political party affiliation? Participate in primaries or caucuses?

It's a relatively innocuous place to start a discussion with a young journalist.

However, we live in an unprecedented time—one when identity is becoming more important and potentially politically divisive. So, as the discussion continues, I complicate the matter. As a feminist who believes in the equality of the sexes, can I carry a tote bag that says "On Wednesdays We Smash the Patriarchy" to an interview? To the grocery store? There are people and sources who view this as opinion and bias.

Then we continue the conversation. Should LGBTIA+ reporters have to identify as such to cover issues that affect their community? To cover unrelated stories? Can people be expected to mitigate themselves? And why is identity considered a bias in the first place?

Take Lewis Wallace. Wallace was a journalist at *Marketplace*—a public radio show from American Public Media that examines the economy and its impact on people. Just days after President Donald Trump was sworn into office in 2017, Wallace posted, "Objectivity is dead, and I'm okay with it," on *Medium*, questioning the role and responsibility of journalists in the world of "alternative facts."

In his post, Wallace (2017a) also disclosed he is transgender and believes he had never had the privilege of appearing neutral.

"Obviously, I can't be neutral or centrist in a debate over my own humanity. The idea that I don't have a right to exist is not an opinion, it is a falsehood," Wallace wrote.

In a subsequent *Medium* post titled "I was fired from my journalism job ten days into Trump," Wallace (2017b) wrote that just hours after publishing the original piece, he was contacted by members of the editorial staff and told that due to a violation of *Marketplace's* ethics code, he would be suspended from the air. The cited violation: *Marketplace's* belief in objectivity and neutrality. The editors, Wallace wrote, were concerned about his assertion "that we shouldn't care, as journalists, if we are labeled 'politically correct' or even 'liberal' for reporting the facts."

Wallace was asked to remove the post. He did. Days later, though, he reposted it, saying, "allowing myself to be intimidated into retracting a thoughtful blog post about ethics felt like one too many compromises, small though it may seem." Soon afterward, he was fired.

In August 2014, a Ferguson, Missouri, police officer shot and killed 18-year-old Michael Brown Jr. His death ignited a movement. Years of protests followed, giving birth to the Black Lives Matter movement. In May 2020, George Floyd was killed by Minneapolis police, and mass action calling for police reform and racial equity was organized nationally and internationally.

In June 2020, NPR and other organizations reported that the *Pittsburgh Post-Gazette* barred a Black female reporter, Alexis Johnson, from covering local racial protests due to a tweet. The tweet read, "Horrifying scenes and aftermath from selfish LOOTERS who don't care about this city!!!!! . . . oh wait sorry. No, these are pictures are from a Kenny Chesney concert tailgate. Whoops."

According to NPR, the paper barred her and a Black photographer, Michael Santiago, from covering further stories about police and racial justice. For context, NPR reported that these were two of the few Black journalists at the paper. "Of the 140 members of the Newspaper Guild of Pittsburgh, 13 are African American" (Folkenflik, 2020a).

While the tweet may have been questionable, the result was that a Black reporter was viewed as being too biased to continue covering the story. The issue does not end there. According to NPR's reporting, digital sports reporter Joshua Axelrod "reported on a man accused of vandalizing and looting stores in downtown Pittsburgh. He tweeted about it, calling the suspect a vulgar slang word." NPR did not broadcast the vulgarity; the tweet itself was pulled down.

Axelrod received a verbal warning about the tweet, but his reporting assignments were not altered. However, he was banned from covering the protests two days later after the newspaper union raised the issue of disparate treatment.

Reporter Madison Lawson has Ulrich congenital muscular dystrophy, or UCMD, a rare form of muscular dystrophy. She uses a wheelchair for mobility and requires oxygen to breathe. We worked on an award-winning podcast called "The Obvious Question," which explored how a disability actually impacts a life—including love, sex and dating, bathrooms, and even being a journalist.

This podcast uses Lawson's experiences and those of other people with disabilities to cover these topics. Lawson says she was motivated to create the podcast, in part, due to problematic interactions with reporters.

For example, one young student reporter at the end of a routine interview with Lawson turned to her and said she had been coached to ask the "obvious question." The reporter blurted out, "So, can you have sex?" Lawson was stunned.

Lawson says she considers her disability a strength, especially when reporting on issues of disability, because she can "start from a place of automatic understanding."

"There is a natural ignorance that comes from not being a part of a community, which makes those stories less accurate," Lawson said. "It makes people feel so much more comfortable [when the reporter has a disability]. 'This person believes me. They have experiences similar to me or they can relate. So, I don't feel like they're coming from a place of pure ignorance. I'm already understood, and this person is going to explain it accurately.' "

Lawson also recalls a time in her journalism school experience when she was working in a professional newsroom and an editor told a colleague that "she has to stop pitching disability stories." The editor was concerned that people would think it was all Lawson was capable of covering.

Lawson says she considers the idea of having an identity as a bias "problematic in and of itself." She wonders if newsrooms are more afraid of reporters with disabilities telling culturally competent stories that point out other reporters' or the organization's implicit privilege. You can hear more from Madison in the episode "How Can You Be a Journalist?"

In the Facebook group "Public Media Journalists," following the 2017 mass shooting in Las Vegas, Nevada, a Vegas-based reporter posted "as a journalist, am I allowed to give blood?"

Admittedly, I, and many others, were caught off guard by the question. Was there a bias in helping others? Was there activism in assisting a community in need? And were there even two sides of this issue—one that supported survivors of the shooting and the other, the shooter?

Micro Issues

1. Lewis Wallace wrote, "It matters who is making editorial decisions: I think marginalized people, more than ever now, need to be at the table shaping the stories the fact-based news media puts out. I think people crave the honesty, the uniqueness, the depth that comes out of bringing an actual perspective to our work. They don't want us to all be white and male, a situation which

creates its own sort of bias toward the status quo, male power and white racism."

Evaluate this comment in terms of Wallace's work as a radio journalist. How might it affect his ability to get sources to talk? To pitch assignments to editors? Would things be different if he were a television reporter?

2. How should editors respond to the criticism that assigning reporters of color to cover racial protests "ghettoizes" those reporters? Would the same criticism be applied to Christians who cover religion?
3. Should journalists vote? Should journalists give blood or contribute to charities? Support your answer with ethical theory.

Midrange Issues

1. When is it appropriate for a journalist to comment on social movements? What if the event was recognized as discriminatory, such as the 2017 neo-Nazi rally in Charlottesville?
2. As noted in the text for this chapter, journalism organizations have attempted—to varying degrees of success—to diversify newsrooms. What sorts of decisions might more diversity in newsrooms effect? How? Would you make the same analysis for strategic communication agencies?
3. By virtue of who is doing the reporting, what sorts of ideas and perspectives do journalists "norm"? How might that influence coverage of nontraditional life circumstances—for example, the "stay-at-home dad" or the "working mother"?
4. Young journalists often are told that they need to "get to know" communities they cover. How does living in a place and belonging to subcommunities within that community inform coverage? Distort it?

Macro Issues

1. What does activism mean for professional journalists and strategic communication professionals? Given your answer, how would you respond to Aristotle's assertion that politics is the most ethical form of human activity?
2. Why is white, cis, nondisabled, and heterosexual considered a default in reporting?
3. Why are identity and life experience considered biases—something to mitigate—instead of something that strengthens and informs reporting and editing?

CASE 6-C

WHERE'S THE LINE? COVERING RACIAL PROTEST ON A COLLEGE CAMPUS

NICOLE KRAFT
Ohio State University

The *Lantern* thought it was covering a straightforward campus protest over racial injustice. Within hours, Ohio State's student media was in the middle of a First Amendment fight.

It started with a public-safety notice. Ohio State reported two sets of students near campus had been called a racial slur and physically assaulted. They identified the suspects as Black but failed to ID the victims, who were white. Public safety resent the release and indicated the action was classified as a "hate crime" due to the racial slurs, which were not identified.

That prompted more than 100 demonstrators to gather outside the president's office to protest racial injustice and call for equal protection of all students, claiming the safety notice negatively and unfairly impacted the perception of Black students on campus.

Lantern reporters chronicled the protest, which included speeches from three people who were appointed members of the undergraduate student government. For all intents and purposes, the writers did a fair and accurate job of coverage.

Or so they thought.

The challenges began to surface with coverage of the second campus protest a week later. *Lantern* reporters arrived on the scene and were surprised to find they were no longer just covering the story. They had become the story.

The protestors immediately faced the camera and proclaimed their names and faces were off-limits for coverage. They were not organizers, just participants. Their lives would be in danger if their faces and names were exposed. Despite protesting in public, they claimed a right to privacy.

The *Lantern* staff listened. They discussed options, which included abiding by their requests, skipping coverage of the event altogether, or limiting exposure of protest attendees but not speakers. The staff decided on option 3. Images of the attendees would be shown from behind to protect their privacy. The speakers, however, had no such privacy protection, and their unobstructed images and names were included.

The result: Students accused the *Lantern* of discriminating against students of color, a petition was launched calling for the media enterprise to be censured, and Editor-in-Chief Sam Raudins became the focal point of prejudice for many Black and brown students.

Student-journalists are trained to be ready for as many scenarios as possible—public meetings, data-driven investigations, family-focused features, even active campus shooters. However, they were not trained for what happens when the community they cover suddenly makes them a focal point and their coverage becomes a societal confrontation.

Student protestors said concerns about faces being photographed and shared put them in danger, as police might use them for identification or future arrests, which is what professor and visual journalist Tara Pixley addressed in *Nieman Reports*: "Each image photographed, published, and circulated has the capacity to both inform a viewing public and inform the police" (Aushana & Pixley, 2020).

Lantern editors also considered the position taken by National Public Radio Public Editor Kelly McBride, who wrote, "Blurring images is a form of photo manipulation that makes them less true, and is generally an unacceptable practice for documentary photography" (McBride, 2020).

In the end, Raudins explained the rationale best in a letter to *Lantern* readers:

> We cover protests by any group, because it is news that happens on our campus. It is our charge and responsibility to cover movements that involve and impact the lives of students. We will report them accurately and fairly, and will uphold the same standard for every group that assembles on our campus.
>
> We want the message of these groups to be heard, and we want Ohio State students, faculty, staff and alumni to look back at The Lantern archives 100 years from now and understand what these times were like. That has been the mission of The Lantern since its inception, and it will be our mission every day moving forward. (Raudins, 2020)

Micro Issues

1. Did *Lantern* photographers have an obligation to protect protestors by blurring their names and faces? Is there an ethical difference between speakers and other protestors?
2. *Lantern* reporters discussed options including abiding by protestors' requests, skipping coverage of the event altogether, or limiting exposure of protest attendees but not speakers. Ultimately, they chose the third option. Was that the most ethical choice? Why or why not?

3. Do you agree with Kelly McBride's statement that "Blurring images is a form of photo manipulation that makes them less true"? Why or why not?

Midrange Issues

1. How are the ethical obligations different for students, as opposed to professional, reporters?
2. What is the role of a student publication in covering its campus? Its city/community?
3. Compare and contrast the decisions made by *Lantern* journalists with those of reporters at the *Daily Northwestern* who apologized for publishing photos of student activists protesting a speech by Attorney General Jeff Sessions in November 2019.

Macro Issues

1. How should reporters cover a story when they become part of the story?
2. Can participants in a public protest still claim privacy rights? If so, under what circumstances? If not, why not?
3. What is the proper relationship between the press and police? Is it okay to publish mugshots, which are taken following an arrest but before conviction? How about descriptions of suspects, which often are vague and could negative influence perceptions of a minority group?

CASE 6-D

SPOTLIGHT: IT TAKES A VILLAGE TO ABUSE A CHILD

LEE WILKINS
University of Missouri

The process of investigative reporting has been the focus of two classic Hollywood films—*All the President's Men* in 1976 and the 2015 Oscar-winning Best Picture *Spotlight*. *All the President's Men* recounted the story of the *Washington Post*'s Watergate coverage, focusing on the external obstacles, specifically corruption in the White House, that journalists Bob Woodward and Carl Bernstein encountered in their reporting.

Spotlight dramatized the investigative reporting process, but instead of focusing on the external obstacles, *Spotlight* focused on the way that community and individual biography shape journalism. In the case of the *Boston Globe*'s investigation of the Catholic Church pedophile priest scandal, the film explores how the history of specific journalists covering specific stories in specific communities shapes those stories—from the "discovery" of a decades-long problem to how the newspaper reported and published what it found.

Early in the film and at the outset of the investigation, one of the characters notes that "your best shot is to try these cases in the press," meaning that it was impossible to challenge the historic and pervasive institution of the Roman Catholic Church and its leaders in Boston without the help of other powerful institutions. Those powerful institutions, including prominent Boston lawyers, made sure that the scandal left a minimal paper trail and, when there were documents, that they sometimes vanished—including from official court records and legal proceedings.

However, if the press was unable or unwilling to take on other powerful institutions over the issue, then the injustice would continue. In the initial phases of the reporting process, multiple characters tell the journalists involved that they believe the *Globe* will simply lack the courage to cover the story in anything other than an episodic fashion, as the paper had for several decades before the investigation uncovered the systemic roots of the scandal itself.

The *Globe*, despite its big-city circulation, envisioned itself as a community newspaper. Within the *Globe*, the six-member *Spotlight* team (reduced to a four-member team for the film) identifies itself as the oldest continuously operating newspaper investigative unit in the United States, with a high degree of autonomy over both story selection and journalistic methods. The staff members, including *Spotlight* team leader Robbie Robinson and the other team members who reported the story, were raised in the Roman Catholic Church, attended Catholic parochial schools, and had deep roots in the community of Boston.

From that personal history emerged a respect for the church itself, its leadership, and a skepticism about the scope of the story that ultimately fueled the reporting of it. Connections to the community also made it possible for powerful people to try to exert pressure on the journalists involved to abandon the story or to downplay it. How that pressure was exerted, and ultimately resisted—what some critics referred to as nongovernmental censorship—is one of the themes of the film.

A second theme is the ethical virtue of listening. The impact of listening as part of the interviewing process, and of doing so without judgment, emerges as the journalists interview the victims of the pedophile priests who recount the details of their molestation in explicit detail. The interviews include difficult questions, and because the victims are recounting events that occurred decades before, the viewer is able to at least superficially gauge the impact the molestation had on people throughout their lives. However, it is the act of listening that ultimately weaves trust among the journalists and the victims they interviewed.

The third theme that emerges is one of persistence, a theme also in *All the President's Men*. "Keep going" becomes the watchword of the reporting process in *Spotlight*, just as "follow the money" did for Watergate. However, the directive to "keep going" also meant that the reporters involved also questioned their own actions when pieces of the story had emerged years before anyone understood either the scope of the story or the problem. Their self-doubt about the quality of their journalism also distinguishes the film's portrayal of journalists in the midst of a big story that even they struggle to believe. Fictionalized, though based on real-life, executive editor Marty Barron, who kept the team focused on the systemic problem rather than the sensational individual stories of abuse, personified the maxim of "keep going until you've got the bigger story" that the *Globe* ultimately reported.

Critics of the film lauded it for its non-glamorized portrayal of journalism and journalists. "They got the journalism right" was one of the most frequent comments about the production.

Micro Issues

1. What are the specific instances in the film where listening without judging is important in reporting the story?
2. What role do family and friendship play in the reporting? Do you believe the journalists handled these conflicts appropriately?
3. At one point in the film, one of the characters says that only an outsider could have uncovered this story. Do you agree?

Midrange Issues

1. Did the *Spotlight* team do the right thing when it abandoned the story to report on 9/11? Why?
2. Use the theory of W. D. Ross to explore how the journalists viewed their duties as they reported the story. Did the ordering of those duties change during the reporting?

3. Evaluate the level of proof that the *Globe* reporters amass to make their story believable. Do you think this is a new standard of "proof" for journalists reporting instances of sexual assault and abuse?

Macro Issues

1. Does this film trivialize the harm of childhood sexual abuse for the sake of profitable entertainment?
2. At one point in the film, one of the characters urges Robinson to look around: "Robbie, this is the church . . . these are good people." Evaluate this rationale as a reason to curtail reporting on this story. Which philosopher would support your decision?
3. Evaluate how community shaped this story? Was it right for the journalists involved to tell their sources they "cared"?

CASE 6-E

CINCINNATI ENQUIRER'S HEROIN BEAT

CHAD PAINTER
University of Dayton

Heroin-related overdose deaths have more than quadrupled since 2010, with nearly 13,000 people dying nationwide in 2015 alone. Some of the greatest increases have occurred among women, the privately insured, and people with higher incomes—demographic groups with historically low rates of heroin use (Centers for Disease Control and Prevention, 2017). In response, the CDC added overdose prevention to its list of top public health challenges, and President Donald Trump created the Commission on Combating Drug Addiction and the Opioid Crisis to study "ways to combat and treat the scourge of drug abuse, addiction and the opioid crisis" (White House, 2017). This designation focused on raising national awareness about the severity of the problem but stopped short of providing additional funding for treatment and research about the opioid crisis.

News media also have responded with new initiatives. Specifically, the *Cincinnati Enquirer*, a daily newspaper covering Cincinnati and its Northern Kentucky suburbs, established the nation's first heroin beat in January 2016. While the heroin and opioid epidemic is a national problem, Ohio—more specifically, southwestern Ohio—is considered its epicenter. Heroin is thought to be the most accessible drug in Ohio (Ohio State Bar Association, 2017), which leads the nation in both opioid and heroin overdose deaths (Kaiser Family Foundation, 2014).

Terry DeMio, the *Enquirer* reporter who heads the heroin beat, said in an interview with the author that the *Enquirer* really is just responding to the community's need for information:

> There's a recognition that, not only is this a crisis, it's a crisis that, even now, is not well understood. I have easily more than 100 and probably well over 100 individuals talking to me, reading my work, people who have families who are addicted or people who are in recovery. In Northern Kentucky, which is where I started, one in three people knows someone addicted to heroin. So, these are our neighbors, and we want to be responsive to our community's needs.

DeMio covers the heroin and opioid epidemic from a public-health angle, not as a crime beat. She often discusses issues such as the need for first responders to carry naloxone, a drug that can block an opioid overdose; medication-assisted instead of abstinence-based treatment; and needle exchanges to help prevent HIV and Hepatitis C in both addicts and non-addicts who can accidentally step on improperly discarded needles. DeMio wants her reporting to help provide solutions to a community that is facing a public health crisis:

> I think the urgency is pretty obvious as far as the fact that this is a public health crisis. I mean, we want to stop the dying and then turn it around. That's my primary focus, which is a public health issue.

In DeMio's coverage, she routinely talks to a wide variety of sources, including addicts and their families, doctors and health-care experts, police officers, and local and state government officials. She said the key to doing this kind of beat is credibility and trust:

> They have to trust you and understand that you care. I think through the work of doing this it shows that we as a newspaper care and that I personally care. I report objectively by, just like any reporter, introducing both sides, being fact based, telling a story which shows the compassion and hopefully gives people clarity about what this really is like for someone to go through. But I don't hesitate to provide resources to people.

The *Enquirer* coverage gained widespread national attention when it published "Seven days of heroin: This is what an epidemic looks like" on Sept. 10, 2017. The 20-page special section, which was supplemented with additional online content, included contributions from more than 60 reporters, photographers, and videographers from the *Enquirer* and colleagues from 10 other news sites affiliated with the Media Network of Central Ohio. (Versions of "Seven days of heroin" appeared in those newspapers as well.) The special section focused on one week in July 2017, a week that included 18 deaths, at least 180 overdoses, more than 200 heroin users in jail, and 15 babies born with heroin-related medical problems.

Micro Issues

1. Evaluate the *Cincinnati Enquirer*'s decision to cover the heroin and opioid epidemic as a public health instead of a criminal issue.
2. How might the *Enquirer*'s reporting influence how the community understands and addresses the heroin and opioid epidemic?
3. How can a newspaper cover the heroin and opioid epidemic consistently without sensationalizing coverage or publishing "addiction porn"?

Midrange Issues

1. The *Enquirer*, like many medium-market newspapers, has made tough budget decisions, including newsroom layoffs and shuttering beats. How should a newspaper balance necessary beats (crime and courts, education, etc.) with important community issues in a time of shrinking newsroom budgets?
2. How should a reporter balance objective reporting with showing compassion and sharing treatment and other resources with sources and their families?
3. This ambitious series was labeled as being financially sponsored by a local hospital. Could this funding in any way have affected the coverage?

Macro Issues

1. In Cincinnati and Northern Kentucky, the majority of heroin and opioid users and overdose victims are middle-class, suburban Whites. How would you respond to criticism that news organizations and other institutions began treating heroin and opioid addiction as a disease instead of a crime once the racial and class demographics changed?

2. Projects such as these often win prizes and even sabbaticals for their authors. Prizes help quality storytelling get recognized, but they also have been the occasion for scandal. On balance, are awards good for the profession?
3. How might the *Enquirer*'s coverage serve as a template for other news organizations that want to start doing the same type of beat coverage in their communities?

CASE 6-F

GOLDIEBLOX: BUILDING A FUTURE ON THEFT

SCOTT BURGESS
Wayne State University

For more than 100 years, boys' toys have included Legos, Erector Sets, and Lincoln Logs—toys that help them build math and engineering skills. Girls, by contrast, played with tiaras, Barbies, and ballet shoes. Debbie Sterling, the founder of the Oakland-based toy company GoldieBlox, sought to change this dichotomy. Sterling started GoldieBlox in 2012, the first girls-only toy company that also develops computer apps and publishes books that focus on keeping girls interested in science (GoldieBlox, 2017).

GoldieBlox wants to "disrupt the pink aisle in toy stores globally" and challenge gender stereotypes "with the world's first girl engineering character," according to the company's website. The company began with $280,000 raised in a Kickstarter campaign after many people were inspired by the company's mission (Sterling, 2013). For the next year, GoldieBlox received a small amount of favorable press as a fun, feminist-oriented business with strong ideals.

That changed in November 2013, when the company released the YouTube video "Girls." In the video, three girls get bored watching a television show in which girls in pink taffeta dresses dance on a sofa. So, with a revised version of the Beastie Boys 1987 song "Girls" playing in the background, they grab work belts, safety goggles, and tools and build an elaborate contraption using many of the pink toys in their house.

The video received more than 8 million views on YouTube and 100,000 shares on Facebook in a few days. The company and its founder were featured on news programs, magazines, and newspapers around the world. While the privately held company does not release sales reports, some estimates suggest that sales tripled immediately following the video. Sterling claimed the company sold every toy it made during the 2013 Christmas season (Li, 2014).

One group, however, remained disappointed in the video: the Beastie Boys. GoldieBlox had not sought permission to use the song, and the band previously had never allowed its music to be used in commercials. Further, when Beastie Boy Adam Yauch died in 2012, he specified in his will that "in no event may my image or name or any artistic property created by me be used for advertising purposes" (Cubarrubia, 2012).

The two remaining band members, Michael Diamond and Adam Horovitz, approached GoldieBlox about the use of their music in the advertisement, and the toymaker responded with a lawsuit claiming fair use.

"As creative as it is," Diamond and Horovitz said in a statement, "make no mistake, your video is an advertisement that is designed to sell a product, and long ago, we made a conscious decision not to permit our music and/or name to be used in product ads. When we tried to simply ask how and why our song Girls had been used in your ad without our permission, YOU sued US" (*New York Times*, 2013).

GoldieBlox, now facing a legal and public relations backlash to a dying man's wishes, took down the video and issued the following statement:

> Although we believe our parody video falls under fair use, we would like to respect his wishes and yours. Since actions speak louder than words, we have already removed the song from our video. In addition, we are ready to stop the lawsuit as long as this means we will no longer be under threat from your legal team. (Michaels, 2013)

The Beastie Boys filed suit against GoldieBlox, claiming copyright infringement (Michaels, 2013). In March 2014, GoldieBlox settled with the Beastie Boys. The company issued an apology and agreed to pay a portion of its proceeds to the Beastie Boys, which in turn would donate that money to charities that furthered development of girls learning science and math (Itzkoff, 2014). (The original video is still available on YouTube.)

Furthermore, the negative publicity from the legal battle with the Beastie Boys also may have put a brighter light on GoldieBlox, which was accused of "pink washing" its toys. Critics accused GoldieBlox of claiming to provide toys for girls that would inspire them to pursue careers in engineering while still perpetuating the very stereotypes the company says it wants to tear down. Pink is used as a primary color in GoldieBlox toys, and among their collection is a kit to build a parade float for princesses. Sterling has fought this criticism, saying in interviews that "girls should be able to design their own princess castles" (Miller, 2013).

Micro Issues

1. Both versions of the GoldieBlox "Girls" video are widely available on the internet. How does the message in the advertisement change without the inclusion of the Beastie Boys song?
2. Compare and contrast the "Girls" advertisement with more traditional "girls' toys" advertising such as commercials for Barbie dolls.

Midrange Issues

1. Do companies claiming to take on social issues have more responsibility for transparency to their customers than companies that do not make such claims?
2. What are the ethical responsibilities of media outlets reporting this case? Should they show the original commercial that includes the Beastie Boys song?
3. Critique the final statement of Sterling above. Does the fact that girls are invited to design mitigate the fact that the project being designed deals in stereotypes?
4. GoldieBlox is a privately held company. Would any of your answers change if this company had stockholders? If so, in what way?

Macro Issues

1. Can a company such as GoldieBlox "disrupt the pink aisle in toy stores" and still use pink as a primary color in its toys?
2. Where should companies draw the line between advertising and activism?
3. Do the creators of the GoldieBlox ads have an obligation to follow the wishes of the Beastie Boys on the use of their music? What about filmmakers?
4. What are the responsibilities of consumers when they make decisions to purchase such products? Is it reasonable to expect the average consumer to be aware of the desires of the Beastie Boys with regard to how their music would be used?

PART II:
APPLICATIONS

Just as the chapters in Part I of this book focused on common philosophical understandings, this portion of the book focuses on discrete subsets of those questions. Strategic communication professionals have to grapple with advocacy. The fact that "the media" are most often a profit-making business sets up a unique set of tensions for the entire industry, explored in the chapter on media economics. Visual information, whether in news or advertising, also stresses our understanding of truth and privacy in the professional world. That visual information, as well as industry economics, likewise invades ethical thinking about art and entertainment. The application of ethical thinking in each of these areas informs thinking more broadly while raising specific questions that are more applicable in some professional activities than others.

7

Strategic Communication

Does Client Advocate Mean Consumer Adversary?

By the end of this chapter, you should be able to

- know how new technologies raise old ethical questions;
- understand balance and cognitive dissonance persuasion theories and their role in persuasion;
- understand the amplified TARES test for evaluating the ethics of individual messages;
- understand why the relationship between the media and public relations is both symbiotic and strained.

REACH OUT AND TOUCH SOMEONE

Most of the readers of this book are in their early twenties and are most often seeking *someone* in addition to the *something* of a college education. Many of you will conduct your search for friends and life partners online—and increasingly on apps such as Tinder and sites such as eharmony. Visitors to that site and others like it pay a subscription fee, complete various sorts of profiles, and are linked with possible matches. The non-virtual world and that human thing called chemistry seem to take it from there.

Not much of an ethical issue involved—that is, until you learn how such websites really make their money. They do it not exclusively through the matching service they advertise but more predominantly by attaching cookies to subscribers' computers and then selling potential behavioral change based on that information—willingly provided in the form of the profile—to marketers who seek a specific demographic, such as people of a certain age, or a certain income, and with specific likes and dislikes. Those electronic lists the websites sell—a process you must agree to in order to use the matching service—and then allow marketers to push specific sorts of messages at you electronically and, at times of their choosing, employing what the industry now terms *behavioral marketing*.

Behavioral marketing, which also is sometimes called behavioral targeting, is used to increase the effectiveness of advertising by tapping into data created by users as they surf the web. When you buy a book on Amazon, you've created a data point that the site's algorithm uses to advertise other similar books. When you "like" a cat video on Facebook, you have sent a signal that you might be interested in ads for cat food or pet adoption. Users somewhat involuntarily create a wealth of data, from whichever websites and pages they visit to the links they click on and the terms they enter into Google or other search engines. This information then can be combined with a person's geography and demographic area, as well as personal information they voluntarily disclose on websites and social media. Publishers love this data; they can charge a premium for targeted ads because consumers are more likely to purchase products from such ads when compared to random advertising. While the marketers never know your specific identity—in other words, your name—they know enough about you for selling purposes, right down to the fact that you like terrier dogs but not cats and that your favorite musician is Taylor Swift.

It's all part of the brave new world of strategic communication, or the seamless connections between what professionals used to refer to as advertising and public relations.

Strategic communication, just like news, is facing a new economic reality: a business model that is no longer successful. What used to be the case—that entertainment or news content either on television or in a print medium was designed to deliver an audience to advertisers—is now increasingly problematic because people are finding ways to dodge persuasive messages as never before. Whether it's ad-free (or nearly ad-free) streaming services such as Netflix and Hulu, or skipping through commercials, or getting news "for free" on the web, strategic communication professionals are being forced to find novel ways to get their messages to "eyeballs"—or people acting in their roles as consumers. Strategic communication professionals also are faced with the reality of an active audience—an audience that not only buys products or services but also expects to be able to evaluate those services and products on sites such as Yelp, which allows consumers to post their unfiltered opinions about local businesses, including restaurants, shops, and other sorts of local services. Local businesses particularly thrive with positive mentions and are punished by negative reviews. Several small business owners have filed lawsuits, complaining that Yelp has a financial interest in the listings, so consumer reviews posted on the site were manipulated depending on which companies advertise on the site—claims that Yelp executives deny, stating that both negative and positive feedback provide authenticity and value. In April 2009, Yelp began allowing local businesses to respond to comments on the site. These audience-based measures of products and services have added new dimensions to efforts to "control the message" that have been part of both advertising and public relations for decades.

These novel approaches can raise serious individual ethical issues—issues that once seemed more the realm of the journalist. Students who once said, "I went into advertising because I don't feel comfortable forcing people to talk to me, and I don't have to think about invading people's privacy," are now facing decisions about whether and how to use computer-based technologies to do precisely those things—only this time to promote sales of various products and lifestyles.

These facts of new media life also do not blunt some of the deepest continuing criticisms of persuasion, that the nature of the persuasive message itself—short, highly visual, and intentionally vague—is overly reliant on stereotypes, spins the truth, glorifies consumerism at the expense of community, and as an institution warps non-persuasive content in significant ways. The ease of bypassing persuasive messages also challenges one of the most significant justifications for advertising: that without the funding it provides, broad-ranging political discourse would not be possible in developed democracies such as the United States. There are similarities between commercial and political advertising; however, they also are ethically distinct. As presidential candidate Adlai Stevenson said in 1952, you shouldn't try to sell a presidential candidate the same way you sell cereal or soap. Therefore, this chapter focuses on commercial advertising while political advertising is discussed earlier in the book.

TECHNOLOGY: A ROOM OF REQUIREMENT OR A SYSTEM OF VALUES?

The ubiquitous nature of social media and other forms of nearly instantaneous news and advertising consumption raises another issue: fake ads. Senator Elizabeth Warren, while running in the 2020 Democratic presidential primary, purchased a series of Facebook ads that falsely claimed that Facebook CEO Mark Zuckerberg had endorsed President Donald Trump for reelection. The ad read:

Breaking news: Mark Zuckerberg and Facebook just endorsed Donald Trump for re-election. You're probably shocked, and you might be thinking, "how could this possibly be true?" Well, it's not. (Sorry.) but what Zuckerberg *has* done is given Donald Trump free rein to lie on his platform and then to pay Facebook gobs of money to push out their lies to American voters. (Epstein, 2019)

Warren only purchased the ads to illuminate an issue with Facebook's attempts to limit fake ads: Its policy exempts politicians from third-party fact-checking, giving them a potential platform to spread disinformation.

The problem with fake ads first surfaced in 2016 following the revelation that Russian companies with ties to the Kremlin purchased divisive, inflammatory, and false ads on Facebook and Twitter in an attempt to tip the presidential election to Donald Trump, as well as to sow social discord throughout the United States. These ads, which were seen by upward of half of US adults, featured hot takes on gun control, race and anti-racist groups, women's rights, immigration, and political rallies, including the "Not My President" and "Down with Hillary!" rallies that didn't exist. The information in these ads was false—including made-up protest groups and events, as well as discredited information. However, some ads were featured prominently on fact-checking sites such as PolitiFact and Snopes, sites that aim to dispel such falsehoods. Google, Facebook, and Twitter all are under scrutiny, including congressional hearings, for how their automated ad systems were used by Russians to spread this false information.

Facebook's ad problems didn't stop there, however. Anyone can create an ad on Facebook; the tool is prominently displayed on its homepage, and it's easy and relatively cheap to use. It's also easy to discriminate. A ProPublica investigation in September 2017 revealed that advertisers can direct their pitches to specific groups—including to people who expressed interest in topics such as "Jew hater," "How to burn Jews," and "History of 'Why Jews ruin the world.'" In November 2017, ProPublica revealed the results of a second investigation, in which its reporters bought rental housing ads on Facebook but asked that certain categories of users—including Blacks, people interested in wheelchair ramps, and Spanish speakers—be excluded, a clear violation of the Fair Housing Act. ProPublica again found problems with Facebook ads in December 2017; this time, employers could target ads to job seekers under 40, allowing advertisers to skirt employment law. The problem comes from automation. Unlike legacy media companies, Facebook uses an algorithm instead of sales representatives. So, instead of a Facebook employee selecting audiences offered to advertisers, ad categories are created automatically based on what users share on Facebook and their other online activity.

Many of these issues arise because technology makes certain activities possible. Such activities, which most often require the enormous data-processing capacities of the computer, also present professionals with two different ways of thinking about technology itself.

The first approach equates technology with efficiency. Those who subscribe to this school of thought assert that technology itself raises no ethical issues, but rather the ethical issues arise in how the technology is put to use. The second approach asserts that any technology is embedded with values. Think of the technology you are using right now: the written word and the printing press. What does writing value? A specific definition of truth, as reviewed in chapter 2 of this book. A specific standard of evidence—for example, written documents and sources for them are important. Some specific ways of organizing the human community and of placing economic value on some activities also are emphasized by the written word. The act of writing and the technology of the printing press have made much of the contemporary human community possible—but those communities privilege some values while minimizing others.

In this view, articulated by French theologian Jacques Ellul, technology is at core a system of values that must be understood before any decision to adopt a specific technology can be made. Failure to understand the values embedded in a technology can have many unintended consequences, some of them quite horrible.

To be a competent and ethical professional does not require you to resolve this deeply philosophical debate. But it does require you to acknowledge that it exists and to think clearly about whether, in the process of claiming efficiency, you have overlooked important questions or values.

THINKING ABOUT THE AUDIENCE: FROM PERSUASION THEORY TO PHILOSOPHICAL ANTHROPOLOGY

Psychologists first began to try to understand persuasion by working with a stimulus–response model. This early behaviorist approach led many to believe that the media could act as a "hypodermic needle" or a "magic bullet," sending a stimulus/message to an unresisting audience. These researchers, called "powerful effects theorists," found examples to support their theory in the success of propaganda during both world wars and in the public panic after Orson Welles's *War of the Worlds* broadcast on Oct. 30, 1938 (though the extent of that panic has been overblown).

However, the stimulus–response model proved to be a poor predictor of much human behavior. Later, communication theorists focused on cognitive psychology. Rather than analyzing persuasion as a simple behavioral reaction to a sufficient stimulus, these scholars theorized that how people think and what they bring to the persuasive situation helped to explain persuasion. According to these theories, people strain toward cognitive balance. Simply put, we are most comfortable when all of our beliefs, actions, attitudes, and relationships are in harmony, a state theorists called "symmetry."

Such theories have become known as "balance theories" because they stress the tendency of people to strive for cognitive balance in their lives. A person achieves balance only when his or her attitudes, information, and actions are in harmony. Leon Festinger (1957) coined the term "cognitive dissonance" to describe the state where a message and an action give conflicting and uncomfortable signals. Think of it as knowing the hazards of smoking but choosing to smoke anyway, setting up a classic brain/action dissonance. The desire to eliminate that dissonance is a strong one, sometimes strong enough to influence purchasing behavior and voting habits—at least some of the time (see figure 7.1).

Advertisers use this theory. Knock a consumer off balance early in the commercial and promise restoration of that balance through the purchase of a product. For instance, the opening scene of a commercial might suggest that your dandruff is making you a social outcast, and the subsequent copy promises you social approval if you use the correct shampoo.

Balance theories also explained why persuasive messages were sometimes quite effective while at other times inconsequential. No consequences to the problem, no lack of balance, and subsequently no sale. This individually

Figure 7.1.   Doonesbury © 1988 G. B. Trudeau. Reprinted with permission of Andrews McMeel Syndication. All rights reserved.

focused approach also provided the ultimate practical justification for advertising: the ancient Roman phrase *caveat emptor*, "Let the buyer beware." The creators of the ads were willing to assume little responsibility for the impact of their work, and academic studies gave them partial cover: If you can't prove that something's been effective, then it's unreasonable to suggest you take some responsibility for it. Even the FTC allows "puffery in advertising but not deception"—but they never tell you where they plan to draw the line.

Anthropologists assert that human rationality exists on equal footing with daily experience, language, and symbols. Culture and our personal experience balance rationality (Wilkins & Christians, 2001). If philosophical anthropology is correct, then ethical analysis of advertising founded in "Let the buyer beware" is morally unsustainable.

Instead, the ethical goal of advertising should be the empowerment of multiple stakeholders—from those who need to buy, those who need to sell, those who live in a community fueled by commerce and tax dollars, and finally those who depend on advertising-supported news to be participatory citizens in a democracy.

If the concept of human being as creator of culture and then a dynamic user of symbols becomes an ethical foundation for thinking about the audience, advertising practitioners should be expected to operate within the following framework:

- Clients and the public need information that gives them "a good reason to adopt a course of action" (Koehn, 1998, p. 106). The reason needs to be non-arbitrary and capable of helping people support one action instead of others.
- Rather than offering only expert opinion, advertising should foster ongoing discussion so that people can explore when options are sound and when practical knowledge (common sense) is superior.
- Advertising, just like news, can help foster a reflective community, including the community of consumers. Just like the Super Bowl results that are discussed at work the next day, often the creative ads that supported it are part of the social experience as well.
- Advertising needs to take seriously the role of culture in our lives. That means that advertising must authentically reflect the diverse voices that comprise our culture.
- Advertising will speak to the role of organizations in our lives. Questions of history and background can be conveyed in ads, but that must be done accurately and in context.

Given these general guidelines, let's explore a specific framework that puts ads to an ethical test.

THINKING ABOUT THE MESSAGE: A SYSTEMATIC TEST

The original TARES test is a checklist of questions the creators of every persuasive message should ask themselves in order to determine the ethical worthiness of the message (Baker & Martinson, 2001). While the TARES test takes its inspiration from the "symbol formation" function of both advertising and news, public-relations practitioners have added the significant element of advocacy to an ethical evaluation of public-relations messages. Advocacy means "understanding and valuing the perception of publics inside and outside organizations" (Grunig, Toth, & Hon, 2000). Advocacy also means communicating those perceptions to other publics, an effort that has become more complex because it involves relationships with multiple stakeholders "in a world of increasingly diverse and more active publics who are empowered by and connected through the Internet" (Fitzpatrick & Bronstein, 2006, p. x).

Those who support the advocacy model argue that any misleading information put out by strategic communications professionals will be somehow "self-corrected" by the gatekeepers of the media or by the self-righting "marketplace of ideas." Those who reject the advocacy model do so on two grounds. First, they assert that advocacy too easily morphs into distortion and lies. Second, they argue that the long-term health of many enterprises, from business to government programs, is ill served by "spin" and better served by honest, timely communication—even at the expense of short-term losses.

Of course, public relations professionals do not enjoy the special status of the "Fourth Estate." Indeed, as advocates of *special* interests—as compared to the *public* interest—they and their clients and employers may have less protection from judicial forays into questions of ethics. Public relations professionals must consider both whether the special obligations associated with the freedom to communicate are being met and whether, in the absence of effective *self*-regulation, the government might step in to hold practitioners accountable for irresponsible behavior. (Fitzpatrick & Bronstein, 2006, p. 16, italics in the original)

To help you think through the ethical issues that persuasion raises—particularly in the world of strategic communication, where most professionals will be asked to meld traditional advertising and public relations—we have connected the approaches in both fields through a single, ethically based test of specific messages.

The first element of the test—**T**—stands for **truthfulness**. Are the claims, both verbal and visual, truthful? If the message communicates only part of the truth (and many ads do this), are the omissions deceptive? Conversely, a message would pass the test if it meets a genuine human need to provide truthful information, even if some facts are omitted. Does the technology used to convey the message obscure or help to reveal the truth about the claims?

In addition, practitioners should be able to verify with clients the truthfulness of client claims, and they should provide information to their audiences that will allow them to verify the truthfulness of claims in messages aimed at the public (table 7.1).

The Cheerios television ads that emphasize eating Cheerios as part of a heart-healthy lifestyle could easily pass the first element of the TARES test. People do have to eat, and the ads provide needed information. The ads also omit some information—for example, the other components of a heart-healthy lifestyle or the fact that other breakfast cereals also meet these requirements. However, the omitted information does not lead the mature consumer to make false assumptions and bad choices.

In addition, telling the truth in times of crisis, such as becoming an advocate rather than an adversary in the long-term health care of a particular client, tests the foremost professional principles for public-relations practitioners. The history of the field would suggest that businesses and agencies whose actions demonstrate that public health and safety are more important than short-term profits—telling the truth even when it hurts—are quite likely to profit and survive in the long term.

Step two in the amplified TARES test—**A** for **authenticity**—is closely linked to step one. Authenticity suggests that it's important not only to do the right thing but also "to do it with the right attitude" (Pojman, 1998, p. 158). We link this notion to the concept of sincerity. First, is there a sincere need for this product within the range of products and services available? Second, are the reasons given to the consumer purchasing the product presented in such a way that they also would motivate the person who developed and wrote the message? Simply put: Would you buy your own reasoning about the uses and quality of the product advertised?

Authenticity, used in this way, is closely linked to disclosure, an important standard for public-relations messages. The ethical end of disclosure is the generation of trust among and between various publics. "Ethical public relations professionals are forthright and honest and counsel clients and employers to adopt responsible communication policies built on principles of openness and transparency" (Fitzpatrick & Bronstein, 2006, p. 13). Disclosure

Table 7.1. The Amplified TARES Test of Ethical Persuasion

T	Are the ad claims **truthful**?
A	Is the ad claim **authentic**?
R	Does the ad treat the receiver with **respect**?
E	Is there **equity** between the sender and the receiver?
S	Is the ad **socially responsible**?

also demands providing information about who is paying for the message and who stands to profit from its success. Direct advertising of pharmaceuticals to consumers—once banned by law—often fails this part of the test.

Let's take a set of strategic communication messages about products designed to help elderly or infirm people live more independently. Although some of these products—for example, devices that turn on lights in response to a hand clap—may seem little more than high-tech toys, anyone with a grandparent in a wheelchair, a sibling crippled by an illness like rheumatoid arthritis, or even a young person suffering from the imposed immobility of a broken leg can readily understand the need for such devices.

Others, such as advertisements for extended-care facilities or supplements to existing insurance plans, attempt to focus on the human desire of independent living. However, if the messages stereotype elderly people as frail, helpless, weak, or easily panicked, or if they knock otherwise healthy individuals off balance to sell a product based on fear, they do not authentically reflect the reality of life beyond age 65. The ad then lacks authenticity based on an unrealistic stereotype of the early retiree. The TARES test would require rethinking the specific appeal in the ad to one that scares and stereotypes less and informs more. For creative people, such a switch is readily accomplished if they think about it. Just as important, a fresher approach might well sell more.

The **R** in the test stands for **respect**—in this case, respect for the person who will receive the persuasive message. However, as a shorthand way of thinking through this element of the test, it might be appropriate for advertising practitioners to ask themselves, "Am I willing to take full, open, and personal responsibility for the content of this ad?"

Take the anti-texting-while-driving public service campaign that began with an ad of an actual car crash, filmed from inside the car, and its devastating aftermath. Even though the ad itself, which originated with a European government and went viral through YouTube, was filmed as a documentary, the campaign was criticized for its "scare" tactics. However, while the campaign relied on fear as a primary emotional tactic, it also provided rational reasons to not text and drive. Even though it was created by a government agency, the ad and its emotional appeal provide evidence of respect for human life.

The **E** in the amplified TARES test stands for **equity**. We conceptualize equity as follows: Is the recipient of the message on the same level playing field as the ad's creator? Or, to correctly interpret the ad, must that person be abnormally well informed, unusually bright or quick-witted, and completely without prejudice? Equity is linked to **access** for public-relations professionals, and it takes its ethical power from the role of free speech in a democratic society. Free people are the autonomous moral actors that philosophers have long insisted must be the foundation of ethical choice, and access to information equalizes an individual's ability to participate in the marketplace of ideas.

Think about this corporate image ad for Mobil Oil—the one with the pristine scenery, glorious sunset, and an oil tanker. The ad claims that by building tankers with double hulls, Mobil has the best interests of the environment at heart. While Mobil's claim that it builds double-hulled tankers is literally true, correctly interpreting the ad requires historical recall. Mobil, and all other oil companies, were required by Congress to build double-hulled tankers after a single-hulled tanker, the *Exxon Valdez*, ran aground in March 1989 and spilled an enormous amount of oil on the Alaskan coast, an environmental disaster of the first magnitude. For the image ad to work, it counts on the average person not knowing—or not being able to connect—legal requirements with corporate behavior. The ad assumes (and actually depends on) an imbalance between the knowledge of the person who created the ad and the consumer. It flunks the concept of equity. Similarly, an airline company that brags about a point of customer service that has actually been codified by the congressionally mandated Passenger Bill of Rights is relying on customer ignorance or forgetfulness to score points for behavior required by law.

Finally, the **S** in the amplified TARES test: Is the ad **socially responsible**? This is perhaps the most difficult element of the test for the simple reason that advertising practitioners have duties to many groups, among them their clients, the agencies for which they work, consumers, people exposed to the ad whether they buy or not, and society at large.

Because this text emphasizes social ethics, we suggest interpreting this portion of the TARES test in the following fashion:

- If everyone financially able to purchase this product or service did so and used it, would society as a whole be improved, keeping in mind that recreation and self-improvement are worthy societal goals?
- If there are some groups in society that would benefit from using this product as advertised, are there others that could be significantly harmed by it? Are there ways to protect them?
- Does this ad increase or decrease the trust the average person has for persuasive messages?
- Does this ad take the notion of corporate responsibility, both to make money and to improve human life and welfare, seriously and truthfully?

For public-relations practitioners, social responsibility also may be defined as **process**, whether public-relations advocacy impedes or contributes to the robust functioning of the marketplace of ideas. An evenhanded process encourages both the journalists who use public-relations-generated information for news stories and various audiences who must rely on those stories as part of their decision-making to use the information provided.

Using this concept of social responsibility should enable you to think ethically about television's decisions to air condom advertising. MTV, the network targeted at teenagers, chose to air such ads in 2000. More traditional network television outlets still do not. Which decision do you believe is more ethically justified? Why? Does the notion of social responsibility, and the process of democratic functioning, have any place in your analysis?

Or try this dilemma: With all the talk about global warming, there is one organism that thrives in a warmer subtropical environment—the mosquito that perpetuates dengue fever, a painful disease totally preventable by mosquito control. Does the "first world" have a right to advertise the comforts of energy consumption when a single-degree change in the world's climate allows more latitudes for the disease-bearing mosquito?

The amplified TARES test is a demanding one. However, asking these questions, particularly during the process of creating an ad, also can be a spur to better, more creative execution and can be rewarded in the capitalistic marketplace. The TARES test may help advertising practitioners warn their corporate clients about the kind of advertising that could do them, as well as society at large, great long-term harm.

ADVERTISING'S SPECIAL PROBLEMS: VULNERABLE AUDIENCES

Advertising in a mass medium reaches large, heterogeneous audiences. Often, advertising intended for one group is seen by another. Sometimes the results are humorous, and maybe even a little embarrassing, as when ads for contraception or personal hygiene products make their way into prime-time programming.

However, in the case of Camel cigarettes' "Joe Camel" ads, this "confusion" of intended audience with actual recipients appeared quite deliberate. In 1997, the Camel company agreed to withdraw the cartoon spokesperson "Joe Camel" from magazines and billboards after internal documents revealed the industry targeted underage smokers, and sales figures bore out its success.

In other cases—for example, the beer industry—no such ban exists. Advertising intended for adults is often seen by those who cannot legally drink but do remember the catchy commercials and the presentation of drinking as something connected with fun and good times. These ads air in a society in which most adult alcoholics report having had their first drink when they were underage.

Are there certain types of audiences that deserve special protection from advertising messages? US law says yes, particularly in the case of children.

Legal restrictions on advertising targeted at children cover everything from Saturday-morning television programming to types of products and the characters that advertisers may employ. Children, unlike adults, are not assumed to be autonomous moral actors. They reason about advertising imperfectly, and in an attempt to protect them, American society has accepted some regulation of commercial speech.

However, the issue gets murkier when the target audience is formed of subgroups of adults—for example, ethnic consumers. Exactly when advertisers began to actively court ethnic consumers is uncertain. Dwight Brooks (1992) quotes a 1940 *BusinessWeek* article that reported that an organization was established in Los Angeles to help guide advertisers who wished to garner the patronage of Black consumers. Amazingly, the businesses were cautioned against using such words as "boss," "boy," and "darkey" in their ads. Instead, the advertisers were urged to refer to Black consumers as "Negroes" who want the same things as other shoppers.

America is on its way to being a nation with no ethnic majority, and the real attempt to court ethnic audiences began when those audiences acquired buying power. Hispanics are now the largest minority in the United States. The buying power of Black consumers now tops more than $300 billion. The Asian American market also has increased substantially.

Yet only a relative handful of advertisements reflect this emerging demographic reality despite studies and surveys showing that consumers, especially millennials, are more likely to purchase products that include diverse families in advertisements. Companies such as Budweiser and 84 Lumber received good reviews following their 2017 Super Bowl ads that directly addressed immigration and diversity. However, commercials designed to appeal to this market segment sometimes employ troubling stereotypes or encounter other difficulties. For example, Dove body lotion apologized after publishing and then pulling an ad where a Black woman, after using Dove, removes her top to reveal a white woman underneath. Dove was especially susceptible to criticism because it also produced a 2011 ad for its body wash depicting a before-and-after picture that charted the transition of a Black woman into a white woman. Pepsi, in a divisive 2017 commercial,

> depicted [Kendall] Jenner drinking a Pepsi and walking through a group of diverse protesting marchers. Eventually, Jenner notices a large group of protesters being watched intently by some police officers. She then pulls off a wig and struts toward one of the officers, hands him a Pepsi, and the protestors cheer wildly. (Ferrucci & Schauster, 2020, p. 1)

After controversy surrounding the commercial ensued, people within and outside the advertising industry argued that the ad violated ethical strategic communication boundaries by co-opting a social issue, acting as a form of cultural appropriation, and serving as an example of brand activism gone awry (Ferrucci & Schauster, 2020). Several commercial (Aunt Jemima, Land O' Lakes), artistic (Dixie Chicks—now the Chicks, and Lady Antebellum—now Lady A), and athletic (Washington Redskins, Cleveland Indians) brands faced similar reckonings in 2020 from consumer backlash over racist or racially charged words or images.

Magazines pointed at teenage girls seldom reflect the reality of teenage bodies. Studies have shown that women who are exposed to such advertising images find their own bodies less acceptable. The same goes for facial features. Scholars have noted that the ideal image of beauty, even in magazines targeted at Blacks, is a Caucasian one of small noses, thin lips, and lighter skin tones. Black women simply don't see themselves in these advertisements. Scholars in cultural studies argue that the impact of these repeated images is "cumulative." Ultimately, culture comes to accept without question what is nothing more than a gender or racial stereotype, and the stereotype ultimately becomes a "truism."

Few scholars have suggested that adults who are minorities need special protection from advertising. What they have noted is that ads that abuse the trust between consumer and advertiser have consequences. In the short term, products may not sell or may become the target of regulation. In the long term, cynicism and societal distrust increase. People sense they are being used, even if they can't explain precisely how. The buyer may resort to avoiding advertising itself rather than using advertising to help make better decisions.

JOURNALISM AND STRATEGIC COMMUNICATION: THE QUINTESSENTIAL STRUGGLE

Public relations began as a profession in the late 19th century when newsmakers sought to find a way to get past journalism's gatekeepers to get their stories told, from simple press releases to elaborate publicity stunts (such as the "torches of freedom" march for women smokers envisioned by Edward L. Bernays in the early years of the 20th century). For the client, public-relations practitioners offered free access to the audience; for the newspapers, they offered "free" news to publishers.

Despite the occasional animosity between journalists and public-relations practitioners, the relationship is truly symbiotic: They simply could not live without each other. No media organization is large enough to gather all the day's news without including several public-relations sources. Business pages are full of press releases on earnings, new product lines, and personnel changes, all supplied by writers not paid by the media. Travel, entertainment, and food sections of newspapers would be virtually nonexistent if not for press releases. However, media outlets provide the all-important audience for an institution wanting the publicity.

With this common need, why are the two professions sometimes at odds? Much of the problem stems from how each of the two professions defines news. To the public-relations professional, the lack of breaking news is newsworthy. Plants that operate safely and are not laying off any employees, nonprofit organizations that operate within budget and provide needed services, companies that pay a dividend for the 15th consecutive quarter are all signs that things are operating smoothly and make for a story that the public should hear. To the journalist, the opposite is true. Plants only make news when they endanger the public safety. Employees are at their most newsworthy when they bring a gun to work, not when they show up every day for 30 years.

Similarly, there is a strained but symbiotic relationship between journalism and advertising. In the commercial press model (which is discussed more in-depth in the media economics chapter), media organizations almost always report and distribute news at a loss, instead making their money by selling readers, viewers, or listeners to advertisers. A similar model also is the norm for online news and social media sites. However, advertisers might try to influence content because they serve as the primary source of income for the mass media (Herman & Chomsky, 2002). Such was the case with "Doctor Patient Unity," a lobbying group funded by doctors and doctor-staffing companies that opposes laws to stop surprise medical bills. The group pulled hundreds of thousands of ad dollars from television network affiliates in Austin, Minneapolis, and Denver after journalists in those markets began reporting stories about the group (Vanderveen, 2019).

Attempts to use ad dollars to influence editorial content (though often unsuccessful) is one major issue. Another modern issue is native advertising, which is sponsor-funded content that matches the form and editorial and design function of news content. In 2020, for example, *Teen Vogue* published on its website the 2,000-word question-and-answer advertorial "How Facebook Is Helping Ensure the Integrity of the 2020 Election." One issue is that the piece wasn't clearly marked, so it initially appeared to be journalistic content; only after publication on the *Teen Vogue* website did editors slap it with a "sponsored content" label before ultimately taking it down. A later statement from *Teen Vogue* editors read as follows:

> We made a series of errors labeling this piece, and we apologize for any confusion this may have caused. We don't take our audience's trust for granted, and ultimately decided that the piece should be taken down entirely to avoid further confusion. (Newton, 2020)

The issue really isn't new, though: David Ogilvy created the famous "Guinness Guide to Oysters" magazine advertorial in 1950. While there must be a clear disclosure such as the label "advertisement" or "sponsored content" to protect consumers from being deceived, native ads are designed to trick readers or viewers into thinking that material presented was created by reporters or other journalists. Further muddying the water is that news organizations have started branded content studios, most notably the *New York Times*'s T Brand Studio, that create and sell native ads, as well as other advertising content. Examples of native ads are almost too numerous to list; consumers see them every day in sponsored posts on Facebook and Twitter, Google text ads in search listings, product placement such as characters eating Reese's Pieces in *E.T. the Extra-Terrestrial*, and in-feed ads such as the recommended content from "Around the Web" found at the end of almost every online news article.

The average news consumer rarely observes this constant struggle for control, yet he or she is affected by it. How should we evaluate a profession with the goal of persuading in a manner that does not look like traditional persuasion or the goal of preventing the dissemination of information that might harm the illusion that has been created? By undermining the concept of independent and authentic news messages accepted as credible by the public, are strategic communication practitioners undermining the central content vehicle for their messages? Doesn't persuasion need the contrast of news to succeed?

More recently, the focus of animosity has centered on the concept of "synergy," or the notion that consumers should receive multiple messages from distinct sources, thereby increasing sales or public perception of particular issues. At the ethical core of synergy is the concept of independence—for the journalists who report on the news and for the consumers of both news and persuasive messages who need to make independent decisions about them. The current economic pressures on both strategic communication and journalism have intensified this tug-of-war over independence.

PERSUASION AND RESPONSIBILITY

Louis Hodges (1986) says that the notion of professional responsibility can be summed up in a single question: To what am I prepared to respond ably? In other words, what have my education and my experience equipped me to do and to assume responsibility for? Ask a strategic communication practitioner, "To what are you ably equipped to respond?" and he or she might answer, "To respond to a crisis for a client" or "To generate favorable media attention for a client" or "To generate increased sales for my client." However, there are greater responsibilities.

Hodges further states that responsibilities come from three sources. First, there are those that are *assigned*, such as employee to employer. Second, there are those that are *contracted*, where each party agrees to assume responsibilities and fulfill them. Third, there are the *self-imposed* responsibilities, where the individual moral actor takes on responsibilities for reasons indigenous to each individual. It is our contention that public relations, practiced ethically, will not only fulfill the assigned or contracted responsibilities with the employer or the paying client but also take on the greater calling of self-imposed responsibilities. These self-imposed responsibilities could include such constructs as duty to the truth and fidelity to the public good. The more self-imposed responsibilities the strategic professional assumes, the more ethical the profession will become as practitioners will see their personal good as being synonymous with the public good.

SUGGESTED READINGS

Duffy, M., & Thorson, E. (eds.). (2016). *Persuasion ethics today.* New York: Routledge.

Fitzpatrick, K., & Bronstein, C. (eds.). (2006). *Ethics in public relations: Responsible advocacy.* Thousand Oaks, CA: Sage.

Hodges, L. (1986). Defining press responsibility: A functional approach. In D. Elliott (ed.), *Responsible journalism* (pp. 13–31). Newbury Park, CA: Sage.

Baker, S., & Martinson, D. (2001). The TARES test: Five principles of ethical persuasion. *Journal of Mass Media Ethics, 16*(2/3), 148–175.

Leiss, W., Kline, S., & Jhally, S. (1986). *Social communication in advertising: Person, products and images of well being.* New York: Methuen.

O'Toole, J. (1985). *The trouble with advertising.* New York: Times Books.

Schudson, M. (1984). *Advertising: The uneasy persuasion.* New York: Basic Books.

CASES

CASE 7-A

FYRE FESTIVAL BECOMES FYRE FRAUD

EMILY HORVATH AND CHAD PAINTER
University of Dayton

The 2017 Fyre Festival started with a social media blitz using the hashtag #FyreFestival and a solid orange block posted by social media influencers. It ended with the hashtag #FyreFraud and pictures of prepackaged sandwiches and FEMA (Federal Emergency Management Agency) tents.

Fyre Festival was the brainchild of Billy McFarland—an entrepreneur turned fraudster—and rapper Ja Rule. They hired social media influencers including Kendall Jenner, Bella Hadid, Hailey Baldwin, and Emily Ratajkowski to promote the festival, mainly on Instagram—although the influencers didn't disclose that they were paid, as required by law. Initially, each influencer posted a solid orange block with the hashtag #FyreFestival, and a video of them running around a tropical beach in bikinis. The hashtag soon went viral.

A social media influencer is a user who has credibility, tools, and authenticity in a specific industry, has access to a large audience, and can persuade and motivate others to act on their recommendations (Digital Marketing Institute, 2018). There are many differences between social media influencers and public relations and advertising professionals; *the major difference is that traditional strategic communicators are paid to develop a campaign to promote a brand while social media influencers are paid to use their *personal* brand to persuade others to buy a product or service.*

In all, there were more than 40,000 posts with the #FyreFestival hashtag, and the event became so big—and with so much upfront cost—that McFarland and Ja Rule couldn't turn back despite obvious warning signs, including experienced event planners telling McFarland that a large-scale festival would take at least a year to plan instead of the two months he allotted. The concept was a luxury music festival on a private island in the Bahamas featuring 33 acts including Pusha T, Tyga, and Blink-182. Tickets ranged from $500 to $1,500, though some spent up to $30,000 for a VIP experience that included being flown to the island on a private jet, housed in luxury cabanas, and served gourmet food and drinks.

However, there were problems with security, food, accommodations, and media services. Also, most of the musical acts pulled out. Once festivalgoers arrived, the more than 5,000 people who purchased tickets were quick to take to social media to air their extreme disappointment. Coming full circle, social media provided a powerful platform to generate a movement from #FyreFestival to #FyreFraud. As a result, the festival was postponed indefinitely and later was canceled.

In March 2018, McFarland pled guilty to one count of defrauding investors and ticket holders. (Later, while out on bail, he pled guilty to defrauding a ticket vendor.) Organizers, including McFarland, were sued for more than $100 million in civil damages. The festival was the subject of two documentaries—Hulu's *Fyre Fraud* and Netflix's *Fyre: The Greatest Party That Never Happened*—as well as an episode on CNBC's *American Greed*.

Micro Issues

1. What, if any, responsibility do Bella Hadid, Hailey Baldwin, and other social media influencers have in the aftermath of #FyreFraud? What is the responsibility of Jerry Media, which created the ad campaign?
2. Should social media companies such as Instagram allow persuasive messages that are not clearly marked as advertising? Why or why not?

Midrange Issues

1. Use the TARES test to evaluate the Fyre Festival social media campaign.
2. Social media creates a two-way communication channel between advertiser and consumer. Evaluate the effectiveness of the #FyreFraud hashtag.
3. Fyre Fest is not the first disastrous music festival. Compare and contrast the advertising and aftermath of Fyre Festival with the pre-social media "Woodstock 1999" featuring Korn and the Red Hot Chili Peppers.

Macro Issues

1. All advertising is regulated by the Federal Trade Commission. How might the FTC better regulate advertising on social media?
2. Fyre Festival was intended as a high-end festival with tickets as much as $30,000. Was Instagram—a free app or website available to anyone with an internet connection—the appropriate venue to advertise the festival? What, if any, responsibility do advertisers have to protect people outside of their target audience—in this instance, people of a lower socioeconomic status—from seeing the message?
3. What is the role of the consumer to verify the claims made in persuasive messages? Is that role different if the message appears on social media as opposed to television or print?

CASE 7-B

THROUGH THE GLASS DARKLY: PELOTON, BODY SHAMING, AND AMERICA'S ODD RELATIONSHIP WITH EXERCISE

LEE WILKINS
University of Missouri

The image itself was hardly atypical. Christmas morning, obviously affluent surroundings, a surprise present for a young mother. She unwraps a Peloton exercise bike that, in 2019, when the television commercial aired, retailed for about $2,400 plus a $39 per month subscription fee for programming on the Wi-Fi-enabled device. The young woman is slender, her muscles are toned, and she appears to have slept the entire night through, a relatively rare experience for many young parents.

As the 30-second spot continues, the young woman rides the bike, sometimes in the morning and some days after work. She takes selfies to document her fitness progress. At the end of a year on the bike, she authors a fitness video for her husband, telling him that she did not realize how much the exercise device would change her.

And then the Twitterverse explodes.

There were multiple criticisms. The young woman, played in the commercial by actor Monica Ruiz, obviously was not overweight and appeared to be in strong physical condition. Why would the spouse of a person who looked like that think she needed to exercise or that she needed more exercise? While weight loss was never a part of the overt appeal in the ad, many who saw it said that Peloton was engaging in a form of body shaming that valued weight loss over health.

Ruiz's performance also was criticized. Some said she looked "scared" when she first started to ride. Ruiz's character was dubbed "the Peloton wife" online.

Then there was the price. The visual imagery in the ad indicated wealth. The couple lived in spacious surroundings—spacious enough to have a separate room for the exercise bike. A Peloton also is pricey. So, a television ad that reached a heterogeneous audience wound up peddling a product that only a few could afford.

The company's stock declined by more than $1 billion following backlash to the ad, although it has since recovered.

The company itself responded. It produced commercials shot in different sorts of homes and reminded critics that gym memberships can cost a lot more than the $39 per month of a Peloton subscription.

Peloton also emphasized that online cyclists often form a genuine and supportive community and that the commercial and subsequent ads were trying to celebrate the mind–body connection. This fairly abstract appeal, one that counters the American notion that exercise is a necessary punishment for indulgence, might have been lost on some viewers. Finally, the company noted that some physical conditions—including diabetes, high blood pressure, and some forms of arthritis—not visible to the naked eye, do afflict the young, and are helped by exercise.

Micro Issues

1. Was broadcast television the most appropriate medium for the Peloton ad? Why or why not?
2. Would the same criticisms have been appropriate if a young man had received the gift? Why or why not?
3. Did the company take the response of the Twitterverse too seriously?

Midrange Issues

1. Should expensive products—such as Pelotons or some cars—deliberately pitch their ads in a non-classist way? Why or why not?
2. Did critics overanalyze a 30-second spot? Did they "see" more than was actually there?
3. As a gender, do females constitute a vulnerable audience because their bodies are so often the focus of many types of interaction?
4. Should the Peloton ad have interspersed other forms of exercise—for example, walking or swimming—as a way to make the point about the connection between exercise and health?

Macro Issues

1. The Peloton ad aired in 2019. How do you think the response to the ad would be different in 2020?
2. Feminist theory suggests decision-makers consider content that focuses on what is possible. Does the Peloton ad do this? Contrast the Peloton approach with other exercise products—for example, Nike's "Just Do It" campaign or the public service campaign "Play Like a Girl."

CASE 7-C

WEEDVERTISING

LEE WILKINS
University of Missouri

In *Nichomachean Ethics*, Aristotle discusses the vice of gluttony, which included drinking too much. For the Greeks, gluttony was a violation of the ethical virtue of moderation—it was too much of a good thing. But, for the Greeks, and for multiple cultures throughout history, it was the excess, not the substance itself, that created potential problems.

Weed was initially used in the United States by Blacks and was adopted by mainstream culture in the 1960s, when it became the drug of choice for baby boomers (Weisman, 2014). Because of its association with marginal and countercultures, as well as its intoxicating effects, possessing, growing, and selling marijuana was criminalized; in fact, for much of the second half of the 20th century, possessing even small amounts of weed was the criminal equivalent of possessing small amounts of heroin, at least in the United States. During this era in US history, it was the substance itself that was at issue.

People smoked dope anyway, and based on personal experience and perhaps some wishful thinking, the 1960s also gave voice to a small political movement that argued for its legalization, claiming it was no more harmful for most people than alcohol and almost certainly much less harmful than tobacco (which by this time had been linked to cancer) and less addictive than heroin. Marijuana laws also were selectively enforced: If you were a person of color and caught with a "baggie" or a "joint," you were far more likely to be criminally prosecuted than if you were a Caucasian caught in the same set of circumstances.

In later decades, the generation that had grown up with illegal—but popular—"Mary Jane" obtained political power. Democratic presidents Bill Clinton and Barack Obama both admitted to smoking weed, although Clinton claimed he "never inhaled." The underground market for the drug remained brisk, and marijuana became an economically viable cash crop (meaning no taxes were paid on the proceeds) in geographic areas as distinct as California, Oregon, and southern Missouri, even though it continued to remain illegal at both local and federal levels. Scientists also systematically began to investigate the anecdotal claims about the drug. Marijuana was found to reduce the pain of cancer and other illnesses and long-term injuries, sometimes when other drugs would not. It did not appear to have the addictive qualities of some more traditional painkillers. Extracts of the plant (those that did not produce a high for the average person) were prescribed for people with certain sorts of seizure disorders. In sum, scientific evidence coupled with personal experience prompted a culture change: Marijuana came to be viewed much more like alcohol, a legal product or, like certain prescription drugs, a medically effective substance, rather than just an underground street drug that put users in jail and landed providers with lengthy felony convictions.

As the way the culture viewed the drug changed, governments also changed their outlook: Alcohol and tobacco produce tax revenue, even though both continue to be regulated. Why not do the same with weed? The political movement to legalize marijuana that originated the 1960s began to see political success as first municipalities and then states began to legalize (but still control) marijuana, initially for medical purposes and then for recreation, in much the same way that states and municipalities regulated alcohol consumption. As of January 2021, 15 states and the District of Columbia have legalized marijuana for recreational use and another 35 states have legalized it for medicinal use (an additional 13 states legalized marijuana for medicinal use but limit the THC content), though it is illegal at the federal level. The political and cultural change had indeed been a long, strange trip.

With legalization at the local and state levels, business sprang up. There were marijuana vacations, where a tour company would pick you up at the airport and take you to various vendors to sample everything from edibles to more traditional ways of consuming the drug. These tour companies would make sure that no one was "high" behind the wheel and also that people were guided through the various kinds and strengths of marijuana available. The experience was very much like a tour of California wine country, only the intoxicant had changed.

However, because the federal government continued to regard the drug as illegal, the clash of federal, state, and local law enforcement expectations resulted in transactions that were conducted only in cash. Businesses could not provide information to potential consumers about their existence or their services. In other words, marijuana-based businesses couldn't advertise.

However, given the history of the past 60 years, there is every reason to believe that the federal government will eventually begin to regulate weed in the same way it regulates alcohol. Whether that change comes in the next year or the next decade, the prospect of advertising weed provides advertising practitioners with a rare opportunity to consider how that product can be effectively and ethically advertised to a growing group of consumers before such advertising becomes widespread.

Micro Issues

1. How is advertising weed like and unlike direct-to-consumer advertising of over-the-counter and prescription drugs?
2. How does the fact that marijuana is a "sin" product like alcohol or gambling influence your approach to developing ads?
3. How does thinking about vulnerable audiences influence your approach to weedvertising?
4. What sorts of images would be appropriate to employ in weedvertisements?

Midrange Issues

1. W. D. Ross provides a set of duties, reviewed in chapter 1. Could weedvertising be said to support any of Ross's duties?
2. Are there some uses of weed that should not be advertised? Compare your response on this question to how you would respond to similar questions about drugs, alcohol, or gambling.
3. Advertisers often employ testimonials in their ads. Would such a strategy be appropriate for weed?

Macro Issues

1. Should the advertising industry develop and enforce its own set of guidelines that regulate weedvertising? What might those guidelines be? How would these guidelines be like or unlike the current guidelines regulating advertising promulgated by the federal government for all products? For products such as alcohol?
2. How would developing a weedvertising campaign be like or unlike a campaign for selling seats on commercial ventures that promise to take passengers to outer space or the moon?

CASE 7-D

KEEPING UP WITH THE KARDASHIANS' PRESCRIPTION DRUG CHOICES

TARA WALKER
St. Bonaventure University

In 2015, Kim Kardashian-West posted a picture of herself on Instagram holding a bottle of pills with the caption, "OMG. Have you heard about this?"

The post touted the drug Diclegis and its benefits for morning sickness. Soon thereafter, Duchesnay, the drug manufacturer, received a warning letter from the Food and Drug Administration saying that the post had been "false and misleading" because it failed to mention the drug's risks. Consequently, Kardashian-West posted a month later describing the potential side effects and the risks associated with Diclegis. She used the hashtag "#correctivead" with the post, and prefaced the list of side effects with the words "for US residents only."

Kardashian-West's original post omitted any warnings, suggesting that Duchesnay deliberately sidestepped the regulations about direct-to-consumer drug advertising. According to Matt Brown, the CEO of Guidemark Health, Duchesnay "took a risk by having Kardashian-West promote the product without safety information." As a result, brand awareness increased substantially. "The concept of 'bad publicity is good publicity' was definitely embraced here," Brown said (McCaffrey, 2015).

Kardashian-West's post is only one event in a long line of controversies associated with direct-to-consumer advertising, or DTCA.

Proponents of DTCA claim that these ads provide an important source of health information, especially for hard-to-reach populations (Lee & Begley, 2010). Additionally, advocates argue such advertising may help undiagnosed patients receive treatment and promote greater adherence to drug regimens (Calfee, 2002; Hoek & Gendall, 2002; Hoek, 2008; Johar, 2012). Critics argue such advertising contributes to high health-care costs, weakens doctor–patient relationships, adds to an unnecessary demand for drugs, and oversimplifies complex health issues (Metzl, 2002; Huh, Delorme, & Reid, 2004; Grow, Park, & Han, 2006; Payton & Thoits, 2011).

Until the early 1980s, prescription drugs had been marketed almost exclusively to doctors. The justification was that consumers did not have the medical knowledge or experience to make decisions about prescriptions. However, cultural changes about patients' rights and the unquestioned authority of doctors in making medical decisions primed the political environment for the acceptance of advertising drugs directly to consumers. In 1985, the FDA loosened regulations (Donohue, 2006). Approved advertising, however, had to include the same information that ads for physicians contained: "a true statement of information in brief summary relating to side effects, contraindications and effectiveness" and a "fair balance" of both the drug's benefits and its risks (FDA/DHHS, 1969). By default, these requirements made it difficult to advertise drugs on television because the safety information could not fit into a television spot.

In 1997, the FDA released a new set of guidelines specifically for broadcast DTCA. These new guidelines suggested that the "brief summary" could be avoided as long as the ad provided information on major side effects and contraindications and gave viewers a way to access the rest of the information. Ads could refer consumers to web pages, a corresponding print ad in a magazine, a toll-free number, and/ or their pharmacists and physicians. These loosened restrictions resulted in drug companies dedicating more of their marketing budgets to television advertising, and less to print (Eaton, 2004, p. 430).

DTCA for prescription drugs is legal only in the United States and New Zealand. Online, however, there are no national borders.

Micro Issues

1. Should pharmaceutical companies develop distinct standards for adverting drugs via social media?
2. Is the omission of a drug's potential risks deceptive?
3. To whom do celebrity endorsers such as Kim Kardashian-West owe loyalty? To the drug manufacturer? To readers or viewers?

Midrange Issues

1. DTCA is legal only in two countries but can be accessed almost anywhere online. What legal restrictions, if any, should be enacted for such advertising online?
2. Evaluate the claim "bad publicity is good publicity" in the context of direct-to-consumer ads.
3. Do drugs constitute a different category of advertised product, and hence require different sorts of standards/regulations compared with other consumer goods? How are drugs like or unlike tobacco and beer, both products whose advertising is more stringently regulated?

Macro Issues

1. How things are sold—the advertising appeal—is one of the enduring ethical issues in advertising. Evaluate the appeal in the original Instagram ad.
2. Does the use of a celebrity endorsement change the nature of direct-to-consumer drugs ads? Why?
3. Does the original ad pass the TARES test? Could any social media ad pass the TARES test?
4. Media organizations now make a great deal of money on the DTCA of drugs. Evaluate the impact of this revenue stream on potential decision-making about printing/broadcasting such ads.

CASE 7-E

BETWEEN A (KID) ROCK AND A HARD PLACE

MOLLY SHOR
Wayne State University

On Sept. 2, 2017, the *Detroit Free Press* published an opinion piece by editorial writer and Pulitzer Prize-winning journalist Stephen Henderson. In his editorial, Henderson questions whether Kid Rock was an appropriate choice for the opening concert at Detroit's Little Caesars Arena, which was built with significant taxpayer support in a city with a large black population.

Henderson wrote:

This is a musician who got rich off crass cultural appropriation of black music, who used to wrap his brand in the Confederate flag—a symbol inextricably linked to racism, no matter what its defenders say—and who has repeatedly issued profane denouncements of the very idea of African Americans pushing back against American inequality.

Henderson called the opening of the arena with Kid Rock as public representative "tone deaf." He not only condemned Kid Rock as spokesperson for such a public opening but also questioned the public and political sensitivity of the Illitch family. As owners of the new arena, and as operators of the Olympia Entertainment Division, the Illitch organization was responsible for booking the concert.

"Having Kid Rock open this arena is erecting a sturdy middle finger to Detroiters—nothing less," Henderson wrote. "And the Ilitches, who've done so much for this city and also taken so much from it, should be the last to embrace that kind of signaling."

In response to the *Detroit Free Press* editorial, Kid Rock's representatives pulled the press credentials for the paper, limiting the newspaper's access to report on the concert and the much-anticipated opening of the arena (Gross, 2017). Journalists still would have access to the concert by buying a ticket and attending with the general public.

Numerous press outlets reported the retaliatory action. In many of the subsequent stories, Kirt Webster, Kid Rock's publicist, said the reason for denying access was that the *Detroit Free Press* "wrote a fucked-up story and allowed it to be published" (Herreria, 2017). The publicist also contended that the paper did not fact-check the article, nor did Henderson report about Kid Rock's local charitable giving. Webster claimed that their response to the article was to show that they would not "reward bad behavior" (Greenwood, 2017).

While the regional editor of the *Detroit Free Press* clarified that Henderson's column was an opinion piece, he also defended the paper's news coverage of the arena opening (Greenwood, 2017).

Webster shuttered his public-relations firm in November 2017 following sexual harassment claims, which he said were egregious and untrue.

Micro Issues

1. Was it reasonable or fair for Kid Rock's representatives to pull the *Detroit Free Press* credentials in response to commentary that they deemed less than favorable?
2. Kid Rock is a musician who uses his art as a platform for uninhibited public speech. Should he therefore be held to a higher standard regarding issues such as media access?
3. Should a hometown newspaper be held to a different standard than a national newspaper when covering local celebrities and civic events?

Midrange Issues

1. Compare this incident to Disney banning the *Los Angeles Times* from movie press screenings following the newspaper's investigation into Disney's Anaheim business dealings.
2. To whom does Kirt Webster owe loyalty? To whom does Kid Rock owe loyalty?

3. What do you see as the differences in getting excluded from a sporting event or public performance and a news event such as a press conference?

Macro Issues

1. What are the options for a newsroom that gets shut out of an event? Do you include that fact in your reporting of the event? Does it become a separate story?
2. Many news outlets have forums for opinion, including editorial pages, on-air commentaries labeled as such, and so on, and one of the oldest tenets of journalism is the independence of this role from outside pressure, whether newsmakers or advertisers. If these clearly labeled opinions begin to affect the ability of reporters to get access to news, what do you do?

CASE 7-F

WAS THAT AN APPLE COMPUTER I SAW? PRODUCT PLACEMENT IN THE UNITED STATES AND ABROAD

PHILIP PATTERSON
Oklahoma Christian University

Michael Scott, the buffoon-like office manager in the Emmy Award-winning NBC comedy *The Office*, shows up at casual Friday encouraging his shocked employees to check out his backside in his new Levi's jeans. In the wildly popular ABC drama/comedy *Desperate Housewives*, Gabrielle (played by Eva Longoria) gets desperate enough for cash to model beside a Buick LaCrosse at a car show and for a mattress firm. In the now-cancelled *American Dreams*, which portrayed American life in the 1960s, such American icons as Campbell's Soup and the Ford Mustang were woven into the show.

Hollywood calls it "brand integration." Its critics—some of them the very writers for shows using product placement—call it much worse. But by any name, the phenomenon is growing. During the 2004–2005 television season, more than 100,000 actual products appeared in American network television (up 28 percent in one year), according to Nielsen Media Research, generating $1.88 billion (up 46 percent in a year) according to PQ Media (Manly, 2005). Advertising agencies have set up product placement divisions. Research organizations have cropped up to take on the task of measuring the effectiveness of product placement. And television shows in the United States seem to have an insatiable appetite for what they offer.

"The fact is, these brands are part of our lives, and brands exist in these television environments, so why not showcase them," said Ben Silverman, chief executive of the firm that produces *The Office* (Manly, 2005, A14).

However, not everyone is pleased. In a 2005 meeting in New York during "Advertising Week," television writers protested outside a panel discussing the state of brand integration in television programming. Among their gripes, they want more of a say in how products will be placed and, inevitably, a share of the profits generated from writing a product into the script.

Most see the move as one of survival. Taking a cue from radio and its "soap operas," the original television shows were named for the sponsors (*The Colgate Comedy Hour* and *Texaco Star Theater*), and the audience had little option but to watch the ads. While commercials undergirded the television industry for the first 50 years, the advent of the remote and, more recently, TiVo has allowed consumers to avoid the very commercials that make the programming free.

"The advertising model of 10 years ago is not applicable today," according to Bruce Rosenblum, president of Warner Bros. Television Group. "At the end of the day, if we are unable to satisfy advertisers' appetites to deliver messages in new ways to the viewer, then we're destined to have a broken model" (Manly, 2005, A14).

However, for government-sponsored television in Europe, the practice of product placement remains a sticky issue.

In a 2005 edition of *Spooks*, a BBC drama, a logo for an Apple computer appeared in early airings of the show and then was removed in subsequent showings after British print media alleged that the Apple logo and others had slipped into BBC programming in exchange for cash and favors, which violates BBC rules. In Germany, firings occurred after public broadcaster ARD was found to have had shows full of illegal product placements for years (Pfanner, 2005).

Not every European country has such a ban. In Austria, public broadcaster ORF airs more than 1,000 product placements a year on its shows, which provides ORF with about $24 million in funds to supplement its budget of approximately $1 billion. ORF says that allowing the placements actually regulates what happens anyway.

"If you don't regulate it, it exists anyway, in a gray zone," said Alexander Wrabetz, chief financial officer for ORF (Pfanner, 2005, A15).

And even within the BBC, which has not announced any intent to change its ban on product placement, there are differing opinions. One BBC executive, speaking to the *International Herald Tribune* off the record, said, "Back in the '50s, everything was called Acme, or we stuck stickers over all the brand names. There isn't a TV company in the world that does that now. Viewers don't find it convincing" (Pfanner, 2005, A15).

Ultimately, success in product placement still comes down to whether the placement fits the plot.

"The needle we have to thread," according to Johnathan Prince, creator of *American Dreams* and now working on Madison Avenue, "is to have brand integration that is effective enough to have resonance, but . . . subtle enough so that it doesn't offend" (Manly, 2005, A16).

Micro Issues

1. Would you personally prefer to go back to the days where made-up names such as "Acme" were placed on products to conceal the true brand names of the products?
2. Does the authenticity that real products such as name-brand computers bring to a television show outweigh the intrusiveness of inserting a product into the plot of a show?
3. Are products placed into television shows the "price" you pay for free television, just as watching 30-second commercials were the "price" your parents and grandparents paid?

Midrange Issues

1. News magazines such as *Newsweek* will often run multipage special sections on issues such as "Women's Health," and all of the ads within the section will be for products promoting women's health. What do you see as the difference between this practice and product placement on television shows?
2. Do you see a difference in whether product placement should occur in scripted dramas and comedies as opposed to reality television?
3. How does product placement in television shows differ from naming sports stadiums or college bowl games after corporate sponsors, where presumably they will be mentioned on air for free during newscasts? Should newscasters avoid the corporate names of these places and events?

4. When a news show ends with rolling credits that attribute the wardrobe of the anchor to a certain store, is that product placement? Is that an intrusion on the objectivity of the news? Justify your answers.

Macro Issues

1. If consumers are "zapping" and "TiVo-ing" through commercials in free television, what will happen to the medium if product placement fails to deliver the needed revenue to keep the programming free? What will happen to the United States if free television is eliminated?
2. In trying to "thread the needle" between effectiveness and offensiveness, what are some of the guidelines you would write for product placement?
3. Is the argument made by Wrabetz in this case an ethical one? Compare the argument to the five standards of the TARES test found in this chapter and see how it measures up.

8

Picture This

Technology, Visual Information, and Evolving Standards

By the end of this chapter, you should be familiar with

- the problems with deepfake technology as it is used in persuasion and entertainment;
- the ethical problems of point of view, file footage, and "eyewash";
- the conundrum of open-source journalism.

Human beings trust what they see. As a species, it's been to our evolutionary advantage to do so. This willingness to trust what we see is what adds to the power of images—both still and moving. However, almost as soon as it was possible to permanently capture an image, a human effort that emerged in the world of fine art but, in the 19th century, began to include the earliest versions of photography, the truthfulness of the image became the focus of debate.

In this early part of the 21st century, we find ourselves in the era of deepfakes, the most recent permutation of fake news (discussed in chapter 2 of this book). In some ways, deepfakes are a 21st-century version of photoshopping, or what was referred to in the 20th century as electronic manipulation. Photo manipulation has a long history, beginning with such crude drawing-board techniques as cropping with scissors and paste and darkroom techniques such as "burning," "dodging," and airbrushing. Technology has made the word "photography"—it literally means "writing with light"—obsolete, as a lighted reality no longer need exist in order for a "photograph" to be created.

Today, deepfakes use a form of artificial intelligence called "deep learning" to render moving images of fake events. For example, you may have seen Jon Snow's moving—and deepfaked—apology for what some thought was the dismal ending of the hit television series *Games of Thrones*. Deepfake technology also can create entirely fictional moving images. Audio can be deepfaked via what is called "voice skins" or "voice clones"—and is most often of public figures. In March 2019, an executive of a UK subsidiary of a German energy firm paid more than $250,000 into a Hungarian bank account after being phoned by a fraudster who mimicked his boss's voice through an audiofake. Similar scams have reportedly been used with WhatsApp.

Philosophically, deepfakes ask us to reconsider how we define truth. As noted in chapter 2, how we define truth has changed through human history. For Plato, the entire concept of deepfakes would have been meaningless because he considered all of what the 21st century defines as reality no more real than the shadows on the wall of a cave. A deepfake would have been another kind of shadow, irrelevant to the concept of the "perfect form." For those of us who have lived in the 20th and 21st centuries, deepfakes challenge two of our contemporary notions of truth: the correspondence theory of truth and the coherence theory of truth, also discussed in chapter 2. Because the human species is so reliant on what it sees for the acts of daily living (think of hunting for food as one example or what we find physically beautiful as another), providing us with compelling visual information that cannot be easily verified or discounted asks us to act in ways counter to daily routines. Deepfakes should correspond to the reality we see; the fact that they do not makes them difficult to dismiss, especially in real time. In fact, deepfakes take advantage of another human trait: People function as cognitive misers, and moving images can overwhelm cognitive capacity, particularly on ethical decisions (Meader, Knight, Coleman, & Wilkins, 2015).

Deepfakes also play havoc with the coherence theory of truth. If you accept a web of information that suggests that people (for example, film stars) will act in a certain way when playing a particular part, a deepfake of that actor in that role—even though physical presence was not possible—becomes acceptable. Diet Coke played with this notion of the coherence theory of truth in the mid-1990s when it photoshopped the images of Hollywood stars of bygone eras into a commercial to dance with Paula Abdul. The result, which actually became the focus of a NOVA special, was both entertaining and commercially successful. However, if you did not have a memory of Groucho Marx (who died before almost everyone reading this book was born), then the guy with the mustache and cigar in that commercial was simply a goofy placeholder, not a creative approach to product sales.

As of this writing, making a deepfake is far from easy or inexpensive. Deepfakes require not only substantial computing power but also expertise. Some deepfakes employ a generative adversarial network, or GAN. This network employs two different artificial intelligence algorithms. The first is fed a stream of "random noise," the second a stream of real images. As the two algorithms "talk" to each other, a process that is repeated quickly and countless times, both algorithms improve until the first—the one that began with random noise—is producing realistic faces or completely nonexistent celebrities. One study found that in 2019 there were about 14,000 deepfake videos circulating online (Panyatham, 2020).

At their current level of sophistication, deepfakes are profitable in two entirely distinct ways. The first is in the entertainment industry, where deepfake technology has been used to recreate images of celebrities who have died while in the midst of significant projects. Disney studios are continuing to experiment with deepfakes that currently are not quite ready for the big screen because of the number of pixels involved in screen-sized images. Digital effect studios such as Industrial Light and Magic are convinced that the technology will eventually save time and money on postproduction. However, the profits from Hollywood are dwarfed by another major and enormously profitable use of deepfake technology: pornography. The AI firm Deeptrace found 15,000 deepfake videos online in September 2019, more than 96 percent of which were pornographic and 99 percent of those deepfakes mapped the faces of female celebrities onto the bodies of porn stars. This use of the technology, asserts Boston University law professor Danielle Citron, is being "weaponized against women."

Photos and video have been what photography researcher Shiela Reaves (1987) called a "controlled liquid." Writing in the infancy of computer manipulation of photography, Reaves foresaw a time when photos would lose their "moral authority." Marshall McLuhan (1964) said more than 70 years ago in his book *Understanding Media* that there would come a time when images would replace bullets in warfare. The power of images is so overwhelming that the George W. Bush administration banned the presence of press photographers at the Air Force base where flag-draped coffins containing the remains of soldiers killed in action in Iraq and Afghanistan arrived almost daily. One military contractor and her husband lost their jobs in Kuwait for leaking such a photo and ultimately allowing it to be run in the *Seattle Times*. Deepfakes of Speaker of the House Nancy Pelosi and former Secretary of State Hillary Clinton have been used as political fundraising vehicles and in campaign commercials.

The war that employs images is a war against trust, an effort to create a zero-trust society where people cannot or no longer bother to distinguish truth from falsehood. The erosion of trust makes it easy to raise doubts about specific events. In 2018, Amnesty International asserted that it had a video that showed Cameroon's soldiers executing civilians. Cameroon's minister of communication dismissed the video as "fake news." As the technology becomes more widespread, deepfakes could be used as evidence in court, particularly in child custody disputes. There are security risks as well; deepfakes can mimic biometric data or otherwise fool systems that rely on facial or voice recognition. "The problem may not be so much the faked reality as the fact that real reality becomes plausibly deniable," notes Professor Lilian Edward of Newcastle University (Sample, 2020).

Spotting a deepfake is not easy, but there are "tells" that the technology is being employed. Among them are these:

- In 2018, US researchers discovered that deepfaked faces don't blink normally, although the technology is developing to mimic "blinks."
- Lip-synching may be "off" or skin tones uneven; inconsistent or strange lighting effects can be another giveaway.
- Fine details such as hair also can be hard to render realistically, as can poorly copied jewelry or teeth.
- Snopes and other websites devoted to the detection of "fake news" also can be used to spot deepfakes. For a fuller checklist on spotting fake news, see chapter 2 of this book.

STREET TAPES AND THE CITIZEN AS PHOTOJOURNALIST: DO WE NEED OPEN-SOURCE ETHICS?

The contrast to deepfakes could not be more evident than found in street tapes: video, most often shot with cell phones, of potentially historic or newsworthy events. Most often street tapes are shot by citizens, sometimes at significant personal risk. Think about the person who, instead of sheltering from the hurricane, tornado, or wildfire, is shooting a cell-phone video of those events and uploading it to Facebook, YouTube, the Weather Channel, or the local television outlet or newspaper. Or the journalists working for those organizations, including storm chasers, one of whom was killed chasing an Oklahoma tornado in 2017.

The most devastating street tapes have been those that document police brutality, including the more than eight-minute tape of the death of George Floyd despite pleas from passersby for the officers to relent in their treatment of him. The George Floyd street tape has a history. In 1992, it was an amateur video, aired first on local and then on national television news, of Rodney King, who was Black, being beaten by uniformed Caucasian police officers. That video, and the subsequent acquittal of the officers, set off a rash of riots in Los Angeles. Since that date, amateur images have chronicled, and sometimes influenced, history. The conditions at Abu Ghraib in Iraq, where prisoners were tortured by US troops, was brought to light by amateur photography "leaked" to investigative reporter Seymour Hersh. In 2010, protests in Tunisia captured by street tapes became one catalyst for the Arab Spring movement. Cell-phone video has captured and then publicized acts of racism by private citizens and public officials alike.

The professional reason for this reliance on visuals is compelling. Study after study has confirmed that newspaper photographs attract reader attention more than even the biggest headlines. Television producers stack newscasts based, in part, on which stories have video and which do not, and stories without any art sometimes do not make the newscast. Public relations professionals now routinely supply video as part of story pitches, particularly for the sorts of stories where journalistic access can be difficult (for example, the coverage of medical news or medical treatments). Eye-catching video on the internet is one of the things that leads to clicks, likes, and sharing. Nowhere is the concept of citizen journalist more accepted than in photography and videography. Cutbacks in photo budgets became a common way for traditional print media to cut costs. In May 2013, the *Chicago Sun-Times* laid off its entire full-time photography staff—including a Pulitzer Prize winner and about 28 photographers. Photojournalism is now a profession staffed almost entirely with freelancers. People are drawn to visuals and, in an era of shrinking staffs, the demand for them from nonprofessional sources has only increased.

Difficult questions emerge. For instance, when a man drove a car into a group of activists in Charlottesville, Virginia, killing one and injuring 19 others, the raw and unedited video of the racially charged violence was available almost immediately online—well before the families of the victims had been notified. Similarly, the mass shooter in Christchurch, New Zealand, livestreamed his attack on Facebook Live. The ethical problems here are not novel. As *Newsweek*'s David Ansen (2006) wrote in his review of the 2006 film *Flags of Our Fathers*, which focused on World War II propaganda:

> What the Pentagon didn't foresee, and couldn't control was the rise of new media—the unfiltered images popping up on the Web, the mini-TV cams put in the hands of soldiers that emerge in the recent documentary, *The War Tapes*. We don't see much of the real war on network TV, but the unauthorized documentaries—*The Ground Truth, Gunner Palace* and many more—come pouring out. . . . It's been the "unofficial media" that have sabotaged the PR wizards in the Pentagon. The sophistication of the spinners has been matched by the sophistication of a media-savvy public. (p. 71)

In the past, the most instantaneous ethical decision in photography was "Shoot or don't shoot?" Garry Bryant (1987), a staff photographer with the *Deseret News* of Salt Lake City, offers the following checklist he goes through "in hundredths of a second" when he reaches the scene of tragedy:

1. Should this moment be made public?
2. Will being photographed send the subjects into further trauma?
3. Am I at the least obtrusive distance possible?
4. Am I acting with compassion and sensitivity?

To this list Bryant adds the following disclaimer:

What society needs to understand is that photographers act and shoot instinctively. We are not journalists gathering facts. We are merely photographers snapping pictures. A general rule for most photojournalists is "Shoot. You can always edit later." (p. 34)

Today, the question has added layers: "Post or don't post?" Or: "Go live or not?" Or: "Can we trust this amateur video?" Decisions that once could be made in the relative calm of the newsroom after a dramatic tragedy now must be made in the field in an increasingly competitive media environment.

The contribution of citizen journalists via street tapes is changing the relationship between journalists and their audiences. After the 2005 subway bombings in London, the perpetrators were identified in part through the use of the more than 1,000 images passengers on the city's underground captured with their cell phones and forwarded to police. Those images also became part of the news. Richard Sambrook of the BBC noted, "People were participating in our coverage in a way that we had never seen before. By the next day, our main evening TV newscast began with a package edited entirely from video sent in by viewers. From now on news coverage is a partnership" (Reuters Institute for the Study of Journalism, 2015).

However, ethical questions of whether it is appropriate for street tapes and cell-phone images to become evidence in police investigations, especially after they have been broadcast as part of news reports, has now become more urgent. Historically, journalists have maintained that they are not an arm of law enforcement. The professional photographer who attempts to perform an ethical triage at the scene of a tragedy might find his career in jeopardy, and that photographer also has failed to capture some of the truth for the reader or viewer. The citizen photojournalist may wrestle with issues of privacy while taking cell-phone video. Both are wrestling with the dilemma of treating every subject as an end and not merely a means to an end.

Some scholars are suggesting that ethical standards, once the exclusive purview of professionals, should in this age of the internet be open-sourced (Ward & Wasserman, 2010). What that means is that ethical standards regarding important issues such as free press/fair trial, exploitation, and privacy would be arrived at through a dialogue with audience members as well as journalists, public relations professionals, and others. What is acceptable in persuasive messages should be the focus of open dialogue between strategic communications professionals, the organizations for which they work, their clients, and their audiences.

Warren Bovée (1991), in an essay entitled "The Ends Can Justify the Means—But Rarely," offers this set of questions to help the photographer—citizen or professional—find the answer:

1. Are the means truly morally evil or merely distasteful, unpopular, and so forth?
2. Is the end a *real* good or something that merely *appears* to be good?
3. Is it probable that the means will achieve the end?
4. Is the same good possible using other means? Is the bad means being used as a shortcut to a good end when other methods would do?
5. Is the good end clearly greater than any evil means used to attain it?
6. Will the means used to achieve the end withstand the test of publicity?

Whether open-sourced ethics is a good idea in philosophical terms, open-source journalism such as street tapes—particularly if it is managed by a more traditional news organization—faces the same ethical tests as more traditional photography does. The premiums are accuracy, fairness, and originality, standards that are no different from those that apply to strategic communication.

SEEING IS BELIEVING: THE PHILOSOPHICAL ISSUES IN POINT OF VIEW

As Arthur Berger points out in *Seeing Is Believing* (1989), because of the many variables in photography—camera angles, use of light, texture, and focus—a picture is always an *interpretation* of reality, not reality itself. He adds that a dozen photographers taking pictures of the same scene would produce different views of the reality of it.

Not only does the camera differ from the eye in its ability to manipulate angle, light, and focus, but cameras also capture an isolated reality by presenting us with a slice of life, free from context. In *About Looking*, John Berger says:

What the camera does, and what the eye can never do, is to fix the appearance of that event. The camera saves a set of appearances from the otherwise inevitable supersession of further appearances. It holds them unchanging. And before the invention of the camera nothing could do this, except in the mind's eye, the faculty of memory. (1980, p. 14)

What the camera—or cell phone—does is provide us with a "point of view"—a physical stance that allows us to see events from a certain perspective. Think about a common local news story—a house fire. Video of that fire will focus on the building that is in flames, the firefighters' efforts, the aftermath. It will not include the rest of the homes on the block—providing they are not on fire, too. Those images are taken from a point of view, and the videographers who shoot them believe that the audience members who see them will understand that the entire block is not on fire. Most often, if the news story is a local house fire, believing that the audience will fix the event in a single geographic context is a good assumption. However, take the local out of the story, and something strange begins to happen to how it is understood. Colorado wildfires are not burning up the entire state. However, residents of other states who see the images, which focus only on the fire itself and those neighborhoods that are threatened or which have been destroyed, can and do believe that the devastation is much more widespread. This does not mean the devastation is not profound, merely that there are enormous parts of the state that are not on fire. In this instance, the point of view of the camera has obscured the complexity and context of the wildfire story.

Telling stories from a point of view is not the exclusive province of the visual portion of the business. Print writers, creative nonfiction writers, those who write memoirs, and most documentarians all exercise point of view. And some of the best journalism written and reported in the past 100 years has succeeded precisely because it adopted a point of view that was outside the mainstream. One such example is one of Gloria Steinem's first magazine stories, "I Was a Playboy Bunny," itself controversial because Steinem went undercover to report the story, including using a false name and deducting four years from her age to get the job. Steinem wrote the seemingly biographical piece when she worked for a month in the New York Playboy Club, and the details she was able to include are among the things that made the piece a success. Readers today sometimes assert that all Steinem did was to chronicle her own experience. However, the piece actually was built on dozens of interviews in addition to Steinem's own observations. Her point of view allowed for new questions to emerge, but she sought the experiences of others as she was analyzing her own. As Steinem said much later in her career, the role of journalism is to get the truth, but first, it's going to piss you off.

Journalism provides context for the ubiquitous images created by professionals and amateurs alike. It's not enough, from an ethical standpoint, to say, "Here's what happened" to an audience that probably knows the news before the newscast airs or the newspaper story goes live online. The audience also knows that photos and video are easily manipulated. Because of this technological context, journalists must say, "Here's why we believe this happened the way you are seeing it."

ENDURING ISSUES: STAGING PHOTOGRAPHS AND VIDEO

Photographer John Szarkowski (1978) writes of "mirror" and "window" photographs, and his 1978 Museum of Modern Art show was entitled "Mirrors and Windows." These two types of photos are also roughly analogous to realistic and romantic photography. According to Szarkowski, window photographs should be as objective a picture of reality as the medium will allow, untouched by the bias of the lens or the photographer. However, the mirror photograph attempts to subjectively recreate the world in whatever image suits the photographer. Anything can be manipulated: light, proportion, setting, even subject.

Each type of photography has a function. A large percentage of the government-commissioned Dust Bowl-era photographs that have seared our memories of the Depression would fit into the mirror category. Photographers searched for settings, posed people, and shifted props to achieve the maximum effect. However, the photos that show us the horrors of war and famine, and arouse public opinion, are windows, where the photographer captures the moment with no attempts to alter it.

The problem comes in the substitution of one for the other. When a photograph has been staged for greater effect, yet is passed off as a window on reality, the viewer has been deceived. Iconic photos such as the Marines raising the flag at Iwo Jima or the young girl crying over the body of the dead student shot by the Ohio National Guard on the campus of Kent State University have been debated for decades about whether they were spontaneous and contextually correct photos. Again, the rise of citizen photojournalists has exacerbated this problem.

"Your work sounds interesting." Francesca said. She felt a need to keep neutral conversation going.

"It is. I like it a lot. I like the road, and I like making pictures."

She noticed he'd said "making" pictures. "You make pictures, not take them?"

"Yes. At least that's how I think of it. That's the difference between Sunday snapshooters and someone who does it for a living. When I'm finished with that bridge

we saw today, it won't look quite like you expect. I'll have made it into something
of my own, by lens choice, or camera angle, or general composition or all of those.
   "I don't just take things as given; I try to make them into something that reflects
my personal consciousness, my spirit. I try to find the poetry in the image."
                                   —Robert James Waller, *The Bridges of Madison County*

Most editors and photographers agree that manipulation or staging of *news photos* is generally more culpable than manipulation or staging of *feature photos,* and this is regardless of source. During the 2003 war in Iraq, Brian Walski, a photojournalist for the *Los Angeles Times*, was fired for combining two similar photographs into one more aesthetically pleasing version. Today, you can find the original photos and the blended composition online. While the resulting photo was so similar to the "real" ones that the difference originally escaped the eye of the *Times* photo editor, a line had been crossed, and the photographer was dismissed.

Walski later told a colleague that "I went from the front line for the greatest newspaper in the world, and now I have nothing. No cameras, no car, nothing" (Irby, 2003).

The reason for the different standard for news photography is a presupposition that *while art may be manipulated, information may not* (Martin, 1991). The problem for audiences is compounded by the fact that entertainment, strategic communication, and the non-news sections of newspapers and magazines make frequent use of these techniques. Confusion over what is appropriate in one context and not another is bound to occur. However, for strategic communication to be effective, it needs to rely on truth, something codes of ethics in many public relations organizations emphasize.

SELECTIVE EDITING

Another ethical question centers on the video editing process: whether editing itself renders a story untrue or unfair. Actually, the term "selective editing" is redundant. *All* editing is selective. The issue is who does the selecting and what predispositions they bring to the process.

A dual standard has emerged between words and photos. The writer is allowed to reorder facts and rearrange details into an inverted-pyramid story on the rationale that the reader wants the most important facts taken out of sequence, and even out of context, and placed first in the story for more efficient reading. The result is praised as good writing and is taught in every journalism program.

However, should a photographer attempt to do the same thing with a camera—rearrange reality to make a more interesting photo or video—the result is called "staged." Our unwillingness to allow visual journalists the same conventions as print journalists says something fundamental about the role of visuals in the news. When a writer edits, it makes for a more readable story, and the act is applauded. When a photographer or video editor does the same thing, he or she is open to accusations of distortion.

That is because we evaluate news photos according to print standards: linear and logical. Yet video and photographs are neither. They have a quality Marshall McLuhan called "allatonceness"—or a cessation of time and space, an all-at-once quality—that we are not quite comfortable with as a technology.

However, as long as readers think that "seeing is believing," that view—whether based in reality or not—becomes a promise between the media and their audiences that photographers and videographers should be hesitant to break. While many photojournalists argue that "seeing is believing" should have never been a cultural truism (Lester, 1992), others argue that we must work within our readers' or viewers' predispositions about the truth of what they see.

In the wake of a large number of entries at the 2015 World Press photo competition being disqualified for having manipulated photos, including the revocation of one first prize, the *New York Times* interviewed several leading photographers in an essay entitled "Staging, Manipulation and Truth in Photography" (*New York Times*, 2015). Their questioning of several of the nation's leading photographers revealed a substantial gap between the various codes of ethics that govern photojournalists and photojournalism contests and what happens in the real world. Stanley Green, a photojournalist and co-founder of Noor Images, told the *Times*, "Setting up photos, where they are completely staged is very widespread. I've seen it done by very well-known photographers." He added, "It seems the honor system is not working."

A 2015 survey answered by more than 1,500 photographers worldwide for the Reuters Institute for the Study of Journalism and the World Press Photo Foundation (Hadland, Campbell, & Lambert, 2015) showed an interesting mix of results on the major ethical questions in the industry. More than three-quarters of those responding said that manipulating or altering photos is wrong and an equal number claimed to have "never" done it; however, more than half of all those responding said they "sometimes" manipulate photos, such as asking people to do actions again or wait to do actions until the photographer is ready. Twelve percent said they did so "at least half the time." While virtually every respondent agreed that the ethical standards of the profession were important, the researchers concluded that they were not always followed in the field.

EYEWASH

Imagine a new government study is released on compulsive gamblers, and you are told to make it into a video package for tonight's news. You might show a woman enjoying herself on a sunny afternoon at the races. Or a man sitting at a slot machine in a casino. While each of their actions takes place in public view, they might or might not be a victim of the syndrome addressed in the article. In this context, the photo is serving the purpose of "eyewash," decoration for a story that bears no genuine relationship to it (see figure 8.1).

While the courts have been ambiguous on the matter of eyewash, the media have created divergent policies to cover the issue. Some newspapers and television stations, for instance, will use no picture not directly related to the story. Others limit the use of file or stock footage to that which is clearly labeled. Others limit the shooting of eyewash only by insisting that it occur in public view.

AESTHETICS AND ETHICS

Taste in spot news photography has been an issue almost from the very start of field photography during the Civil War. For years, newspapers and morning television news shows used the "Post Toasties Test" to determine the photos or video that accompanied early morning news stories. The test gets its name from a popular breakfast cereal and is a sensitivity test for media that might be at the breakfast table, from newspapers to television and even websites. The test asked the question "Does this need to be shown at breakfast?" Or "Should children see this over their morning breakfast?"

However, according to Louis Hodges (1997), no photographer or photo editor has identified "what exactly what we mean by 'in bad taste.' The closest they come is to note that people do not want bloody pictures at the breakfast table."

Figure 8.1. Calvin and Hobbes © 1992 Watterson. Reprinted with permission of Andrews McMeel Syndication. All rights reserved.

Hodges argues that many issues in visual journalism that appear to be lapses in ethics are actually differences in opinion over matters of aesthetics—the ancient Greek branch of philosophy that considered beauty and what is beautiful and also whether beauty could be objectified or codified so that everyone could agree on its qualities. Hodges suggests that many works that are considered "unethical" are often merely "unbeautiful," adding that it may be easier to discern what is unethical than what is ugly. Hodges uses this illustration:

> The mushroom cloud from the atomic bomb, for example, has always appeared beautiful to me. Those pictures led to moral rejoicing that the war was about over, and my father would soon be coming home. For others, the cloud is symbolic of human evil, power and inhumanity.

An agreement on aesthetics is one of the most difficult in all of philosophy. Modern philosopher Elmer Duncan (1970) claims that even if we agree on the principles of "goodness" in aesthetics in art (e.g., a "good" painting should have balance and unity), we would not be able to definitely call it "good" or "bad" without committing what philosophers call the "naturalistic fallacy"—namely, that the "good" is a simple, irreducible concept that cannot be defined in terms of any other concept. When a photo or video is called "unethical" by viewers, it is often based on an indescribable quality inherent to the viewer and is neither shared universally nor defensible logically. It really is a matter of taste.

CONCLUSION

The debate over visual ethics is emotionally charged and entwined with technology. Simultaneously, the consumer of news photography is sometimes presented with a product too raw to be watched and at other times too polished to be believable. Visuals that accompany strategic communication messages often suffer from the reverse problem. Professionals should consider operating under this version of Kant's categorical imperative: *Don't deceive a trusting audience with manipulated reality and don't offend an unsuspecting audience with your gritty reality.* Photographers are dealing with a trust that readers and viewers have placed in them. If that trust is betrayed, it will be slow to return.

SUGGESTED READINGS

Berger, A. (1989). *Seeing is believing*. Mountain View, CA: Mayfield.
Berger, J. (1980). *About looking*. New York: Pantheon Books.

Journal of Mass Media Ethics. (1987). Spring–Summer. Special issue on photojournalism.

Lester, P. (1991). *Photojournalism: An ethical approach*. Hillsdale, NJ: Lawrence Erlbaum Associates.

Lester, P. (2003). *Images that injure*. 2nd edition. Westport, CT: Greenwood Press.

Newton, J. (2000). *The burden of visual truth: The role of photojournalism in mediating reality*. Hillsdale, NJ: Lawrence Erlbaum Associates.

Reuters Institute for the Study of Journalism (2015). How mobile phones are changing journalism practice in the 21st Century. Retrieved from http://www.reutersinstitute. politics.ox.ac.uk.

CASES

CASE 8-A

NEW YORK TIMES ENDS POLITICAL CARTOONS

CHAD PAINTER
University of Dayton

The *New York Times* announced that it would stop running daily political cartoons in its international edition on July 1, 2019.

The announcement followed public and internal backlash over an April 2019 cartoon by Portuguese cartoonist António Moreira Antunes. That cartoon, which originally was published in the Lisbon, Portugal, newspaper *Expresso*, depicted Israeli Prime Minister Benjamin Netanyahu as a guide dog leading a blind Donald Trump. Netanyahu was depicted wearing a blue Star of David dangling from his collar, and Trump was shown wearing a yarmulke.

Critics, including *Times*'s editorial writers such as Bret Stephens, blasted the cartoon for being anti-Semitic. The *Times* opinion editors wrote a statement saying, in part:

> Such imagery is always dangerous, and at a time when anti-Semitism is on the rise worldwide, it's all the more unacceptable. We have investigated how this happened and learned that, because of a faulty process, a single editor working without adequate oversight downloaded the syndicated cartoon and made the decision to include it on the Opinion page.

Editorial Page Editor James Bennet said in a statement that the *Times* would "continue investing in forms of opinion journalism, including visual journalism, that express nuance, complexity and strong voice from a diversity of viewpoints."

The *Times* previously ended political cartoons in its national US edition, though Jake Halpern and Michael Sloan won the 2018 Pulitzer Prize for editorial cartooning for their graphic-narrative series chronicling a Syrian refugee family as they adjusted to their new life in the United States.

Political cartoons often are controversial. For example, a 2018 Mark Knight cartoon in an Australian newspaper was decried as racist. He depicted a monstrous, animalistic Serena Williams with exaggeratingly large lips and ears throwing a temper tantrum by stomping on her tennis racket while her pacifier lies nearby. In September 2005, Muslims in Denmark and around the world protested—at times violently—after the Danish newspaper *Jyllands Posten* published 12 editorial cartoons depicting the Prophet Muhammad (a blasphemy in most Islamic traditions). The office of the French satirical paper *Charlie Hebdo* was firebombed in June 2011, and in January 2015 gunmen killed 12 people and injured 11 others after forcing their way into the paper's offices. *Charlie Hebdo* had reprinted the Danish cartoons and then continued to publish deliberately offensive anti-Islamic cartoons in subsequent years. Seven people were arrested in September 2020 after a man attacked two people outside the former *Charlie Hebdo* offices. The magazine, which is now housed in an undisclosed location, had republished some of the cartoons during the trial of the 2015 attackers.

In the United States, the Supreme Court generally has protected the free speech rights of political cartoonists. For example, the 1988 *Hustler v. Falwell* case centered on the parody ad "Jerry Falwell talks about his first time," which included having sex with his mother in an outhouse. Falwell was a prominent Southern Baptist preacher and founder of the "Moral Majority," a right-wing Christian political organization with ties to Ronald Reagan and the Republican Party. Falwell sued Larry Flynt, the publisher of the pornographic magazine *Hustler*, for intentionally inflicting emotional stress, but US Supreme Court Justice William Rehnquist ruled that there must be a free trade of ideas even if there is emotional distress. Rehnquist specifically wanted to protect political cartoons, which he held constituted an important forum for political discussion though they often were based on unfortunate physical traits or events.

Micro Issues

1. Was the *New York Times*'s decision to end political cartoons justified? Was it an overreaction?
2. Do you think the *New York Times* would have faced similar backlash if it described Netanyahu as a "guide dog leading a blind Donald Trump" instead of depicting it? Why or why not?
3. Canadian political cartoonist Michael de Adder was "let go" from Irving-owned Brunswick News Inc. just days after his cartoon depicting US President Donald Trump playing golf next to the bodies of two migrants went viral. He tweeted that, for the year before his firing, none of his Trump-focused cartoons had been selected for publication. Do these editorial actions constitute censorship of political speech? Contrast your answer to this question to how you evaluated the *Times*'s decision.

Midrange Issues

1. Is António Moreira Antunes's cartoon anti-Semitic? How might your answer change if it depicted a Muslim or another racial or religious minority?
2. In your opinion, what is the proper balance between free speech and decency? How is that balance different for a private individual, a celebrity, and a public official?
3. Compare and contrast the *Times*'s actions with those of the *Pittsburgh Post-Gazette*, which fired cartoonist Rob Rogers in 2018 following a series of anti-Trump cartoons.

Macro Issues

1. The first political cartoon in the United States was published in 1754. What, if anything, is lost if newspapers stop running political cartoons? Contrast the *Times*'s decision with other newspapers, including the *Washington Post*, that continue to publish political cartoons.
2. What would Immanuel Kant say about the *Times*'s decision to stop running political cartoons? What would John Stuart Mill say? A feminist ethicist?
3. How does a visual image of something—say an image of a particular deity—differ ethically from saying the same thing in words without images?

CASE 8-B

DID YOU MEME THAT? THE UNHOPPY LIFE OF PEPE THE FROG

LEE WILKINS
University of Missouri

Even the concept of "meme" is a mash-up. One base of the word comes from the Greek *mimema*, meaning that which is imitated. The second base is from English: the word *gene*, meaning biological, genetically influenced inheritance. Put the two together, and a meme is most commonly defined as an idea, behavior, or style that becomes a fad and spreads by means of imitation from person to person within a culture and often carries symbolic meaning representing a particular phenomenon or theme. Other definitions emphasize that the culture or behavior a meme represents is a "nongenetic" imitation. Still others emphasize that memes often are humorous, many with a satirical edge that melds elements of popular culture to generate a meaning.

There are websites that will help you build individual memes. Because memes are most often a composite of preexisting visual elements, it's not clear that they can be copyrighted as original work. However, they are widely shared. In fact, it's likely that your Twitter feed, Instagram account, or the text chains on your cell phone include multiple memes right now.

Because memes are visual, they are created to convey meaning without words. They are symbols, and it's the concept of symbol that's important for journalists and strategic communicators. Symbols seldom mean just one thing. They take advantage of the sort of creative vagueness that advertising practitioners have employed for decades. In fact, much of the meaning symbols produce originates in the mind of the audience members who perceive them. It's what you—the viewer—bring to the message. Or, as fictional Harvard University symbologist Robert Langdon notes in his lecture that opens the film *The Da Vinci Code*, the same symbol has been with humanity for millennia, but its meaning changes with history and context. What was a good luck symbol to the Egyptians—the swastika—becomes a symbol of hatred and death in the Third Reich.

Which brings us to Pepe the Frog.

The green dude was created by artist Matt Furie in 2005 as a comic depiction of one of the most common stereotypes of college life—drinking, eating pizza, smoking pot, and being harmlessly gross, especially when urinating. In fact, Pepe's original tagline—"feels good man"—emerged from the "what you do when you've had too much beer" activity. Pepe was amorphous and anthropomorphic, a sort of frog version of the frat boys in *Animal House*.

Pepe and his catchphrase became so popular by 2008 that new iterations of Pepe (none of them created by Furie) emerged: sad, smug, and angry. As Pepe moved across the internet in subsequent years, he was appropriated by denizens of some of its darker alleys, including 4chan, where Pepe was given a Hitler mustache and his catchphrase replaced with "Kill Jews Man." Pepe could be found dressed in an SS uniform, or a Ku Klux Klan robe and hood, or standing outside a burning World Trade Center dressed as an orthodox Jew.

Pepe then moved to Twitter, where he regularly posted messages supporting white nationalism and anti-immigrant views. During the 2016 election cycle, Donald Trump Jr. posted a photo on Instagram of himself and other Trump supporters as "The Deplorables"—a play on the film *The Expendables*. Pepe was included in the post.

In September 2016, the Anti-Defamation League designated Pepe a hate symbol. What was unique about Pepe is that his symbolic impact was confined almost exclusively to social media.

Furie, who was largely unaware of Pepe's evolution, was horrified at the designation because it was so far outside his original, non-hateful intent.

> To have it evolve into what it is today, it's a nightmare. . . . It's kind of my worst nightmare . . . to be tangled in forever with a symbol of hate. . . . I'm a life-long artist. Hate and racism couldn't be further from something on my radar. (Roy, 2016)

Furie stopped drawing Pepe about 2012, long before he became a hate symbol. Furie also looked for ways to rehabilitate Pepe's image, including filing lawsuits he could not afford because no one had figured out how to stop this sort of expropriation in an online world.

Pepe's story was chronicled in the 2020 documentary *Feels Good Man*. Director Arthur Jones said that he built the film to explore how a propaganda machine—in this case, the alt-right—made Furie and others feel unsure, dumb, and ridiculous. In the film, and in subsequent interviews, Furie shares his own frustration at trying to rehabilitate Pepe by flooding the internet with positive Pepe images. It was a largely futile effort, as those who had appropriated Pepe fought back to reclaim him from the "normies."

However, the film has a happier ending. Pepe was appropriated by pro-democracy demonstrators in Hong Kong in 2019, something the filmmakers and Furie himself did not anticipate. On Twitch in 2020, Pepe memes appeared to have become apolitical, until Pepe resurfaced on a T-shirt worn by one of the insurgents who invaded the US Capitol in January 2021.

Micro Issues

1. How much responsibility should Furie assume for Pepe? For the use of the altered images by others?
2. How do you define the concept of hate symbol? What ethical principles inform your decision?
3. What should photojournalists consider when photographing events where political symbols are a part of the background?

Midrange Issues

1. How are memes like and unlike the political cartoons described in Case 8-A?
2. Do you think memes should be copyrighted?
3. Examine section 230 of the 1996 Communications Decency Act. How might changing that section to make social media companies legally liable for their content have helped Furie?
4. Does the use of Pepe by those supporting democracy in Hong Kong rehabilitate the image for Americans?

Macro Issues

1. Watch the documentary *Feels Good Man*. Does seeing Pepe in historical context change your understanding of the concept of memes?
2. Scholars have suggested that media ethics needs to expand to include input from audience members. How should that proposal be evaluated in light of Pepe's history?
3. Few ethical theories examine the concept of creativity. Does creativity have a moral dimension? If so, what might that be?
4. Pepe was captured by the dark corners of the internet. Should such "corners" be allowed to continue to exist in the United States? What are the normative implications of your answer?

CASE 8-C

REMEMBER MY FAME: DIGITAL NECROMANCY
AND THE IMMORTAL CELEBRITY

SAMANTHA MOST
Wayne State University

In 2013, Universal Pictures put the production of its film *Furious 7* on hold after Paul Walker, one of the film's stars, died. Two years later, the movie was released to solid reviews while grossing more than $1 billion worldwide. To complete Walker's scenes, Universal asked Walker's brothers to fill in the role, using computer-generated imagery (CGI) to fuse Walker's facial image over body doubles. Walker's brothers provided voiceover for the character.

This concept actually wasn't new. Universal began using celebrity images posthumously in 1966 when the corporation sold merchandise depicting deceased actor Bela Lugosi in his portrayal of Count Dracula (Petty & D'Rozario, 2009).

Digital necromancy is the term used to describe the use of a deceased celebrity's likeness in many kinds of mediated messages. Films such as *Furious 7* and the *Star Wars* "backstory" *Rogue One* successfully resurrected the images of deceased actors—in those cases, Walker and Peter Cushing, respectively. In 2013, an ad for the whiskey brand Johnnie Walker Blue employed the image of Bruce Lee more than 40 years after his death to promote the product. Marilyn Monroe's image is widely used in ads.

Scholars note that the use of such images—which some have termed "delebs"—raises ethical questions. They note that the likeness of a dead celebrity is often less expensive to acquire and is a safe bet for maintaining a sound reputation that, in turn, means less potential blowback for a brand that inadvertently uses the image of a living celebrity who becomes caught up in some sort of scandal.

Micro Issues

1. Is there an ethical difference if the celebrity's family refuses to consent to the use of the image rather than cooperating with the effort, as was the case in *Furious 7*?
2. Should creative projects such as films be treated differently regarding the use of deceased celebrity images compared to

commercial projects such as ads? What philosophical theory justifies your response?
3. Is there an ethical distinction between selling a still image and an image that moves and speaks? Justify your answer.

Midrange Issues

1. In *Furious 7*, the producers justified the use of Walker's CGI image by noting that the use allowed the multi-episode plot to be brought to a conclusion, which fans expected. Evaluate this justification.
2. If the use of a "delebs" image was done poorly in a technological sense—in other words, if the use of the image was not made a seamless part of the film or advertising content—would that change your ethical evaluation?
3. Dead celebrities are cheaper to employ. Should this economic reality be a part of the justification for using such images?

Macro Issues

1. Digital necromancy raises issues of truth telling. Discuss those issues from the point of view of content creators and from the point of view of audience members. Refer to the conceptualizations of truth outlined in chapter 2.
2. Can a deceased celebrity make an authentic claim for the selling of a particular product?
3. In 1984, California passed the Celebrity Rights Act, which protected the rights of the deceased celebrity up to 50 years after his or her death (Petty & D'Rozario, 2009). Should the use of these sorts of images be legally constrained? Why?

CASE 8-D

PROBLEM PHOTOS AND PUBLIC OUTCRY

JON ROOSENRAAD
University of Florida

Campus police at the University of Florida were called on a Saturday to a dorm to investigate "a large amount of blood on the floor of a women's bathroom." According to police reports, they determined that the blood "appeared to have been from a pregnancy miscarriage" and began searching the dorm area. Sometime later a police investigator searching through a trash dumpster behind the dorm found bloody towels, plastic gloves, and a large plastic bag containing more towels and the body of a 6- to 7-pound female infant.

Police discovered no pulse. Rigor mortis had set in. After removing the body from the bag, the police briefly placed the body on a towel on the ground next to the dumpster. The photographer for the student paper, the *Independent Florida Alligator,* arrived at this time and photographed the body and dumpster.

Later on Saturday, the 18-year-old mother was found in her dorm bed and taken to the university's hospital. The hospital exam revealed "placenta parts and the umbilical cord in her," and she was released later in good health. A local obstetrician contacted about the case said that judging by the size of the infant, it was likely a miscarriage and not an abortion. The infant was determined to be about seven months developed.

The story began on the front page of the Monday issue, across the bottom of the page, under the headline "UF police investigate baby's death at dorm." It jumped inside to page 3 and was accompanied by the photo (see figure 8.2).

It was a dramatic photo, contrasting two well-dressed detectives and one uniformed policeman with the naked body and contrasting the fragile human form with the harsh metal dumpster filled with pizza and liquor boxes. The photo was played 7 by 5 inches.

The story was well written and the photo dramatic but likely offensive to many—potentially so offensive that the newspaper's staff debated most of Sunday about how to use it. The editor decided to run it, but, in an unusual move, she wrote an editor's column explaining why that appeared on the opinion page of the same issue. It showed a scene readers might expect but not on a college campus. It showed that supposedly sexually educated and sophisticated college students still need help. The editor wrote:

> Even with these legitimate reasons we did not run the picture on the front page. This is partially in response to our concern that we do not appear to be exploiting this picture to attract readers. . . . We also examined the photographer's negatives to see if there were any less graphic prints. . . . Is the message perceived by the reader worth the shock he or she experiences? After pondering what we feel is a very profound photo, we decided there is. This was a desperate act in an area of society where it is not expected. The picture shows it.

Figure 8.2. **Photo courtesy of the** *Independent Florida Alligator*. **Used with permission.**

The local daily covered the story Monday in a police brief. No photo ran. It was determined that the body was from a miscarriage. The woman involved left school. The campus paper got several letters critiquing its coverage of the story. Many chose to criticize the editors for running the photo, while some praised the staff for pointing out the problem and for listing places on campus where sex and pregnancy counseling was available. Some letters did both.

An example of some of the outrage over the running of the photo by the *Alligator* came from a female student who called the coverage "the most unnecessary, tactless piece of journalism I've ever encountered." Another letter from a male student called the photo "in poor taste and extremely insensitive." The writer added, "There are times when good, sound judgment must override 'hot' copy."

Perhaps the most pointed comment came from a female writer who added 24 other names to her letter. The letter stated:

> The incident *could* have been used to remind people that they need to take responsibility for their own sexuality. The story *could* have been used as a painful reminder that there are many un-educated, naïve people out there who need help. But, unfortunately, the *Alligator* chose to sensationalize the story with a picture, completely nullifying any lesson whatsoever that might have been learned.

Micro Issues

1. Should the photographer have taken the picture? Justify your answer.
2. Is this a legitimate story, and if so, does it belong on page 1?
3. If this was the only photo available, did the paper then have to run it?
4. Various letters to the editor called the photo "unnecessary," "tactless," and "insensitive." What would you say to those charges if you were on the staff?

Midrange Issues

1. Does running the photo inside lessen any criticism of poor taste? Did its placement mitigate any ethical criticism?
2. If the staff was so unsure, was the editor correct in writing a same-day rationale for its publication?
3. Critique the reasoning stated by the editor in running the photo. What moral philosophy, if any, would lead one to agree with the action?

Macro Issues

1. Should a paper play a story and photo such as this to crusade about a problem?
2. Is the perceived social value of such a picture worth more than the shock and criticism?
3. Was the writer correct in her assessment that the shock of the photo negated any good that might have been done by the story?
4. Should a campus newspaper have a different standard—of taste, play, news value—than a "regular" daily?

CASE 8-E

ABOVE THE FOLD: BALANCING NEWSWORTHY PHOTOS WITH COMMUNITY STANDARDS

JIM GODBOLD, MANAGING EDITOR
Eugene Register-Guard, Eugene, Oregon

JANELLE HARTMAN, REPORTER
Eugene Register-Guard, Eugene, Oregon

Author's Note: *On Nov. 10, 1993, a nightmare unfolded in Springfield, Oregon, a quiet town adjoining the university community of Eugene, as Alan McGuire held his 2-year-old daughter, Shelby, hostage in their house. By the end of the standoff, both were dead, and the media had captured some horrific photos.*

Seven children had died as a result of child abuse in Lane County, Oregon, in the 20 months prior to that day, and the media had just witnessed the eighth. Jim Godbold was the assistant managing editor of the Eugene Register-Guard *at the time. The remarks below are from an interview with him months after the event.*

Godbold: The call came over the police scanner shortly after noon. We responded to a hostage situation, a man holding someone at knifepoint in a Springfield neighborhood. We knew it was probably 20 minutes from the *Register-Guard* in the best of possible circumstances, so we really scrambled. Photographer Andy Nelson and police reporter Janelle Hartman went as fast as they could to the area.

We got there when the police were trying to set up a perimeter to get people away from the area. It was real pandemonium right when Andy arrived. The situation didn't unfold for more than a few minutes before there was a burst of flame inside the house that caught the attention of the police officers, and they immediately made the decision that they were going to have to go inside.

A group of officers ran at the door, and then all of a sudden Alan McGuire, the man who was in the house, came hurtling through the front window on fire. I am not even sure if police officers knew how many people were in the house at the time. [Earlier,] his wife had escaped from the home. She had been held at knifepoint and bound, and she had somehow gotten out, and she had let police know that their 2-year-old daughter, Shelby McGuire, was in the house.

Shelby was a hostage and being held at knifepoint. Police saw her and tried to set up a telephone line so they could negotiate with McGuire, but the events unfolded rapidly, and after Alan McGuire jumped through the front window, police broke down the door. Two officers hauled McGuire's flaming body to the ground and tried to douse the flames with a garden hose. Inside the house, one of the officers saw Shelby McGuire sitting upright on the couch. She had a plastic grocery produce bag over her head, and it apparently had been duct-taped in some fashion, maybe around the neck.

They immediately tore the bag away. A detective picked Shelby up and sprinted out of the house with her. It was at that moment that Andy Nelson snapped his picture of one of the officers with Shelby's body in his arms, running out, two other officers standing on the side of the doorstep, another officer with a hose near Alan McGuire, and Alan lying on the ground. The flames were now out, but the charred and still-smoking body was present in the viewfinder as Andy snapped the picture (see figure 8.3).

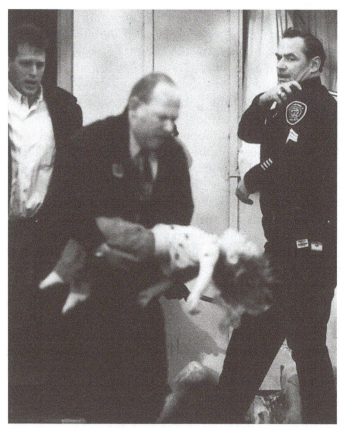

Figure 8.3. Photo courtesy of the *Eugene Register-Guard.* **Used with permission.**

At that moment, the officer with Shelby McGuire, the 2-year-old, began mouth-to-mouth resuscitation on the front lawn. Andy subsequently took a photograph of that. Then they rushed both Alan and Shelby McGuire to the hospital. We did not know Shelby's condition. The police didn't respond about whether she was able to be resuscitated.

We have a standing policy at the newspaper that as a general rule we don't run photographs of dead bodies of children. That immediately triggered the kind of review that we would go through to determine where this particular incident was going to stand up on our policy, whether or not anyone was going to argue for publication or against publication.

We began to talk about the policy and the potential community reaction that we might face. The discussion was pretty brief. The photo was so compelling and the situation that it sprang from so horrifying that we began looking at the photograph and saying,

"Well, I don't know, but look at what the photo has captured."

"People are going to be upset."

"This is potentially a photograph of a dead 2-year-old child."

"Look at the concern and the expression on the police officers' faces. This is an example of what they deal with day in and day out. They are up against this kind of domestic violence hostage situation and people don't realize that."

So, the debate was intense and yet pretty short. We prepared a selection of pictures, and we brought those to the then-managing editor Patrick Yak and made the case that this is going to be a tough photograph for us to run. This is going to be one that we are going to have to be prepared to defend. But we believe it's that kind of exception to the rule that we look for.

The public response to the publication of the Shelby McGuire photograph was unprecedented in my 22 years in journalism and unprecedented at this newspaper. I have not come across a case, having been shown a number of them subsequently, that is of the magnitude per capita of reader response to a single photographic image. We received on the order of 450 telephone calls that began the moment people got the newspaper, which started at 6 a.m. First, they came into our circulation department. The circulation department switchboard became overloaded and gave them the main newsroom switchboard, which didn't open until 7:30. At 7:30 when they threw the switch, all 20 of our incoming phone lines lit up, and the calls began to roll over into a holding pattern that had never been utilized by our switchboard before.

I was called at home by Al Gimmell, the corporate controller, who said, "We are inundated with telephone calls. We need some help." So I immediately came in to try to handle telephone calls, and I tried to find the time in between phone calls to call other editors in, but the calls were coming so rapidly that every time I hung up it rang again. When I picked up my voicemail messages, I had 31 unanswered messages, and that was probably 7:45 in the morning.

The range of responses wasn't monolithic, except in their anger. But the anger came from different places. For some people, the anger came from a belief that we had simply stooped to a tremendously sensational graphic crime picture trying to sell newspapers. For others, the anger came from the terrible sense of violation that the surviving mother and brother of Shelby McGuire would have to wake up to the morning after their ordeal and see this on the front page of the hometown newspaper (see figure 8.4).

Another component argued that this was wholly inappropriate for the kind of newspaper the *Register-Guard* has been and continues to be. That 5-year-olds and 6-year-olds were sharing the newspaper at the breakfast table, and parents were finding themselves in a position of having to explain this horrifying incident and having the question "How is the little girl?" asked again. And there was also a range of responses from people who were themselves victims of domestic violence or spouses of victims or had family members who were involved in it. For them, it was a combination of anger and pain.

I spoke with literally dozens of people through tears. It was an emotional response that was overwhelming, and people were extremely upset by the picture. Most asked the question "Why? I need to understand why the newspaper published this picture."

Figure 8.4. **Photo courtesy of the** *Eugene Register-Guard.* **Used with permission.**

We were really, I think, at a loss initially to respond to that question. I think a lot of that had to do with being, in a very real sense, out of touch with a substantial number of readers. The kind of reaction that we had was not anticipated by anyone in the news department.

If we were presented with a similar situation and a similar photograph today, we would absolutely not do it the way that we did it in the Shelby McGuire case. Thousands of our readers have defined for us a boundary in this community and for this newspaper that I don't think, until we began to see it materialize, we had any sense of exactly where it was.

Micro Issues

1. Look at the photos that accompany this text. The photo of the officer carrying out Shelby McGuire ran in full color above the fold, two-thirds of the page wide and 6 inches tall. Does a photo of that size over-sensationalize the story?
2. The photo of Sergeant Swenson's attempts to resuscitate Shelby ran below the fold in a small two-column photo. Why do you think, the decision was made to run this photo smaller and lower?

Midrange Issues

1. Does the fact that Shelby died influence your decision on whether to run the photos? If so, in what way?
2. Does the fact that at least one television station and the local Springfield newspaper were there with photographers influence your decision to run the photos? If so, in what way?
3. Does the fact that seven other children had died in Lane County in less than two years affect your decision to run the photos? If so, in what way?
4. The biweekly *Springfield News* chose to run a front-page photo of Alan McGuire falling out of the front window of his home, his badly burned flesh still in flames. However, they covered the front page with a wrapper that read "Caution to Readers" and explained the content of the stories and photos underneath the wrapper. Critique that approach to handling the story.
5. A local television station showed a few seconds of the scene described above after warning viewers of the violent nature of the video that followed. The station got fewer than 20 complaints. How do you explain the vast difference in the reaction to the broadcast and print photos?

Macro Issues

1. What are the privacy rights of
   a. Shelby McGuire?
   b. Shelby McGuire's mother and 4-year-old brother?
   c. Sergeant Swenson?
2. Critique the argument that these photos should be shown because they illustrate the type of tragedy that law enforcement officers are often called upon to handle.
3. Critique the argument that these photos should be shown because they illustrate the horror of domestic violence.
4. Critique the statement that "if we were presented with a similar situation and a similar photograph today, we would absolutely not do it the way that we did it in the Shelby McGuire case." In your opinion, is that based on sensitivity to reader concern or caving in to reader pressure?

CASE 8-F

HORROR IN SOWETO

SUE O'BRIEN, FORMER EDITORIAL PAGE EDITOR
The Denver Post

On Sept. 15, 1990, freelance photographer Gregory Marinovich documented the killing, by a mob of African National Congress supporters, of a man they believed to be a Zulu spy.

Marinovich and Associated Press reporter Tom Cohen spotted the man being led from a Soweto, South Africa, train-station platform by a group armed with machetes and crude spears. Marinovich and Cohen continued to witness and report as the man was stoned, bludgeoned, stabbed, doused with gasoline, and set afire.

It was one of 800 deaths in two months of factional fighting among Blacks as rival organizations vied for influence in the declining days of apartheid.

The graphic photos stirred intense debate among editors. In one, the victim, conscious but stoic, lies on his back as a grinning attacker poises to plunge a knife into his forehead. In the final photo of the series, the victim crouches, engulfed in fire.

As the series was transmitted, several member editors called to question what the photographer was doing at the scene—could he in any way have stopped the attack? In response, an advisory went out on the photo wire, saying Marinovich had tried to intervene and then, when told to stop taking pictures, had told mob leaders he would stop shooting only when they "stopped hurting that man."

Decisions on what to do with the photos varied across the country, according to a survey. If any pattern emerged, it was that newspapers in competitive markets such as Denver, Minneapolis-St. Paul, and New York were more likely to go with the harsh graphics.

The burning photo was the most widely used, the stabbing the least. Several editors said they specifically rejected the stabbing as too extreme.

"It showed violence and animalistic hatred," said Roman Lyskowski, graphics editor for the *Miami Herald.*

"That's not as unusual an image as that knife sticking right out of the skull," said another editor, who agreed that the stabbing was much more disturbing than the burning, saying he recalled immolation pictures from the Vietnam era.

When the Soweto series cleared at the *Miami Herald,* the burning photo was sent to Executive Editor Janet Chusmir's home for her approval. At her direction, the immolation picture ran on the front page, but below the fold and in black and white. The detail revealed in color reproduction, Chusmir and her editors agreed, was too graphic (see figure 8.5).

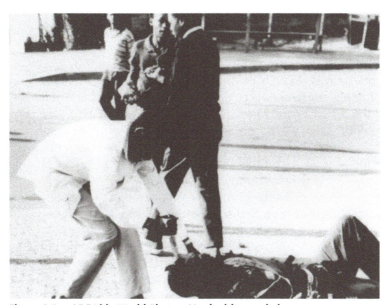

Figure 8.5. AP/Wide World Photos. Used with permission.

At the *Los Angeles Times* and *Dallas Morning News*, however, the burning photo ran above the front-page fold—and in color.

The *St. Paul Pioneer Press* chose the stabbing for front-page color.

"I look at the moment that the photo freezes on film," said News Editor Joe Sevick. "Rarely do you see a photo where a knife is about to go into somebody."

The photo ran in color on the *Pioneer Press* front page, accompanied by the story Cohen had written on the attack and a longer story on the South African government's attempt, announced that day, to crack down on Black-on-Black violence.

In Denver, at the *Rocky Mountain News*, Managing Editor Mike Madigan wanted to run a comprehensive package on the Soweto story. The tabloid's only open page was deep in the paper, but a page 3 box referred readers to the story with a warning the photos were "horrific and disturbing." Inside, stories on the attack and government crackdown and an editor's note on Marinovich's intervention accompanied three photos: the victim being led away from the train station, the stabbing, and the burning.

Most papers that ran the more challenging photos involved top management in the decision. Frequently, top editors were contacted by telephone, or came in from home, to give the photos a final go-ahead.

In most newsrooms, the burning or stabbing photos made it to the news desk for approval or rejection. But there, they sometimes were killed abruptly.

"The editors at that point said no," one picture editor reported. "They would not take the heat."

Several editors deferred to the so-called Post-Toasties Test.

"The question is 'Which of those photos would help tell the story without ruining everyone's breakfast?'" asked Rod Deckert, managing editor of the *Albuquerque Journal*.

One editor said his paper is especially likely to de-emphasize disturbing material in the Sunday paper, which children often read with their parents. But many editors who rejected the more brutal pictures said the Post-Toasties Test is irrelevant.

"If you're putting out a paper in New York and don't have something that's going to cause some discomfort over breakfast, then you're probably not putting out the full paper you should," said Jeff Jarvis, Sunday editor at the *New York Daily News*. "I don't think the breakfast test works for [today]."

Others cited distance tests. Some newspapers, in deference to victims' families, are less likely to use death photos from within their own circulation areas. Another editor, however, said his paper is *less* likely to run violent photos unless they are local and have a "more immediate impact on our readership."

Newspapers also differed widely on how they packaged the Soweto story. Some accompanied a photo series with the Cohen and crackdown stories, and a note on Marinovich's intervention. Some ran a single photo, often the burning, with only a cutline and a brief reference to the train-station incident in the "crackdown" story. Two respected big-city dailies, which omitted any reference to the Soweto attack in their accompanying stories, ran cursory cutlines such as "Violence continues: A boy runs away as an ANC supporter clubs a Zulu foe who was beaten, stabbed and set ablaze."

Although 41 papers used at least one of the Marinovich photos, only four—the *Charlotte Observer*, *Akron Beacon-Journal*, *Rocky Mountain News*, and *USA Today*—told the story of Marinovich's attempt to halt the attack (see figure 8.6).

Among collateral considerations at many news desks was the coverage of South African troubles that had gone before. At least one editor said the Soweto photos, which followed several other beating and killing photographs from South Africa that had been used earlier in the week, were "just too, too much."

Figure 8.6. AP/Wide World Photos. Used with permission.

With only three exceptions, editors said race did not figure in their considerations. One white editor said the fact that both attackers and victim were Black deprived the series of clarity.

"You don't have a sense of one side against another. You don't have a sense of right or wrong."

Two editors who identified themselves as Black, however, argued for aggressive use of the photos. Both work in communities with significant Black populations.

"I think Black readers should be more informed about this," one said. "Across the board, Black Americans don't realize what's going on with the Black-on-Black violence."

Front-page placement and the use of color frequently triggered reader objections, but the adequacy of cutline information and accompanying copy also appear significant. The *Albany Times Union* was flooded by phone protests and subscription cancellations. Two other papers perceiving significant reader unrest—the *Dallas Morning News* and *Los Angeles Times*—ran the burning photo in color on their front pages. However, each of the three papers also ran the front-page photos with only cutline accompaniment, referring readers inside to the stories that placed the images in context.

In retrospect, *Rocky Mountain News*'s Madigan said he was very pleased with the final Soweto package and readers' reaction to it.

> It wasn't so much the idea that "yeah, we ran these really horrific pictures and, boy, it knocked people's socks off." I don't think that was the point. I think it was more the way we handled it. Just one word or the other can make a terrific difference in whether the public starts screaming "sensationalize, sensationalize," or takes it as a thoughtful, important piece of work, which is what we were after.

Micro Issues

1. In all but the most important stories, would you support a ban on dead-body photos in your newspaper or newscast?
2. Some editors believe it is their ethical duty to avoid violating readers' sense of taste or compassion. Others argue that it is their duty to force society to face unpleasant truths, even if it means risking reader anger and rejection. Whose side would you support?
3. Many readers suspect that sensational photos are chosen to sell newspapers or capture rating points by appealing to morbid tastes. Do you believe they're right?

Midrange Issues

1. Editors sometimes justify running graphic photos by saying they can provide a "warning bell," alerting people to preventable dangers in society. What values might the Soweto photographs offer readers?
2. Is the desire to avoid offending readers an ethical consideration or a marketing consideration?
3. Is it appropriate to base editorial decisions on what readers are likely to be doing at home: to edit newspapers differently, for instance, if they are likely to be read at the breakfast table, or present newscasts differently if they are to air during the dinner hour rather than later in the evening?
4. As an editor, would you be more likely to run a photograph of someone being murdered if the event happened in your own community, or if it happened thousands of miles away and none of your readers would be likely to know the victim or his family?
5. Do you see any distinction in
   a. whether a violent photo is run in color or black and white?
   b. whether it is run on the front page or on an inside page?

Macro Issues

1. Is aesthetic, dramatic, or photographic value ever reason enough to run a picture, regardless of how intrusive it may be or how it may violate readers' sensitivities?
2. Is it your responsibility as an editor to find out if a photographer could have saved a life by intervening in a situation rather than taking pictures of it? Is that information you need to share with your readers?
3. Is it your responsibility as an editor to find out if the presence of the camera at the scene in any way helped incite or distort an event? Is that information you need to share with your readers?
4. When dramatic photographs are printed, how important is it for readers or viewers to be told all the background of the story or situation?

9

Media Economics

The Deadline Meets the Bottom Line

By the end of this chapter you should be familiar with

- the economic realities of the social responsibility theory of the press;
- the economic and legislative initiatives that have combined to place control of information in the hands of fewer and larger corporations;
- how various mediums have coped with the current economic and technological realities of media;
- the "stakeholder" theory of economic success.

OF MARKETS AND MORALS

Let's say you're a famous Broadway producer—Joe Papp—and in the mid-1970s decide that while Broadway productions are terrific, it would be even better if the average New Yorker could see classics for free. Shakespeare in the Park was born. Each summer, New York City's Public Theater puts on free outdoor Shakespeare performances in Central Park, subsidized by taxpayer dollars. All New Yorkers have to do is stand in line—and sometimes it's a long one—to get the tickets.

Enter Craigslist and services that will wait in line for you: at a cost of $125 per hour. Suddenly, the free tickets weren't so free. New York is not the only place you can hire someone to stand in line. Washington, D.C., has an industry fueled by Linestanding.com where surrogates will stand in line for seats to US Supreme Court arguments or congressional hearings. Homeless people are often hired to do the work. And, of course, if you want to move to the front of the line at Disney World, you just have to pay more for the tickets. Or if you want to drive in the high occupancy lane in some metropolitan areas—without benefit of a car pool—you can pay for the privilege, even if there is no one in your vehicle but you.

What's wrong with that? In a market economy, goods and services change hands and no one really gets hurt. Or do they? In the case of Shakespeare in the Park, New York Attorney General (later Governor) Andrew Cuomo pressured Craigslist to stop the ads, arguing that selling tickets that were meant to be free deprived New Yorkers of one of the more unusual benefits of their political community.

The chance to stand in line to see Al Pacino play Shylock is something that should not be for sale, according to Harvard political philosopher Michael Sandel. In his bestselling 2012 book *What Money Can't Buy: The Moral Limits of Markets*, Sandel argues that, in this century, economic language— where literally everything has to be marketed and incentivized—has not only crowded out moral thinking but sometimes changed our conception of what it means to have a good life in the sense that Aristotle meant it: to have a life with authentic flourishing. Whether it's paying kids to get good grades, the naming opportunities for everything from sports stadiums to national parks to newborns, to the selling of everything from blood to kidneys, Sandel argues that there are places and areas of life where the market simply doesn't belong.

Sandel notes two sets of basic objections to thinking that everything should be the subject of commerce. The first is the notion of fairness, which is highlighted by the example of hiring someone to stand in line for a free ticket. Those with money move to the front. Shakespeare might have objected (after all, he wrote jokes for the groundlings who couldn't afford the expensive seats); Sandel most certainly does. Line jumping is just not fair. In addition, it's coercive—those involved in the case, the citizens of New York, haven't given their permission for "free" tickets to be sold to the highest bidder. They also have no recourse to change the system that emerges unless they become unwilling participants.

The second set of objections to thinking about everything in terms of a market begins with the capacity to fuel corruption. This objection is not new. Paying money for priestly indulgences in the Roman Catholic Church, a corruption of the concept of forgiveness of sins, is one of the reasons for the Protestant Reformation more than 500 years ago. God, and forgiveness, simply could not and should not be bought—even though they were for sale. As Sandel notes, you can buy sports memorabilia or even a sports team. What you cannot do is buy the actual experience of hitting a home run in the World Series or scoring the winning touchdown in the Super Bowl. Moneyball will take you only so far, and the experiences are not equivalent.

In many areas of life, money does not incentivize better behavior. Students who were offered a monetary incentive to raise money for a charity raised less money than those who were offered nothing. Citizens of a community in Switzerland volunteered to become the locus of a nuclear waste repository, but they turned down the same proposal when it was presented to them with an economic inducement. In 2012, Alvin Roth won the Nobel Memorial Prize in Economic Sciences in part for his pioneering work that created an efficient and moral market for kidney donors moved by altruism but lacking a specific person in their lives who needed the kidney at that time. The New England Program for Kidney Exchange was born. However, when the same problem was presented to them with an economic inducement, they turned the proposal down. Traditional economists tend to think that qualities such as altruism, generosity, solidarity, and civic duty are scarce. Sandel argues that they are like a muscle: They grow with repeated use. They speak to notions of the good life, and when market language is substituted for the language of morals, our concept of the good life itself is degraded. Corruption and degradation are the second set of reasons that market thinking fails to capture what human beings truly want and need.

Sandel concludes his book with the following:

> The disappearance of the class-mixing experience once found at the ballpark represents a loss not only for those looking up but also for those looking down. Something similar has been happening throughout society. At a time of rising inequality, the marketing of everything means that people of affluence and people of modest means lead increasingly separate lives. . . . Democracy does not require perfect equality, but it does require that citizens share in a common life. . . . For this is how we learn to negotiate and abide our common differences, and how we come to care for the common good. (2012, p. 203)

A LEGACY OF RESPONSIBILITY

The *social responsibility theory of the press* was developed in the 1940s by a panel of scholars, the Hutchins Commission, with funding from Henry Luce, the conservative founder of *Time* magazine. Social responsibility theory envisioned a day when an active recipient of news and information was satisfied by a socially responsible press. According to the Hutchins Commission, media have the following five functions in society:

1. to provide a truthful, comprehensive and intelligent account of the day's events in a context that gives them meaning;
2. to serve as a forum for exchange of comment and criticism;

3. to provide a representative picture of constituent groups in society;
4. to present and clarify the goals and values of society; and
5. to provide citizens with full access to the day's intelligence.

Social responsibility theory, however, has a fundamental flaw: It gives little attention to modern media economics. This omission occurred in part because multinational corporations and chain ownership were still on the horizon when the Hutchins Commission worked. Because the theory was developed early in the McCarthy period, there was also an unwillingness to link economic and political power for fear of being labeled Marxist. This omission means that *the social responsibility theory does not deal with the realities of concentrated economic power*, particularly in an era when information has become a valuable commodity.

As the mass media became enormous, economically powerful institutions, they joined what political scientist C. Wright Mills (1956) called the "power elite," a ruling class within a democratic society. Time has proved Mills right. Power is found not only in the halls of government but also on Wall Street. And power is found not only in money or armies but also in information. Media organizations, precisely because they have become multinational corporations engaged in the information business, are deeply involved in this power shift.

Today, the media are predominantly corporate-owned and publicly traded, with media conglomerates among the largest (and until recently, the most profitable) of the world's corporations. The corporate owners of the average news operation are more insulated from contact with news consumers than virtually any other business owner in America. And there are fewer of those owners. Most local media outlets are owned by one of five multinational corporations, and each has become increasingly larger in an attempt to gain market efficiencies.

A handful of media conglomerates—NewsCorp, Viacom/CBS, Comcast/NBCUniversal, AT&T/Time Warner, and the Walt Disney Corporation—own the vast majority of media, including newspapers, broadcast and cable television networks, radio stations, movie and music studios, and book publishers. Other media organizations have a virtual stranglehold on various mediums—from the Sinclair Broadcast Group in local television to iHeartMedia in commercial radio. Even these conglomerates pale in market size when compared to the internet behemoths collectively known as the FAANG (Facebook, Apple, Amazon, Netflix, and Google) group. To illustrate, the combined worth of the five major media conglomerates—which, again, collectively own the vast majority of media—is *less* than that of Amazon, Apple, or Alphabet (the parent company of Google), each of which is worth more than $1 *trillion*. In October 2020, the US Department of Justice sued Google, alleging that it used unfair practices to preserve its search and advertising monopoly (Ghaffary & Molla, 2020). Two months later, the Federal Trade Commission and 48 state attorneys general demanded that Facebook sell Instagram and WhatsApp, stating that those acquisitions were a prime example of Facebook's "buy or bury" strategy for eliminating competition (Nylen, 2020). This consolidation of voices might limit the marketplace of ideas, especially when ownership has a decided partisan and political bias.

These corporations typically adhere to market philosophies (Barnouw, 1997). Commercial news organizations concurrently trade in four markets: the market for audience, competing for readers and viewers; the stock market, because most firms trade stock and desire higher valuations; the advertising market, because firms compete for advertising revenue; and a market for sources, competing for information to disseminate (McManus, 1994). According to market theory, these four markets should operate efficiently and consistently to produce high-quality news that aligns with public interest; however, a focus on profitability and serving the market often conflicts with serving the public (Barnouw, 1997; McManus, 1994).

This emergence of media as economic and political power brokers leads to the question of how a powerful institution such as the mass media, which traditionally has had the political role of checking other powerful institutions, can itself be checked. Can the watchdog be trusted when it is inexorably entwined with the institutions it is watching? For instance, NBC removed legendary sportscaster Bob Costas from the Super Bowl and its *Sunday Night Football* broadcast after he delivered an on-air commentary about the link between football and chronic traumatic encephalopathy (CTE) following the release of the 2015 film *Concussion*. Costas has covered almost every sporting event—from the Super Bowl, World Series, and NBA Finals to the Olympics and Kentucky Derby—winning 28 Emmys and 8 National Sportscaster of the Year awards. NBC, however, is paying the NFL more than $3 billion for the right to air games on Sundays and, at the time of Costas's commentary, was negotiating to expand its NFL package to Thursday (which ultimately didn't happen). Costas eventually left NBC, ending a nearly 40-year relationship with the network (Fainaru-Wada, 2019).

When the social responsibility theory was framed in the 1940s, the primary informational concern was scarcity: People might not get the information they needed for citizenship, and until recently, government agencies such as the FCC were still basing policy decisions on the scarcity argument when any consumer with cable or a satellite dish knew otherwise. Today, however, the primary informational concern is an overabundance of raw data: People might not filter out what they need through all the clutter. Media and their distribution systems changed, but the theory remained silent, especially about the role of profit.

The clash of large, well-financed institutions over control of information is a modern phenomenon. Classical ethical theory, which speaks to individual acts, is of little help in sorting out the duties and responsibilities of corporations (larger than most nations) that control the currency of the day: information. Americans are unwilling to accept government as the solution to counter the concentrated economic power of the media, and government has been hesitant to break up the large media conglomerates. Europeans have taken a different view, in many cases using tax dollars to support a government-controlled broadcast system. In some cases, such as the Scandinavian countries, tax dollars also support newspapers—with the goal of sustaining multiple, distinct voices in the public sphere (Picard, 1988).

HYPER-COMPETITION AND ITS IMPACT ON NEWS

Legacy journalists, those who did not come of age as "digital natives," and the news organizations that employ them face a huge shift in the assumptions about what makes news media profitable and praiseworthy. Legacy journalism emerged from an era of low-to-moderate economic competition. Even though specific rivalries often were intense, they were local and definitely not across media platforms. Individual organizations competed for consumer satisfaction and time, consumer spending, content, advertisers, and employees. More than 30 years ago, media scholar Steve Lacy (1989) predicted these low-to-moderate competitive environments would produce a quality news product based on individual organizations' financial commitment to news, which in turn was perceived as being useful by audience members and sustained by a journalistic culture that valued excellence and public service.

However, low-to-moderate competition no longer exists in the contemporary media marketplace. Instead, we now live in an era of hyper-competition, much of it provided by web access. In hyper-competition, *supply substantially exceeds demand so that a large percentage of the producers in the market operate at a financial loss*. Classical economic theory holds that hyper-competition cannot exist permanently. However, news and information are not traditional economic commodities; they are called "experience and credence" commodities, meaning that a consumer cannot judge whether the product actually meets his or her individual needs until he or she has invested in and spent time with the product. News also is linked to social welfare, a category of products with significant external values not readily captured by price point or profit margin.

John McManus argued that, beginning in the 1980s, news organizations began moving toward making news "explicitly a commodity" (1994, p. 1). Journalists in a market-driven newsroom, McManus argued, would select stories for the "issues and events that have the greatest ratio of expected appeal for demographically desirable audiences" (1994, p. 114). In other words, the first goal of journalists would not be informing the public. Instead, it would be providing news that could entice more readers or viewers. More readers or viewers, in turn, would lead to increased profitability. Journalism, historically, aims to inform citizens and assist in strengthening democracy. Market-driven journalism, however, was not a service to the public. Instead of informing readers or viewers, market-driven news organizations entertain while possibly informing.

The current state of media financial affairs can be summarized as an emphasis on corporate responsibility to the stockholders of publicly traded corporations. In stockholder theory, corporations and their leaders have a single, overriding, and legally binding promise to those who purchase stock: increase the share price. Milton Friedman, who first articulated the theory, suggests that increasing the share price is *the* promise that managers make. Whatever is legally done to promote that end is ethically right.

Business ethicist Patricia H. Werhane (2006) has a different vision of the traditional stakeholder map. She says that some sorts of businesses—such as healthcare—have a public responsibility that extends beyond individual stockholders. These companies, she says, should operate from an "enriched stakeholder" model as opposed to a "profit-driven stockholder" model. The enriched stakeholder model puts something other than the corporation at the center of the "stakeholder" map (for healthcare, she suggests the patient) and rings that central stakeholder with government, investors, the court system, medical professionals, insurance companies, managed-care plans, and others. By changing the stakeholder map, Werhane suggests that other "promises" surface and that other measures of success emerge.

The stakeholder model of media economics has much to recommend it. At the center of the map are citizens and community. Around the center is a ring, including audiences, creative artists, stockholders, governments, nongovernmental organizations, journalists, strategic communication professionals, corporate managers, and employees. By asking what benefits citizens living in communities the most, media corporate managers would begin to use a different gauge of success that does not place profit first in every situation. Media corporations would no longer search for a one-time "hit" that can be packaged, imitated, and mass reproduced. Instead, they would make smaller investments in a variety of experiments, allowing creativity and connection to community to help determine what works for both stakeholders and stockholders and what does not.

From the level of the individual journalist or strategic-communication profes-sional to the organizations that employ them, today there are multiple experiments with "new" business models. One example is civic news organizations such as the American Journalism Project, which aims to create a new public-service model built on investing in nonprofit, nonpartisan news organizations. In 2019, the project announced its first 11 grants to local news organizations—including WyoFile, VTDigger, and the *Connecticut Mirror* (Leonhardt, 2019). Another is the Brick House Media Cooperative, an online publishing cooperative where news organizations and journalists pool and share subscribers, revenues, and expenses in order to lower costs and, by extension, the price of a subscription (and where one subscription bypasses the paywall of every news site within the collective). While it is difficult to categorize new business models, they share an attempt to shift the costs of producing and distributing content to the indi-vidual listener/reader/viewer rather than to advertisers. New business models are producing some efforts that, just a few decades ago, were seen as an unprof-itable backwater or completely ethically forbidden. Documentary films were once a staple of art film houses, attracting small audiences. Today, they take on issues of public importance, combining traditional news gathering efforts with Hollywood-style cinematic techniques. Some are financially successful, and some, such as Josh Fox's *Gasland* (2010), have influenced public policy. Podcasts thrive as well in outlets such as NPR, where consumer suggestions are sometimes the starting point for NPR documentaries, a polar opposite of the "agenda setting" role of the press that media theorists wrote about in the latter part of the 20th century (see figure 9.1).

Other examples are all across the media landscape. The *New York Times* now has an "Op Docs" section attached to the more traditional opinion page. Niche sites such as FiveThirtyEight and Jezebel have become successful enough that they have been purchased by mainstream news organizations, often with little change to content or frequency from the days before they found financial secu-rity. Popular YouTube stars such as Felix Arvid Ulf Kjellberg (better known

Figure 9.1. Non Sequitur © 2008 Wiley Ink, Inc. Distributed by Andrews McMeel Syndication. Reprinted with permission. All rights reserved.

as PewDiePie) make salaries rivaling those of the most successful Hollywood actors, and comedians such as Aziz Ansari of *Parks and Recreation* and Derek Waters of *Drunk History* launched their careers with internet-based short films. And almost everyone, from the folks who sell you household products to the stodgiest of the "old guard" newsrooms, is experimenting with reader/viewer/listener engagement. From allowing consumers to comment on stories to pretesting news programming, or developing ad messages, the public now has a say in what "news" is.

The result is what at least one scholar has called "liquid journalism" where

traditional role perceptions of journalism influenced by its occupational ideology—providing a general audience with information of general interest in a balanced, objective and ethical way—do not seem to fit all that well with the lived realities of reporters and editors, nor with the communities they are supposed to serve. (Deuze, 2008, p. 848)

When news organizations, and even individual journalists, worry about their "brand" rather than the public they serve, something essential has changed. Perhaps the most troubling element in this strand of research in media economics is that the public appears not to value—or sometimes even to recognize—that quality is declining. In hypercompetitive situations, ethics takes a back seat to survival, and the common good becomes the loser in the process.

TELEVISION: CONGLOMERATION, CONSOLIDATION, AND SURVIVAL

Television, a medium that began its existence as a free service brought to the public by willing advertisers, has morphed into something that nine out of ten Americans now pay for twice—once with their cable or satellite bills and, for most, twice with their attention to advertising. Yet, television, particularly at the network or cable levels where programming is produced, is always in search of more efficiency and revenue streams.

Take the two entities that are the original television networks: NBC and CBS. In the past decade, both have acquired more assets, from publishing houses to cable networks to content distributors. Both also have launched their own online streaming platforms. The goal of all this financial activity is not only to find profit centers but also to create vertically integrated companies with diverse sources of income. Consider this scenario:

- By acquiring production facilities, networks can now own the shows they broadcast, a new phenomenon cutting deeply into the old system of buying programs from independent producers who took the risks in order to reap the possible rewards if shows were picked up.

- By acquiring cable stations such as Comedy Central (owned by Viacom/ CBS), networks control outlets for their shows as they go into the lucrative phases of syndication, taking advantage of legislation that ended the FCC's old Financial Interest and Syndication Rules prohibiting networks from being syndicators.
- By acquiring the maximum number of local television stations owned by law, networks have a built-in advantage for uploading news when it happens in a market where they own a station, something that Rupert Murdoch's Fox brand has perfected even after getting a late start in the market.
- By acquiring the rights to broadcast major and minor sports, amateur and professional alike, both of the traditional two, NBC and CBS, launched their own 24/7 cable sports networks to rival ESPN, which is owned by another traditional network, ABC.
- By acquiring aftermarket distributors, networks make money on rentals and sales of boxed DVD sets of popular series after their original airing. Even series that were closed after two or three seasons find an afterlife in boxed sets.
- By licensing shows to streaming services such as Netflix, Amazon Prime, and Hulu, networks have yet another revenue stream to make money from popular (and sometimes unpopular) television programs. Disney and cable networks including HBO and Showtime have launched their own streaming services. Of course, the major streaming services also program original content, including rebooting hit TV shows such as *Fuller House* and *Gilmore Girls*, as well as series such as *Arrested Development* and *Longmire*, which failed to find more than a cult following when they originally aired on broadcast and cable networks.

The result of vertical integration is a pair of companies that have survived in the broadcasting industry for nearly a century and that can now control a product from the filming of the pilot episode to the last airing of the syndicated show or personal download, sometimes decades from now. And it must be emphasized that much of what is now possible in the bullet points above has only recently been made possible by FCC and court rulings as well as generous antitrust rulings. NBC and CBS are but two "legacy" media corporations to have acquired their way to financial success.

Media consolidation allows for a diversification of income. In the case of NBC, after the acquisition of Universal Studios, revenues went from 90 percent advertising-based to 50 percent, with the remainder coming from subscriptions, admissions, licensing, and other ancillary income. By weaning themselves away from advertising, media companies have hedged against the vagaries of recession. This shift also has an impact on the advertising industry, which has seen a large increase in layoffs, furloughs, and other cost-cutting measures—a trend that was exacerbated in 2020 by the COVID-19 pandemic.

Conglomeration, consolidation, and the aftermarket added more revenue streams and made things more predictable for stockholders. However, not everyone is happy with the direction media ownership is taking. Groups as diverse as the National Organization for Women and the National Rifle Association criticized and challenged changes in ownership limits proposed by the FCC. *Columbia Journalism Review* editor-at-large Neil Hickey (2001) summed up the fears of many when he concluded,

> What we risk over the long haul is ownership creep that may eventually see the end of the few remaining rules, and with them, the public's right to the widest possible array of news and opinion—at which point, robust, independent, antagonistic, many-voiced journalism may be only a memory.

NEWSPAPERS: WHAT COMES AFTER THE PENNY PRESS?

Financing the American media through advertising is so deeply ingrained in the system that it is hard to imagine any other way. Yet, newspapers in America were supported solely by their readers for more than a century. Incidentally, in 1920, the then secretary of commerce Herbert Hoover argued for commercial-free radio, a funding formula that would have likely failed or at the least changed the medium entirely.

The legacy funding formula for most newspapers was created more than 175 years ago when Benjamin Day, publisher of the *New York Sun*, started the "penny press" revolution by lowering the price of his newspaper to a penny at a time when his competition was selling newspapers for a nickel. He gambled that he could overcome the printing losses with additional advertising revenue—if circulation increased. When his gamble paid off, virtually every publisher in town followed his lead.

What Day did was farsighted. By pricing their products at or below the cost of printing, publishers cast their economic future with advertisers, which demand "eyeballs" and paid circulation guaranteed by the Audit Bureau of Circulation. The system worked as long as circulation increased to cover the rising costs of covering the news. However, readership peaked more than three decades ago, and newspapers began shedding costs. Some sold to chains. Others combined with rivals in "joint operating agreements" (JOA), which were, in effect, a congressionally approved exception to antitrust laws.

Under a JOA, rival papers could combine press operations, billing operations, and so forth, but act as rival newspapers in their quest for news. With more than 30 years of history to evaluate the impact of the JOA legislation, what scholars and stockholders now know is that no joint operating agreement has allowed both newspapers to survive indefinitely under the new financial arrangement. Still others became "ghost papers," publishing under the same name but with less quality, quantity, and scope of editorial content (Abernathy, 2020). One example is the *Ithaca Journal*, which has just one reporter, and no locally based editor or publisher, to cover a town with 30,000 residents—swelling to 60,000 when Cornell University and Ithaca College are in session (Edmonds, 2020).

Such consolidation efforts were not nearly enough to survive the onslaught of the web and a business model that provided news—an expensive commodity to produce—for free online. Layoffs and hiring freezes became a fact of life at large and award-winning papers such as the *Los Angeles Times* and the *Chicago Tribune*, as well as smaller community papers. National papers, such as the *New York Times* and *Washington Post*, have found success with online subscription models; audiences are willing to pay for quality journalism. However, small- and medium-market papers continue to struggle to find a way to "monetize" the internet operation. Attempts to gain more readers by being more convenient eventually became a way for many to not pay for news content at all. Although ads were possible and even abundant on newspaper websites, advertisers were loath to pay the same amount that audited readership had commanded. Major newspapers such as the *Rocky Mountain News* in Denver folded. Some, such as the *Wall Street Journal*, decreased their page size while most decreased their page count, beginning a cycle where a smaller "news hole" required fewer journalists. Other papers, most notably the *New Orleans Times Picayune*, went to less-than-daily circulation in an attempt to survive. In all, almost 25 percent of US newspapers have closed since 2004, including 70 dailies and more than 2,000 weeklies or non-dailies.

The local newspaper in most communities had long been a monopoly operation, with returns of greater than 20 percent annually common before the bleeding of circulation and advertising. Even after cutbacks, newspapers still boast a "name brand" in most communities and the largest reporting staff in any given local market. Economically, small-market dailies are actually thriving financially. However, with readers decreasing, some newspapers are increasingly putting video segments on their websites in an attempt to siphon viewers from local nightly newscasts. How this even more expensive use of the web will play out is unknown, but it does demand that journalists be cross-trained for the new media reality as newspapers add video and sound and television stations add print stories to their websites.

THE STATE OF MEDIA ECONOMICS—THE CASE OF ONE STATE

Ohio is a good test market—in fact, its capital city, Columbus, is a long-time test market for products ranging from MTV to the latest Starbucks latte. One reason is that its demographics typically have mirrored national averages. Another is that it's a state with both big cities and large swaths of rural farming communities. Ohio is also a major presidential swing state: It has voted for the presidential elect in all but five elections since the US Civil War. What has happened to legacy media organizations in Ohio also is illustrative of larger trends across the United States.

The *Columbus Dispatch* and *Cincinnati Enquirer*—daily newspapers in the state's first and third most populous cities—are both owned by Gannett. Gatehouse Media bought Gannett for $1.1 billion in November 2019 (though the merged company kept the more prestigious Gannett name), becoming by far the nation's largest newspaper company. It owns more than 260 daily newspapers, including *USA Today*, as well as hundreds of weeklies.

The few remaining reporters for the *Cleveland Plain Dealer*, Ohio's largest newspaper and home to the nation's first News Guild, were told in April 2019 that they were no longer allowed to cover Cleveland, Cuyahoga, and Summit counties, or anything that might be considered a "statewide" issue. Those areas were now the domain of the non-union sister outlet Cleveland. com. Both the *Plain Dealer* and Cleveland.com are owned by Advance Publications, a New York-based media conglomerate that has been trying for years to break the Cleveland union.

Atlanta-based Cox Media sold its television holdings to the private-equity firm Apollo Global Management for $3.1 billion in November 2019. That sale, however, was problematic for the completely converged Dayton newsroom, which included newspaper (*Dayton Daily News*), television (WHIO), radio (WHIO AM 1290 and News 95.7), and digital (Dayton.com) journalists. The sale violated an FCC rule that prohibited ownership of a daily newspaper and TV station in the same market. (Cox Media was grandfathered in because it owned the *Dayton Daily News* and WHIO before the rule was established in 1975.) Apollo's original plan was to scale back publication of the newspaper, as well as its sister publications, the *Hamilton Journal-News* and *Springfield News-Sun*, to three days a week. The FCC approved this plan, but there was an uproar from Dayton leaders and residents. So, Apollo sold the papers *back* to Cox, which kept the daily publication schedule.

None of these papers are locally owned. However, Ohio is fairly lucky compared to other states. Nationwide, 225 counties do not have a local newspaper, and more than 1,500 counties (about half of those in the United States) have only one, usually a weekly. This lack of local news is important for a few reasons. First, local newspapers are still the most significant providers of journalism in local communities. In one study, newspapers, which made up roughly 25 percent of the sample of local media outlets, accounted for nearly 60 percent of the local news stories, including nearly 50 percent of the original news stories, in the database (Napoli & Mahone, 2019). The loss of local newspapers, and the corresponding growth of news deserts, also has been correlated to increases in the cost of local government (Capps, 2018) and higher levels of political partisanship (Hitt, Darr, & Dunaway, 2019). Further compounding the issues, a wealth of hyper-partisan media—typically funded and operated by government officials, political candidates, political action committees, and political parties—has popped up in swing states, including two in Ohio and another in Cincinnati's northern Kentucky suburbs, filling the local and state informational vacuum with political propaganda while masquerading as traditional, nonpartisan news (Mahone & Napoli, 2020).

NEW MEDIA, OLD ISSUES

Publishers, editors, and reporters at legacy news organizations have long argued that the current crisis is economic, not journalistic. Financial woes, they assert, are the result of Craigslist and Monster siphoning off classified ads, Match and eHarmony taking personal ads, and car dealerships and grocery stores realizing that it is more cost effective to create their own websites than to advertise in print or on television. The hope was that a new generation of online media companies would help fill some of the void left by shrinking newsroom budgets.

However, new media companies are facing many of the same issues as their legacy counterparts. In 2019, for example, Buzzfeed laid off 15 percent of its staff, and *HuffPost*'s parent company, the Verizon Media Group, cut 7 percent. One year earlier saw a round of layoffs at online and legacy heavyweights, including CNN, *Glamour*, *GQ*, Into, Lenny Letter, Mic, the *New York Daily News*, The Outline, Refinery29, Rookie, *Teen Vogue*, Vox, *Vanity Fair*, *Vice*, and *Vogue* (Knibbs, 2019). BuzzFeed and *Vice* both missed 2017 revenue targets by 15–20 percent. Mashable, once valued at $250 million, sold in November 2017 for only $50 million.

One major issue facing new, and legacy, media is that consumers, especially in the desired 18–29 age demographic, are increasingly getting their content online. Network and cable television now compete with internet media from Amazon Video, Disney, Hulu, iTunes, Netflix, Sling TV, and YouTube. Cable subscriptions have decreased quarterly since 2010 (Spangler, 2017).

Platforms such as Facebook and Google compete with publishers for advertising content, so, in essence, online publishers (much like their legacy counterparts before them) are paying to produce content while Facebook and Google reap most of the monetary rewards. In 2020, the Australian Competition and Consumer Commission drafted a news media bargaining code that would force Google and Facebook to pay for news on their sites to help fund public-interest journalism. Facebook retaliated by threatening to ban publishers and Australian citizens from sharing local and international news on Facebook and Instagram (Nicholls, 2020). The display-advertising model, which led to a destructive race for "clicks," is outdated and ineffective. Some sites—from Mashable to MTV News—pivoted to video in the hope that video ads would be more appealing and, therefore, more lucrative, than their display counterparts. All must find a workable revenue model, with subscriptions, memberships, events, nonprofit status, and venture capital—or some combination of all of the above—being the most likely economic fix, at least in the short term.

SOCIAL RESPONSIBILITY IN THE NEW MEDIA WORLD

Stakeholder theory is far from a reality in the media universe. Good journalism is expensive, and in an era of declining subscriptions and ad revenues, few newsrooms enjoy budgets as large as in past years. Television networks have closed entire bureaus, and many newspapers have pulled back on overseas correspondents, leaving coverage of foreign news to the wires and CNN. The current era of cutbacks and consolidations has been noted by media researcher Robert McChesney (1997), who makes this analogy:

> Imagine if the federal government demanded that newspaper and broadcast journalism staffs be cut in half, that foreign bureaus be closed, and that news be tailored to suit the government's self-interest. There would be an outcry that would make the Alien and Sedition Acts, the Red Scares and Watergate seem like child's play. Yet when corporate America aggressively pursues the exact same policies, scarcely a murmur of dissent can be detected in the political culture.

The effect of cutbacks is lost news for the consumer. One photojournalist, Brad Clift, told the authors that he went to Somalia months before US troops were dispatched, using his own money because he felt the starvation there was an underreported story. Only an occasional network crew and a handful of newspapers pursued the Somalia story before former president George H. W. Bush committed US troops to the region in December 1992. Most news organizations, such as this photojournalist's employer, declined to cover the emerging story, pleading that they had depleted their international budgets by covering Operation Desert Storm. However, other approaches and organizations are emerging—funded by cooperative agreements among news organizations and sometimes foundations. They have produced excellent journalism. Some, such as ProPublica, have won prestigious awards, including the Pulitzer Prize.

In reading the Society of Professional Journalists code of ethics, two of the "guiding principles" of journalism speak directly to the ethics of media economics: (1) seek truth and report it as fully as possible and (2) act independently. Seeking the truth can be personally and financially expensive, something that stakeholder theory demands and stockholder theory avoids.

Some media companies *have* learned the lesson. McKinsey and Company (National Association of Broadcasters, 1985) studied 11 of the nation's great radio stations and reported what made an excellent radio station. Their findings were as follows:

- The great radio stations were audience-oriented in their programming.
- The great radio stations were community-oriented in their promotions.

Great radio stations had a knack for becoming synonymous in their communities with charitable events and community festivities even without an immediate return on investment. The attitude is summed up by WMMS (Cleveland) general manager Bill Smith:

> If you want a car to last forever, you've got to throw some money back into that car and make sure that it's serviced properly on a continual basis. Otherwise, it's going to break down and fall apart. We know that we're constantly rebuilding the station one way or another. We throw the profit to the listening audience[,] . . . to charities, to several nonprofit organizations, to free concerts or anything to affect the listeners of Cleveland as a whole . . . because they identify us as being community-minded.

In the past decade, the one area of radio listenership that has shown steady growth is National Public Radio (NPR), whose more than 1,000 member stations constitute a daily national audience larger than the television networks, according to Nielsen, NPR affiliates are the highest-rated radio station in several local markets. NPR—which unlike the BBC in England receives almost no government funding—is an avowed proponent of the stakeholder model of media economics.

Uplifting examples are far too rare. Entry-level salaries for journalists in both print and broadcast are far too low—under $30,000 in one survey—draining the industry of the talent that might solve some of the seemingly unsolvable problems. However, a strong democracy requires a strong media, and valid solutions must be found.

The stakes could not be higher.

SUGGESTED READINGS

Auletta, K. (1991). *Three blind mice: How the TV networks lost their way.* New York: Random House.

Bagdikian, B. H. (2000). *The media monopoly* (6th ed.). Boston: Beacon Press.

Cranberg, G., Bezanson, R., & Soloski, J. (2001). *Taking stock.* Ames: Iowa State University Press.

McChesney, R. W. (1991). *Rich media, poor democracy: Communication politics in dubious times.* Urbana: University of Illinois Press.

Mills, C. W. (1956). *The power elite.* New York: Oxford University Press.

Picard, R. G. (2010). *The economics of financing media companies.* New York: Fordham University Press.

Sandel, M. (2012). *What money can't buy: The moral limits of markets.* New York: Faffaf, Straus and Giroux.

Spence, E. H., Alexandra, A., Quinn, A., & Dunn, A. (2011). *Media, markets, and morals.* London: Wiley-Blackwell.

CASES

CASE 9-A

TWITTER'S TRUMP PROBLEM

CHAD PAINTER
University of Dayton

Twitter permanently suspended Donald Trump's personal account on Jan. 8, 2021, "due to the risk of further incitement of violence" (Twitter, 2021). The decision followed the Jan. 6 attack on the US Capitol, which was fostered—at least in part—by Trump's rhetoric online and offline. On Jan. 6, Twitter took down a video of Trump praising the rioters and falsely claiming election fraud, and the social media company suspended him from tweeting for 12 hours.

Twitter, however, isn't alone. Other social media and online companies—including Amazon, Facebook, Instagram, Pinterest, Shopify, Snapchat, TikTok, Twitch, and YouTube—have permanently or temporarily suspended Trump.

Twitter's ban is not without financial consequences for the company. For example, its stock, which is publicly traded, dropped 6 percent on the first day of trading since it banned Trump. Its stock price continued to drop from $52 a share on Jan. 8, 2021, to $44 on Jan. 19. As of this writing, the price has not recovered. Facebook, Pinterest, and Snapchat also lost value, but not to the extent of Twitter (Bursztynsky, 2021).

One reason for the price drop is that Donald Trump's personal Twitter account had 88.5 million followers—just more than 25 percent of Twitter's 330 million total users. His official presidential account had 33.3 million followers in January 2020. The White House account had 26.1 million followers during his last month in office. (The @POTUS and @WhiteHouse accounts were not suspended, but both did transfer to Biden's communication team following his Jan. 20 inauguration.)

Those numbers are problematic for Twitter, which makes money through selling users' behavioral patterns to advertisers. The more engagement—the depth of involvement with the site measured by retweets, replies, likes, and time spent on the platform, among other things—a person has with the platform, the better for Twitter. Trump drove engagement in his political base, as well as opponents who often "hate tweeted" responses to his posts.

Twitter also has a financial stake in the debate about Section 230 of the 1996 Communications Decency Act, which protects internet companies from legal liability for user-generated content. Trump and his allies—falsely claiming that social media companies censor them—want to repeal Section 230. Others—including Twitter's Jack Dorsey and Facebook's Mark Zuckerberg—think the law should be revisited and possibly amended or replaced, but not repealed. Many on the left also favor this reform, which, as of this writing, has yet to be codified in legislation. The bottom line for Twitter and other social media platforms is that keeping Trump happy—or at least not angry—is good for business.

In June 2020, Twitter announced that tweets by world leaders would stay online if they have a "clear public interest value"—even if those tweets violate the platform's policies. When, for example, a political leader violates the platform's rules of spreading misinformation, Twitter might add a disclaimer providing context, hide the offending tweet behind a warning label, or limit its spread by preventing people from liking, replying, or retweeting it. "Direct interactions with fellow public figures, comments on political issues of the day, or foreign policy saber-rattling on economic or military issues are generally not in violation" of the rules, according to Twitter.

Donald Trump consistently broke Twitter's rules while he was president. For example, in the week after the Nov. 3 presidential election, Twitter flagged 39 Trump tweets for spreading baseless accusations of voter fraud, falsely claiming victory, and casting doubt on the validity of mail-in ballots. Trump's Twitter misbehavior, however, started long before the election. During unrest and violence following the police killing of George Floyd in Minneapolis, Trump tweeted that "when the looting starts, the shooting starts" on May 29, 2020. Twitter flagged the tweet, stating that it violated rules about "glorifying violence." Trump's team escalated the dispute by tweeting the same message on the official White House account, but it again was flagged by Twitter (see figure 9.2).

Perhaps the most egregious example came when Trump accused MSNBC host Joe Scarborough of potentially murdering Lori Klausutis, who died from a fall when she hit her head on a desk while she was an aide for then-US Representative Scarborough in 2001. The fall was the result of an undiagnosed heart condition. Trump began attacking Scarborough in 2020 when the host criticized Trump's COVID-19

Figure 9.2.

Figure 9.3.

response and anti-immigration policies. The continued attacks and innuendos by Trump prompted Klaustutis's widow to write a personal letter to Twitter CEO Jack Dorsey asking him to intervene (see figure 9.3).

Twitter responded on May 26, stating that it would not take action on Trump's tweets.

Twitter's fairly hands-off approach to tweets by world leaders does not apply to ex-public officials.

Micro Issues

1. Donald Trump had 88.5 million Twitter followers. What role, if any, should a person's number of followers play in deciding actions for tweets that violate Twitter's terms of use?
2. Are disclaimers, warning labels, and preventing actions such as retweets effective? Why or why not? Provide evidence to support your answer.
3. Should Twitter have permanently suspended Donald Trump's account? Did it wait too long? How would your answer change if Twitter waited until after Joe Biden's inauguration?
4. What standard of truth do you think tweets should be held to?

Midrange Issues

1. Is it ethically fair for Twitter to have one set of rules for political leaders and another for everyone else? How might Michael Sandel answer that question?
2. How would you define "clear public interest value"? How is your definition similar to or different from Twitter's?
3. Is there an ethical difference between tweeting misinformation (i.e., voter fraud), threats (i.e., "when the looting starts, the shooting starts"), and conspiracy theories (i.e., accusing Scarborough of murder)?

Macro Issues

1. Do social media platforms have a social responsibility to provide truthful information? How is that responsibility similar to or different from the obligations of news media?
2. Twitter CEO Jack Dorsey, while testifying before Congress, said that eliminating Section 230 would likely result in "increased removal of speech, the proliferation of frivolous lawsuits, and severe limitations on our collective ability to address harmful content and protect people online." Evaluate this statement.
3. Is there an ethical distinction between Donald Trump and administration officials tweeting from @realDonaldTrump (his personal account) or @POTUS or @WhiteHouse? Should there be a distinction?
4. Should the income from social media platforms be taxed to support fact-based journalism, similar to the support for the BBC or media organizations in Sweden and Finland?

CASE 9-B

WHEN INVESTIGATIVE REPORTING IS BAD FOR BUSINESS

CHAD PAINTER
University of Dayton

In November 2019, *Bloomberg News* announced a 2020 election policy forbidding investigations of potential Democratic presidential nominees. *Bloomberg News* had a long-standing policy to avoid probing Michael Bloomberg—the former New York City mayor and billionaire publisher of his own namesake news organization—so they would be hands off for all other Democratic presidential contenders in order to level the playing field after Bloomberg announced his own candidacy. They would, however, continue to investigate the Trump administration (Darcy, 2019).

When some reporters expressed concern about the hands-off approach, Bloomberg said they "just have to learn to live with some things."

"They get a paycheck," Bloomberg told *CBS This Morning*'s Gayle King. "But with your paycheck comes some restrictions and responsibilities" (Darcy, 2019).

Bloomberg dropped out of the presidential race on March 4, 2020, following losses in all but American Samoa on Super Tuesday; he later endorsed Joe Biden and donated $18 million to the Democratic National Committee. *Bloomberg News* reporters resumed coverage of the Democratic contenders after Bloomberg dropped out of the race.

Bloomberg's prohibition against investigating Democratic candidates is not, however, the first time he has meddled in newsroom operations.

In 2013, Bloomberg LP (the parent company of *Bloomberg News*) targeted China as a growing market and strategic priority for its main product, Bloomberg Terminals. Subscribers pay $20,000 annually for each terminal, which provides specialized financial data and analysis (Folkenflik, 2020b).

So, Bloomberg and his editors killed an investigative series about the accumulation of wealth by Communist Party elites in China following backlash by the Chinese government (Folkenflik, 2020b). The Chinese ambassador to the United States warned Bloomberg executives against publishing the series. Following the publication of the first story in the series, Chinese authorities searched Bloomberg's news bureaus, delayed visas for reporters, and ordered state-owned companies not to sign leases for Bloomberg terminals (Folkenflik, 2020b).

The series focused on ties between Chinese leaders—including the family of Chinese President Xi Jinping—and businessman Wang Jianlin. According to a subsequent story in the *New York Times*, relatives of high-ranking party members invested in Jianlin's company Dalian Wanda just before its initial public offering; the company appreciated to more than $1.1 billion once it was listed.

In October 2013, Bloomberg Editor-in-Chief Matthew Winkler—in a private conference call with senior news executives in New York, as well as the China-based investigative team—expressed concern about the consequences of publishing additional pieces of the investigation.

"It is for sure going to, you know, invite the Communist Party to, you know, completely shut us down and kick us out of the country," Winkler said. "So, I just don't see that as a story that is justified" (Folkenflik, 2020b).

Publicly, Bloomberg editors said at the time that the story didn't run because it needed more reporting. However, Winkler's private comments suggest that the real motivation was the potential loss of business in China.

In late 2013, *Bloomberg News* suspended and later fired Beijing correspondent Mike Forsythe, accusing him of leaking the controversy to other news outlets. Forsythe now works for the *New York Times*.

Micro Issues

1. Should *Bloomberg News* have forbidden investigations of potential Democratic presidential nominees once Michael Bloomberg entered the race? Should they also have halted investigations into Donald Trump?
2. Do reporters give up some speech rights in exchange for their paycheck?
3. China is a major business market because of its population of more than 1.4 billion people. What role, if any, should access to that market play in editorial decisions by news organizations?

Midrange Issues

1. When, if ever, should a newsroom report on its publisher if he/she is running for public office? If he/she owns international businesses?
2. Bloomberg is not the first publisher to slant news coverage of China. Evaluate the role of Henry Luce and *Time* magazine in its coverage of the Chinese Communist revolution. Have the ethical standards for publishers changed in the past 50 years?

3. Is it a conflict of interest for a publisher to run for public office? For a reporter or editor?

Macro Issues

1. Evaluate Bloomberg's editorial decisions based on stockholder theory versus stakeholder theory?
2. Does the fact that Bloomberg LP is a privately held company make any difference to your ethical analysis? Compare Bloomberg's relationship with Bloomberg LP and Jeff Bezos's relationship with the *Washington Post* in reporting political news.
3. Should the ethical strictures that apply to news workers apply equally to managers and owners? Do you think your response is practical, considering the current ownership structure of most media organizations?

CASE 9-C

AND THE OSCAR REJECTS . . . FRIDA MOM

CHAD PAINTER
University of Dayton

Companies are willing to pay a premium to reach the 18 million people who tune in annually to the Oscars telecast. In 2020, Oscars ads sold for $2.6 million for a 30-second spot.

One company, however, was shut out at the Oscars. The Academy of Motion Picture Arts and Sciences rejected a Frida Mom ad for being "too graphic with partial nudity and product demonstration."

In this 60-second ad, a new mother struggles to use the bathroom following childbirth. The spot centers on a new mother who is woken up during the night by her crying newborn. She gets out of bed to use the bathroom. Her postpartum belly is visible, and she is wearing ill-fitting mesh underwear with bulky pads. Most of the ad takes place in the bathroom, where the new mom struggles to urinate (a common problem following childbirth) and uses a poorly designed peri bottle—a squirt bottle that allows a woman to clean her bottom easily and gently after childbirth—that requires a lot of dexterity and flexibility to use. The ad ends with the tagline "Postpartum recovery doesn't have to be that hard" and a shot of a variety of Frida Mom products (Seligson, 2020).

In an email to Frida Mom, the Oscars suggested the company consider advertising "an alternative product in their portfolio" or a "kinder, more gentle portrayal of postpartum" (Seligson, 2020).

Frida Mom executives said they wanted to show postpartum recovery in unsparing detail. The ad, however, was criticized by some mothers (although others strongly supported it), who said that postpartum is almost never as difficult as depicted in the ad, that hospitals and doctors do help new mothers, and that the ad depicted new mothers as weaker and more helpless than they actually are. There also was criticism about the cost of the product—Frida Mom's "Labor and Delivery + Postpartum Recovery Kit" sells for $99.99, making it a luxury that only certain classes of women can reasonably afford.

"The ad you're about to watch was rejected by ABC & the Oscars from airing during this year's award show," the company wrote on Instagram after posting the video. "It's not 'violent, political' or sexual in nature. Our ad is not 'religious or lewd' and does not portray 'guns or ammunition.' 'Feminine hygiene & hemorrhoid relief' are also banned subjects" (Henderson, 2020).

Frida Mom CEO Chelsea Hirschhorn said she thought networks and advertising boards are "cautious against polarizing the broadest base that they have, so some of these topics generate very polarizing opinions. I don't happen to think pregnancy and postpartum are one of them" (Seligson, 2020).

The ad has been viewed more than 4.3 million times since it was posted online.

Micro Issues

1. The Frida Mom ad was rejected because it was "too graphic." Compare it to ads—for example, ads about prescription drugs including those that treat erectile dysfunction—that did run during the Oscars telecast.
2. Frida Mom has received a wealth of free advertising—in terms of both news stories and the 4.3 million times its ad has been viewed online. What are the ethical issues, if any, of using the Oscars rejection to garner free publicity?
3. Should Frida Mom have reshot the ad to depict a "kinder, more gentle portrayal of postpartum"? What are the ethical implications of reshooting the ad? Of not reshooting it?

Midrange Issues

1. Would the Frida Mom ad pass the Post Toasties Test (discussed in chapter 8)? Why or why not?
2. Many 2020 Oscar ads—including Nike's commercial narrated by Serena Williams and Cadillac's commercial featuring victorious women at an awards ceremony and in a boxing ring—were directed at female viewers. What are the economic advantages of targeting women in the Oscars telecast? What are the ethical implications of your answer?
3. Thinx created the ad "MENstruation," which showed an alternate world where men menstruate. It was rejected by CBS but ran on networks including NBC, Bravo, MTV, E!, and TLC. Did companies such as Frida Mom and Thinx cross an ethical line with their ads? Where is that line?

Macro Issues

1. Frida Mom executives said they wanted to show postpartum recovery in unsparing detail. What is the role of truth telling in advertisements? How is that similar to and/or different from truth telling in news?
2. Is the Frida Mom ad socially responsible? Why or why not?
3. Evaluate the Frida Mom ad in terms of feminist ethics.

CASE 9-D

WHO CONTROLS THE LOCAL NEWS? SINCLAIR BROADCAST GROUP AND "MUST-RUNS"

KEENA NEAL
Wayne State University

Americans take for granted that the news they watch on their local NBC, ABC, CBS, or Fox affiliate is local. But what if what we watch on our local news is produced at the corporate headquarters of the broadcaster rather than by local reporters and producers?

In May 2017, Sinclair Broadcasting Group brokered a $3.9 billion deal to buy Tribune Media's 42 television stations. (Tribune terminated the sale agreement in August 2018 following pushback from the FCC and Department of Justice.) Sinclair, the largest owner of local television stations in the United States, would have reached nearly three out of four homes in the country (Zhou, 2017). Sinclair has largely operated in small to medium markets, often owning multiple stations within one market. The addition of Tribune Media's stations would have given Sinclair access to the three largest markets in the nation: New York, Los Angeles, and Chicago (Folkenflik, 2017). A look at the holdings of each company also reveals that the merged group would have owned at least two television stations with fully staffed newsrooms in many small- to mid-sized markets. Under the deal, Sinclair also would have assumed $2.7 billion in Tribune Media's debt.

Critics argue Sinclair uses its television stations to promote right-wing propaganda. After the 9/11 attacks, Sinclair required its anchors and reporters to read positive messages supporting then President George W. Bush's campaign against terrorism. In 2004, when ABC's *Nightline* devoted an entire episode to soldiers killed in the Iraq war, Sinclair barred its local ABC affiliates from airing the program. Nationwide, local anchors read a segment in April 2018 denouncing "the troubling trend of irresponsible, one-sided news stories plaguing our country" in which "the media use their platforms to push their own personal bias and agenda to control 'exactly what people think.' "

The company produces "must-run" content it distributes to its 173 stations. For example, the "Bottom Line with Boris" feature commentary from Boris Epshteyn, Sinclair's chief political analyst and former staff assistant to President Donald Trump, must air nine times per week. Epshteyn "reliably parrots the White House on most issues," including claiming that former FBI Director James Comey's Capitol Hill testimony "was more damaging to Hillary Clinton and former Attorney General Loretta Lynch than to the president" (Gold, 2017). Sinclair denies any partisan tilt to its programming and defends its "must-run" practice, stating, "We stand by our approach to sharing content among our stations to supplement the excellent work our newsroom staffs do every day in service to their communities" (Gold, 2017).

Consumer advocate groups opposed the Sinclair-Tribune merger because the combined company would have surpassed the federally mandated maximum reach of 39 percent of national TV homes (Snider, 2017a). Sinclair-Tribune would have owned and/or operated more than 200 stations and reached 72 percent of US households. The increase in stations could have permitted Sinclair to demand larger payments to pay-TV operators that wanted to retransmit their programming, the cost of which ultimately could be passed down to the American consumer (Snider, 2017b).

Democratic senator Dick Durbin of Illinois urged the FCC to block the proposed purchase, writing that the deal would "threaten diversity and localism in broadcasting, ignore the unique concerns and interests of local audiences and harm competition" (CBS, 2017). Additionally, the attorneys general in four states (Illinois, Maryland, Massachusetts, and Rhode Island) announced their opposition, contending the merger would have increased market consolidation, reduced consumer choice, "and threaten[ed] the diversity of voices in media" (Johnson, 2017a). The attempt to close the Sinclair-Tribune merger came at a time when four other huge media outlets were attempting mergers of their own. Both AT&T and Time Warner (Kang & de la Merced, 2017) and Disney and 21st Century Fox (Delk, 2017) were running into congressional resistance in their attempts to merge into two more media behemoths. Both of those deals eventually were approved.

Recently, the Republican-led FCC has relaxed several long-established rules designed to protect against monopoly and ensure diverse content in local media. In April 2017, the FCC reversed a 2016 rule that limits the number of television stations a broadcaster can buy (Shepardson, 2017), and, in October 2017, it "rescinded a 78-year-old rule that required broadcasters to maintain a local studio in communities where they're licensed, overturning a requirement to deliver strong local content" (CBS, 2017). In November 2017, the FCC voted to allow broadcasters to own newspapers in the same market and two of the top four stations in a city (Johnson, 2017b).

Micro Issues

1. What are the advantages and disadvantages of local ownership for television stations? What are the advantages and disadvantages of a broadcast company producing content for stations across the United States?
2. Critics charge that Sinclair censors alternative viewpoints, requires its stations to air conservative content, and exercises corporate control over local news content. How might these arguments influence your answer to the previous question?

Midrange Issues

1. Evaluate Illinois senator Dick Durbin's statement that the merger would "threaten diversity and localism in broadcasting, ignore the unique concerns and interests of local audiences and harm competition."

2. What is the value of local autonomy for journalists and producers? Discuss using the concepts of public service, credibility, and trust.
3. Do you see a difference in mergers that involve journalism, such as the Sinclair merger with Tribune, and mergers that are largely about entertainment, such as AT&T/Time Warner and Disney/21st Century Fox?

Macro Issues

1. Who were the stakeholders in the proposed merger? How should their interests have been weighed by the FCC?
2. Would Immanuel Kant approve the merger? Would John Stuart Mill?
3. The "39 percent" rule is designed to limit monopolization of news. Should this rule still be enforced in the digital age when citizens can access virtually any news media via the internet? Why or why not?

CASE 9-E

CONTESTED INTERESTS, CONTESTED TERRAIN: THE *NEW YORK TIMES* CODE OF ETHICS

LEE WILKINS
University of Missouri

BONNIE BRENNEN
Marquette University

In January 2003, the *New York Times* broke with a lengthy tradition and published its new ethics code on the web. The *Times*'s decision was an important one, for ethics codes are often controversial in both their creation and their application. However, ethics codes can be an important marker of specific social practices created under particular social, economic, and political conditions at distinct times in history.

For example, in 1933, members of the American Newspaper Guild crafted one of the first ethics codes developed by journalists rather than managers. That code suggested the "high calling" of journalism had been tarnished because news workers had been pressured by their employers to serve special interests rather than the public good. Conflict of interest was centered on the relationship between reporters and sources, and the code made a particular point that business pressures were putting undue stress on newsrooms. The code recommended that to combat business pressures the news should be edited "exclusively in newsrooms."

Ethics codes in general are controversial among professionals and scholars. Some maintain that ethics codes are nothing more than generalized aspirations—too vague to be of any use when specific decisions must be made. Others insist codes can be helpful to beginning journalists, photographers, and public relations practitioners—that they provide some guidance in the form of rules that can be internalized as media professionals gain expertise and experience. And still others see ethics codes as a manifestation of the ideology of an era—more about power and politics than ethics.

The new *Times* code linked its creation to the public perception of the "professional reputations of its staff member(s)." The code was directed to "all members of the news and editorial departments whose work directly affects the content of the paper."

The code focused primarily on conflict of interest. In fact, the code did not mention accuracy and fairness and devoted only a single sentence to privacy. However, when addressing conflict of interest, the code was both specific and detailed. The *Times* code considered the impact that spousal relationships might have on news coverage. It also addressed whether journalists working abroad should abide by the ethics and mores of the countries in which they are stationed, most of which do not provide the equivalent of First Amendment protections.

The code required staff members to disclose yearly speaking fees in excess of $5,000 and prohibited staff members from accepting gifts, tickets, discounts, or other "inducements" from organizations the *Times* covered. Staff members could not invest in companies they covered, and payment for favorable or altered coverage was specifically forbidden.

However, staff members were allowed to do certain sorts of unpaid work—for example, public relations for a child's school fundraising event. But *Times* staffers were forbidden to give money to candidates or causes, march in support of public movements, or appear on radio and television shows to voice views that went beyond those of the paper. When family members, such as spouses, participated in such activities, *Times* staffers were required to disclose those activities to management and recuse themselves from certain sorts of coverage.

The *Times* code was protective of the newspaper's position in the marketplace. Staffers were prohibited from disclosing confidential information about the operations, plans, or policies of the newspaper to other journalists. Such questions were to be referred to management. If readers asked such questions, *Times* staffers were encouraged to respond "openly and honestly." *Times* staff members also were prohibited from doing freelance work for any media outlet that competed with the *Times*.

> Staff members may not appear on broadcasts that compete directly with the *Times*'s own offerings on television or the Internet. . . . As the paper moves further into these new fields, its direct competitors and clients or potential clients will undoubtedly grow in number.

Micro Issues

1. Should managers and owners be subject to a code of ethics, particularly for publications as influential as the *Times*?
2. Why is the notion of perception—as opposed to action—important in considering the issue of conflict of interest?
3. Should the *Times* code have addressed a variety of common journalistic issues—such as accuracy, fairness, and privacy?

Midrange Issues

1. Disclosure is often suggested as a remedy for conflict of interest. Evaluate this remedy.
2. Should conflict of interest rules be different at a small newspaper as opposed to the *Times*?
3. Does the *Times* code infringe on staffers' First Amendment rights? Do journalists give up some of their rights as citizens in order to do the work of journalism?
4. Are there instances when recusing oneself from an assignment is unsatisfactory? What should journalists do if such a case arises?
5. Should a conflict of interest extend as far as prohibitions against a journalist being an officer in the parent–teacher association (i.e., PTA or PTO) of his or her child's school? An officer in your local homeowners' association? Does the potential for those organizations to get involved in the news pages (i.e., teacher problems, zoning protests) influence your decision?

Macro Issues

1. What are the specific historical developments in the field of journalism that may have promoted the development of this particular version of the *New York Times* code?
2. Research indicates that codes that are developed by the newsroom have a much better chance of influencing behavior than codes

that are superimposed by management. If the *Times* had used this approach, would it have "discovered" the actions of reporters such as Jayson Blair (details of the Blair case may be found on the internet)?

3. Does the *Times* code place the organization's financial health on equal footing with the public trust? Is that appropriate?

The *New York Times* Social Media Policy: Everything We Do Is Public

In October 2017, the *New York Times* expanded its existing ethics policies to cover social media. *Times* executive editor Dean Baquet, himself a prize-winning investigative reporter, presaged the change with some comments at a George Washington University forum where he said *Times* reporters should not be able to say anything on social media platforms that they would not be able to say in the pages of the newspaper.

In a preface to the changes, Baquet wrote:

> Social media plays a vital role in our journalism. On social platforms, our reporters and editors can promote their work, provide real-time updates, harvest and curate information, cultivate sources, engage with readers and experiment with new forms of storytelling and voice.
>
> We can effectively pull back the curtain and invite readers to witness, and potentially contribute to, our reporting. We can also reach new audiences.
>
> But social media presents potential risks for *The Times*. If our journalists are perceived as biased or if they engage in editorializing on social media, that can undercut the credibility of the entire newsroom.
>
> We've always made clear that newsroom employees should avoid posting anything on social media that damages our reputation for neutrality and fairness.

The guidelines apply to all *Times* employees. They specifically require the following:

- In social media posts, our journalists must not express partisan opinions, promote political views, endorse candidates, make offensive comments or do anything else that undercuts the *Times'* journalistic reputation.

- Our journalists should be especially mindful of appearing to take sides on issues that the *Times* is seeking to cover objectively.

- These guidelines apply to everyone in every department of the newsroom, including those not involved in coverage of government and politics.

The new social media policy also offered advice to *Times* journalists, particularly the women on the staff, about how to handle trolls who, in the heat of the 2016 election, suggested through internet memes that rape would be an appropriate response to stories written by women that readers might disagree with.

The decision by editors to try to tamp down social media posts by *Times* reporters dated at least to September 2016, when the public editor, the *Times*'s version of an ombudsman, wrote that *Times* editors had cautioned reporters about stating opinions regarding then-candidate Donald Trump's tweets.

Some media outlets, among them Fox News, called the guidelines a "fig leaf" that could not obscure what Fox and others have called the *Times*'s left-leaning reporting.

In an article in the *Columbia Journalism Review*, reporter Mathew Ingram noted the changes at the *Times* were connected to Trump's continuing campaign against what he called "the failing New York Times." However, the article noted that such restrictions were unlikely to convince readers that journalists were "objective." The piece also noted that such restrictions would not allow *Times* journalists and others to use social media to its fullest potential. However, Ingram noted that there were financial implications:

> This flawed approach is even more dangerous for publishers who, like the *Times* and the [*Wall Street*] *Journal*, are relying increasingly on subscriptions, membership fees, and other relationship-based models for their continued economic survival.

How do you convince people to support you in such a way? By building a relationship with them, one that encourages them to believe you share a worldview, or at least that you can be trusted. And how do you do that? Not by pretending you have no opinions, but by being as honest as possible—asking for feedback and admitting when you make a mistake. In other words, by being human.

Micro Issue

1. How is the *Times*'s social media policy like or unlike its general ethics policy?

Midrange Issue

1. Should journalists, in order to practice journalism, give up their First Amendment rights on social media platforms?

Macro Issue

1. Is objectivity the appropriate professional standard in a century increasingly dominated by social media and where fact and opinion continue to blur? If your answer is no, what do you think might be an appropriate preliminary substitute?

CASE 9-F

AUTOMATED JOURNALISM: THE RISE OF ROBOT REPORTERS

CHAD PAINTER
University of Dayton

Traditionally, workers considered most at risk of being replaced by machines performed physical jobs in predictable environments, such as operating machines in a factory or preparing fast food. Today, however, another kind of worker is at least partially replaceable: the news reporter.

News organizations, including the Associated Press, Reuters, the *Los Angeles Times*, the *Washington Post*, and *USA Today*, have begun experimenting with automated content-generating systems for fairly boilerplate stories such as earning reports and simple sports recaps.

Content-generation systems such as Narrative Science and Automated Insights can produce short articles with structured data. These systems comb data feeds for facts and trends and then meld that information with historical and contextual data to form narrative sentences (Keohane, 2017). For example, the *Washington Post* uses a program called Heliograf. Editors create narrative templates for stories and then tap Heliograf into a source of structured data such as VoteSmart.org. Heliograf can identify relevant data, match it to corresponding phrases from the narrative template, merge the data and the phrases, and publish the resulting story across different platforms (Keohane, 2017). There is a better-than-average chance that you have read a Heliograf-created article; the program wrote and published more than 850 articles in 2016 about the Rio Olympics, congressional and gubernatorial races, and Washington, D.C., area high school football games.

The rise of robots does not mean the fall of reporters, however. Heliograf, for example, includes a function to alert reporters if it finds data anomalies such as a wider margin of victory than expected in a gubernatorial race (Keohane, 2017). In 2014, Reuters created News Tracer, a program that tracks social media, specifically Twitter, for breaking news. The program can track 500 million tweets daily in real time, and it alerted Reuters reporters to hospital bombings in Aleppo and terrorist attacks in Nice and Brussels before other media outlets were aware of the stories (Stray, 2016). Similar programs can scan data and documents to make connections for complex investigative projects and evaluate the truthfulness of statistical claims (Stray, 2016).

In these cases, automation creates leads, not stories. In other words, robots can report a figure but cannot interpret its meaning. Humans still have to do the in-depth work of talking to sources, piecing together data points from multiple inputs, and drawing evidence-based conclusions. Robots can write formulaic stories, but at least so far humans are needed to write profiles, trend pieces, and analyses. As Kevin Roose writes, "Rather than putting us out of work, it might free us up to do more of the kinds of work we actually *like*." The Associated Press estimates that automation has reduced reporters' time spent covering corporate earnings by 20 percent while also increasing accuracy (Moses, 2017).

Still, reporters are unconvinced that robot reporters are good for journalism. In one recent study, journalists expressed concerns that robots could produce a high volume of stories that negatively impact the news agenda:

> We believe robo-journalism will be used more often to produce simple factual reports, increase the speed with which they are published, and to cover topics currently below the threshold of reportability. . . . However, the increased volume of news resulting from automation may make it more difficult to navigate a world already saturated with information, and actually increase the need for the very human skills that good journalists embody such as news judgement, curiosity, and skepticism. (Scott, 2017)

Micro Issues

1. Should news organizations identify stories generated by automated programs?
2. Ken Schwencke developed an algorithm called Quakebot for the *Los Angeles Times* to quickly write articles about any LA-area earthquakes. The program plugs in relevant data to an existing

template and publishes the story under Schwencke's byline. Is this practice ethical reporting? Does it make an ethical difference that Schwencke wrote the algorithm? Why or why not?

Midrange Issues

1. Beginning reporters typically are assigned to write the formulaic stories. What are the advantages and disadvantages of having automated programs produce these stories instead of assigning them to beginning reporters?
2. How does your answer to the previous question change if and when automated programs advance to the point where they can write more complex pieces such as profiles, trend pieces, and analyses?
3. Do automated content systems prioritize information from certain kinds of sources? Evaluate how this kind of privilege might influence the news agenda or certain types of stories.
4. Programs such as this might allow media to get "hyper-local" in its coverage—for example, by producing news stories for each student on the honor roll. Is this a good use of the tool, or does this just add to the clutter some predict will come from automated reporting?

Macro Issues

1. Evaluate the statement that the number of articles produced by automated journalism could "make it more difficult to navigate a world already saturated with information."
2. Most newsrooms experimenting with automated reporting are large, national organizations such as the Associated Press and the *Washington Post*. Does the use of automation give these organizations an unfair advantage over small- and medium-market organizations that cannot invest in similar programs?
3. At the end of chapter 2, there is a list of ethical news values. Examine how robot-generated stories might and might not fulfill those values.

10

The Ethical Dimensions of Art and Entertainment

By the end of this chapter you should be able to

- understand the link between aesthetics and excellent professional performance;
- explain Tolstoy's rationale for art and apply it to issues such as stereotyping;
- understand the debate over the role of truth in popular art;
- understand the impact of economics on artistic vision.

In the last century, the primary use of media shifted from distributing information to providing entertainment and popularizing culture. In this chapter, we examine the ethical issues from the field of aesthetics. We will apply these principles, plus some findings from social science, to the art and entertainment industries, focusing on the responsibilities of both creators and consumers of entertainment.

AN ANCIENT MISUNDERSTANDING

Plato didn't like poets. His reasoning was straightforward: Poets, the people who dream, were the potential undoing of the philosopher king. They were rebels of the first order, insurrectionists on the hoof. He banned them from the Republic.

Plato's skepticism is alive today. Few weeks elapse without a news story about an artist or entertainment program that has offended. You are probably familiar with at least some of the following:

- When late-night talk shows were forced to produce content from their homes due to COVID-19, ABC's Jimmy Kimmel announced that he would donate to an organization providing COVID-19 relief each night while also urging viewers to do the same. Most notably, Kimmel's show raised more than $8,000 for Meals on Wheels, $16,000 for Feeding America, and $17,000 for World Central Kitchen. Kimmel has a history of advocacy on his show, including monologues about healthcare and gun control. In April and September 2017, an exasperated and impassioned Kimmel discussed his infant son, who had open-heart surgery in April and whose medical coverage could be severely limited if the Affordable Care Act was repealed. During his Oct. 2, 2017, opener, a clearly emotional Kimmel focused on the mass shooting in his Las Vegas hometown, calling on politicians to pass "common sense" measures to limit similar catastrophes. Proponents applauded Kimmel for using his platform to discuss important national topics. Opponents said that he is an entertainer who should stick to making people laugh.
- Universal Pictures delayed the scheduled Sept. 27 release of the film *The Hunt*, which centered on coastal elites hunting "deplorables" for sport, following mass shootings in El Paso, Texas, and Dayton, Ohio, as well as angry tweets from President Trump stating that Hollywood "is Racist at the highest level" and that the film was "made in order to inflame and cause chaos" (Dessem, 2019). The film eventually was released March 13, 2020, to mixed reviews and a $15 million gross at the box office, attributed at least in part to movie theaters closing due to the COVID-19 pandemic.
- Pop-country band Lady Antebellum changed its name to Lady A after increased national conversations about race and criticisms that its name romanticized ideas of a pre-Civil War, slave-owning South (Wang & Millman, 2020). The band also was criticized for its new name because Anita White, a Black blues and R & B singer, has performed and recorded under the name Lady A for more than 20 years. The singer and the band are suing each other over rights to the name.
- Attempts to ban books, even classics such as *Catcher in the Rye* or *Lady Chatterley's Lover*, from public or school libraries for being too sexually explicit. Recently, Harry Potter books were the focus of mostly unsuccessful attempt to ban books, a move led largely by conservative Christians.
- The controversy over government funding of art that some claim is obscene.
- Calls by conservatives and liberals to boycott television networks and their advertisers over allegedly objectionable content. This practice is similar to "cancel culture," which refers to the practice of withdrawing support (e.g., not purchasing tickets to movies or concerts, or watching

TV shows) from celebrities and other public figures who have said or done something offensive or objectionable.

- The furor over rappers, television producers, and filmmakers whose homophobic, misogynistic, and sometimes clever content offends many while earning nominations for the industry's top awards.
- While these examples come from the West, other cultures and political systems show the same tendencies. In 2012, the Russian punk band Pussy Riot received a two-year jail term for its criticism of Russian President Vladimir Putin's policies.
- In China, architect and sculptor Ai Weiwei, a member of the team that designed the 2008 Olympic stadium nicknamed "The Bird's Nest," was arrested and held without charge for more than two months in 2011 in response to his protests about the Chinese government's lack of action after devastating earthquakes and his allegations of government corruption.
- The producers of *Big Brother* in Germany were criticized for withholding news about the COVID-19 pandemic from 14 contestants who entered the show's sequestered house when cases were first being reported outside of Wuhan, China. The contestants only were told about a worldwide pandemic—which, at the time, included 6,000 cases and 13 deaths in Germany—live on-air.

Like Plato long ago, those who would restrict the arts do so because they mistrust the power of the artist or even the audience to link emotion and logic in a way that stimulates a new vision of society, culture, or individuals.

OF TOLSTOY AND TELEVISION

Tolstoy was the sort of artist Plato would have feared. In his famous essay "What It Art?" Tolstoy (1960) argued that good art had one dominant characteristic: It communicated the feelings of the artist to the masses in the way that the artist intended.

> To evoke in oneself a feeling one has once experienced and having evoked it in oneself then by means of movements, lines, colors, sounds or forms expressed in words, so to transmit that feeling that others experience the same feeling—that is the activity of art. . . . Art is a human activity consisting in this, that one may consciously by means of certain external signs, hand on to others feelings he has lived through, and that others are infected by these feelings and also experience them.

Tolstoy's standard was so demanding that he rejected the works of both Shakespeare and Beethoven as incapable of being understood by the masses.

Tolstoy's rationale is particularly pertinent to photographers and videographers who, through their visual images, seek to arouse emotion as well as inform. Haunting pictures of starvation from the Third World have launched international relief efforts. Televised images of Hurricane Katrina's victims spurred the resignation of some of FEMA's top officials—and affected the 2006 election. Award-winning dramas such as the play *Angels in America*, movies such as *Dallas Buyer's Club* and *Philadelphia*, the AIDS quilt, and obituaries of famous artists who have succumbed to AIDS have all aroused both our intellects and our emotions about the disease. Similarly, the opioid overdose deaths of Prince and Philip Seymour Hoffman, as well as great journalistic and fictional work about the spread of heroin and opioids across the United States, has both brought the epidemic to the public consciousness and helped frame it as a public health crisis instead of a law enforcement issue. They invite action. Television and film documentaries have made viewers more aware of the plight of the mentally ill and homeless, raised important public policy questions, and occasionally made us laugh through a unity of purpose and craft.

Such work reminds readers and viewers of the moral power of art by putting us in touch with characters and situations sometimes more complex than our own lives. By thinking about these fictional characters, we enlarge our moral imaginations.

Unfortunately, Tolstoy's assertion that great art is defined by how it is understood by an audience also includes a genuine dilemma. Even if given Tolstoy's life experiences, many readers could not articulate the deep truths about human nature Tolstoy wrote about in *War and Peace*. Worse yet, it is nearly impossible to sell those insights to a sometimes lukewarm public, or to produce them on demand for an hour a week, 36 weeks a year. The result is popular art that loses its critical edge and takes shortcuts to commonplace insight. In fact, some mass-communication scholars have argued that the unstated goal of popular art is to reinforce the status quo; popular culture, they say, blunts our critical-thinking abilities (see figure 10.1).

Figure 10.1. Calvin and Hobbes © 1990 Watterson. Reprinted with permission of Andrews McMeel Syndication. All rights reserved.

What Is Art?

Philosophers, sociologists, and artists have debated the meaning of art for hundreds of years. Prior to the Industrial Revolution, art was something only the well educated paid for, produced, and understood. Mozart had to capture the ear of the emperor to get a subsidy to write opera. Such "high" or "elite art" provided society with a new way to look at itself. Picasso's drawings of people with three eyes or rearranged body parts literally provided Western culture with a new way of seeing. Michelangelo's paintings and sculpture did the same thing in the Renaissance. But patronage had disadvantages. The patron could restrict both subject matter and form, a reality depicted in the film *Amadeus* where the emperor informed Mozart that his work, *The Marriage of Figaro*, had "too many notes." Gradually, artists discovered that if they could find a way to get more than one person to "pay" for the creation of art, artistic control returned to the artist. The concept of "popular art" was born. Scholars disagree about many of the qualities of elite and popular art; some even assert that popular art cannot truly be considered art. While both kinds of art are difficult to define, the following list outlines the major differences between popular and elite art and culture:

1. Popular art is consciously adjusted to the median taste by the artist; elite art reflects the individual artist's vision.
2. Popular art is not abstruse, complicated, or profound; elite art has these characteristics.
3. Popular art conforms to majority experience; elite art explores the new.
4. Popular art conforms to less clearly defined standards of excellence, most often linked to commercial success; elite art is much less commercially oriented, and its standards of excellence are consistent and integrated.
5. Popular artists know that the audience expects entertainment and instruction; elite artists seek an aesthetic experience.
6. The popular artist cannot afford to offend its target audience; the elite artist functions as a critic of society, and his or her work challenges and sometimes offends the status quo.
7. Popular art often arises from folk art; elite art more often emerges from a culture's dominant intellectual tradition.

Today, mass media have become the primary cultural storytellers of the era. Nearly half a century ago, Jacques Ellul (1965) argued that, in a modern society, storytelling is an inevitable and desirable tool to stabilize the culture. This "propaganda of integration" is not the deliberate lie commonly associated with propaganda but the dissemination of widely held beliefs to the culture at large. Aesop's fables and the early *McGuffey Readers* influenced generations of Americans with subtle (or not) messages that reinforced the social structure. This is precisely where the entertainment media get their power—not in the overt messages but in the underlying assumptions that (if unchallenged) will become widely held societal values. For instance, entertainment content can reinforce the status quo by constantly depicting certain social groups in an unflattering and unrepresentative way, presenting a distorted picture of reality. Groups as disparate as Muslims and evangelicals have chafed under depictions (or omissions) that reinforce cultural stereotypes despite evidence to the contrary.

At least some such distortion is the natural outcome of compression. Just as substances such as rubber change form when compressed, so do media messages. Given only 15 seconds to register a message in a commercial, an advertising copywriter will resort to showing us the presumed stereotype of a librarian, a mechanic, or a pharmacist. Using stereotypes as a form of mental shorthand is a natural way media work and was noted as early as 1922 by Walter Lippmann in *Public Opinion*. Lippmann said that we are all guilty of defining first and seeing second.

Soon, we expect reality to imitate art. Internationally, it is now common for those with a media following—often from entertainment programming—to run for and be elected to public office. Closer to home, news anchors began sitting on their suit jackets—sitting on the hem prevents the collar from riding up on the neck—after seeing the characters Tom Grunick and Aaron Altman do so in the 1987 film *Broadcast News*. Mass communicators know the power of stereotypes and deeply held notions and use them. According to Tony Schwartz (1973), advertising messages are often constructed backward. The communicator actually starts with what the receiver knows—or believes he knows—and then constructs a message that fits within that reality. Schwartz calls it hitting a "responsive chord." Time is saved in plucking the chords already deeply held by the public rather than challenging stereotypes. So pimps are Black, terrorists are Middle Eastern, women are subservient, and no one challenges the unstated assumptions. The audience gets the idea of a pimp or a terrorist, but notions of racism and worse have been planted as well. While these images suit the artist's purposes, they are problematic.

TRUTH IN ART AND ENTERTAINMENT

No question in the field of aesthetics is more thoroughly debated with less resolution than the role of truth in art. Most philosophers seem to agree that artists are not restricted to telling the literal truth. Often artists can reveal a previously hidden or veiled truth, providing a new way of looking at the world or understanding human nature that rings deeply true.

Just how much truth should the audience expect from entertainment? How entertaining should the audience expect truth to be? There are several opinions. At one point on the continuum is the argument that there is no truth requirement at all in art. At another point on the continuum is the belief that there must be one accepted truth for all. Compounding the problem is that often the audience doesn't care when the lines of truth and entertainment are blurred.

The Daily Show and Modern "Mock" News

We live in a society saturated with mock news programming. While a tradition of satirical news stretches at least as far back as the Greeks, the most famous example of modern satire is *The Daily Show*. Created as a spoof on local news with host Craig Kilborn in 1996, the show reached national prominence when Jon Stewart took over the anchor seat in 1998 and refocused content to concentrate on national affairs. Stewart's mock news footprint continues today with his hand-picked successor, Trevor Noah, at *The Daily Show*, as well as former correspondents Samantha Bee and John Oliver hosting similar shows on different networks.

The brilliance of *The Daily Show* and its ilk is that these programs so closely mimic the structure and substance of "real" news. *The Daily Show* features the same structure of headlines, special reports, breaking news, and correspondents "on location" as network and cable broadcast news (Barbur and Goodnow, 2011; Hess, 2011; McGeough, 2011). "Mock" news programs also cover the same types of stories—politics and elections, foreign affairs, news media, and policy issues— as traditional news broadcasts while skewering political actors such as politicians, journalists, economists, consultants, and corporatists (Barbur and Goodnow, 2011; Compton, 2011; Spicer, 2011). By playing the role of real reporters, and by playing that role so well as to often be indistinguishable from their traditional counterparts, mock journalists suggest that "real" journalists also simply are playing a role (Baym, 2005).

The overarching social critique of mock news programs is that the modern news industry, driven by commercial pressures, the quest for ratings, and the near impossibility of filling a 24-hour news hole with substantive programming, often eschews substance for style (Hess, 2011). News networks, according to this critique, forgo hard news for the "infotainment" of popular culture and moralistic fights on highly contrived events (Hess, 2011; McBeth and Clemons, 2011).

Satirical programs, however, do more than critique. They also educate otherwise tuned-out citizens who come for the humor but stay for policy information and discussions of media and the electoral process (Caufield, 2008). These mock television programs can influence viewers' evaluations of political candidates, perceptions of certain institutions, interest in campaigns, and support for specific policies (Compton, 2011). That sort of civic engagement and media literacy is no laughing matter.

Should there be a truth standard in art? The tendency of the status quo to impose a specific moral "truth" on the masses has been common to many cultures and political systems across the ages. In *Republic*, Plato had Socrates argue against allowing children to hear "casual tales . . . devised by casual persons." The Third Reich burned books deemed unsuitable for reading. In the United States, the battle historically has raged over library books. Classics such as *Huckleberry Finn, Of Mice and Men, The Grapes of Wrath*, and *The Merchant of Venice* are but some of the long-revered and award-winning works that now face censorship by various school systems. The American Library Association reports that incidents of book banning now reach more than a thousand annually, with little legal intervention. The US Supreme Court has not heard a book-banning case since allowing a lower court ruling to stand in 1982.

Protests began early in the history of television. The 1951 show *Amos 'n' Andy* was condemned by the National Association for the Advancement of Colored People for depicting "Negroes in a stereotyped and derogatory manner." In the 1960s, the United Church of Christ successfully challenged the license renewal of WLBT in Jackson, Mississippi, on the grounds that the owners had blatantly discriminated against Blacks.

In the latter half of the 20th century, a variety of special-interest groups used subtler methods to influence entertainment programming. Some, such as the Hispanic advocacy group Nosotros, worked closely with network bureaucracies, previewing potentially problematic episodes of entertainment programs, often altering program content before it reached the airwaves. Not all protests involve censoring a program. Some want to make sure that programming airs, such as advocacy groups who lobby advertisers and affiliates to ensure the airing of certain shows or inclusion of certain controversial characters in prime time. Others simply want characters of a certain race to be played by an actor of that same race. (The same is true for characters with a disability to be played by actors with that disability.) The latest iteration of the controversy occurred when Gal Godot, who is Israeli, was cast to play the titular role in a remake of a film about the Egyptian queen Cleopatra (who most famously was played by the white American actress Elizabeth Taylor in 1963).

New York Times television critic Jack Gould framed the problem of artistic accountability in the early days of these advocacy groups, arguing that such agreements held

> latent dangers for the well-being of television as a whole. An outside group not professionally engaged in theatre production has succeeded in imposing its will with respect to naming of fictional characters, altering the importance of a leading characterization and in other particulars changing the story line. (Montgomery, 1989, p. 21)

And for the artist trying to create in the medium, network attempts to "balance" competing advocacy-group interests had come close to recreating the patronage system, albeit a far more sophisticated one with government as the patron.

The struggle over content becomes even more acute when governmental sponsorship is at stake. Some argue that because tax dollars are extracted from all, the programs they fund should be acceptable to all. Federal support for programs such as the National Endowment for the Arts (NEA) repeatedly has been questioned in Congress. Conservatives objected to funding artists such as photographer Robert Mapplethorpe, whose blend of homoerotic photos and traditional Judeo-Christian symbols offended many. Eventually, the criticism was a factor in the resignation of one of the NEA's directors, John E. Frohnmayer.

The government also censors directly. On multiple occasions, Infinity Broadcasting was fined several hundred thousand dollars for disc jockey Howard Stern's on-air profanity and offensive racial slurs. Stern protested that the FCC's action amounted to an enforcement of political correctness. But others noted that Stern most often castigated disadvantaged people and groups. By 2006, Stern had left terrestrial radio and its rules for satellite radio, where he found a fat payday, artistic freedom, and a much smaller audience.

In 2006, with the Broadcast Decency Enforcement Act, Congress raised the fine for a single count of indecency from $27,500 to $325,000. Because of the potential liability for crippling fines, producers of live programming such as the Grammys and the Oscars were forced to put a delay on their broadcasts to bleep out what the courts called "fleeting expletives" or nudity.

MOVIES AND MUSIC: BLOCKBUSTERS AND SUPERHEROES

Digital technology sent shock waves throughout all media industries; however, the strongest tremors were felt in the entertainment business. There, digital technology arrived at the same time a handful of global companies took control of about 85 percent of the record industry. The rationale for the consolidation in the music industry was that profits from established labels and artists would be used to promote new talent. However, the corporate approach meant that managers now focused on quarterly profits and selling records rather than making music and promoting art.

Corporations wanted blockbuster hits. They were difficult and expensive to make and promote and impossible to predict. Walmart, the largest retailer of music in America, wanted to make its profits from the industry while carrying only about 2 percent of all releases available in a single year (Anderson, 2006).

Chris Blackwell, who began a small record label in the 1970s and sold it to PolyGram in 1989, said,

> I don't think the music business lends itself very well to being a Wall Street business. You're always working with individuals, with creative people, and the people you are trying to reach, by and large, don't view music as a commodity but as a relationship with a band. It takes time to expand that relationship but most people who work for the corporations have three-year contracts, some five, and most of them are expected to produce. What an artist really needs is a champion, not a numbers guy who in another year is going to leave. (Seabrook, 2003, p. 46)

Other industries are affected by the new economic realities as well. Major studios no longer want to make medium-budget films—from $40 million to $80 million. Instead, they prefer smaller films for $10 million or less and "blockbuster" films with budgets of $100 million or more. Films in the middle—particularly the $40 to $60 million range—are now considered too risky to make by many producers and some studios.

Plus, investors want films with a built-in audience, so a huge percentage of the nation's screens are filled with sequels, comic-book heroes, and action-adventure movies known to be big in foreign distribution. For instance, in 2019, each of the top 10 grossing movies was a sequel of a previous movie, a remake of an earlier film, or a tie-in with a fictional book or comic-book character. Most of these top 10 eventually will see yet another sequel as long as audiences are willing to pay. So the surprise 2014 hit *Guardians of the Galaxy* (grosses of $333 million) becomes *Guardians of the Galaxy Vol. 2* (grosses of more than $385 million), and a planned *Vol. 3*, while the photo-realistic computer-animated version of *The Lion King* raked in more than $500 million. The urge to create a sequel is irresistible for Hollywood. Such movies, regardless of their merit, consume a huge proportion of available screens—leaving art films, indies, and the like pushed aside. In addition, promotional budgets for potential blockbusters have become so bloated that smaller films with more modest budgets tend to get lost in the noise. These promotions create large opening weekends that are typically followed by drop-offs in attendance of up to 70 percent as the word of mouth gets out that some films are not that good.

The effect of this trend was that mid-priced, independent films, with fewer explosions and with no-name actors, have less chance of being made than ever before. True, there was the occasional medium budget breakout, but the entertainment industry, focused as it was on the "blockbuster" business model, continued to play it safe. The same mentality is true of music and book publishing, where fewer producers meant fewer outlets for artists and a dumbing down of content to please a mainstream audience. The impact of COVID-19 already has produced significant economic fallout in the film industry, and two of the largest theater chains in the United States declared bankruptcy in 2020. Broadway went dark for more than a year; so did Lincoln Center and the American Ballet Theater, which reported losing more than $45 million in December 2020, in part because it could not stage its annual *Nutcracker* production.

Meanwhile, another threat to the digital entertainment industries started emerging in the 1990s. Piracy and sharing of digital files sent music CD sales plummeting and threatened movies as download speeds and storage space allowed for the transfer of very large files. Those who did buy their music legally through iTunes, Rhapsody, or some other source opted to pay less than a dollar for a tune they liked instead of nearly $20 for the corresponding CD. Many music fans forego purchase altogether and stream music through sites such as Pandora or Spotify. In 2002, the industry shipped 33.5 million copies of the year's 10 best-selling CDs, barely half the number it had shipped in 2000. Today, that number has been halved again, with a "best-selling" CD often registering sales in the tens of thousands compared to chart-topping "albums" in the early rock era that routinely sold millions of copies.

The music industry—from producers to radio station owners—was slow to realize that consumers had forever changed the way they would buy and listen to their music. Sir Howard Stringer, chairman of the Sony Corporation of America, called downloaders "thieves" and compared them to those who shoplift from stores. The recording industry initially filed suit against some select downloaders and was successful in shutting down the very popular, but ultimately illegal, file-sharing site Napster. However, a pricing structure that made downloading inexpensive, combined with the emergence of popular devices to play it on such as the iPod (itself now obsolete due to advances to the iPhone), seemed a more effective—and more profitable—remedy. A look at the top 10 formats in radio, available at several industry websites, validates the fact that it is a medium with an aging audience.

On an industry-wide level, new artists, especially those who don't fit the corporate view, will find the internet to be a two-edged sword. It will give them the publicity they need at an affordable cost, but it will allow for file sharing or dollar downloads that make it virtually impossible to make significant sums of money. As is often the case in the mass media, the development and adoption of a new medium or delivery technology has unanticipated consequences for existing media and formats. For music, the solutions are elusive, and the stakes are high. Will creative people, who find their energies unusable in the music industry, turn to other mediums, or will the industry—and most importantly, consumers—find a way to reward the creators of this most personal of mediums?

COP TV: ENTERTAINMENT, INFOTAINMENT, OR NEWS?

In his ingenious Academy Award–winning script, *Network* (1976), the late writer-director Paddy Chayefsky envisioned a time when the lines would be blurred between entertainment and news, rendering them indistinguishable. However, Chayefsky was wrong in one detail. News did begin to take on the look of entertainment (as he predicted it would, to great satirical effect), but he did not predict that entertainment would also begin to look like news with the two meeting somewhere in the middle.

Consider these current and former shows: *America's Most Wanted*, which ran for 25 seasons, in which audience members were encouraged to help police by calling in tips; *Unsolved Mysteries* (now rebooted on Netflix), with its focus on the criminal and the paranormal; *TMZ on TV*, a celebrity gossip show heavy on mugshots, police reports, and drunken rants by the rich and famous; *Inside Edition*, a voyeuristic look at stories dubbed "too hot to handle" for traditional network news and which featured a pre-Fox News Bill O'Reilly and NBC and CBS reporter and anchor Deborah Norville as hosts; and others of the same breed, including *COPS* (which was cancelled after 31 years following protests against police brutality after a Minneapolis police officer killed George Floyd), *The First 48*, *Bait Car*, *America's Dumbest Criminals*, and any number of other spin-offs. Or consider *Dateline*, which blurred the lines of entertainment programming and the apprehension of would-be child molesters duped onto the show's set.

Then came YouTube, where virtually no event was outside the range of cameras and videos shot by amateurs. These videos often found their way into the mainstream media.

In what genre do these shows belong? Is it news or entertainment when Hawaiian police arrest the co-stars of *Dog the Bounty Hunter* for illegal detention and conspiracy? Which set of standards of truth should the producer of that show (and others like it) operate under—the artistic license of entertainment or the more rigorous truth standard of news? When *Dateline* sets up one of its "stings" with the internet promise of sex to would-be predators, have they crossed the line from entertainment to entrapment? Is it the truth that the television show prevented a crime, or is it the truth that the show caused someone to act in a criminal fashion?

The blending of facts and entertainment is not restricted to the small screen. Films such as *Bombshell*, *Harriet*, *Ray*, *Walk the Line*, *The Alamo*, *The Social Network*, *Lincoln*, and *American Sniper* reflect a particular artistic vision based on fact. That blending of fact and fiction becomes more pronounced in films such as *Moneyball* that include characters such as Billy Beane and Art Howe, based on real people, and other characters, such as Jonah Hill's Peter Brand, who are composites of several real-life baseball executives. Such depictions simplify and overly dramatize historical facts, foregoing context and complexity in favor of a sharp focus on a few select individuals. Fact and fiction also blend when actual journalists portray themselves in fictional television series and movies. For example, John King, Soledad O'Brien, Kelly O'Donnell, Rachel Maddow, Sean Hannity, Morley Safer, Candy Crowley, and George Stephanopoulos all played themselves—almost always in a brief cameo—during the six-season run of the Netflix series *House of Cards*. O'Brien, Hannity, Wolf Blitzer, Katie Couric, Lester Holt, and Chris Matthews all have appeared in more than three films or television series, and CNN's Larry King alone has more than 30 film credits to his name.

Based-on-reality films and reality-based television shows differ in format and content, but they are alike in invoking the license allowed entertainment programming while retaining the authority of fact—a risky combination. By blending information and entertainment, the possibility for abuse of an unsuspecting audience exists. To understand how this happens, we look to the theory of "uses and gratifications." Phrased simply, the theory says audience members will use the media to gratify certain wants and needs. People bring something to the message, and what they bring influences what they take away.

For example, seeking news and information is a common use of the media, with the expected gratification of getting information necessary for living one's life, from traffic to weather to news about government. Entertainment is another common media use, with its own gratification of happiness, sorrow, or any other emotion evoked by entertainment media—something Tolstoy said was the basic aim of the audience.

Infotainment keeps the look of news yet airs the content of lowbrow entertainment juxtaposing traditional uses and gratifications. With a look of authority (an anchor's desk, a courtroom, a police precinct) and the hype of their importance (e.g., "200 lives saved so far!"), these shows appear to be useful for acquiring information. However, by invoking their license as entertainment, such shows are free to bypass accuracy, fairness, balance, and other standards normally associated with news and to focus on more sensational elements to garner larger ratings.

Consequently, infotainment, while fundamentally flawed, gets widely accepted as fact. *New York Times* columnist A. M. Rosenthal (1989) compared airing these tabloid television shows to buying news programming "off the shelf." Stations should add the disclaimer, "We did not put this stuff in the bottle, whatever it is," Rosenthal added.

REALITY TELEVISION: OXYMORON, PROFIT CENTER, AND USING THE AUDIENCE

They eat cows' lips, let their families pick their mates, and routinely lie about their financial and physical assets. They are Americans with talent. They are seven strangers who stop being polite and start getting real. They race, they sing, and they dance. It's all part of the reality television craze that has made strong inroads into prime-time entertainment programming. The craze began with the wildly successful *Survivor* series, which ran first as a summer replacement show and garnered ratings that impressed network executives. *Survivor* quickly spawned other reality shows, among them *Amazing Race*, *American Idol*, *Big Brother*, *Dancing with the Stars*, *Keeping Up with the Kardashians*, *America's Got Talent*, *The Voice*, and *The Masked Singer*.

Why the rush to reality programming? Ratings and money. For three decades, traditional network television programming lost audience share to cable television, TiVo, and the internet. At their height, the original three American networks—ABC, CBS, and NBC—could count on attracting approximately 90 percent of American homes with televisions on any given evening; the rest tuned into a few fledgling independents playing reruns. Today, the audience for five broadcast networks (including Fox and CW) has plunged to less than half of all households, with the number slipping every season.

Traditional cable outlets such as HBO, TNT, and USA—and later online streaming websites such as Netflix, Amazon Prime, Disney+, and Hulu—got into original scripted programming, cutting further into the audience for scripted entertainment, often sweeping the industry's awards along the way. The reason for the immediate artistic success was a matter of sheer economics: It was easier to program a few hours of quality television a week than to try to program three hours every night as the traditional networks have done for years.

Compounding the problem, those who continued to watch the traditional networks were an older demographic not popular with advertisers. For the networks, reality television was a chance to pull viewers away from cable and computers and back to their programming at a cost lower than scripted television series. Not only did reality shows draw viewers, but the age of the audience they drew centered on 18–49-year-olds, a ratings bonanza in the preferred demographic, and a potent inducement to produce more reality programming. Of course, streaming services, especially Netflix, have entered—and started to dominate—the "reality" game with popular, binge-worthy shows such as *The Great British Baking Show*, *Love Is Blind*, *Tidying Up with Marie Kondo*, and a rebooted *Queer Eye*.

Reality programming was not only popular but also cheap to produce. There was little need to pay writers, and the actors who populated them worked for scale or prizes. Unlike the *CSI* and *Law and Order* franchises, where the popularity of the show caused cast salaries to skyrocket, programs such as *Pawn Stars*, *Ice Road Truckers*, and *The Deadliest Catch* got great ratings for minor networks with few of the traditional costs of scripted programming with sets to be built, outdoor permissions to be sought, and so forth.

However, using cheaply produced reality programming to garner ratings has had consequences. Quality shows such as *Modern Family* and *Breaking Bad* were expensive to produce, and it often took time to find an audience sufficient to sustain these shows. What the producers hoped for was a chance to air enough episodes—typically 60 or more—to make it to the lucrative syndication market, DVD box sets, and licensing deals with streaming services, where they live on for years and produce a sizable return on the initial investment. What networks ordered were 12 episodes with options for more at a later date—a clause that kept writers and others tied to the show and kept lives in limbo until the network exercised or failed to exercise the option.

By eating up entire chunks of the network schedule, reality television pushed many quality shows into an early retirement and kept many more out of production. The result now is fewer quality programs in syndication and fewer producers of quality shows able to get their product onto the schedules of the major networks now infatuated with reality. Quality writers fled to the movies or to the cable channels willing to try scripted television. For example, Netflix outbid HBO and AMC for David Fincher's *House of Cards* by guaranteeing, before a single episode was produced, to air two seasons and 26 episodes. The light-viewing months of the summer were once a time when networks took some chances on genre-defining shows to see if they could find an audience. Now that season is given over to "star-making" shows that turn immediate profits with no regard for the future.

If they didn't add to the nation's intellect, reality shows have added to American slang. Getting "voted off the island" became a catchphrase for everyone from politicians to news journalists. "You're fired" entered the American vernacular from *The Apprentice*, starring future president Donald Trump, who continued to use the line while commander in chief.

The "new" reality television was really a second pass at the genre. The first attempt took place in the 1950s with quiz shows such as *21* and *The $64,000 Question*. These shows were enormously popular and, as it turned out, could be rigged. Popular contestants were given the answers to general-knowledge questions beforehand. What the audience saw was a scripted contest with the winner predetermined. Winners came back from week to week, and some gained a national following. Not surprisingly, the predetermined winner was the one the producers believed would sustain the ratings or increase them. The quiz show scandals, as they are referred to in media history, were followed by congressional hearings, ruined careers, and even legislation.

The new reality shows suffered from some of the same problems. When it was discovered that those who advanced on one or more popular reality shows had actually been determined in advance, it became national news. Soon after, audiences learned that participants in the various reality shows were not always novices to the medium but were often recruited from ranks of fledgling actors. Furthermore, the notion of spontaneity, crucial to getting the audience to believe the premise of the reality show, was false. The producers of shows such as *Survivor*, *The Real World*, and the like most often shot hundreds of hours of video with a predetermined "storyline" to edit into an allegedly spontaneous program.

Some reality shows were based on legally questionable premises, such as the series that proposed to capture men hiring prostitutes—the reality of "johns"—or cop shows that allowed media to capture arrests inside homes only to be successfully sued for invasion of privacy later. Some shows seemed notable for their complete lack of a moral compass or made us more like voyeurs than traditional viewers. There is little to nothing socially redeeming about TLC's freak show parade of *My Big Fat Fabulous Life*, *Sister Wives*, and many other similar series. *Temptation Island* put couples and relationships in physical and emotional jeopardy for the entertainment of the audience. ABC halted filming of *Bachelor in Paradise*, a spin-off of the popular dating game show, after allegations that the crew might have filmed one cast member sexually assaulting another. Still, America watched even as lives were altered irreparably.

In June 2009, a record 10.6 million people tuned into the TLC show *Jon and Kate Plus 8* to learn that Jon and Kate Gosselin were calling it quits after 10 years of marriage, including several years that were documented on television. The concept was a reality series of two parents and their eight children on a $1.1 million Berks County, Pennsylvania, home built in part with television funds. At the time of their divorce, papers filed by the couple indicated that they had long lived separate lives, including the possibility that they had been misleading the public about their marriage for up to two years before the filing—a claim disputed by the lawyers as mere "legalese." In an interview with *People* magazine, Kate didn't blame the ubiquitous cameras for the failure of the marriage, saying that the divorce would have happened with or without the television show, which was consistently one of the top shows for the TLC network.

Reality television raises an important ethical question: What constitutes reality? Kris Bunton and Wendy Wyatt (2012) raise other important questions in their philosophical approach to the ethics of reality television. For example, do reality programs stereotype participants or activities? Even though participants sign legal waivers that are 20–30 pages long, do reality programs invade privacy? Can contestants ethically give away the sort of access the shows require? Does reality television inspire us—particularly if we have talent or can create a team that functions well under original circumstances and stress? Suzanne Collins, whose successful book trilogy begins with *The Hunger Games*, takes on many of these same questions in fictional form, often with disturbing answers. Collins has said that she wrote the series, in part, as a response to reality television and that her early literary influences included George Orwell's *1984*.

The early part of this century has been a scary time, and watching bachelors and bachelorettes find "true love" is a lot easier than taking the chance of going on a first date. However, that scary first date has the chance of turning into something wonderful or awful. Truth in relationships matters because it's how people form connections. Reality television is people, inside a box, having a planned and edited experience. That planning wasn't about truth. It wasn't even particularly personal.

THE DOCUMENTARIAN: ARTIST OR JOURNALIST?

Perhaps no media genre blends art and journalism together as does documentary film. In fact, if you ask a documentarian—particularly a fledging one—to define a professional role, directors, producers, and editors are quite likely to say that they are producing art that sometimes looks like journalism. Yet, as scholarship and professional conferences suggest (Aufderheide, 2005), documentarians share many of the same ethical questions as their journalistic first cousins. However, because many of them are either self-taught or the product of film programs, they stumble into the same ethical questions with relatively little guidance.

Documentarians generally agree that they are truth tellers, but that the truth they seek is not necessarily objective in the way that journalists traditionally have defined it. Rather, documentarians seek to tell truth from a point of view influenced by context, something that is discussed more extensively in the chapter about visuals. It is not unreasonable to suggest that multiple documentaries can be made about what is essentially the same subject—for example, Oregon's controversial assisted suicide law—each one taking a point of view. However, documentarians assert that the best documentary film is one that acknowledges, and sometimes deeply examines, views in opposition to the director's point of view. The *New York Times*, in 2011, began a new feature on its opinion pages: op docs, where citizens and professionals were invited to provide editorial commentary in the form of short documentaries on subjects of public importance.

Documentary links facts to beliefs and opinions in important ways. Documentarians also wrestle with how deeply involved they should become with the subjects of their films. For example, the director and producer of *Born into Brothels* (2004), Zana Briski, as part of her film, recounts her personal efforts to get the children of Indian sex workers into school so they could escape the poverty and work choices the Calcutta slums seem to provide. Michael Moore does not hide his personal opinions in films such as *Roger and Me* (1989), where his anger at General Motors CEO Roger Smith's decision to close a Flint, Michigan, factory is palpable throughout. Moore, a Flint resident, honed his reporting chops with the alternative newsweekly *The Flint Voice*, and his radical roots are forefront in his films. Documentarians often invest their own funds and months of their unpaid time to capture images, scenes, and dialogue that make a narrative work. This commitment to a single source and point of view is rare for journalists and can blur the line between essential source and friend. On the one hand, documentarians are concerned about exploiting those whom they become close to. This concern is especially present in documentaries about artists who are reclusive (e.g., Sixto Rodriguez in *Searching for Sugar Man*, the titular subject in *Finding Vivian Maier*), have a history of mental illness (e.g., *The Devil and Daniel Johnston*, about an eccentric songwriter with a history of schizophrenia), or both (e.g., *In the Realms of the Unreal*, about Henry Darger, who created the epic "Vivian Girls" artbook). On the other hand, they worry about becoming the prisoner of a single point of view, or of a source who likes to be on camera to the point that the director loses control over the content of the film itself.

Editing also raises a host of issues for documentarians: everything from the often in-your-face shots of people in joy or pain to the construction of a narrative that requires significant omissions and emphases for aesthetic purposes that edge the resulting film away from the initial truth, or just the well-rounded examination, that both the filmmaker and the sources sought. Adding music, archival footage, and building a narrative structure all require hours in the editing room and, as documentaries have become more profitable, significant investment in production values and postproduction efforts. Raising the money to make these sorts of films is not easy, and documentarians also worry about becoming the intellectual and artistic hostages of those who fund their work. For example, documentarian Craig Atkinson accused Netflix of blacklisting his film *Do Not Resist*, about the militarization of police and the protests in Ferguson, Missouri, after he turned down their offer to buy his film and brand it as a Netflix Original, because the streaming service required full creative control.

There also is the role of emotion in documentary film. These are films that are designed to provoke audience response. Strategic communication professionals would recognize the call to action embedded in many documentaries. Documentarians seek to overtly link emotion, fact, logic, and action in a way that journalism, perhaps with the exception of investigative reporting, seldom does. Along the way, there are real ethical questions that are not readily answered by the too common response "But, I am an artist." In the documentary *Inside Job*, which won an Academy Award in 2010, the filmmakers accepted the Oscar by noting that no one had yet been jailed in the financial scandal that precipitated the recession of 2008. The film was an artistic success; however, its political impact was less successful. If Plato were alive today, there is little doubt that documentary film, through its artistry as well as investigations, would be on the list of highly suspect professions in the modern-day democratic republic.

AESTHETICS IS AN ATTITUDE

Artists see the world differently. While most people perceive only what is needful, the artist works with what some have called an "enriched perceptual experience." This aesthetic attitude is one that values close and complete concentration of all the senses. An aesthetic attitude is a frankly sensual one, and one that summons both emotion and logic to its particular ends.

For example, the theater audience knows that Eugene O'Neill's plays are "merely" drama. However, they also provide us with an intense examination of the role of family in human society—an experience that is both real and personal to every audience member. Such intense examination is what gives the plays their power to move an audience.

The makers of mediated messages, whether they are the executive producers of a television sitcom or the designers of a newspaper page, share this aesthetic impetus. These mass communicators are much like architects. An architect can design a perfectly serviceable cube-like building, one that withstands the elements and may be used for good ends. But great buildings—St. Paul's Cathedral in London or Thomas Jefferson's home at Monticello—do more. They are tributes to the human intellect's capacity to harmoniously harness form and function.

In fact, philosophers have argued that what separates the commonplace from the excellent is the addition of an aesthetic quality to what would otherwise be a routine, serviceable work. These qualities of excellence have been described as:

- an appreciation of the function realized in the product;
- an appreciation of the resulting quality or form; and
- an appreciation of the technique or skill in the performance.

These three characteristics of aesthetic excellence characterize excellence in mass communication as well.

Take the newspaper weather page. *USA Today* literally recalibrated the standard from tiny black-and-white agate type to a colorful full page. They understood what the late political columnist Molly Ivins knew: When people aren't talking about football, they talk about the weather. They devoted more space to it and printed it in color. They added more information in a more legible style and form. In short, they gave newspaper weather information an aesthetic quality. While much about *USA Today* has been criticized, its excellent weather page has been copied.

Although mass-communication professionals are infrequently accused of being artists, we believe they intuitively accept an aesthetic standard as a component of professional excellence. As philosopher G. E. Moore (1903, p. 83) noted in *Principia Ethica*:

> Let us imagine one world exceedingly beautiful. Image it as beautiful as you can; put into it whatever on this earth you most admire: mountains, rivers, the sea, suns and sunsets, stars and moon. Imagine these all combined in the most exquisite proportion so that no one thing jars against another, but each contributes to increase the beauty of the whole. And then imagine the ugliest world you can possibly conceive. Imagine it just one heap of filth, containing everything that is most disgusting to you for whatever reason, and the whole, as far as may be, without one redeeming factor. . . . Supposing [all that] quite apart from the contemplation of human beings; still it is irrational to hold that it is better that the ugly world exists than the one which is beautiful.

Substitute film, record, poem, news story, photograph, or advertising copy for Moore's word "world," and we believe that you will continue to intuitively agree with the statement. While we may disagree on what specifically constitutes beauty in form and content, the aesthetic standard of excellence still applies.

Philosopher John Dewey (1932/2005) noted, "Aesthetic experience is a manifestation, a record and celebration of the life of a civilization, a means of promoting its development, and is also the ultimate judgment upon the quality of a civilization." In an interview on the PBS series *The Promise of Television*, commentator Bill Moyers (1988) said,

The root word of television is vision from afar, and that's its chief value. It has brought me in my stationary moments visions of ideas and dreams and imaginations and geography that I would never personally experience. So, it has put me in touch with the larger world. Television can be a force for dignifying life, not debasing it.

Though Moyers's comments were made specifically about television, the same argument can be made for a good book, a favorite magazine, music, or a film. And whether the media are a force for dignifying humanity or debasing it is largely in the hands of those who own and work in them.

SUGGESTED READINGS

Bunton, K., & Wendy, W. (2012). *Reality television: A philosophical examination.* New York: Continuum International.

Calvert, C. (2000). *Voyeur nation: Media, privacy and peering in modern culture.* Boulder, CO: Westview Press.

Jensen, J. (2002). *Is art good for us?* Lanham, MD: Rowman & Littlefield.

Medved, M. (1992). *Hollywood vs. America.* New York: HarperCollins.

Montgomery, K. C. (1989). *Target: Prime time. Advocacy groups and the struggle over entertainment television.* New York: Oxford University Press.

Postman, N. (1986). *Amusing ourselves to death: Public discourse in the age of television.* New York: Penguin Books.

CASES

CASE 10-A

DOCUMENTING CULTURE CLASH IN *AMERICAN FACTORY*

Emily Callam and Chad Painter
University of Dayton

The 2019 Academy Award-winning documentary *American Factory* introduces viewers to the transition of a large factory in Dayton, Ohio, from General Motors Company to Fuyao Glass America, a Chinese company. The film attempts to capture an all-encompassing view of this transition as it depicts the effects it has on everyone from the CEO of the company to both American and Chinese workers on the factory floor. Lifestyles and workplace cultures clash as the productivity levels of those in the United States do not nearly reach those of China. *American Factory* is the first film produced by Barack and Michelle Obama's production company, Higher Ground Productions. It began streaming on Netflix in August 2019.

The former GM plant was purchased in 2014 by Chinese billionaire Cao Dewang. His company, Fuyao, employs 2,300 Americans and 200 Chinese workers in the Dayton-area factory, making it the world's largest complex devoted to producing automotive safety glass.

Filmmakers Julia Reichert and Steven Bognar—who are based in Yellow Springs (about 30 minutes from Dayton) and teach at Dayton's Wright State University—have had a long fascination with the factory. Their previous documentary *The Last Truck: Closing of a GM Plant* (2010) was shot in the same factory and focused on the automotive manufacturer's 2008 decision to close it.

Dayton once had been a manufacturing giant; it had been home to six Fortune 500 companies and the largest concentration of General Motors employees outside of Michigan. That began to change in the 1970s and accelerated in the 1990s, with major employers such as National Cash Register, Mead Paper Company, Delco, and General Motors either leaving Dayton or substantially reducing their workforces in the city. Dayton's population has dropped by more than 100,000 people since 1960.

Reichert and Bognar filmed *American Factory* from 2015 to 2017 in both Dayton and China. They were given almost unfettered access to everything and everyone in the Dayton factory. The resulting documentary "provides a snapshot of the struggle between labor and management that is both timeless and distinctly of its time. Even more surprisingly, it does so in a manner that is often engaging and entertaining, considering the subject matter" (Sobczynski, 2019).

That snapshot includes frank discussions about race, class, and culture. The Americans must learn to assimilate to Chinese work culture and foreign leadership. They earn significantly lower wages than they were accustomed to while working for General Motors, are stymied in their attempts to unionize, and uneasily adjust to unstable employment and at times unsafe working conditions. Chinese Fuyao workers who move to America must learn to live and work in a new culture while they are separated—often for months—from their families.

"And so *American Factory* is only nominally a film about America. The part that is astonishing about *American Factory* is seeing everything about the United States through the eyes of Chinese factory workers and managers arriving to reopen and restaff a plant in the rust belt.

American Factory is the view we never get. Americans know how they feel about competing with China. But we don't know how China feels about working with America" (Urstadt, 2019).

Micro Issues

1. Julia Reichert and Steven Bognar live and work near Dayton and codirected a previous short documentary about the factory and its workers. What are the advantages to their "insider" knowledge about the city and the factory? What are the disadvantages?
2. *American Factory* was distributed through Netflix (and viewed by individuals or small groups) instead of through movie theaters (and viewed by large crowds). How might that distribution change the viewing experience? How might it change conversations about the film?
3. As you watch the film, note the visual images of American workers and Chinese workers. How do those images reaffirm or contradict your view of the two cultures? How are they different from what you might find in popular films?

Midrange Issues

1. What would Tolstoy say about *American Factory*?
2. Is *American Factory* journalism? Should documentaries be held to the standards of journalism?
3. *American Factory* was produced, in part, by Barack and Michelle Obama, and it was released during an escalating trade war between America and China. As an ex-president, should Obama be commenting on international labor issues? How might your answer change if *American Factory* was a fictional film instead of a documentary?
4. Does the depth of the cultural dimension of the factory workplace portrayed in the film change your understanding of the competitive economic environment in China? In the United States? How might this be reflected in news stories you would write? What ethical values are reflected in your answer?

Macro Issues

1. Is *American Factory* truthful? How might someone watching this film in China answer that question?

2. Evaluate *American Factory* in terms of social justice. What might John Rawls, Amartya Sen, or Martha Nussbaum say about the film?
3. *One Child Nation*, a documentary about China's one-child policy that was reversed several years ago, also provides an in-depth look at some elements of Chinese culture. Contrast what you learned about China in *American Factory* with those of *One Child Nation* (available on Amazon). How are you developing your own version of "the truth" about contemporary Chinese culture?

CASE 10-B

THE *DAILY SHOW*'S ONE-CLIENT LEGAL TEAM

CHAD PAINTER
University of Dayton

Trevor Noah and his *Daily Show* team bought full-page ads on Aug. 27, 2020, in the *New York Times*, *Washington Post*, and *Los Angeles Times* to "promote" their new law firm—Trevor Noah & Associates & Sons Presidential Attorneys. The ads were timed to coincide with Donald Trump's nomination acceptance speech at the Republican National Convention.

The text of the ad reads, "Are you a soon-to-be ex-president? About to lose legal immunity? Has your lawyer gone to jail? Call the very fine people on YOUR side." Noah and his team say they can defend clients against "Corruption," "Mega-corruption," "Emoluments (we know what that is!)," "Shady rich guy tax stuff," "Obstruction of justice (same price for multiple counts!)," "You told people to inject bleach for some reason," and "Mail murder." They also promise to "get you off . . . and you won't even have to pay us $130,000."

The ad also features the phone number 1-210-WH-CRIME. It is a working number, and callers are prompted to press 1 if they are president, and 2 if they are not president. Pressing 1 prompts the following prerecorded message from Noah:

Hello, Mr. President. I'm Trevor Noah, managing partner of Trevor Noah and Associates and Sons. Have you ever been to Uganda, sir? It's a beautiful country with a strong goat-based economy. And most important, it does not extradite to the United States. At any time on or before January 20th 2021, I can transport you and any members of your family you actually like to Uganda. I can provide the service for, I don't know, $10 million. Let me know. Oh, and if you made a mistake, and you're not actually the president, press or say two now. Otherwise, goodbye, Mr. President. (Haysom, 2020)

Pressing 2 prompts a cheery woman saying, "Congratulations on not being the president. Goodbye."

Trump left office with a looming impeachment trial—his second—as well as a host of legal problems. While Trump was in office, he was protected from criminal liability by a Department of Justice policy that shields presidents from indictment while they are serving as president; however, that protection does not extend to ex-presidents. So, Trump could face federal and/or state charges for inciting the Jan. 6 riot at the US Capitol and for his phone call pressuring Georgia Secretary of State Brad Raffensperger to "find" votes and declare him the winner of that state's presidential election (Thomson-DeVeaux, 2021). He also could face several potential financial crimes in Manhattan related to tax fraud, his dealings with the Trump Organization, and his alleged hush-money payments to porn star Stormy Daniels and *Playboy* model Karen McDougal (Cuza, 2021).

Micro Issues

1. How is this ad more effective than if the *Daily Show* had aired a segment on Trump's legal issues? How is it less effective?
2. Why do you think the ad was released to correspond with Trump's speech at the Republican National Convention? Would it have been more or less effective at other points in the campaign (for example, before the first presidential debate)?
3. Months after this ad appeared, President Trump was impeached a second time. Should Noah consider a repeat?
4. What do you think is the purpose of this ad? Can it pass the TARES test outlined in chapter 7?

Midrange Issues

1. How should the *Daily Show* balance entertainment and journalism/news? To what extent should a news parody show adhere to conventional journalistic standards?
2. Evaluate the fact claims made in the ad. To what standards of truth should Noah and other mock newscasters be held?
3. To whom does Trevor Noah owe loyalty? How does that answer change if Noah is considered a journalist as opposed to a comedian?

4. Is ridicule ethical? If your answer is yes, are there certain people or groups for whom if might be considered unethical? If your answer is no, does that eliminate all forms of biting, humorous criticism?

Macro Issues

1. In *Amusing Ourselves to Death*, Neil Postman argues that public discourse about politics, news, religion, education, and commerce increasingly is mediated through entertainment programming. Evaluate his argument in regard to *The Daily Show*.
2. What is the role of a political satirist in modern political debate and discussion? How does Noah fulfill (or not fulfill) that role?
3. The *Daily Show* has inspired similar mock news programs in France, Germany, Hungary, Pakistan, Israel, Japan, and Canada. What might a similar ad look like in one of those countries?
4. There is substantial research to suggest that the most significant effect of advertising is to reinforce previously held opinion. Considering this likely impact, evaluate audience response to this ad. Do you think the ad accomplished Noah's goals?
5. Compare this ad with those of the Lincoln Project, focused on Trump's 2020 campaign. Which do you think is the more socially responsible? Effective? In the realm of political persuasion, is it ethical for effectiveness to supersede social responsibility?

CASE 10-C

#OSCARSSOWHITE: REPRESENTATION IN THE CREATIVE PROCESS

LEE WILKINS
University of Missouri

In January 2015, April Reign ended a single tweet with the hashtag #OscarsSoWhite. Reign, at the time managing editor of Broadway Black, viewed the Academy Award nominations as essentially erasing people of color from the film industry.

While the viral hashtag began in 2015, there was still a great deal of discussion about the composition of those who vote for the Academy Awards five years later (as of this writing, the Academy is still predominantly a Caucasian-dominated organization), as well as the appropriateness and impact of the movement itself.

First, there was a discussion of "hashtag activism." This critique asserted that merely retweeting or otherwise using the hashtag was a poor substitute for actual, in-person activism. In response, some actors and directors boycotted the 2015 awards ceremony; others refused the boycott because they said it was a "slap in the face" to host Chris Rock.

Second, there was the criticism that the hashtag didn't really get at the core of the problem: the composition of the Hollywood elite that funds films and otherwise makes decisions about everything from which films get made to publicity budgets. The argument was that diversity needed to find a home with those who controlled the industry rather than those in front of or behind the camera. In subsequent interviews, Reign noted that this debate may present a false choice:

> I think that this is an issue that can be addressed on many fronts. There is a need for the academy to be more diverse and for them to represent the people who watch the films that they nominate and that they support.

And then there were the ripples in the creative pond. In announcing the nominees for the best director category in 2019, writer and actress Issa Rae announced the nominees and then said, "congratulations to those *men*," a direct reference to the fact that the women who directed some of that year's most financially successful and critically acclaimed films were not included. This critique about the lack of representation of women in categories as diverse as film editing, screenwriting, and producing had a history at least as long as the #OscarsSoWhite protest. These inequalities include film animation and special and computer-based effects, each of which always has been dominated by Caucasians.

The years between 2015 and when you are reading this case have marked uneven changes in the Academy and awards nominees. In the incredibly competitive business of narrative filmmaking, creatives of color continue to assert that they must be better than their Caucasian counterparts in order to land the same jobs and to receive the same recognition. They argue that certain kinds of stories don't get told—or are told only from a predictable point of view. The industry itself continues to struggle with how to recoup the enormous financial investment in "blockbuster" films, a problem that has been exacerbated with the COVID-19 pandemic. Lower-budget films continue to struggle to find financial support, and there is a great deal of uncertainty about whether physical theaters (the multiplex) will survive financially in a post-COVID world.

Micro Issues

1. What philosophical theory supports the concept of #OscarsSoWhite?
2. Could the same critique of the film industry also be applied to television? To book publishing? To the music industry?
3. Define diversity. How does #OscarsSoWhite fit—or not fit—your definition?

Midrange Issues

1. When you decide to purchase a ticket to a film or attend a film festival, what guides your decisions?
2. Are there films directed at "minority" audiences—for example, *Black Panther* or *Little Women*—that you have decided not to view because you think you won't be interested? How would you evaluate those decisions in light of #OscarsSoWhite?
3. Elliot Page, who starred as a pregnant teenager in *Juno* and can be seen in the Netflix series *The Umbrella Academy*, announced he was transgender in December 2020. How does the announcement change your view of him as an actor? How should Hollywood reward him for his critically acclaimed work?

Macro Issues

1. Is it important for Black actors to be given roles that represent events that "happened" to Black people?
2. The Globe Theater in London has staged Shakespeare's *The Taming of the Shrew* with an all-female cast. What would Tolstoy say about such an effort? How does such casting challenge audiences to "suspend disbelief"? How does an emphasis on representation challenge this notion?
3. In music, genres that were considered the province of minority communities—for example, jazz or rap—have deeply influenced music in other genres and in subsequent decades. How does the concept behind #OscarsSoWhite inform these types of creative movements?

CASE 10-D

GET OUT: WHEN THE HORROR IS RACE

MICHAEL FUHLHAGE
Wayne State University

LEE WILKINS
University of Missouri

The 2017 horror film *Get Out*, made by first-time director/writer Jordan Peele for $4.5 million—a very modest budget by current standards—grossed more than $254 million worldwide. While profitability is one mark of success in Hollywood, the film also received critical acclaim. After its Sundance Film Festival preview in January 2017, it received the Oscar for Best Original Screenplay and three other Oscar nominations, two Golden Globe nominations, and more than 20 other nominations from a variety of groups for acting, directing, the music, and the screenwriting.

However, more than that, it was a film that made people think—an uncomfortable essay on the actual bodies of Black people being colonized by white minds.

Most critics interpreted the film as a commentary on how Caucasian liberals can make life unintentionally difficult for Blacks. A *Guardian* reviewer noted, "It exposes a liberal ignorance and hubris that has been allowed to fester. It's an attitude, an arrogance which in the film leads to a horrific final solution, but in reality, leads to a complacency that is just as dangerous." In an interview with CBS News, Peele explained that the film reflected "my truth as a Black man. My perspective that I haven't seen in film before."

The film plays on references to other films that make political and/or social points, among them the original *Invasion of the Body Snatchers*, *The Stepford Wives*, and *Guess Who's Coming to Dinner*.

Much of *Get Out*'s commentary about race is tucked into the film's visuals. The movie opens with a young Black man walking down a street in a tidy suburban neighborhood. He's followed by a white sports car and eventually kidnapped off the street by a man wearing a medieval helmet suggestive of a knight.

The next scene shows a young couple in an urban environment. She's bringing him breakfast in preparation for a weekend of meeting her family—upscale liberals, by her description of it. "Do they know I'm Black?" asks Chris Washington, played by Daniel Kaluuya. He doesn't really receive an answer from his girlfriend, Rose Armitage (Allison Williams)—although that answer becomes clear by the end of the film.

On the drive to the weekend of introductions, their car runs into a deer—a foreshadowing of the plot to come. The police officer who stops at the scene of the accident plays on all of the tropes of the current "arrested for driving while Black" incidents common in the United States, while Rose keeps the cop from getting ID from Chris by arguing that he wasn't even driving so he shouldn't have to show proof of anything. Of course, it turns out that Rose played the white-privilege card for the selfish reason of preventing a paper trail in the event that Chris's absence was noted once her real reason for taking him home is revealed. The stone planters on the porch of her family's country home are adorned with the Omega symbol, the last letter of the Greek alphabet, foreshadowing that the Armitage house is "the end."

Dean and Missy Armitage, Rose's dad and mom, say the kinds of inadvertently embarrassing things to Chris that parents typically say when their child brings home a significant other. But their comments devolve into ambiguously racist asides. Then Missy offers to hypnotize Chris, supposedly for the well-meaning purpose of helping him quit smoking, eventually doing it without his consent. All the while, she drinks tea in bone china—sugar and tea having been the colonial products that formed the commercial chains of the slave trade in the western hemisphere. It turns out that the Armitages see Black bodies as commodities, just like tea, for consumption and profit.

When Chris is hypnotized, his mind "falls" into the sunken place, a mental state that leaves his body paralyzed. His consciousness is capable of witnessing what is happening around him, but it is incapable of controlling his body. The context and visuals are a callback to the captivity of Africans who, similarly, lacked control over their own bodies as they were transported in the holds of slave ships.

And the help—both Black—are simply odd. The caretaker, Walter, uses an archaic vocabulary to describe Rose—"one of a kind, top of the line, a dog-gone keeper!" The housekeeper, Georgina, obeys orders to the letter, prompting Chris to muse to himself that she "missed the [civil rights] movement."

From this point on in the film, the real intent of the family weekend emerges: A "family reunion" turns out to be a viewing period for bidders to assess Chris, the main attraction in a silent auction reminiscent of those during the slave trade. Again, the cultural stereotype of Blacks as "strong physically" becomes part of the plot. The goal, immortality—or at least greatly extended life—through a very immoral means is revealed. Walter and Georgina are actually the bodies of Black victims used to extend the lives of Rose's grandparents. That fate awaits Chris unless he can avoid it in the only way possible: get out!

Peele initially wrote two endings for the film but settled on the happier one because he was concerned about how the film would be received by Caucasian moviegoers. Regardless of which ending you prefer, the movie stands as a disturbing satire of American horror movies with the message that Blacks can rely only on themselves to overcome exploitation by the very people who claim to want to help them.

Micro Issues

1. If you have seen the film, how many of the visual cues did you recognize as symbols of racial oppression or white privilege?
2. W. E. B. Du Bois wrote about what he called double consciousness—the idea that Blacks simultaneously lived with the identity of an American and a Black person, an individual feeling of being divided into multiple parts so it was impossible to have a single unified identity. How is that concept woven into the film? Do you find it meaningful today?
3. Evaluate Jordan Peele's decision to use a happier ending for the film in order to make it more palatable for Caucasian audiences.

Midrange Issues

1. Peele has said that he wrote the film to illustrate a system that is dominated by white power. Do you think a horror film is an effective vehicle for such a social critique?
2. Some reviewers have noted that the film also illustrates an additional social problem: the fact that Blacks constitute about 14 percent of the US population but more than 24 percent of Americans "missing" due to some form of criminal activity. Contrast this film with *Wind River*, a drama that makes the same point with regard to Native Americans. Which do you believe is more effective?
3. Compare and contrast the social and political message of *Get Out* to similar films, such as *Invasion of the Body Snatchers*, *The Stepford Wives*, and *Guess Who's Coming to Dinner*.

Macro Issues

1. Audience response to *Get Out* varied. One of the authors of this case saw the film in Detroit, where the largely Black audience cheered at the ending. The other saw the film in a Midwestern college town where the audience did not applaud at the ending. What might be the reasons for such divergent responses?

2. *Get Out* takes a historic injustice and gives it a modern expression. How are the various theories of justice outlined in the text reflected in the film?
3. If you were unaware of racial exploitation before seeing the movie, what is your responsibility given your awareness of Peele's interpretation of America?

CASE 10-E

TO DIE FOR: MAKING TERRORISTS OF GAMERS IN *MODERN WARFARE 2*

PHILIP PATTERSON
Oklahoma Christian University

The scene on the screen is brutal. Bullets fly indiscriminately. Bodies fall to the floor. An airport terminal becomes a killing field for Russian terrorists who want the massacre to incite a US–Soviet war. Fortunately, it's only a game—*Call of Duty: Modern Warfare 2*—but one with very real decisions that have to be made by the viewer/gamer.

At the beginning of the mission, entitled "No Russian," the player is only a bystander as Russian terrorists fire randomly and ruthlessly into crowds at a fictitious Russian airport terminal. But the player quickly discovers that he or she can fire as well—only not at the perpetrators, but at the civilians. In one of the most controversial "first-person shooter" gaming decisions of all time, *Modern Warfare 2* (*MW2*) allows players to decide whether to join in the carnage.

First-person shooter (FPS) games had been a staple of video gaming since the earliest days of the industry, beginning with *Maze War*, released in 1974. Today, FPS games are the most commercially viable of all video games, accounting for 27 percent of all video game sales in 2016, according to statista.com. But prior to *MW2*, the target of the shooting had been enemy combatants, fleeing criminals, zombies, and the like. Few FPS games and no bestsellers had featured the gamer firing at innocent bystanders.

MW2 challenged that convention. Here is a description of the gamer's option according to a reviewer for the gaming website kotaku.com:

> Bullets unload on an unsuspecting crowd, and the body count quickly begins to rise. Most players, thinking they needed to play along, probably decided to start shooting—at the time, I did. But the

game never forces you do *anything*, and it's entirely up to the player whether a single shot is fired from their gun. Dozens of people will die, regardless of what you decide to do, but active participation is left to the player. (Klepek, 2015)

In some locations, becoming an active shooter was *not* left up to the player. In Japan and Germany, if a player attempted to join the shooting, he or she was met with a "mission failed" screen, the game having been altered at the insistence of the government. The entire segment was removed from versions released in Russia.

One of the game's designers, Mohammad Alavi, said in an interview that he took pride in forcing players to make an uncomfortable decision, telling interviewer Matthew Burns (2012), three years after the release of the game:

In the sea of endless bullets you fire off at countless enemies without a moment's hesitation or afterthought, the fact that I got the player to hesitate even for a split second and actually consider his actions before he pulled that trigger—that makes me feel very accomplished.

Despite the controversies surrounding the game—or perhaps because of them—sales were brisk. The game grossed $310 million on Nov. 10, 2009, the first day of its release, and has since earned more than $1 billion. It was well reviewed, including winning "Game of the Year" honors from several retail and fan sites online. Eight years after its release, *Call of Duty: Modern Warfare 2* ranked as the 24th best-selling game of all time, selling nearly 23 million units. Industry estimates placed the cost of developing *MW2* at $40–$50 million along with a marketing budget of $200 million to launch the game.

Knowing that some players would choose not to shoot at the civilians in the terminal, the designers of *MW2* allowed players to bypass the "No Russian" segment and still move on in the game. Before starting the game, players were shown a screen that read:

Disturbing Content Notice

Some players may find one of the missions
disturbing or offensive. Would you like to have
the option to skip this mission?
[You will not be penalized in terms of Achievement
or game completion]
The options given the player were these:
Yes, ask me later
No, I will not be offended

All "unlockables" were removed from the segment and a player could reach the highest levels of the game and earn the highest rewards even if they chose to either skip "No Russian" or not participate as a shooter in the segment.

One of the detractors of the civilian violence in *Call of Duty: Modern Warfare 2* is Walt Williams, lead writer for the 2012 game *Spec Ops: The Line*. Williams, who would write the killing of civilians into his war game (crossing "the line" in the game's title), criticized the "No Russian" sequence of *MW2* for its "clumsiness" (Hamilton, 2012). In commenting on the civilian violence in that earlier game, he told a reviewer for kotaku.com:

> The thing that got me the most was that you could opt out of playing it. And that struck me as saying, "We wanted to do something that would cause controversy, but it's actually not necessary to the game, which is why you don't have to play it."

FPS games are often debated in the aftermath of mass shootings such as one in Las Vegas, Nevada, in the fall of 2017. In that event, a lone gunman shot into a crowd of 22,000 outdoor concertgoers from a high floor of a nearby hotel, killing 58 of them and injuring 546. While no direct evidence links FPS games to events such as Las Vegas, researchers note the similarities of such random shootings to FPS games and claim that hours of playing such games can desensitize the player to real-world violence.

In the case of *MW2*, the controversy is not merely a hypothetical debate. On July 22, 2011, Anders Behring Breivik, a far-right Norwegian terrorist, killed eight persons in a car bomb in Oslo and then killed 69 participants of a Worker's Youth League summer camp at an outing on an island 24 miles away. He would later claim to have been motivated in the attack by the game, but no evidence has been produced that supports the claim. Though he is still alive in prison today, he has been diagnosed as a paranoid schizophrenic and has never been questioned further about the relationship of the game to his actions.

Micro Issues

1. Should FPS games be regulated? If so, in what way?
2. Should the killing of innocent bystanders be banned in FPS games?
3. The game was modified in Japan and Germany and banned in Russia. Critique the actions of these countries in their actions toward this game.

Midrange Issues

1. What does the decision by the developers to make the segment optional say to you?
2. Critique the claim of Breivik above. Is it credible to you? Does it have any bearing on whether FPS games should be regulated?
3. Critique the remarks of Williams above. He allowed the killing of civilians in his game while criticizing the violence of *MW2*. Do you see a difference in the two games?

Macro Issues

1. Violence has long been a part of art and entertainment. What standards, if any, should we place on the artist in terms of how much violence we wish to see in our art?
2. Do you place any credibility in the research that indicates that violence in games, on television and movie screens, and so forth, desensitize the audience to violence in real life?

CASE 10-F

THE ONION: FINDING HUMOR IN MASS SHOOTINGS

CHAD PAINTER
University of Dayton

A lone gunman opened fire Oct. 1, 2017, during the Route 91 Harvest Music Festival in Las Vegas, killing 58 and injuring 546. News coverage was nearly around the clock, mostly following a similar, well-rehearsed playbook, according to the *Washington Post*:

> Deploy reporters to the scene quickly. Interview eyewitnesses and families of the victims and the shooters. Check social media for clues to the attackers' identity. Bring on the law enforcement experts for comment. (Farhi, 2015)

Coverage was a bit different, however, for one "news" organization. In *The Onion*, readers were greeted with a familiar headline: "'No Way to Prevent This,' Says Only Nation Where This Regularly Happens." The full text of less than 200 words reads:

> LAS VEGAS—In the hours following a violent rampage in Las Vegas in which a lone attacker killed more than 50 individuals and seriously

injured 400 others, citizens living in the only country where this kind of mass killing routinely occurs reportedly concluded Monday that there was no way to prevent the massacre from taking place. "This was a terrible tragedy, but sometimes these things just happen and there's nothing anyone can do to stop them," said Iowa resident Kyle Rimmels, echoing sentiments expressed by tens of millions of individuals who reside in a nation where over half of the world's deadliest mass shootings have occurred in the past 50 years and whose citizens are 20 times more likely to die of gun violence than those of other developed nations. "It's a shame, but what can we do? There really wasn't anything that was going to keep these individuals from snapping and killing a lot of people if that's what they really wanted." At press time, residents of the only economically advanced nation in the world where roughly two mass shootings have occurred every month for the past eight years were referring to themselves and their situation as "helpless."

The Onion had published versions of the same story several times, changing only the date, location of violence, and number of people killed. The story was first published after a May 23, 2014, attack at the University of California where a gunman killed six people and injured 14 others. It later ran, almost verbatim, after the June 17, 2015, shooting at the Emanuel African Methodist Episcopal Church in Charleston, South Carolina; the Oct. 1, 2015, shooting at Umpqua Community College in Oregon; the Dec. 2, 2015, shooting at a Christmas party for the San Bernardino County Department of Public Health; the Feb. 14, 2018, shooting at Parkland High School; and the Aug. 3, 2019, shooting at a Walmart in El Paso, Texas.

The Onion has not run the story after every mass shooting; notably, it didn't appear after the June 12, 2016, Orlando nightclub attack. The repetition, though, underscores the problem that mass shootings are a regular occurrence in US life. *Onion* managing editor Marnie Shure told *Vice* in a September 2017 interview that "by re-running the same commentary, it strengthens the original commentary tenfold each time. In the wake of these really terrible things, we have this comment that really holds up." The not-so-subtle commentary is an attempt by *Onion* writers to tap into a shared sense of frustration coupled with futility and hopelessness. The satire here is not just used for humor; instead, it has a larger purpose regarding social and political life (Feinberg, 1967).

The Onion, which dubs itself "America's Finest News Source," is a satirical website that covers both real and fictional current events in the tone, format, and design of traditional news organizations such as the Associated Press. It came to national prominence for its acclaimed coverage of the 9/11 terrorist attacks; *Onion* writers were among the first humorists to address the attacks and their aftermath.

Micro Issues

1. Does *The Onion*'s mass shooting story gain or lose impact with each retelling?
2. The story is fictional, though it does include real information, including statistics. Does this blending of fiction and nonfiction aid or detract from the overall message? Compare this story to news coverage of these shootings that appeared in local newspapers.

Midrange Issues

1. *The Onion* publishes the story after only some mass shootings. Discuss this editorial strategy.
2. Does *The Onion*'s approach trivialize these events? What might be the impact of this story on the victims' families should they see it?
3. Is *The Onion*'s story fake news?

Macro Issues

1. What are the ethical implications of using humor to discuss mass shootings or other tragic events?
2. Compare *The Onion*'s coverage of mass shootings to that provided by columnists such as Nicholas Kristof of the *New York Times*. Evaluate their effectiveness as a form of political communication as outlined in chapter 5.
3. Satire typically has a larger social or political purpose. Discuss that purpose in relation to mass shootings.

11

Becoming a Moral Adult

By the end of this chapter, you should be able to

- know the stages of moral development as described by Piaget and Kohlberg;
- have a deeper understanding of the ethics of care;
- understand the stages of adult moral development;
- understand how these theories have been applied to journalists' and strategic communications professionals' ethical thinking.

Graduation is not the end of the educational process; it is merely a milestone marking the beginning of a new era of learning. College studies should not only equip you for entry into or promotion within the workforce but also equip you to be a lifelong learner.

The same is true about moral development. There is no "moral graduation" marking you as an upright person capable of making right choices in life's personal and professional dilemmas. It's a lifelong process. Where you are now is a function of both age and experience, but the person you are now is not the person you will be 10 years from now. Growth may, and probably will, change your decisions. This process is not inevitable, but it is desirable. Moral adulthood does not coincide with age or with certain sorts of legal status—for example, the ability to register and vote or enlist in the armed forces. We can all think of people who do not behave as moral adults well into their 40s and 50s, and we also can think of people whom we "look up" to in their decision-making regardless of chronological age. Moral adulthood

349

is as much something that we aspire to as it is a "label" marking something we have achieved. Contemporary scholarship suggests moral development begins within the mind-enhanced brain (Gazzaniga, 2011).

This chapter is designed to provide you with an overview of some psychological theories of moral development. It attempts to allow you to plot your own development not only in terms of where you are but also in terms of where you would like to be.

BASIC ASSUMPTIONS ABOUT MORAL DEVELOPMENT: THE RIGHTS-BASED TRADITION

People can develop morally just as they can learn to think critically (Clouse, 1985). Scholars base this assertion on the following premises, some of which are now being challenged in the literature.

First, *moral development occurs within the individual*. Real moral development cannot be produced by outside factors or merely engaging in moral acts. People develop morally when they become aware of their reasons for acting a certain way. Second, *moral development parallels intellectual development*. Although the two may proceed at a slightly different pace, there can be little moral development until a person has attained a certain intellectual capacity. For this reason, we exempt children and people of limited mental ability from some laws and societal expectations. While you can be intelligent without being moral, the opposite is not as likely. Third, *moral development occurs in a series of hierarchical stages*. Each level builds on the lower levels; there is no skipping of intermediate stages. Fourth, *moral development is prompted by internal conflict*. "A fundamental reason why an individual moves from one stage to the next is because the latter stages solve problems and inconsistencies unsolvable at the present developmental stage" (Kohlberg, 1973, p. 13). Just as a baby learns strategies other than crying to get its needs met, the developing moral being learns more complex behaviors when older, more elementary strategies no longer work (see figure 11.1).

The two most cited experts in the field of moral development did their work decades and continents apart and yet came to remarkably similar conclusions. Jean Piaget conducted his research in Switzerland in the 1930s by watching little boys play marbles, and Lawrence Kohlberg studied Harvard students in the 1960s. They are often called "stage theorists" for their work in identifying and describing the stages of moral development.

Figure 11.1. Calvin and Hobbes © Watterson. Distributed by Universal Uclick. Reprinted with permission. All rights reserved.

THE WORK OF PIAGET

Piaget watched as boys between the ages of 3 and 12 played marbles, and he tested his assumptions about their playground behavior in follow-up interviews. The box on the next page presents the basics of Piaget's theory.

The children under ages 5 to 7 didn't really play a game at all. They made up their own rules, varied them by playmate and game, and delighted in exploring the marbles as tactile objects.

The younger boys, ages 7 and 8, did follow the rules and played as if violations of the rules would result in punishment. Boys in this heteronomous stage believed the rules were timeless, handed down from some "other," and that "goodness" came from respecting the rules. Boys in this stage of moral development believed "Right is to obey the will of the adult. Wrong is to have a will of one's own" (Piaget, 1965, p. 193).

Children progressed to the next stage of moral development at about age 11 when the boys began to develop notions of autonomy. They began to understand the reasoning behind the rules (i.e., fair play and reciprocity) that were the foundation of the rules themselves. Children in this stage of moral development understood that the rules received their power from their internal logic, not some outside authority.

These children had internalized the rules. Understanding the reasons for the rules allowed the boys to rationally justify violating them. For example, children in this stage of moral development allowed much younger children to place their thumbs inside the marble circles, a clear rule violation. But the younger boys' hands were smaller and weaker, and by allowing them a positional advantage, the older ones had—in contemporary language—leveled the playing field. They had ensured fairness when following the rules literally would have made it impossible (see table 11.1).

Although Piaget worked with children, it is possible to see that adults often demonstrate these stages of moral development.

Take the videographer whose primary motivation is to obtain a great shot, regardless of the views of those he works with or his story subjects. This journalist operates within an egocentric moral framework that places the primary emphasis on what "I" think, "my" judgment, and what's good for "me."

Beginning journalists, the ones who find themselves concerned with the literal following of codes of ethics, may be equated with the heteronomy stage of development. This journalist knows the rules and follows them. She would never accept a freebie or consider running the name of a rape victim. It's

Table 11.1.   Piaget's Stages of Moral Development

Early Development (before age 2)
Interest in marbles is purely motor (e.g., put the marbles in your mouth).

First Stage: Egocentrism (years 3–7)
Children engage in "parallel play"; there is no coherent set of rules accepted by all. The moral reasoning is "I do it because it feels right."

Second Stage: Heteronomy (years 7–8)
Children recognize only individual responsibility; obedience is enforced through punishment.
Each player tries to win.
Rules are regarded as inviolate, unbreakable, and handed down from outside authority figures, usually older children.
The children do not understand the reason behind the rules.

Third Stage: Autonomy (begins about age 11)
Children internalize the rules; they understand the reasons behind them.
They develop an ideal of justice and are able to distinguish between individual and collective responsibility.
They ensure fair play among children.
Children can change the rules in response to a larger set of obligations.
Authority is internal.
Children understand universal ethical principles that transcend specific times and situations.
Children internalize the rules; they understand the reasons behind them.

against organizational policy, and heteronomous individuals are motivated by such outside influences.

Just as the boys at the third stage of moral development were more willing to alter the rules to ensure a fair game for all, journalists at the final stage of moral development are more willing to violate professional norms if it results in better journalism. The journalist at this stage of moral development has so internalized and universalized the rules of ethical professional behavior that he or she can violate some of them for sound ethical reasons.

However, people seldom remain exclusively in a single stage of moral development. New situations often cause people to regress temporarily to a previous stage of moral development until enough learning can take place so that the new situation is well understood. Perhaps the immediacy of the internet or the power of social networking sites at first caused such a regression for some. In any case, such regression would not include behaviors that would be considered morally culpable under most circumstances—for example, lying or killing—even despite the new context.

THE WORK OF KOHLBERG

Harvard psychologist Lawrence Kohlberg mapped six stages of moral development in his college-student subjects. Table 11.2 outlines Kohlberg's stages of moral development, divided into three levels.

Kohlberg developed a lengthy set of interview questions to allow him to establish which stage of moral development individual students had achieved. He asserted that only a handful of people—for example, Socrates, Gandhi, Martin Luther King, and Mother Teresa—ever achieved the sixth stage of moral development. Most adults, he believed, spend the greater portion of their lives in the two conventional stages where they are motivated by society's expectations.

Doing right, fulfilling one's duties, and abiding by the social contract are the pillars upon which the stages of Kohlberg's work rest. Under Kohlberg's theory, as you develop, more activities fall under the realm of duty than before. For instance, reciprocity is not even a concept for individuals in the earliest stage, yet it is an essential characteristic of people in the upper stages of moral development. Conversely, acting to avoid punishment is laudable for a novice yet might not be praiseworthy for a news director—or a videographer—functioning at a more advanced stage. The further up Kohlberg's stages students progressed, the more they asserted that moral principles are subject to interpretation by individuals and subject to contextual factors and yet able to be universalized.

Kohlberg's stages are descriptive and not predictive. They do not anticipate how any one individual will develop, but they suggest how most will develop. Kohlberg's formulation has much to recommend it to journalists, concerned as they are with concepts such as free speech, the professional duty to tell the truth, and their obligations to the public and the public trust. However, Kohlberg's work was not without its problems. At least two aspects of his research troubled other moral development theorists (see table 11.2).

Many scholars have argued that any general theory of moral development should allow people who are not saints or religious leaders to attain the highest stages of moral development. History is replete with examples of ordinary people taking extraordinary personal or professional risk for some larger ethical principles. Some felt that Kohlberg's conceptualization—unlike Piaget's—was too restrictive.

Still more troubling was that, in repeated studies, men consistently scored higher than women on stages of moral development. This gender bias in

Table 11.2.　The Six Moral Stages of Kohlberg

LEVEL 1: PRECONVENTIONAL

Stage 1: Heteronymous morality is the display of simple obedience.

Stage 2: Individualism is the emergence of self-interest. Rules are followed only when they are deemed to be in one's self-interest and others are allowed the same freedom. Reciprocity and fairness begin to emerge, but only in a pragmatic way.

LEVEL 2: CONVENTIONAL

Stage 3: Interpersonal conformity is living up to what others expect, given one's role (e.g., "brother," "daughter," "neighbor," etc.). "Being good" is important, and treating others as you would have them treat you becomes the norm.

Stage 4: Social systems is the recognition that one must fulfill the duties to which one has agreed. Doing one's duty, respect for authority, and maintaining the social order are all goals in this level. Laws are to be upheld unilaterally except in extreme cases where they conflict with other fixed social duties.

LEVEL 3: POSTCONVENTIONAL

Stage 5: Social contract and individual rights is becoming aware that one is obligated by whatever laws are agreed to by due process. The social contract demands that we uphold the laws even if they are contrary to our best interests because they exist to provide the greatest good for the greatest number. However, some values such as life and liberty stand above any majority opinion.

Stage 6: Universal ethical principles self-selected by each individual guide this person. These principles are to be followed even if laws violate those principles. The principles that guide this individual include the equality of human rights and respect for the dignity of humans as individual beings regardless of race, age, socioeconomic status, or even contribution to society.

Kohlberg's work prompted discussion about a different concept of moral development founded on notions of community rather than in the rights-based tradition. It is called the "ethics of care."

PARALLEL ASSUMPTIONS ABOUT MORAL DEVELOPMENT: THE ETHICS OF CARE

The psychologists who developed the ethics of care disagree with at least two of the fundamental assumptions underlying Piaget and Kohlberg. First, they say, moral development does not always occur in a series of universal, unvarying, and hierarchical stages. Second, moral growth emerges through understanding the concept of community, not merely through conflict. The rights-based scholars believe that moral development emerges from a proper understanding of the concept "I." Proponents of the ethics of care say that moral development arises from understanding the concept of "we."

Although the ethics of care was developed in the 20th century, the notion that ethics should consider emotion has a 300-year history. Discounting emotion is the dominant intellectual approach in philosophy; Descartes's dictum of "I think, therefore I am" is the most succinct explanation of that approach. However, more than 300 years ago, David Hume, in his attempt to develop a naturalistic approach to ethical thinking, proposed that ethics account for emotion, what Hume called the "moral sentiments." Chief among those sentiments was "sympathy," which Hume theorized was the root of both love and hate. He theorized that people regulated their "sympathetic reactions" by mentally employing "the general point of view"; this can be interpreted as an effort to derive ethical principles from generalized sympathetic responses. Like today's feminists, Hume insisted that understanding ethical actions must begin with observing the natural world. During his life, this focus on "sympathy" and a naturalistic epistemology was discounted and ridiculed. However, Hume's work influenced both Immanuel Kant and Charles Darwin. Today, Hume's approach is considered a precursor to cognitive science and an inspiration for several types of ethical theory.

Carol Gilligan (1982) provides the clearest explanation of the ethics of care, which is summarized in chapter 1. Gilligan argued that the moral adult is the person who sees a connection between the "I" and the "other." For example, Gilligan presented women with Kohlberg's classic ethical dilemma: the case of the desperate man and the greedy pharmacist. In this scenario, a man with a terminally ill spouse doesn't have enough money to purchase an expensive and lifesaving drug. When he explains the situation to the pharmacist, the pharmacist refuses to give him the medication. Under Kohlberg's system, it would be ethically allowable for a man at the highest stages of moral development to rationalize stealing the drug, an act of civil disobedience for a greater good. However, women made this particular choice less often. Instead, they reasoned that the most ethical thing to do was to build a relationship with the pharmacist, to form a community in which the pharmacist viewed herself as an active part. In that situation, the women reasoned, the pharmacist ultimately would give the man the drug in order to maintain the connection.

Gilligan proposed that the women's rationale was no more or less ethically sophisticated than that expected under Kohlberg's outline. However, it was different, for it relied on different ethical constructs. Whether those differences emerged as the result of how women are socialized in Western culture (an assertion that has often been made about Gilligan's work) remains open to debate. For our purposes, the origin of the distinction—and whether it is truly gender-linked—is not as important as the content.

Gilligan's notion of moral development is not neatly tied into stages. Her closest theoretical counterpart is probably the theory of communitarianism (see chapter 6 for a description) with its emphasis on connection to community and its mandate for social justice.

If you were to carve stages from Gilligan's work, they would resemble

- **first**—an ethic of care where the moral responsibility is for care of others before self;
- **second**—an acknowledgment of the ethic of rights, including the rights of self to be considered in ethical decision-making; and
- **third**—a movement from concerns about goodness (women are taught to believe that care for others is "good" while men are taught that "taking care of oneself" is good) to concerns about truth.

A complete sense of moral development, Gilligan observed, requires the ability "to [use] two different moral languages, the language of rights that protects separations and the language of responsibilities that sustains connection" (Gilligan, 1982, p. 210). In fact, she has asserted that moral reasoning at its highest level includes equal elements of care (feminist theory) and rights and responsibilities (much of classical, ethical philosophy) and the ability to know when it is appropriate to apply a specific set of theories to a particular problem.

Graduate students who studied with Gilligan have expanded her work. In *Women's Ways of Knowing*, one of the most central findings is that women who have been the subject of sexual abuse or have lived in poverty are less likely to achieve an understanding of the "truth" of care. Neither Piaget nor

Kohlberg investigated what might forestall moral development; it has taken feminist ethics to consider the question and develop theory in response. However, there is no empirical reason to believe that the negative life experiences that blunted women's moral growth might not have an equally negative impact on men. It is important to note that negative or difficult life experience can (but does not always) stunt moral thinking.

Political science professor Joan Tronto has distinguished four phases of care, and philosopher Virginia Held has asserted that care is a distinct normative theory that can be applied to political policy among other things. The concept of care, when applied to journalism and strategic communication, can influence everything from the news agenda to authentic advertising appeals. Contemporary journalists have struggled with the issues of connection. As noted in chapter 1, care is affirmative. It allows moral thinking to consider the question of what might be possible if things "went right." Feminist philosopher Martha Nussbaum's substantial body of work employs both classical and feminist approaches to undergird her intellectual effort. Nussbaum's overarching project is what is called the "capabilities approach," or a way of organizing political and economic structures to promote human flourishing, what Nussbaum describes as 10 capabilities. Among those are freedom of speech, the freedom to assemble, and the ability to control—and to see reflected in others in community—the narrative of one's life. These capabilities implicate the work of journalists and strategic communication professionals, and they do so by calling on the moral imagination.

Nussbaum concludes her 2001 book, *Upheavals of Thought: The Intelligence of Emotions*, with a plea to idealism tempered by mercy and love of real life in all its contradictions and messiness. She lobbies for an idealism stripped of disgust for real people confronting daily problems. While Nussbaum uses the word "love" throughout the book, the concept of care works equally well in her explanations. Ethical thinking that articulates a balance between the ideal and the real, that accounts for logic and emotion, that promotes some actions while restraining others, and that evaluates the structures within which people live and work is the contribution of Nussbaum's efforts, and of feminist ethics, more generally. It suggests that media professionals consider both the individual and the institution when they make ethical decisions and that they acknowledge that emotion, particularly caring for the truth of the individual, is an essential part of ethical thinking. If journalism as a profession is to mature ethically (or even survive economically), it must see itself as the vehicle to help people become the citizens they can be and to help reconnect and sustain communities that have become increasingly fragmented.

With the election of President Barack Obama, followed by the near-depression of 2008–2009 and economic slump for the decade thereafter, and continuing with the election of President Donald J. Trump, the United States has found itself in an intense conversation about values, rights, community, and class. The Black Lives Matter movement has shared a mediated stage with neo-Nazis, white supremacists, and anarchists who have problematized the First Amendment and our human connection to one another in ways that have challenged journalistic values, norms, and routines. A *Newsweek* essay from 1992 anticipated these developments and the media's role in them:

> Television brought the nation together in the '50s; there were evenings when all of America seemed glued to the same show—Milton Berle, "I Love Lucy" and yes, "Ozzie and Harriet." But cable television has quite the opposite effect, dividing the audience into demographic slivers.... Indeed, if you are a member of any identifiable subgroup—black, Korean, fundamentalist, sports fan, political junkie—it's now possible to be messaged by your very own television and radio stations and to read your own magazines without having to venture out into the American mainstream. The choices are exhilarating, but also alienating. The basic principle is centrifugal: market segmentation targets those qualities that distinguish people from each other rather than emphasizing the things we have in common. It is the developed world's equivalent of the retribalization taking place in Eastern Europe, Africa and Asia. (Klein, 1992, pp. 21–22)

DEVELOPING AS AN ETHICAL PROFESSIONAL

In the 1970s, James Rest, a psychology professor at the University of Minnesota, took Kohlberg's schema of moral development and used it to create a paper-and-pencil test to measure moral development among various professions. In the ensuing years, the test, called the Defining Issues Test (DIT), has been administered to more than 40,000 professionals, among them doctors, nurses, dentists, accountants, philosophers and theologians, members of the US Coast Guard, surgeons, veterinarians, graduate students, junior high students, and prison inmates. Those taking the test read four to six scenarios and are then asked to make a decision about what the protagonist should do and then to rate the factors that influenced that decision. Because the test is based on Kohlberg's work, those test takers who rely on universal principles and who consider issues of justice score well. Most people who take the DIT score in the range of what Kohlberg would have called conventional moral reasoning—stages 3 and 4 of his scale.

Wilkins and Coleman (2005) asked journalists to take the DIT and compared journalists' scores to those of other professionals. Journalists do well on the DIT, scoring below only three other professions: philosophers/

theologians, medical students, and practicing physicians. Because the single biggest predictor of a good score on the DIT is education, and journalists as a group have less formal education than the three professions with scores "above" them, the findings are significant. Other professions—for example, orthopedic surgeons—scored lower than journalists on the test. In a follow-up study, public-relations professionals also did well on the DIT (Coleman & Wilkins, 2006). These findings have been replicated fairly consistently for advertising executives (Castleberry, French, & Carlin, 1993; Schauster, Ferrucci, Tandoc, & Walker, 2020) and public-relations executives (Lieber, 2008; Plaisance, 2015). Cunningham (2005) did find that advertising professionals demonstrated considerably lower ethical reasoning scores than most other tested professions and adults in general. Advertisers' scores, though, mostly aligned with those of other business professionals. This group did score lower on ethical reasoning when presented with advertising-specific dilemmas, suspending moral judgment to instead focus on the financial implications of a decision for themselves and their clients.

The scenarios on the DIT are not directed at any particular profession but rather determine how people think about "average" moral questions. When journalists are presented with scenarios that deal directly with journalism—for example, problems involving the use of hidden cameras or whether to run troubling photographs of children—they score even better. So do public-relations professionals. In these tests, journalists and public-relations professionals often score in the fourth and fifth stages of Kohlberg's moral development schema. In an interesting side note, scholars found that having a visual image, such as a photograph, of some of the stakeholders in an ethical dilemma elevates ethical reasoning. However, research also has found that moving images can degrade ethical thinking just as still images can promote it (Meader, Knight, Coleman, & Wilkins, 2015).

Other scholars have studied journalists' ethical decision-making. Investigative reporters make moral judgments about the subjects of their stories even though they are reluctant to drop their professional objectivity when they talk about their work (Ettema & Glasser, 1998). Another study found that journalists who have been sued for invasion of privacy don't often think about the ethical issues their reporting creates (Voakes, 1998). This leads to an indirect but plausible conclusion that solid ethical thinking may keep journalists out of court.

The decisions made by journalists and public relations professionals—the moral judgments as opposed to moral development—also have been examined by scholars. In a series of studies of journalism students, Coleman (2011a, 2011b) found that Caucasian students tended to use lower-level ethical reasons when their decisions involved photographs of Black subjects.

The same was not true for Black students. Follow-up studies documented that professionals from minority communities used the same quality of ethical reasoning regardless of the ethnicity of the subjects of their coverage. These studies suggest that in-group and social-identity theories that have traditionally studied only Whites "do not apply the same way to the moral judgment processes of minorities" (Coleman & Wilkins, 2020, p. 53).

Finally, research shows that journalists do agree on what constitutes "good work" in their profession—an emphasis on truth telling, taking a role as government watchdog, investigative reporting, and treating the subjects with dignity. However, journalists believe that the single biggest threat to maintaining professional excellence is the increasing pressure to make a profit. Journalists are out of joint with a mission that includes the competing interests of public service and profit-making (Gardner, Csikszenthmihalyi, & Damon, 2001). How that tension is resolved is the essential question facing news operations today. Taking inspiration from the feminist assertion that theory emerges from lived experience, Patrick Plaisance has studied professional moral exemplars. He found that a combination of internal abilities (e.g., the ability to remain resilient in the face of challenges), a supportive work environment, and a sense of journalism as a "mission" rather than a job has allowed individual professionals to make solid ethical choices throughout their careers as well as at particularly contentious decision points (Plaisance, 2015).

WHERE DO YOU GO FROM HERE?

William Perry (1968) postulates that one of the major accomplishments of college students is to progress from a simple, dualistic (right versus wrong) view of life to a more complex, mature, and relativistic view. Perry states that students must not only acknowledge that diversity and uncertainty exist in a world of relativism but also make a commitment to their choices (i.e., career, values, beliefs, etc.) out of the multiplicity of "right" choices available.

Unlike physical development, moral development is not subject to the quirks of heredity. Each individual is free to develop as keen a sense of equity as any other individual, yet not all reach their full potential. Kohlberg (1973) claims we understand messages one stage higher than our own. Through "aspirational listening"—picking a role model on a higher level—you can progress to a higher stage of moral development. This observation is not new. In fact, Aristotle suggested that virtues could be learned by observing those who possess them.

This book uses the case-study method. Often in case studies it is the reasoning behind the answer rather than the answer itself that is the best determiner of moral growth (Clouse, 1985). *An important part of moral development is the recognition that motive, not consequence, is a critical factor in deciding whether an act is ethical.*

Elliott (1991) illustrates the difference in the following scenario. Imagine a situation where you are able to interview and choose your next-door neighbor. When you ask Jones how she feels about murder, she replies she doesn't kill because she would go to jail if she got caught. When you interview Smith, he says he doesn't kill because he believes in the sanctity of life. It takes little reflection to decide which neighbor you would prefer. Elliott concludes, "Ethics involves the judging of actions as right or wrong, but motivations count as well. Some reasons for actions seem better or worse than others" (1991, p. 19).

To the above quote we might add, "and some justifications are more deeply rooted in centuries of ethical thought than others." The goal of this book—and probably one of the goals your professor had for this class—is to ensure that your choices are not merely "right," as that's a debate for the ages, but to ensure that your choices are grounded in the ethical theories that have stood the test of time and are not subject to the vagaries of current popular thought. The work of Kohlberg and Piaget suggests that your journey is not finished, but that you *have* started. And with the set of tools you have now acquired, you have an excellent chance of reaching your destination.

SUGGESTED READINGS

Belenky, M. F., Clinchy, B. M., Goldberger, N. R., & Tarule, J. M. (1988). *Women's ways of knowing: The development of self, voice and mind.* New York: Basic Books.

Coles, R. (1995, September 22). The disparity between intellect and character. *The Chronicle of Higher Education.*

Ettema, J., & Glasser, T. (1998). *Custodians of conscience: Investigative journalists and public virtue.* New York: Columbia University Press.

Gardner, H., Csikszentmihalyi, M., & Damon, W. (2001). *Good work: When excellence and ethics meet.* New York: Basic Books.

Gazzaniga, M. S. (2011). *Who's in charge? Free will and the science of the brain.* New York: HarperCollins.

Gilligan, C. (1982). *In a different voice: Psychological theory and women's development.* Cambridge, MA: Harvard University Press.

Wilkins, L., & Coleman, R. (2005). *The moral media.* Mahwah, NJ: Lawrence Erlbaum Associates.

References

Abernathy, P. M. (2020). The rise of the ghost newspaper. Retrieved from https://www.usnewsdeserts.com/reports/expanding-news-desert/loss-of-local-news/the-rise-of-the-ghost-newspaper/.

Abrams, R. (2020, January 27). Washington Post suspends a reporter after her tweets on Kobe Bryant. *Washington Post*. Retrieved from https://www.nytimes.com/2020/01/27/business/media/kobe-bryant-washington-post-felicia-sonmez.html.

Allcott, H., & Gentzhow, M. (2017). Social media and fake news in the 2016 election. *Journal of Economics Perspective, 31*(2), 211–236.

Anderson, C. (2006). *The long tail: How the future of business is selling less of more.* New York: Hyperion.

Andrews, T. A. (2017, August 2). Why a TV station flew a drone over Kentucky governor's home. *Washington Post*. Retrieved from https://www.washingtonpost.com/news/morning-mix/wp/2017/08/02/why-a-tv-station-flew-a-drone-over-kentucky-governors-home/?utmterm=.66f9db179c40.

Angwin, J., Larson, J., Mattu, S., & Kirchner, L. (2016, May 23). Machine bias: There's software used across the country to predict future criminals. And it's biased against blacks. *ProPublica*. Retrieved from https://www.propublica.org/article/machine-bias-risk-assessments-in-criminal-sentencing.

Ansen, D. (2006, October 23). Inside the hero factory. *Newsweek*, 70–71.

Arendt, H. (1970). *The human condition.* Chicago: University of Chicago Press.

Aufderheide, P. (2005). *Reclaiming fair use.* Oxford: Oxford University Press.

Aushana, C., & Pixley, T. (2020, July 13). If photojournalism wants to draw attention to social justice, it must also look at the unintended harm photography can cause. *Nieman Reports*. Retrieved from https://niemanreports.org/articles/protest-photography-and-black-lives-matter/.

Axelrod, R. (1984). *The evolution of cooperation.* New York: Basic Books.

Baker, S., & Martinson, D. (2001). The TARES test: Five principles of ethical persuasion. *Journal of Mass Media Ethics, 16*(2 & 3), 148–175.

References

Barbur, J. E., & Goodnow, T. (2011). The arête of amusement: An Aristotelian perspective on the ethos of *The Daily Show*. In T. Goodnow (ed.), The Daily Show *and rhetoric: Arguments, issues, and strategies* (pp. 3–18). Lanham, MD: Lexington Books.

Barnes, B. (2020, October 8). Harry and Meghan get an apology after suing paparazzi. *New York Times*. Retrieved from https://www.nytimes.com/2020/10/08/business/harry-meghan-paparazzi-lawsuit.html?smid=em-share.

Barnouw, E. (1997). *Conglomerates and the media*. New York: New Press.

Baym, G. (2005). *The Daily Show*: Discursive integration and the reinvention of political journalism. *Political Communication, 22*(3), 259–276.

Bennett, W. (1993). *The book of virtues: A treasury of great moral stories*. New York: Simon and Schuster.

Benoit, W. (1999). *Seeing spots: A functional analysis of presidential television advertisements*. Westport, CT: Praeger.

Berger, A. (1989). *Seeing is believing*. Mountain View, CA: Mayfield.

Berger, J. (1980). *About looking*. New York: Pantheon Books.

Billings, A. C. (2003). Portraying Tiger Woods: Characterizations of a "Black" athlete in a "White" sport. *Howard Journal of Communications, 14*(1), 29–37.

———. (2004). Depicting the quarterback in black and white: A content analysis of college and professional football broadcast commentary. *Howard Journal of Communications, 15*(4), 201–210.

Billings, A. C., & Eastman, S. T. (2003). Framing identities: Gender, ethnic, and national parity in network announcing of the 2002 Winter Olympics. *Journal of Communication, 53*(4), 569–586.

Bok, S. (1978). *Lying: Moral choice in public and private life*. New York: Random House.

———. (1983). *Secrets: On the ethics of concealment and revelation*. New York: Vintage.

Borden, S. L. (2009). *Journalism as practice: MacIntyre, virtue ethics and the press*. Burlington, VT: Ashgate.

Bovée, W. (1991). The end can justify the means—but rarely. *Journal of Mass Media Ethics, 6*(3), 135–145.

Bowen, E. (2019, October 27). Rep. Katie Hill, facing an ethics investigation, says she will resign. National Public Radio. Retrieved from https://www.npr.org/2019/10/27/773942001/rep-katie-hill-facing-an-ethics-investigation-says-she-will-resign.

Breslow, J. (2020, January 24). Pompeo won't say whether he owes Yovanovitch an apology. "I've done what's right." National Public Radio. Retrieved from https://www.npr.org/2020/01/24/799244678/pompeo-wont-say-whether-he-owes-yovanovitch-an-apology-i-ve-done-what-s-right?utm_campaign=storyshare&utm_source=twitter.com&utm_medium=social.

Brooks, D. E. (1992). In their own words: Advertisers and the origins of the African-American consumer market. Presented at the Association for Education in Journalism and Mass Communication, 1992, Montreal.

Bryant, G. (1987). Ten-fifty P. I.: Emotion and the photographer's role. *Journal of Mass Media Ethics, 2*(2), 32–39.

Bunton, K., & Wyatt, W. (2012). *Reality television: A philosophical examination.* New York: Continuum International.

Burns, M. (2012). A sea of endless bullets: Spec Ops, No Russian and interactive atrocity. Retrieved from https://www.magicalwasteland.com/notes/2012/8/2/a-sea-of-endless-bullets-spec-ops-no-russian-and-interactive.html.

Bursztynsky, J. (2021, January 11). Twitter shares close down more than 6% first trading day after Trump ban. CNBC. Retrieved from https://www.cnbc.com/2021/01/11/twitter-shares-drop-in-first-trading-day-after-trump-ban.html.

Cain, B. (2017, August 14). He's the Raleigh man behind the Twitter account outing racists—and "I'm not going away." *Raleigh News Observer.* Retrieved from http://www.newsobserver.com/news/local/article167142317.html.

Calfee, J. E. (2002). Public policy issues in direct-to-consumer advertising of prescription drugs. *Journal of Public Policy & Marketing, 21*(2), 174–193.

Capps, K. (2018, June 5). Uncovering the financial impacts of local news deserts. *Pacific Standard.* Retrieved from https://psmag.com/economics/economic-damage-from-losing-local-news.

Carey, J. W. (1989). Review of Charles J. Sykes' Profscam. *Journalism Educator, 44*(3), 48.

Caron, C. (2017, August 13). Heather Heyer, Charlottesville victim, is recalled as "a strong woman." *New York Times.* Retrieved from https://www.nytimes.com/2017/08/13/us/heather-heyer-charlottesville-victim.html.

Cassier, E. (1944). *An essay on man.* New Haven, CT: Yale University Press.

Castleberry, S. B., French, W., & Carlin, B. A. (1993). The ethical framework of advertising and marketing research practitioners: A moral development perspective. *Journal of Advertising, 22*(2), 39–46.

Caufield, R. P. (2008). The influence of "infoenterpropagainment": Exploring the power of political satire as a distinct form of political humor. In J. C. Baumgartner & J. S. Morris (eds.), *Laughing matters: Humor and American politics in the media age* (pp. 3–20). New York: Routledge.

CBS. (2017, May 8). Sinclair to buy Tribune Media, expanding its local TV reach. CBS News. Retrieved from https://www.cbsnews.com/news/sinclair-to-buy-tribune-media-expanding-its-local-tv-reach/.

Centers for Disease Control and Prevention. (2017). Retrieved from https://www.cdc.gov/drugoverdose/data/heroin.html.

Christians, C. G. (1986). Reporting and the oppressed. In D. Elliott (ed.), *Responsible journalism* (pp. 109–130). Newbury Park, CA: Sage.

———. (2010). The ethics of privacy. In Christopher Meyers (ed.), *Journalism ethics: A philosophical approach* (pp. 203–214). Oxford: Oxford University Press.

Christians, C. G., Ferré, J. P., & Fackler, M. (1993). *Good news: Social ethics and the press.* New York: Oxford University Press.

Christians, C. G., Glasser, T., McQuail, D., Nordenstreng, K., & White, R. A. (2009). *Normative theories of the media: Journalism in democratic societies.* Champaign: University of Illinois Press.

Clouse, B. (1985). *Moral development.* Grand Rapids: Baker Book House.

Coleman, R. (2011a). Color blind: Race and the ethical reasoning of blacks on journalism dilemmas. *Journalism & Mass Communication Quarterly, 88*(2), 337–351.

Coleman, R. (2011b). The moral judgment of minority journalists: Evidence from Asian American, Black, and Hispanic professional journalists. *Mass Communication and Society, 14*, 578–599.

Coleman, R., & Wilkins, L. (2006). *The moral development of public relations practitioners*. Presented to the Association for Education in Journalism and Mass Communication, August 2006, San Francisco.

———. (2020). Moral development: A psychological approach to understanding moral decision making. In C. G. Christians & L. Wilkins (eds.), *The Routledge handbook of mass media ethics* (pp. 43–58). New York: Routledge.

Compton, J. (2011). Introduction: Surveying the scholarship on *The Daily Show* and *The Colbert Report*. In A. Amarasingam (ed.), *The Stewart/Colbert effect: Essays on the real impacts of fake news* (pp. 9-23). Jefferson, NC: McFarland & Company.

Corbett-Davies, S., Pierson, E., Feller, A., & Goel, S. (2016, October 17). A computer program used for bail and sentencing decisions was labeled biased against blacks. It's actually not that clear. *Washington Post*. Retrieved from https://www.washingtonpost.com/news/monkey-cage/wp/2016/10/17/can-an-algorithm-be-racist-our-analysis-is-more-cautious-than-propublicas/.

Craft, S. (2017). Distinguishing features: Reconsidering the link between journalism's professions status and ethics. *Journalism and Communication Monographs, 19*(4), 260–301.

Cubarrubia, R. J. (2012, August 9). Adam Yauch's will prohibits use of his music in ads. *Rolling Stone*. Retrieved from https://www.rollingstone.com/music/news/adam-yauchs-will-prohibits-use-of-his-music-in-ads-20120809.

Culver, K. B., & Duncan, M. (2017). *Newsrooms should build trust with audiences in drone journalism*. Retrieved from https://ethics.journalism.wisc.edu/dronejournalism/.

Cunningham, A. (2005). Advertising practitioners respond: The news is not good. In L. Wilkins & R. Coleman (eds.), *The moral media: How journalists reason about ethics* (pp. 114–124). Mahwah, NJ: Lawrence Erlbaum Associates.

Cunningham, B. (2003). Re-thinking objectivity. *Columbia Journalism Review*, July/August, 24–32.

Cuza, B. (2021, January 22). Trump, in Palm Beach, won't be able to escape his legal troubles in New York. Spectrum News NY1. Retrieved from https://www.ny1.com/nyc/all-boroughs/news/2021/01/22/trump--in-palm-beach--won-t-be-able-to-escape-his-legal-troubles-in-new-york.

D'Angelo, C. (2017, July 4). Journalist who exposed the racist creator of Trump's CNN tweet gets death threats. *Huffington Post*. Retrieved from https://www.huffingtonpost.com/entry/jared-sexton-trump-cnn-tweetus595a6656e4b0da2c7324d3d6.

Darcy, O. (2019, December 6). Mike Bloomberg to Bloomberg News reporters upset over not being able to probe Democrats: "With your paycheck comes some restrictions." CNN. Retrieved from https://www.cnn.com/2019/12/06/media/michael-bloomberg-reporters-investigate-democrats/index.html.

Davies, J. C. (1963). *Human nature in politics*. New York: John Wiley.

Deitsch, R. (2017, October 9). ESPN suspends Jemele Hill two weeks for violating social media policy. *Sports Illustrated*. Retrieved from https://www.si.com/tech-media/2017/10/09/jemele-hill-suspend-espn.

Delk, J. (2017, December 16). Antitrust calls for hearing on Disney deal to buy Fox assets. *The Hill*. Retrieved from http://thehill.com/blogs/blog-briefing-room/365227-antitrust-senator-wants-investigation-of-disney-deal-to-buy-fox.

Denham, B. E., Billings, A. C., & Halone, K. K. (2002). Differential accounts of race in broadcast commentary of the 2000 NCAA Men's and Women's Final Four Basketball Tournaments. *Sociology of Sport Journal, 19*(3), 315–332.

Dessem, M. (2019, August 10). Universal cancels upcoming movie *The Hunt* after presidential tweetstorm. *Slate*. Retrieved from https://slate.com/culture/2019/08/the-hunt-canceled-universal-craig-zobel-betty-gilpin-hilary-swank.html.

de Tocqueville, A. (1985). *Democracy in America*. New York: George Dearborn.

Deuze, M. (2008). The changing nature of news work: Liquid journalism and monitorial citizenship. *International Journal of Communication, 2*, 848–865.

Dewey, J. (1932/2005). *Art as experience*. New York: Penguin Putnam.

Digital Marketing Institute. (2018, November 27). 9 of the biggest social media influencers on Instagram. Retrieved from https://digitalmarketinginstitute.com/blog/9-of-the-biggest-social-media-influencers-on-instagram#:~:text=A%20social%20media%20influencer%20is,act%20based%20on%20their%20recommendations.&text=Their%20audience%20isn't%20limited,followers%20who%20share%20their%20content.

Dionne, E. J. (1991). *Why Americans hate politics*. New York: Simon & Schuster.

———. (1996). *They only look dead*. New York: Simon & Schuster.

Dixon, T., & Linz, D. (2000). Overrepresentation and underrepresentation of Blacks and Latinos as lawbreakers on television news. *Journal of Communication, 50*(2), 131–154.

Donohue, J. (2006). A history of drug advertising: The evolving roles of consumers and consumer protection. *Milbank Quarterly, 84*(4), 659–699.

Douglas, D. M. (2016). Doxing: A conceptual analysis. *Ethics and Information Technology, 18*(3), 199–210.

Duncan, E. (1970). Has anyone committed the naturalistic fallacy? *Southern Journal of Philosophy, 1*(1/2), 49–61.

Dyck, A. (1977). *On human care*. Nashville: Abingdon.

Eastman, S. T., & Billings, A. C. (2001). Biased voices of sports: Racial and gender stereotyping in college basketball announcing. *Howard Journal of Communications, 12*(4), 183–201.

Eaton, M. L. (2004). *Ethics and the business of bioscience*. Stanford: Stanford University Press.

Edmonds, R. (2020, June 10). At Gannett's Ithaca Journal, local news staffing is down to one reporter. Poynter Institute. Retrieved from https://www.poynter.org/locally/2020/at-gannetts-ithaca-journal-local-news-staffing-is-down-to-one-reporter/.

Elliott, D. (1991). Moral development theories and the teaching of ethics. *Journalism Educator, 46*(3), 19–24.

Ellis, E. G. (2017, August 17). Whatever your side, doxing is a perilous form of justice. *Wired.* Retrieved from https://www.wired.com/story/doxing-charlottesville/.

Ellul, J. (1965). *Propaganda.* Trans. by K. Kellen & J. Lerner. New York: Alfred A. Knopf.

Emerson, J. (2006). *The Bridge.* Retrieved from http://www.rogerebert.com/reviews/the-bridge-2006.

Entman, R., & Rojecki, A. (2000). *The black image in the white mind.* Chicago: University of Chicago Press.

Epstein, K. (2019, October 13). Elizabeth Warren's Facebook ad proves the social media giant still has a politics problem. *The Washington Post.* Retrieved from https://www.washingtonpost.com/politics/2019/10/12/elizabeth-warrens-facebook-ad-proves-social-media-giant-still-has-politics-problem/.

ESPN (2017). ESPN's social media guidelines. Retrieved from https://www.espnfrontrow.com/2017/11/espns-social-media-guidelines/.

Ettema, J., & Glasser, T. (1998). *Custodians of conscience: Investigative journalists and public virtue.* New York: Columbia University Press.

Fainaru-Wada, M. (2019, February 10). Bob Costas, unplugged. From NBC and broadcast icon to dropped from the Super Bowl. ESPN. Retrieved from https://www.espn.com/espn/otl/story/_/id/25914913/inside-story-how-legendary-nfl-broadcaster-bob-costas-ended-excised-football-nbc-espn.

Fallows, J. (1996). *Breaking the news: How the media undermine American democracy.* New York: Pantheon.

Farhi, P. (2015, December 3). Media falls into pattern with coverage of mass shootings. *Washington Post.* Retrieved from https://www.washingtonpost.com/lifestyle/style/media-fall-into-pattern-with-coverage-of-mass-shootings/2015/12/03/ab5001e6-9a09-11e5-94f0-9eeaff906ef3_story.html?noredirect=on&utm_term=.8205f74aa3b8.

———. (2017, September 20). ESPN likes opinionated personalities. Until it doesn't. Just ask Jemele Hill. *Washington Post.* Retrieved from https://www.washingtonpost.com/lifestyle/style/espn-likes-opinionated-personalities-until-it-doesnt-just-ask-jemele-hill/2017/09/20/906ca3d8-9ce7-11e7-8ea1-ed975285475e_story.html?noredirect=on&utm_term=.59b282b227a1.

Feinberg, L. (1967). *Introduction to satire.* Ames: Iowa State University Press.

Feng, Y. (2020). Learning from Confucius: Moral self-cultivation (Xiuji) and its application in media ethics education. Presented at the Association for Education in Journalism and Mass Communication, August 2020, San Francisco (virtual).

Ferrucci, P., & Schauster, E. (2020). Keeping up with the ethical boundaries on advertising. Big soda, metadiscourse, and paradigm repair. Presented at the Association for Education in Journalism and Mass Communication, August 2020, San Francisco (virtual).

Ferrucci, P., Tandoc, E., Painter, C., & Leshner, G. (2013). A black and white game: Racial stereotypes in baseball. *Howard Journal of Communications, 24*(3), 309–325.

Ferrucci, P., Tandoc, E., Painter, C., & Wolfgang, D. (2016). Foul ball: Audience-held stereotypes of baseball players. *Howard Journal of Communications, 27*(1), 68–84.

Festinger, L. (1957). *A theory of cognitive dissonance.* Stanford: Stanford University Press.

Fiegerman, S., & Byers, D. (2017). Facebook, Twitter, Google defend their role in election. *CNN*, October 31, 2017. Retrieved from http://money.cnn.com/2017/10/31/media/facebook-twitter-google-congress/index.html.

Fischer, C. T. (1980). Privacy and human development. In W. C. Bier (ed.), *Privacy: A vanishing value?* (pp. 37–46). New York: Fordham University Press.

Fitzpatrick, K., & Bronstein, C. (eds.). (2006). *Ethics in public relations: Responsible advocacy.* Thousand Oaks, CA: Sage.

Fletcher, G. P. (1993). *Loyalty: An essay on the morality of relationships.* New York: Oxford University Press.

Folkenflik, D. (2017, May 8). Sinclair Broadcast Group has deal to buy Tribune Media's TV stations. National Public Radio. Retrieved from https://www.npr.org/sections/thetwo-way/2017/05/08/527462015/sinclair-broadcast-group-has-deal-to-buy-tribune-medias-tv-stations.

———. (2020a, June 8). Editors barred a Black reporter from covering protests. Newsroom rebelled. National Public Radio. Retrieved from https://www.npr.org/2020/06/08/872234014/editors-barred-a-black-reporter-from-covering-protests-then-her-newsroom-rebelle.

———. (2020b, April 14). Bloomberg News killed investigation, fired reporter, then sought to silence his wife. National Public Radio. Retrieved from https://www.npr.org/2020/04/14/828565428/bloomberg-news-killed-investigation-fired-reporter-then-sought-to-silence-his-wi.

———. (2020c, November 4). How did news networks handle Trump's false victory claims? National Public Radio. Retrieved from https://www.kqed.org/electionupdates.

Food and Drug Administration, Department of Health and Human Services (FDA/DHHS). (1969). Regulations for the Enforcement of the Federal Food, Drug, and Cosmetic Act and the Fair Packaging and Labeling Act. Federal Register 34:7802.

Foundation for Individual Rights in Education. (2020, October 26). FIRE, NAJA and SPLC letter to Haskell Indian Nations University. Retrieved from https://www.thefire.org/fire-naja-and-splc-letter-to-haskell-indian-nations-university-october-26-2020/.

Gans, H. (1979). *Deciding what's news: A study of CBS Evening News, NBC Nightly News, Newsweek and Time.* New York: Vintage.

Gardner, H., Csikszenthmihalyi, M., & Damon, W. (2001). *Good work: When excellence and ethics meet.* New York: Basic Books.

Gazzaniga, M. S. (2011). *Who's in charge? Free will and the science of the brain.* New York: HarperCollins.

Gert, B. (1988). *Morality, a new justification of the moral rules.* New York: Oxford University Press.

Ghaffary, S., & Molla, R. (2020, October 20). Why the US government is suing Google. *Vox*. Retrieved from https://www.vox.com/recode/21524710/google-antitrust-lawsuit-doj-search-trump-bill-barr.

Gilens, M. (1999). *Why Americans hate welfare: Race, media and the politics of anti-poverty policy*. Chicago: University of Chicago Press.

Gilligan, C. (1982). *In a different voice: Psychological theory and women's development*. Cambridge, MA: Harvard University Press.

Glasser, T. L. (1992). Objectivity and news bias. In E. D. Cohen (ed.), *Philosophical issues in journalism* (pp. 176–185). Oxford: Oxford University Press.

Glionna, J. (2006, April 28). Uproar over film of Golden Gate suicides. *Los Angeles Times*. Retrieved from http://articles.latimes.com/2006/apr/28/local/me-bridge28.

Gold, H. (2017, July 10). Sinclair increases "must-run" Boris Epshteyn segments. *Politico*. Retrieved from https://www.politico.com/blogs/on-media/2017/07/10/boris-epshteyn-sinclair-broadcasting-240359.

Goldberg, J. (2019, December). The places where the recession never ended. *The Atlantic*. Retrieved from https://www.theatlantic.com/magazine/archive/2019/12/tara-westover-trump-rural-america/600916/?utm_source=feed.

GoldieBlox. (2017). About GoldieBlox. Retrieved from https://www.goldieblox.com/pages/about.

Graham, D. A. (2020, May 27). CNN is picking ratings over ethics. *The Atlantic*. Retrieved from https://www.theatlantic.com/ideas/archive/2020/05/cnns-cuomo-no-no/612103/.

Grcic, J. M. (1986). The right to privacy: Behavior as property. *Journal of Values Inquiry*, *20*(2), 137–144.

Green, S. (1999, September 1). Media's role in changing the face of poverty. *Neiman Reports*. Retrieved from http://niemanreports.org/articles/medias-role-in-changing-the-face-of-poverty/.

Greenwood, M. (2017, September 12). Kid Rock denies press credentials to Detroit paper. *The Hill*. Retrieved from http://thehill.com/blogs/in-the-know/in-the-know/350326-kid-rock-denies-press-credentials-to-detroit-paper.

Gross, A. (2017, September 12). Kid Rock denies Detroit Free Press credentials for Little Caesars Arena concert. *Detroit Free Press*. Retrieved from http://www.freep.com/story/news/local/michigan/detroit/2017/09/12/kid-rock-detroit-free-press-credentials-lca-concert/657462001/.

Gross, K., & Aday, S. (2003). The scary world in your living room and neighborhood: Using local broadcast news, neighborhood crime rates, and personal experience to test agenda setting and cultivation. *Journal of Communication*, *53*(3), 411–426.

Grow, J. M., Park, J. S., & Han, X. (2006). Your life is waiting! *Journal of Communication Inquiry*, *30*(2), 163–188.

Grunig, L., Toth, E., & Hon, L. (2000). Feminist values in public relations. *Journal of Public Relations Research*, *12*(1), 49–68.

Gurevitch, M., Levy, M., & Roeh, I. (1991). The global newsroom: Convergences and diversities in the globalization of television news. In P. Dalhgren & C. Sparks (eds.), *Communication and citizenship*. London: Routledge.

Gutwirth, S. (2002). *Privacy and the information age*. Lanham, MD: Rowman & Littlefield.

Haddad, T. (2019, November 1). Watch Katie Hill's defiant resignation speech before backing Trump impeachment inquiry "on behalf of the women of the United States of America." *Newsweek*. Retrieved from https://www.newsweek.com/watch-katie-hill-defiant-resignation-speech-before-trump-impeachment-vote-1469122.

Hadland, A., Campbell, D., & Lambert, P. (2015). The state of news photography: The lives and livelihoods of photojournalists in the digital age. Retrieved from https://reutersinstitute.politics.ox.ac.uk/our-research/state-news-photography-lives-and-livelihoods-photojournalists-digital-age.

Haiman, F. (1958). Democratic ethics and the hidden persuaders. *Quarterly Journal of Speech, 44*(4), 385–392.

Halberstam, D. (2001). *War in a time of peace*. New York: Scribner.

Halone, K. K., & Billings, A. C. (2010). The temporal nature of racialized sport consumption. *American Behavioral Scientist, 53*(11), 1645–1668.

Hamilton, K. (2012, July 24). How to kill civilians in a war game. *Kotaku*. Retrieved from https://kotaku.com/5928765/how-to-kill-civilians-in-a-war-game.

Hare, K. (2020, June 10). Gannett took mugshot galleries off former GateHouse sites yesterday. Poynter Institute. Retrieved from https://www.poynter.org/reporting-editing/2020/gannett-took-mugshot-galleries-off-former-gatehouse-sites-yesterday/.

Harp, D., Bachmann, I., & Loke, J. (2014). Where are the women? The presence of female columnists in U.S. opinion pages. *Journalism & Mass Communication Quarterly, 91*(2), 289–307.

Harris, L. (2019, November 6). Correcting the record. *Columbia Journalism Review*. Retrieved from https://www.cjr.org/criticism/felicia-sonmez-metoo.php.

Hart, A. (2003). Delusions of accuracy. *Columbia Journalism Review*, July/August, 20.

Haynes, H., & Dargan, J. (2020). WPR Source demographic survey shows need for improvement. Wisconsin Public Radio. Retrieved from https://www.wpr.org/wpr-source-demographic-survey-shows-need-improvement#report.

Haysom, S. (2020, August 27). Trevor Noah is trolling Trump with a full-page legal ad in the "New York Times." *Mashable*. Retrieved from https://mashable.com/article/daily-show-trump-legal-ad-new-york-times/.

Henderson, C. (2020, February 7). Oscars reject postpartum ad as "too graphic," raising ire from Busy Philipps, supporters. *USA Today*. Retrieved from https://www.usatoday.com/story/entertainment/celebrities/2020/02/07/oscars-reject-post-partum-ad-being-too-graphic-busy-phillips-react/4696560002/.

Herman, E. S., & Chomsky, N. (2002). *Manufacturing consent: The political economy of the mass media*. New York: Pantheon.

Herreria, C. (2017, September 13). Kid Rock bans newspaper from his concert after critical column. *Huffington Post*. Retrieved from https://www.huffingtonpost.com/entry/kid-rock-bans-detroit-free pressus59b8b6b3e4b086432b027dcc.

Hess, A. (2011). Breaking news: A postmodern rhetorical analysis of *The Daily Show*. In T. Goodnow (ed.), The Daily Show *and rhetoric: Arguments, issues, and strategies* (pp. 153–170). Lanham, MD: Lexington Books.

Hess, S. (1981). *The Washington reporters*. Washington, DC: The Brookings Institution.

Hickey, N. (2001). The cost of not publishing. *Columbia Journalism Review*, November–December.

Hitt, M. P., Darr, J., & Dunaway, J. (2019, March 26). Why losing our newspapers is breaking our politics. *Scientific American*. Retrieved from https://www.scientificamerican.com/article/why-losing-our-newspapers-is-breaking-our-politics/.

Hobbes, T. (1651/1985). *Leviathan*. New York: Penguin Classics.

Hodges, L. W. (1983). The journalist and privacy. *Social Responsibility: Journalism, Law, Medicine, 9*, 5–19.

———. (1986). Defining press responsibility: A functional approach. In D. Elliott (ed.), *Responsible journalism* (pp. 13–31). Newbury Park, CA: Sage.

———. (1997). Taste in photojournalism: A question of ethics or aesthetics? In *Media ethics: Issues and cases* (3rd ed., pp. 37–40). New York: McGraw-Hill.

Hoek, J. (2008). Ethical and practical implications of pharmaceutical direct-to-consumer advertising. *International Journal of Nonprofit and Voluntary Sector Marketing, 13*(February), 73–87.

Hoek, J., & Gendall, P. (2002). To have or not to have? Ethics and regulation of direct to consumer advertising of prescription medicines. *Journal of Marketing Communications, 8*(2), 71–85.

Holden, S. (2006, October 27). That beautiful but deadly San Francisco span. *New York Times*. Retrieved from http://www.nytimes.com/2006/10/27/movies/27brid.html.

Huh, J., Delorme, D., & Reid, L. (2004). The information utility of DTC prescription drug advertising. *Journalism and Mass Communication Quarterly, 81*(4), 788.

Irby, K. (2003, April 2). L.A. Times photographer fired over altered image. *Poynter*. Retrieved from https://www.poynter.org/news/la-times-photographer-fired-over-altered-image.

Itzkoff, D. (2014, March 18). Beastie Boys and toy company settle lawsuit over ad's use of "Girls." *New York Times*. Retrieved from https://artsbeat.blogs.nytimes.com/2014/03/18/beastie-boys-and-toy-company-settle-lawsuit-over-ads-use-of-girls/.

Iyengar, S. (1991). *Is anyone responsible?* Chicago: University of Chicago Press.

Jamieson, K. H. (1992). *Dirty politics*. New York: Oxford University Press.

———. (2000). *Everything you think you know about politics . . . and why you're wrong*. New York: Basic Books.

Johar, K. (2012). An insider's perspective: Defense of the pharmaceutical industry's marketing practices. *Albany Law Review, 76*(1), 299–334.

Johnson, T. (2017a, November 3). Four state attorneys general oppose Sinclair-Tribune merger. *Variety*. Retrieved from http://variety.com/2017/politics/news/sinclair-tribune-merger-opposiion-attorneys-general-1202606391/.

————. (2017b, November 16). FCC relaxes media ownership rules in contentious vote. *Variety*. Retrieved from http://variety.com/2017/politics/news/fcc-media-ownership-rules-sinclair-broadcasting-1202616424/.

Kaid, L. L. (1992). Ethical dimensions of political advertising. In R. E. Denton (ed.), *Ethical dimensions of political communication* (pp. 145–169). New York: Praeger.

Kaiser Family Foundation. (2014). *Opioid overdose deaths by type of opioid*. Retrieved from http://kff.org/other/state-indicator/opioid-overdose-deaths-by-type-of-opioid/?currentTimeframe=0.

Kang, C., & de la Merced, M. J. (2017, November 20). Justice Department sues to block AT&T-Time Warner merger. *New York Times*. Retrieved from https://www.nytimes.com/2017/11/20/business/dealbook/att-time-warner-merger.html.

Keller, S. (2007). *The limits of loyalty*. Cambridge: Cambridge University Press.

Keohane, J. (2017, February 16). What news-writing bots mean for the future of journalism. *Wired*. Retrieved from https://www.wired.com/2017/02/robots-wrote-this-story/.

Klein, J. (1992, June 8). Whose values? *Newsweek*, 19–22.

Klepek, P. (2015, October 23). That time *Call of Duty* let you shoot up an airport. *Kotaku*. Retrieved from https://kotaku.com/that-time-call-of-duty-let-you-shoot-up-an-airport-1738376241.

Knibbs, K. (2019, January 26). Buzzfeed layoffs are a bad sign for online news. *The Ringer*. Retrieved from https://www.theringer.com/tech/2019/1/26/18198621/buzzfeed-news-layoffs-digital-media-economy.

Koehn, D. (1998). *Rethinking feminist ethics*. New York: Routledge.

Kohlberg, L. (1973). The contribution of developmental psychology to education. *Educational Psychologist*, *10*, 2–14.

Kovach, B., & Rosenstiel, T. (2010). *Blur: How to know what's true in the age of information overload*. New York: Bloomsbury.

Lacy, S. (1989). A model of demand for news: Impact of competition on newspaper content. *Journalism Quarterly*, *66*(1), 40–48.

Landler, M. (2017, September 14). Trump resurrects his claim that both sides share blame in Charlottesville violence. *New York Times*. Retrieved from https://www.nytimes.com/2017/09/14/us/politics/trump-charlottesville-tim-scott.html.

Lazer, D., Baum, M. A., Benkler, Y., Berinsky, A. J., Greenhill, K. M., Menczer, F., et al. (2018). The science of fake news. *Science*, *359*(380), 1094–1096.

Lebacqz, K. (1985). *Professional ethics: Power and paradox*. Nashville: Abingdon Press.

Lee, D., & Begley, C. E. (2010). Racial and ethnic disparities in response to direct-to-consumer advertising. *American Journal of Health-System Pharmacy*, *67*(14), 1185–1190.

Lee, S. T. (2005). Predicting tolerance of journalistic deception. *Journal of Mass Media Ethics*, *20*(1), 22–42.

Legum, J. (2017, October 10). ESPN struggles to explain how Jemele Hill violated its social media policy. *Think Progress*. Retrieved from https://thinkprogress.org/espn-jemele-hill-social-media-policy-3412c0e2a1d4/.

Len-Ríos, M., Hinnant, A., & Jeong, J. Y. (2012). Reporters' gender affects views on health reporting. *Newspaper Research Journal, 33*(3), 76–88.

Leonhardt, D. (2019, December 10). Save local journalism! *New York Times.* Retrieved from https://www.nytimes.com/2019/12/10/opinion/local-news.html?smid=em-share.

Leshner, G. (2006). The effects of dehumanizing depictions of race in TV news stories. In A. Reynolds & B. Burnett (eds.), *Communication and law: Multidisciplinary approaches in research* (pp. 233–252). New York: Routledge.

Lester, P. (1992). *Photojournalism: An ethical approach.* Hillsdale, NJ: Lawrence Erlbaum Associates.

———. (1996). *Images that injure.* Westport, CT: Greenwood Press.

Levin, A. (2017, June 21). Exclusive: Prince Harry on chaos after Diana's death and why the world needs "the magic" of the royal family. *Newsweek.* Retrieved from https://www.newsweek.com/2017/06/30/prince-harry-depression-diana-death-why-world-needs-magic-627833.html.

Levitsky, S., & Ziblatt, D. (2018, January 21). This is how democracies die. *Guardian.* Retrieved from https://www.theguardian.com/us-news/commentisfree/2018/jan/21/this-is-how-democracies-die.

Li, S. (2014, December 14). Toy makers learn that construction sets aren't just for boys. *Los Angeles Times.* Retrieved from http://www.latimes.com/business/la-fi-girls-toys-20141214-story.html.

Liberman, N., Trope, Y., & Stephan, E. (2007). Psychological distance. In A. W. Kruglanski & E. T. Higgins (eds.), *Social psychology: Handbook of basic principles* (pp. 353–381). New York: Guilford Press.

Lieber, P. S. (2008). Moral development in public relations. Measuring duty to society in strategic communication. *Public Relations Review, 34*(3), 244–251.

Linsky, M. (1986). *Impact: How the press affects federal policymaking.* New York: W. W. Norton.

Lippmann, W. (1922). *Public opinion.* New York: Free Press.

———. (1982). *The essential Lippmann.* Cambridge, MA: Harvard University Press.

Loftus, T. (2017a, August 2). Courier-Journal files complaint after public blocked from board visit to Matt Bevin's home. *Louisville Courier-Journal.* Retrieved from https://www.courier-journal.com/story/news/politics/2017/08/02/courier-journal-appeals-exclusion-inspection-matt-bevins-home/534585001/.

———. (2017b, July 19). A restored mansion or house in disrepair? Board to hear arguments Wednesday on value of Bevin's Anchorage home. *Louisville Courier-Journal.* Retrieved from https://www.courier-journal.com/story/news/2017/07/19/gov-matt-bevin-anchorage-home-hearing-decide-value-set-wednesday/491123001/.

Lowery, W. (2020, June 29). A reckoning over objectivity, led by Black journalists. *New York Times.* https://www.nytimes.com/2020/06/23/opinion/objectivity-black-journalists-coronavirus.html.

Mahone, J., & Napoli, P. (2020, July 13). Hundreds of hyperpartisan sites are masquerading as local news. This map shows if there's one near you. *NiemanLab.* Retrieved from https://www.niemanlab.org/2020/07/

hundreds-of-hyperpartisan-sites-are-masquerading-as-local-news-this-map-shows-if-theres-one-near-you/.

Mahoney, R. (2020, August 27). The Bucks stop play and demand that the real work begins. *The Ringer*. Retrieved from https://www.theringer.com/nba/2020/8/27/21403744/nba-milwaukee-bucks-strike-jacob-blake.

Manly, L. (2005, October 3). U.S. network TV shows turn props into dollars. *International Herald Tribune*.

Martin, E. (1991). On photographic manipulation. *Journal of Mass Media Ethics*, *6*(3), 156–163.

Marx, G. T. (1999). What's in a name? *The Information Society*, *15*(2), 99–112.

Mattin, D. (2007, February 10). The Bridge. BBC. Retrieved from http://www.bbc.co.uk/films/2007/02/12/thebridge2007review.shtml.

May, W. F. (2001). *Beleaguered rulers: The public obligation of the professional*. Louisville: Westminster John Knox Press.

McBeth, M. K., & Clemons, R. S. (2011). Is fake news the real news? The significance of Stewart and Colbert for democratic discourse, politics, and policy. In A. Amarasingam (ed.), *The Stewart/Colbert effect: Essays on the real impacts of fake news* (pp. 79-98). Jefferson, NC: McFarland.

McBride, K. (2020, June 18). Should images of protestors be blurred to protect them from retribution? National Public Radio. Retrieved from https://www.npr.org/sections/publiceditor/2020/06/18/879223467/should-images-of-protesters-be-blurred-to-protect-them-from-retribution.

McCaffrey, K. (2015, September 15). Kim stands corrected: The limits of corrective promotion. *MM&M*. http://www.mmm-online.com/campaigns/kardashian-diclegis-duchesnay-corrective-advertising/article/438723/.

McChesney, R. (1997). *Corporate media and the threat to democracy*. New York: Seven Stories Press.

McGeough, R. (2011). The voice of the people: Jon Stewart, public argument, and political satire. In T. Goodnow (ed.), The Daily Show *and rhetoric: Arguments, issues, and strategies* (pp. 113–127). Lanham, MD: Lexington Books.

McLuhan, M. (1964). *Understanding media: The extensions of man*. New York: Signet Books.

McManus, J. (1994). *Market-driven journalism: Let the citizen beware?* Thousand Oaks, CA: Sage.

Meader, A., Knight, L., Coleman, R., & Wilkins, L. (2015). Ethics in the digital age: A comparison of the effects of moving images and photographs on moral judgment. *Journal of Media Ethics*, *30*(4), 234–251.

Media Matters Staff. (2017, September 19). Bill O'Reilly uses Today show appearance to attack a woman who reported him for sexual harassment. Media Matters for America. Retrieved from https://www.mediamatters.org/nbc/bill-oreilly-uses-today-show-appearance-attack-woman-who-reported-him-sexual-harassment.

Merrill, J. C. (1974). *The imperative of freedom: A philosophy of journalistic autonomy*. New York: Hastings House.

Metzl, J. M. (2002). Selling sanity through gender: The psychodynamics of psychotropic advertising. *Journal of Medical Humanities*, *24*(1), 79–103.

Meyers, C. (2003). Appreciating W. D. Ross: On duties and consequences. *Journal of Mass Media Ethics*, *18*(2), 81–97.

Michaels, S. (2013, December 12). Beastie Boys countersue GoldieBlox for toy video royalties. *The Guardian*.

Miller, C. (2013, November 20). Ad takes off online: Less doll, more awl. *New York Times*. Retrieved from https://bits.blogs.nytimes.com/2013/11/20/a-viral-video-encourages-girls-to-become-engineers/.

Mills, C. W. (1956). *The power elite*. New York: Oxford University Press.

Molotch, H., & Lester, M. (1974). News as purposive behavior: On the strategic use of routine events, accidents and scandals. *American Sociological Review*, *39*, 101–112.

Montgomery, K. C. (1989). *Target: Prime time. Advocacy groups and the struggle over entertainment television*. New York: Oxford University Press.

Moore, G. E. (1903). *Principia ethica*.

Moses, L. (2017). The Washington Post's robot reporter has published 850 articles in the past year. Retrieved from https://digiday.com/media/washington-posts-robot-reporter-published-500-articles-last-year/.

Moyers, B. (1988). Quoted in *The promise of television*, episode 10. Produced by PBS.

Napoli, P., & Mahone, J. (2019, September 9). Local newspapers are suffering, but they're still (by far) the most significant journalism producers in their communities. NiemanLab. Retrieved from https://www.niemanlab.org/2019/09/local-newspapers-are-suffering-but-theyre-still-by-far-the-most-significant-journalism-producers-in-their-communities/.

National Association of Broadcasters. (1985). *Radio: In search of excellence*. Washington, DC: NAB.

Nelkin, D. (1987). *Selling science: How the press covers science and technology*. New York: W. H. Freeman.

Neville, R. C. (1980). Various meanings of privacy: A philosophical analysis. In W. C. Bier (ed.), *Privacy: A vanishing value?* (pp. 26–36). New York: Fordham University Press.

Newsom, D., Turk, J. V., & Kruckeberg, D. (1996). *This is PR: The realities of public relations*. Delmont, CA: Wadsworth.

Newton, C. (2020, January 9). How Facebook's ad in Teen Vogue came back to haunt it. *The Verge*. Retrieved from https://www.theverge.com/interface/2020/1/9/21056988/facebook-teen-vogue-ad-debacle.

New York Times. (2015, October 16). Staging, manipulation and truth in photography. *New York Times*. Retrieved from https://lens.blogs.nytimes.com/2015/10/16/staging-manipulation-ethics-photos/?r=0.

Nicholls, R. (2020, August 31). If Facebook really pulls news from its Australian sites, we'll have a much less compelling product. *The Conversation*. Retrieved from https://theconversation.com/if-facebook-really-pulls-news-from-its-australian-sites-well-have-a-much-less-compelling-product-145380.

Nissenbaum, H. (2010). *Privacy on context: Technology, policy and the integrity of social life*. Stanford: Stanford Law Books.

Nuccitelli, D. (2014, May 23). John Oliver's viral video: The best climate debate ever. *The Guardian*. Retrieved from https://www.theguardian.com/environment/ climate-consensus-97-per-cent/2014/may/23/john-oliver-best-climate-debate-ever.

Nussbaum, M. (2001). *Upheavals of thought: The intelligence of emotions*. Cambridge: Cambridge University Press.

———. (2006). *Frontiers of justice: Disability, nationality and species membership*. Cambridge, MA: Harvard University Press.

———. (2013). *Creating capabilities: The human development approach*. Cambridge, MA: Belknap Press.

———. (2015). *Political emotions: Why love matters for justice*. Cambridge, MA: Belknap Press.

———. (2016). *Anger and forgiveness: Resentment, generosity, justice*. Oxford: Oxford University Press.

Nylen, L. (2020, December 13). Behind Washington's one-eighty on Facebook: A rethink of monopoly power. *Politico*. Retrieved from https://www.politico.com/ news/2020/12/13/facebook-antitrust-flip-flop-444652.

Ohio State Bar Association. (2017). *Fighting Ohio's heroin epidemic*. Retrieved from https://www.ohiobar.org/NewsAndPublications/OhioLawyer/Pages/Fighting-Ohios-heroin-epidemic.aspx.

Oldenquist, A. (2002). Loyalties. In I. Primoratz (ed.), *Patriotism* (pp. 25–42) Amherst, NY: Humanity Books.

Panyatham, P. (2020, March 10). Deepfake technology in the entertainment industry: Potential limitations and protections. Arts Management & Technology Laboratory. Retrieved from https://amt-lab.org/blog/2020/3/deepfake-technology-in-the-entertainment-industry-potential-limitations-and-protections.

Park, S., Holody, K., & Zhang, X. (2012). Race in media coverage of school shootings: A parallel application of framing theory and attribute agenda setting. *Journalism & Mass Communication Quarterly, 89*(3), 475–494.

Patterson, P. (1989). Reporting Chernobyl: Cutting the government fog to cover the nuclear cloud. In L. M. Walters, L. Wilkins, & T. Walters (eds.), *Bad tidings: Communication and catastrophe*. Mahwah, NJ: Lawrence Erlbaum Associates.

Patterson, T. (1980). *The mass media election*. New York: Prager.

Payton, A. R., & Thoits, P. A. (2011). Medicalization, direct-to-consumer advertising, and mental illness stigma. *Society and Mental Health, 1*(1), 55–70.

Pederson, D. M. (1999). Model for types of privacy by privacy functions. *Journal of Environmental Psychology, 19*(4), 397–405.

Perry, W. G., Jr. (1968). *Forms of intellectual and ethical development in the college years: A scheme*. New York: Holt, Rinehart and Winston.

Petty, R., & D'Rozario, D. (2009). The use of dead celebrities in advertising and marketing: Balancing interests in the right of publicity. *Journal of Advertising, 38*(4), 37–49.

Pfanner, E. (2005, October 3). Product placements cause a stir in Europe. *International Herald Tribune*. Retrieved from https://archive.nytimes.com/www.nytimes.com/ iht/2005/10/03/business/IHT-03products03.html?pagewanted=all.

Piaget, J. (1965). *The moral judgment of the child*. Trans. by M. Gabain. New York: Free Press.

Picard, R. (1988). *The ravens of Odin: The press in the Nordic nations.* Ames: Iowa State University Press.

Plaisance, P. L. (2015). *Virtue in media: The moral psychology of excellence in news and public relations.* New York: Routledge.

Pojman, L. (1998). *Ethical theory: Classical and contemporary readings.* Belmont, CA: Wadsworth.

Priest, S., & Hall, A. (2007, February 18). Soldiers face neglect, frustration at Army's top medical facility. *Washington Post.* Retrieved from http://www.washingtonpost.com/wp-dyn/content/article/2007/02/17/AR2007021701172.html.

Rada, J. A., & Wulfemeyer, K. T. (2005). Color coded: Racial descriptors in television coverage of intercollegiate sports. *Journal of Broadcasting & Electronic Media, 49*(1), 65–85.

Radin, M. J. (1982). Property and personhood. *Stanford Law Review, 34*(5), 957–1015.

———. (1993). *Reinterpreting property.* Chicago: University of Chicago Press.

———. (1996). *Contested commodities.* Cambridge, MA: Harvard University Press.

Rainville, R., & McCormick, E. (1977). Extent of racial prejudice in pro football announcers' speech. *Journalism Quarterly, 54*(1), 20–26.

Raudins, S. (2020, September 17). Letter from the editor: *The Lantern*'s coverage of protests and their participants. *The Lantern.* Retrieved from https://www.thelantern.com/2020/09/letter-from-the-editor-the-lanterns-coverage-of-protests-and-their-participants/.

Rawls, J. (1971). *A theory of justice.* Cambridge, MA: Harvard University Press.

Reaves, S. (1987). Digital retouching: Is there a place for it in newspaper photography? *Journal of Mass Media Ethics, 2*(2), 40–48.

Reuters Institute for the Study of Journalism. (2015). How mobile phones are changing journalism practice in the 21st Century. Retrieved from www.reutersinstitute.politics.ox.ac.uk.

Robinson, M., & Sheehan, G. (1984). *Over the wire and on TV.* New York: Basic Books.

Rose, M., & Baumgartner, F. (2013). Framing the poor: Media coverage and US poverty policy 1960–2008. *Policy Studies Journal, 41*(1), 22–53.

Rosen, J. (2000). *The unwanted gaze: The destruction of privacy in America.* New York: Random House.

Rosenthal, A. M. (1989, October 10). Trash TV's latest news show continues credibility erosion. Syndicated column by *New York Times News Service.*

Ross, W. D. (1930). *The right and the good.* Oxford: Clarendon Press.

Roy, J. (2016, October 11). How "Pepe the Frog" went from harmless to hate symbol. *Los Angeles Times.* Retrieved from https://www.latimes.com/politics/la-na-pol-pepe-the-frog-hate-symbol-20161011-snap-htmlstory.html.

Royce, J. (1908). *The philosophy of loyalty.* New York: Macmillan.

Russell, B. (ed.). (1967). *History of Western philosophy.* New York: Touchstone Books.

Sample, I. (2020, January 13). What are deepfakes—and how can you spot them? *Guardian.* Retrieved from https://www.theguardian.com/technology/2020/jan/13/what-are-deepfakes-and-how-can-you-spot-them.

Sandel, M. J. (1982). *Liberalism and the limits of justice*. Cambridge, MA: Harvard University Press.

———. (1996). *Democracy's discontent: America in search of a public philosophy*. Cambridge, MA: Harvard University Press.

———. (2012). *What money can't buy: The moral limits of markets*. New York: Farrar, Straus and Giroux.

Schauster, E., Ferrucci, P., Tandoc, E., & Walker, T. (2020). Advertising primed: How professional identity affects moral reasoning. *Journal of Business Ethics*. Advance online publication: https://doi.org/10.1007/s10551-020-04429-0.

Schoeman, F. D. (ed.). (1984). *Philosophical dimensions of privacy: An anthology*. New York: Cambridge University Press.

Schudson, M. (1978). *Discovering the news*. New York: Basic Books.

Schwartz, T. (1973). *The responsive chord*. Garden City, NY: Anchor Press.

Scott, C. (2017). Report: Robot journalism will continue to grow in newsrooms despite its limitations. Retrieved from https://www.journalism.co.uk/news/report-robot-journalism-s-limitations-not-halting-its-onward-march/s2/a700429/.

Seabrook, J. (2003, July 7). The money note. *New Yorker*, 46.

Seligson, H. (2020, February 19). This is the TV ad the Oscars didn't allow on air. *New York Times*. Retrieved from https://www.nytimes.com/2020/02/19/us/post-partum-ad-oscars-frida.html.

Sen, A. (2009). *The idea of justice*. Cambridge, MA: The Belknap Press.

Shepard, S. (2017, October 18). Politico Poll: 46 percent think media make up stories about Trump. *Politico*. Retrieved from https://www.politico.com/story/2017/10/18/trump-media-fake-news-poll-243884.

Shepardson, D. (2017, November 1). Sinclair Broadcast Group praises FCC media ownership, TV rule changes. *Reuters*. Retrieved from https://www.reuters.com/article/us-tribune-media-m-a-sinclair-ma/sinclair-broadcast-group-praises-fcc-media-ownership-tv-rule-changes-idUSKBN1D1645.

Shihipar, A. (2017, October 25). Antifa history and politics: A historian weighs in. *Teen Vogue*. Retrieved from https://www.teenvogue.com/story/antifa-history-and-politics-explained.

Siegel, J. (2020, October 28). The narcissism of the *New York Times*' foreign coverage. *Tablet*. Retrieved from https://www.tabletmag.com/sections/news/articles/narcissism-nyt-foreign-coverage.

Silverman, C. (2015, February 15). Lies, damn lies, and viral content. *Columbia Journalism Review*. Retrieved from https://www.cjr.org/tow_center_reports/craig_silverman_lies_damn_lies_viral_content.php.

Smith, C. (1992). *Media and apocalypse*. Westport, CT: Greenwood Press.

Snider, M. (2017a, August 7). Two big reasons Sinclair-Tribune TV merger should be nixed, opponents say. *USA Today*. Retrieved from https://www.usatoday.com/story/money/business/2017/08/07/two-big-reasons-sinclair-tribune-tv-merger-should-nixed-opponents-say/546158001/.

———. (2017b, May 7). $4 billion TV deal creates nation's largest broadcaster. *USA Today*. Retrieved from https://www.usatoday.com/story/money/business/2017/05/07/sinclair-broadcasting-buy-tribune-media-4-billion-deal-reports-say/101409222/.

Sobczynski, P. (2019, August 21). American Factory. Roger-Ebert.com. Retrieved from https://www.rogerebert.com/reviews/american-factory-movie-review-2019.

Spangler, T. (2017). Cord-cutting explodes: 22 million U.S. adults will have canceled cable, satellite TV by end of 2017. *Variety*. Retrieved from http://variety.com/2017/biz/news/cord-cutting-2017-estimates-cancel-cable-satellite-tv-1202556594/.

Spencer, J. (2001, October 11). Decoding bin Laden. *Newsweek*. Retrieved from http://www.nbcnews.com/id/3067564/t/decoding-bin-laden/#.WznMMtIzY2w.

Spicer, R. N. (2011). Before and after *The Daily Show*: Freedom and consequences in political satire. In T. Goodnow (ed.), The Daily Show *and rhetoric: Arguments, issues, and strategies* (pp. 19-41). Lanham, MD: Lexington Books.

Steiner, L. (2020). Feminist media ethics. In C. G. Christians & L. Wilkins (eds.), *The Routledge handbook of mass media ethics* (pp. 433–452). New York: Routledge.

Sterling, D. (2013). *TED Talk: Inspiring the next generation of female engineers.* Retrieved from https://www.youtube.com/watch?v=FEeTLopLkEo.

Stewart, E. (2020, January 29). The controversy over a Washington Post reporter's Kobe Bryant tweets, explained. *Vox*. Retrieved from https://www.vox.com/2020/1/27/21083682/kobe-bryant-felicia-sonmez-tweets-washington-post-twitter.

Stone, I. F. (1988). *The trial of Socrates*. Boston: Little, Brown.

Stoycheff, E. (2016). Under surveillance: Examining Facebook's spiral of silence effects in the wake of NSA internet monitoring. *Journalism & Mass Communication Quarterly*, *93*(2), 296–311.

Stray, J. (2016). The age of the cyborg. *Columbia Journalism Review*. Retrieved from https://www.cjr.org/analysis/cyborgvirtualrealityreuterstracer.php.

Su, A. Y. (2020, January 22). Harvard students form coalition supporting slave photo lawsuit demands. *Harvard Crimson*. Retrieved from https://www.thecrimson.com/article/2020/1/22/harvard-coalition-free-renty/.

Szarkowski, J. (1978). *Mirrors and windows*. New York: Museum of Modern Art.

Tannen, D. (1999). *The argument culture: Stopping America's war of words*. New York: Ballantine Books.

Thomson-DeVeaux, A. (2021, January 20). Trump is leaving office with a bunch of legal problems—and we're not just talking about impeachment. FiveThirtyEight. Retrieved from https://fivethirtyeight.com/features/trump-is-leaving-office-with-a-bunch-of-legal-problems-and-were-not-just-talking-about-impeachment/.

Thorson, E., Duffy, M., & Schumann, D. W. (2007). The internet waits for no one. In D. W. Schumann & E. Thorson (eds.), *Internet advertising: Theory and research* (pp. 3–14). New York: Routledge.

Tolstoy, L. N. (1960). *What is art?* Trans. by A. Maude. New York: MacMillan.

Toulmin, S. (1988). The recovery of practical philosophy. *The American Scholar*, Summer, p. 338.

Tur, K. (2017). *Unbelievable: My front row seat to the craziest campaign in American history*. New York: HarperCollins.

Twitter. (2021, January 8). Permanent suspension of @realDonaldTrump. Retrieved from https://blog.twitter.com/en_us/topics/company/2020/suspension.html.

Urstadt, B. (2019, September 10). Why we should all watch "American Factory." National Public Radio. Retrieved from https://www.npr.org/sections/money/2019/09/10/759152615/why-we-should-all-watch-american-factory.

US Census Bureau. (2020). Income, poverty, and health insurance coverage in the United States: 2019. Retrieved from https://www.census.gov/newsroom/press-releases/2020/income-poverty.html.

van den Hoven, J. (2008). Moral methodology and information technology. In K. E. Himma & H. T. Tavani (eds.), *The handbook of information and computer ethics* (pp. 49–68). Hoboken, NJ: John Wiley.

Vanderveen, C. (2019, October 11). We ran a story on a political group buying loads of ads. That political group decided to take its money elsewhere. KUSA-TV. Retrieved from https://www.9news.com/article/news/local/next/we-ran-a-story-on-political-group-doctor-patient-unity-that-political-group-decided-to-take-its-money-elsewhere/73-a0817d7b-4ac3-4a7d-9d02-caf43546328c.

Voakes, P. S. (1998). What were you thinking? A survey of journalists who were sued for invasion of privacy. *Journalism & Mass Communication Quarterly, 75*(2), 378–393.

Wallace, L. (2017a, January 27). Objectivity is dead, and I'm okay with it. *Medium*. Retrieved from https://medium.com/@lewispants/objectivity-is-dead-and-im-okay-with-it-7fd2b4b5c58f.

Wallace, L. (2017b, January 31). I was fired from my journalism job ten days into Trump. *Medium*. Retrieved from https://medium.com/@lewispants/i-was-fired-from-my-journalism-job-ten-days-into-trump-c3bc014ce51d.

Wang, A. X., & Millman, E. (2020, June 12). Lady Antebellum is now "Lady A." But so is a blues singer who's used the name for 20 years. *Rolling Stone*. Retrieved from https://www.rollingstone.com/pro/news/lady-antebellum-lady-a-country-blues-1013919/.

Ward, S. J. (2004). *The invention of journalism ethics*. Montreal: McGill-Queens University Press.

Ward, S. J. A., & Wasserman, H. (2010). Toward an open ethics: Implications of new media platforms for global ethics discourse. *Journal of Mass Media Ethics, 25*(4), 275–292.

Waters, S. (2020). The ethical algorithm: Journalist/whistleblower relationships explored through the lens of social exchange. *Journalism & Communication Monographs, 22*(3), 172–245.

Weaver, D. H., Beam, R. A., Brownlee, B. J., Voakes, P. S., & Wilhoit, G. C. (2007). *The American journalist in the 21st century: U.S. news people at the dawn of a new millennium (LEA's Communication Series)*. Mahwah, NJ: Lawrence Erlbaum Associates.

Weaver, D. H., & Wilhoit, G. C. (1996). *The American journalist in the 1990s: US news people at the end of an era*. Mahwah, NJ: Lawrence Erlbaum Associates.

Weisman, R. (2014, April 13). Are baby boomers ready to give marijuana a second chance? *Boston Globe*. Retrieved from https://www.bostonglobe.com/business/2014/04/12/baby-boomers-who-moved-may-ready-give-marijuana-second-chance/8UcflcGP1dKkanaLuX6wOM/story.html.

Werhane, P. (2006). Stockholder ethics in health care. Presented at the Association of Applied and Professional Ethics, February 2006, San Antonio, TX.

White House. (2017). President's commission on combating drug addiction and the opioid crisis. Retrieved from https://www.whitehouse.gov/ondcp/presidents-commission.

Wilkins, L. (1987). *Shared vulnerability: The mass media and American perception of the Bhopal disaster*. Westport, CT: Greenwood Press.

Wilkins, L. (2009). Carol Gilligan: Ethics of care. In C. G. Christians & J. C. Merrill (eds.), *Ethical communication: Moral stances in human dialogue* (pp. 33–39). Columbia: University of Missouri Press.

Wilkins, L., & Christians, C. G. (2001). Philosophy meets the social sciences: The nature of humanity in the public arena. *Journal of Mass Media Ethics*, *16*(2/3), 99–120.

Wilkins, L., & Coleman, R. (2005). *The moral media*. Mahwah, NJ: Lawrence Erlbaum Associates.

Wilkins, L., & Patterson, P. (2020). Toward an institution-based theory of privacy. In C. Christians & L. Wilkins (Eds.), *The Routledge handbook of mass media ethics* (pp. 374–387). New York: Routledge.

Williams, B. A. (2009). The ethics of political communication. In L. Wilkins & C. G. Christians (eds.), *Handbook of mass media ethics*. New York: Taylor & Francis.

Women's Media Center. (2019). The status of women in U.S. media 2019. Retrieved from https://womensmediacenter.com/reports/the-status-of-women-in-u-s-media-2019.

Woodward, K. (1994, June 13). What is virtue? *Newsweek*, 38–39.

Wooley, S., & Howard, P. (2017). Executive summary: Oxford Computational Propaganda Project. Retrieved from http://comprop.oii.ox.ac.uk/wp-content/uploads/sites/89/2017/06/Casestudies-ExecutiveSummary.pdf.

Zhou, L. (2017, August 4). Sinclair's assist from the FCC. *Politico*. Retrieved from https://www.politico.com/tipsheets/morning-tech/2017/08/04/sinclairs-assist-from-the-fcc-221710.

Zillman, D. (1999). Exemplification theory: Judging the whole by some of its parts. *Media Psychology*, *1*(1), 69–94.

Zuboff, S. (2019). *The age of surveillance capitalism: The fight for a human future at the new frontier of power*. New York: Public Affairs, Hachette Book Group.

Index

Lightning Source UK Ltd.
Milton Keynes UK
UKHW021254191022
410734UK00008B/20